Quality, TQC, TQM

A Meta Literature Study

Robert E. Kemper

The Scarecrow Press, Inc.
Lanham, Md., & London
1997

SCARECROW PRESS, INC.

Published in the United States of America
by Scarecrow Press, Inc.
4720 Boston Way
Lanham, Maryland 20706

British Library Cataloguing in Publication Information Available

Library of Congress Cataloging-in-Publication Data

Kemper, Robert E.
Quality, TQC, TQM : a meta literature study / Robert E. Kemper.
p. cm.
Includes bibliographical references.
ISBN 0-8108-3346-8 (alk. paper)
1. Total quality management—Bibliography. 2. Quality control—Management—Bibliography. 3. Bibliographic citations—Statistics. I. Title.
Z7164.07K35 1997
[H62.15]
016.6585'62—dc21 97-16754
CIP

ISBN 0-8108-3346-8 (cloth : alk. paper)

™ The paper used in this publication meets the minimum requirements of American National Standard for Information Sciences—Permanence of Paper for Printed Library Materials, ANSI Z39.48–1984.
Manufactured in the United States of America.

CONTENTS

PREFACE

The effort represented by *Quality, TQC, TQM: A Meta Literature Study* is a simple one, to cite and summarize important approaches, classifications, articles, researchers and writers, subtopics, and sources about quality.[*] A number of definitions of quality exist. To keep the approach simple, an authoritative source is cited (Flexner, Stuart Berg. [Ed.] [1993] *Random House Unabridged Dictionary*. Second edition. Newly revised and updated. New York: Random House) for a definition:

> qual•i•ty: **1**. A characteristic or attribute of something; property; a feature. **2**. The natural or essential character of something. **3**. Excellence; superiority. (p. 1579).

Then an authoritative business source is cited (Certo, Samuel C. [1994] *Modern Management: Diversity, Quality, Ethics, and the Global Environment*. Boston: Allyn and Bacon):

> qual•i•ty: The extent to which a product, service, or organization does what it is supposed to do—how closely and reliably it satisfies the specifications to which it is built. (p. 466)

In this study, quality is interchangeable with other terms found in the literature: property, attribute, character, and trait. The process of quality includes at least six other variables defined as follows:

> ef•fec•tive•ness: **1**. The degree to which managers attain organizational objectives; it is doing the right things. (Certo [1994], p. 466) **2**. Ability to be proactive, begin with the end in mind, put first things first, think win/win, seek first to understand and then be understood, synergize, and develop a habit of renewal. (Covey, Stephen R. Covey [1989] *The Habits of Highly Effective People: Powerful Lessons in Personal Change*. New York: Simon and Schuster, p. 52-53)

---

[*]When quality is used, the reference is to the dictionary definition. On the other hand, when quality[1] is used, the reference is to something else, which is described later in the book.

ef•fi•cien•cy: **1**. The degree to which organizational resources contribute to production; it is doing things right. (Certo [1994], p. 466) **2**. Getting more done in less time using less resources. (Covey, Stephen R., A. Roger Merrill, and Rebecca R. Merrill. [1994] *First Things First*. New York: Simon and Schuster. p. 26)

lead•er•ship: **1**. Doing the right things. **2**. Deals with the top line. **3**. Determines whether the ladder is leaning against the right wall. **4**. Vision, destination, compass. **5**. Driven by a set of principles or directions. **6**. Problem solvers. (Covey 1989, p. 101)

man•age•ment: **1**. Doing things right. **2**. Efficiency in climbing the ladder of success. **3**. Driven by a roadmap. **4**. Producers. (Covey 1989, p. 101)

as•ser•tive: Concern with one's own outcome. (Kemper, Robert E. and Deborah A. Codding [1994] *The Conflict: The People Who Nobody Knows*. New York: McGraw-Hill. p. 15)

co•op•er•a•tive: Concern with the outcomes of others. (Kemper and Codding, p. 15)

The intended audience for this book is fourfold: (1) people, in general, interested in learning about quality; (2) managers, supervisors, and their subordinates who practice, or should practice, quality routinely; (3) researchers investigating quality; and (4) students seeking an imaginative area for interesting study and research.

To identify quality publications for review, the study began with a list of books, books of readings, journals, other reports, chapters on management, production and operations management textbooks featuring an add-on chapter on quality, and studies necessary for an undergraduate and a graduate course in quality management. The trade books included in the list were required textbooks in existing management courses. The original list of periodical readings was also required reading for students enrolled in quality-management classes. An example of an add-on chapter on quality in a production and operations management textbook is chapter 3 in William Stevenson's fourth edition (1993) of *Production/Operations Management* published by Irwin. References in the publications were searched and the process repeated until no new studies were found. Although there are many more quality publications in the literature, this study uses 127 important sources to compile the chapter "Citations." The 127 items appear in bold face type in the "Citations" chapter. Each item was cited at least three times among all publications. The 309 items referred to in the "Quality Meta Study" chapter were written by 192 authors. Each author was cited more than five times. The 192 authors are identified on pages 28-29. On those pages, the number of publications written appears between [ ] and the total number of citings between { }. The publications appeared in 195 journals, 24 professional and society proceedings and transactions, 5 dissertations, and 157 books. The 309 important citations are identified in "Citations" by bold-face type. Two were published in the 1930s, 1 in the 1940s, 3 in the 1950s, 8 in the 1960s, 16 in the 1970s, 120 in the 1980s, and 159 in the 1990s. These authors cited 1,512 publications.

Concerning the significant sources listed on pages 25-27, 2 were published in the 1930s, 2 in the 1950s, 4 in the 1960s, 7 in the 1970s, 49 in the 1980s, and 63 in the 1990s. These sources supply a listing of the most-cited authors and researchers, pages 28-29; a listing of the most-cited professional associations and societies, page 30; a listing of the 360 most-cited publishers, pages 31-32; and a listing of the most-cited periodical sources, pages 33-34. These listings formed the basis for differentiating among the various approaches to or classifications of quality. These approaches and classifications are discussed in the "Quality Meta Study" chapter.

Inclusion in the review set required presence of these variables: (1) continuous improvement, (2) organizational systems, and (3) internal and external customer values. Continuous-improvement variables include customer loyalty, individual and group growth and development, and productivity. Organizational-systems variables refer to suppliers, customers, the technological culture, leadership, structure, vision, mission, and rewards. Internal- and external-customer values include fear, competition, joy of work, pride in workmanship, motivation, trust, ethics, sentiments, interactions, activities, and processes. Some variables serve as both explanatory and performance characteristics. For example, some publications use growth as a performance measure; others use it as an explanatory measure.

The reader might note the absence of many studies and papers presented at various annual conferences (Academy of Management, Decision Sciences, and so forth); such items have been excluded because they are not cited often in the proceedings of those conferences. Also excluded are the majority of studies and publications that focus on activity-based costing and activity-based management. Although there is minor duplication of some citations, there does not appear to be a direct correlation between quality and activity-based activities. This is not to say that there should be a correlation; it just means that those studying activity-based activities have not found the primary quality literature. Those interested in activity-based costing are referred to (Kemper, Robert E. and Michael R. Wunsch [1998] *Activity-Based Costing (ABC): A Meta Study*. Lanham, MD: Scarecrow Press).

The present study identifies 5,839 publications—1 was published in 1830, 1 in 1886, 2 between 1890 and 1899, 1 between 1900 and 1909, 7 between 1910 and 1919, 12 in the 1920s, 21 in the 1930s, another 59 in the 1940s, 266 in the 1950s, 443 in the 1960s, 1,060 in the 1970s, 3,706 in the 1980's, and 1,205 so far in the 1990s.

As the methodology process continued, the results from many partially comparable empirical studies examining relationships between similar variables were systematically combined and integrated. This meta study provides some clues about the natural parentage of recent publications while controlling crudely for variations in citation rates in different disciplines and for unique antecedents. The procedure and the analysis—citation indexing—are the work of Eugene Garfield.

The theory of citation indexing is that the key to locating the important papers in a field of study rests in the cited references (footnotes and bibliographies) found in books, journal articles, presentations at meetings and conferences, research reports, case studies, and experiential exercises. Garfield's theory is that by checking citations, a diligent researcher uncovers the most cited references, thereby identifying the top-notch papers in a field. Such a process also locates chief researchers, writers, publishers, journals, associations, and societies. Hence, *citation indexing* was chosen as the meta-analysis methodology to *identify the present state of quality knowledge*.

Identifying the universe of quality theory for students of management at any level is difficult. As a result, justifying any particular sample of publications as "representative" of the quality universe is also difficult. The procedures used here were selective rather than random. The purpose was to establish a list of publications that met three criteria: (1) they should be primarily concerned with organizational behavior, (2) they should be highly regarded, recent items, and (3) they should represent a variety of disciplinary and methodological foci.

To differentiate one quality approach from another, each publication was searched for the variables of leadership (doing the right things), of management (doing things right), of win-lose orientation, of organizations (centralization/decentralization), of assertiveness (concern with one's own outcome), and of cooperativeness (concern with the outcomes of others). An investigation was conducted to determine whether these variables were treated as independent or dependent variables. There is some confusion in the literature as to whether the quality movement is a new philosophy or just a traditional management approach that has been tampered with. What was desired was to find that the new philosophy takes uncoordinated knowledge and directs it into a system of quality leadership and management useful for predicting the needs of internal and external organizational customers.

As the study of quality variables continued, a set of approaches and classifications in which almost all quality literature fits was found. The result is as follows:

- *Quality*[1], doing the right things and doing them effectively, is analyzed in 50 publications and shows a clear direction. Quality[1], a top-strategy approach, includes works by, about, and based on the works of W. Edwards Deming and a number of his followers. Included in quality[1] are such strategic topics as ethics, trust, fear, pride, loyalty, and variation. Note that the study distinguishes this quality approach from the generic term quality by placing the superscript [1] after the word quality. Hereafter, such a distinction will be made when referring to the generic term quality and the quality[1] approach.

- *TQC (Total Quality Control),* analyzed in 116 publications, is a leadership movement led by the Japanese. It is based upon a system for integrating the quality development, quality maintenance, and quality-improvement efforts of groups in an organization to economically achieve production and service levels that result in full customer satisfaction. Major subtopics of the TQC literature include just in time (JIT), benchmarking, empowerment, teams, and quality circles.

- *TQM (Total Quality Management)*, doing things right with an emphasis on efficiency, is analyzed in 93 publications. It emphasizes consistent achievement of higher performance. TQM cited literature can be divided into strategic and operational segments. Major subtopics of the TQM literature include JIT, benchmarking, empowerment, teams, and quality circles.

- *Reengineering* is the fundamental rethinking and radical redesign of business *processes* to achieve dramatic improvements in critical, contemporary measures of performance, such as cost, quality, service, and speed. This quality approach is billed as process-based thinking and is both strategic and operations oriented.

- A way to examine quality management and organizations in the 1990s is to use the *Malcolm Baldrige National Quality Award* criteria. Initiated on August 20, 1987, with the enactment of U. S. Public Law 100-17, the Baldrige's purpose is to recognize firms that are leaders in providing increased quality and value to their customers in an internationally competitive era. The literature identifies the Baldrige as process-based management with strategic as well as operational orientations.

- *ISO* is a comprehensive standard specifying the management systems and processes a firm must possess to market certain products in the European Union (EU). Without International Standards Organization (ISO) 9000 certification, a firm with regulated products in the health, safety, or environmental sectors may be prohibited from marketing its products in Europe.

- The *zero-defects* movement is anchored by Philip B. Crosby. Under this approach, quality is defined as conformance to requirements and the system for achieving quality is prevention. The zero-defects movement is designed to structure and position the organization for operational improvements and improved communication.

- Some thinkers and writers prefer the term *continuous improvement* rather than quality, TQC, and TQM. Continuous improvement is preferred because it is less ambiguous than quality and more descriptive of the actual level of commitment required to make things happen. Often, continuous improvement and quality are used interchangeably. One writer, Eliyahu M. Goldratt, is included in this component simply because he has not named the philosophy he prescribes. He sometimes refers to it as throughput theory, other times as theory of constraints, and even other times simply as continuous improvement.

- *QFD (Quality Function Deployment)* is a new-product-development system that helps engineers determine what customers really want and translates those preferences into engineering requirements.

To differentiate one quality approach from another, a distinction is made as to whether the quality variables are treated as dependent or independent variables. Measured at the doing-the-right-thing level, top-strategy approaches have a significant influence on loyalty, individual and group growth and development, and productivity. Factors identified by the citation methodology to increase knowledge and direct it into a system of quality leadership and management include, but are not limited to, ethics, trust, fear, pride, loyalty, and variation. Doing the right things is a way of life. It pervades interpersonal relations, organizational processes, international discretion, cultural diversity, and values. A sense of what is good is the key to quality[1]. Quality[1] is life; it happens for a person at home and at work. A person takes her or his given behavior to work and is faced with the required behavior of the organization. What emerges will be value driven by all participants in the workplace. There is no recipe for implementing doing-the-right-things quality[1]. To be successful at doing the right things, leaders must develop profound knowledge of an organization. The leader must understand variation, systems, prediction, constraints, and psychology. The leader and her or his organization are always in transition—constant improvement is the agenda each day.

The citation methodology for doing things right identified systematic, company-wide, continuous-improvement efforts; self-directing work teams; employee-involvement programs; flexible manufacturing; quick changeover; customer focus; supplier integration; and cycle-time reduction components of total quality control and management. Major subtopics of the doing-things-right literature include JIT, benchmarking, empowerment, teams, quality circles, and continuous improve-ment.

Processes are increasingly being seen as the way to organize a firm. Viewing the materials-transformation process in terms of activities tied to transforming materials into something of value for the customer is a process view. The advantage of concentrating on processes is that they enable the organization to focus on the customer. Process methodology is positively related to organizational performance. Though this methodology is potentially useful, it demonstrates a lack of research in the area; more work is needed, for ultimately these concerns will translate into challenges for all areas of management, including more effective work and job design, and the selection, use, training, development, and motivation of employees.

The citing methodology also identified other process-oriented approaches that used standards to specify the management systems and processes a firm must possess to provide external customers with quality products and services. One process-oriented approach to quality management is found in the "zero defects" movement. Zero defects requires a identifiable flow of events moving toward a conformance standard. The worker's job is to meet the performance standard with no defects while management's job is to improve the flow of events so that zero defects can be achieved. Quality is destroyed by non-conformance to performance standards. There are four absolutes of zero-defects management: conformance to requirements, prevention, zero defects performance, and the price of non-conformance. Relationships and quality are two keys to successful zero-defects leadership. The zero-defects plan for quality improvement is: management commitment, quality-improvement teams, measurement, cost of quality, awareness, corrective action, zero-defects planning, employee education, zero-defects day, goal setting, error-cause removal, recognition, quality councils, and do it all again.

Some thinkers and writers prefer the term *continuous improvement* rather than *quality* because continuous improvement is more descriptive of the actual level of commitment required to make things happen. Continuous improvement requires each of the following: customers come first, company must innovate constantly, quality must be designed into products and services, everything has to be improved continually, safe-work/open-work environment (absolute necessities), messenger is not to be shot, Japanese are not to be imitated, time is used wisely, long-term improvements are not to be sacrificed for short-term profits, and quality is not enough.

Few publications address new-product development that helps engineers determine what customers really want and translate that into engineering requirements. Company-wide quality, focus on the customer, and translation of quality perceptions into product characteristics and then into the manufacturing process are positively related to successful performance.

Identifying the universe of quality theory for students of leadership and management at any level is difficult. As a result, justifying any particular sample of works as "representative" of the universe is also difficult. The procedures used here were selective rather than random. The goal was to establish a list of materials that met three criteria: (1)

they should be primarily concerned with organizational behavior; (2) they should be highly regarded, recent volumes; and (3) they should represent a variety of disciplinary and methodological foci.

Citation analysis, like most research methods, has certain inherent shortcomings. Establishing a truly new quality model is generally infeasible because authors pick and choose particular factors of performance. This process results in a comparison of "theories" in a "compare-and-contrast" framework. The quality literature is large, and several branches have a long history. Since a meta study depends heavily on published literature, quantitative comparison of quality models is difficult, principally because model specifications differ widely. The quality literature abounds with knowledge, great knowledge, but there appears to be no coordination of the pieces. Researchers, of course, are influenced by existing work in which a series of results tend to be highly biased. Among these biases are publication, control, quality and statistical independence, and heterogenous measures.

The reviewing process may exclude publications because a writer or researcher is not diligent and is not accurate in bibliographical citings. Much could be learned from Goldratt (1994), Goldratt and Fox (1986), and Goldratt and Cox (1984, 1992). However, Goldratt and his coauthors fail to cite what may be important sources. An overzealous desire for rigorous methodology may lead editors to reject rich, broad-sweeping, holistic manuscripts that provide field integration by virtue of the many variables studied, while they publish instead narrowly defined, intellectually vapid research reports.

The "Quality Meta Study" chapter examines the results of the final compilation—it identifies the features of recent fashionings in the citations. The "Subject Index" provides subject access to the citations and the "Cocontributor Index" provides access to coauthors, joint authors, editors, and joint editors of quality literature. The "Citation Style Configurations" unfolds the mysteries of the different forms of citations. The "Citations" chapter lists the references found in quality literature. It does not represent all quality literature for it results from researcher citations rather than an on-line search of the collection of the major libraries in the world. Every cocontributor is identified.

CITATION STYLE CONFIGURATIONS

Each bibliographic citation contains the *author's(s') name* (if given); the *date of publication*; the *title of the article* (if printed in a journal); the *name of the journal*; the *name of the book* (if it is a book); the *name of the editor(s)* (if the book is a collection of articles); the *edition of the book* (if the edition is not the first); the *volume number* (when the volume number is given); the *issue number and/or issue date*; the *page numbers* (if appropriate); the *place of publication* (if a book); the *name of the publisher* (if a book); a *multiple-citing number* (the number of times the particular entry was cited in different books, journals, book collections, law cases, and unpublished papers and dissertations, for example [*2]). When the entry appears in **bold face** it is considered a significant citation. Citations without an author are integrated among all entries in alphabetical order.

Single-author entries with more than one publication listed are arranged by publication date with the earliest date listed first. When an author has written both single-author works and multi-author, the single-author works are listed first. Multi-author works are arranged in simple alphabetical order according to *The Chicago Manual of Style.* (1982) [Thirteenth edition. Chicago: IL: University of Chicago]. To distinguish one author with the same surname as another author, complete forenames have been used when appropriate and when available.

Sample Entries

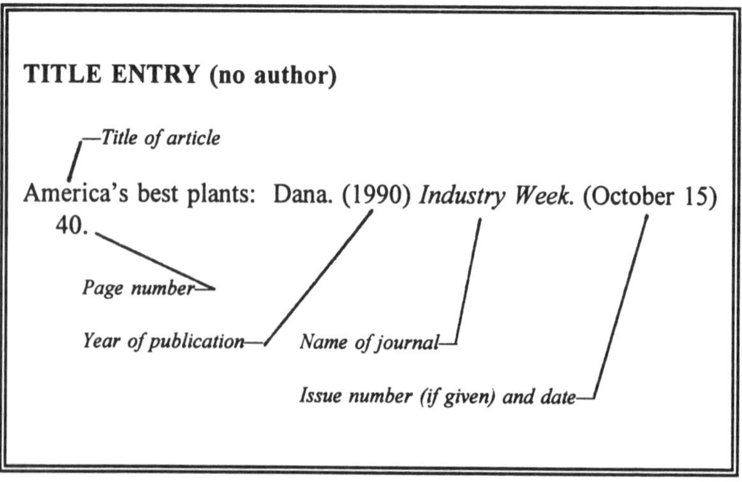

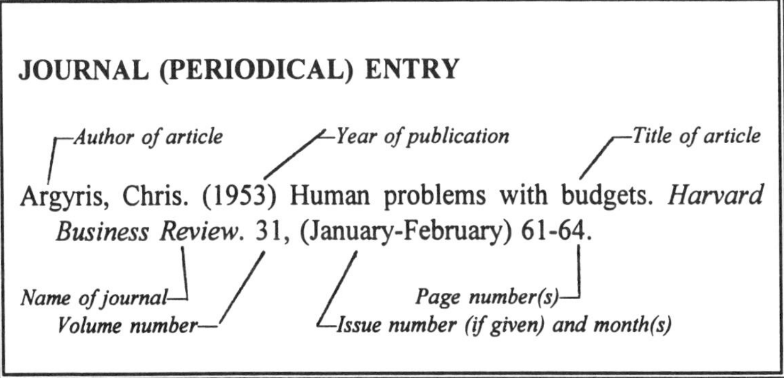

BOOK ENTRY

Author(s) of book *Date of publication* *Title of book*

Band, William A. (1991) *Creating Value for Customers: Designing and Implementing a Total Corporate Strategy*. New York: John Wiley.

Place of publication *Publisher*

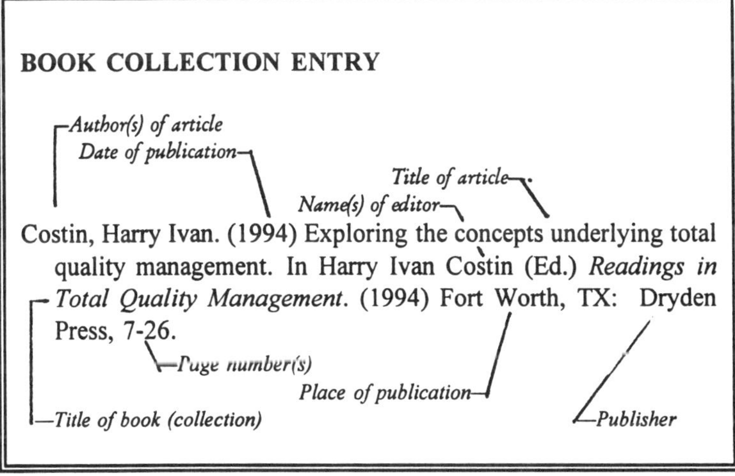

UNPUBLISHED PAPERS AND DISSERTATIONS

Author(s) *Date of presentation* *Title of presentation*

Dechant, K., and V. J. Marsick. (1991) In search of the learning organization: Toward a conceptual model of collective learning, Proceedings, Eastern Academy of Management, Annual Meeting, Hartford, CT. (May).

Name of meeting where paper was presented

Author(s) of article *Date of presentation* *Title of presentation*

Daniels, R. M., A. R. Dennis, G. S. Hayes, J. F. Nunamaker, Jr., and J. S. Valacich. (1991) Enterprise analyzer: Electronic support for group requirements elicitation. In Proceedings of the Twenty-Fourth Annual Hawaii International Conference on System Sciences. New York: IEEE Computer Society Press.

Location and name of publisher

Author *Date of dissertation* *Title of dissertation*

De Simone, Mary Joan Orzolek. (1994) An ethnographic study of the formation of a continuous improvement facilitator's group in higher education. Unpublished Ph.D. dissertation, University of Maryland, College Park, MD. (*2)

Multiple-citing number

Name of college or university

ACKNOWLEDGMENTS

The key to the successful completion of any endeavor is good people. I surrounded myself with good people—family, friends, and trusted colleagues. My family is Joyce, Michele, and Daniele. Joyce made sure the proper software was loaded on my computer and each did its job. Efficient and effective was Northern Arizona University (NAU) librarian Hank Hassell. Hank is a librarian's librarian. He was quick and accurate with answers to exacting and onerous bibliographical questions.

Dr. Michael R. Wunsch (NAU) was just a great friend. Dr. Ronald Gunderson (NAU) made sure that I had the release time and the resources to work on the book during several academic semesters.

QUALITY META STUDY

INTRODUCTION

This is the age of "new paradigms in business." The old paradigms, according to publishers Butterworth and Heinemann, preached short-term goals, rigid culture, product orientation, internal focus, regional emphasis, top-down management, procedural bias, management by numbers, one-win competition, and aggressive values. The "new paradigms," suggest the foregoing publishers, are corporate/individual vision, flexible culture, market orientation, external focus, global emphasis, employee empowerment, risk bias, and collaboration (analysis, intuition, harmony, trust, honesty, and compassion). Quality, also a new paradigm, is the "hot" concept. In Arizona there is the Governor's Advisory Council on Quality and its functional arm, the Arizona Quality Alliance. Northern Arizona University (NAU) has its quality unit—**QU**ality **i**n **L**earning and **L**eadership (QUILL), and the College of Business Administration's MBA program has built its quality perspective around Baldrige's systems' view. One of NAU's undergraduate business professors requires students to read Deming (1994) as well as Hammer and Champy (1993), and another has written and requires students to read Kemper and Codding (1994). W. L. Gore (Flagstaff) requires its managers to read Goldratt (1992), and Prent Corporation (Flagstaff) as well as Gore are ISO 9000 certified.

Rather than being "new," however, quality is quite historic. Juran (1995) wrote that quality has an evolution, is marked by trends, and has a future direction. He traces quality to each of the following: ancient Chinese history, ancient Israel, Greek temples and theaters, early India, Scandinavian shipbuilding, ancient Rome, Germany, Arsenale of the Venetian Republic, clocks in the Netherlands, Russia, cathedral building in France, the United Kingdom, the Czechs' mining as well as beer and sugar production, Japan, and the United States. Burkett (1991) traces quality principles to the Bible. Among the quality principles he cites from there are business bondage, personal lifestyle goals, hiring and firing decisions, corporations as well as partnerships, and retirement.

The study of quality provides a remarkable meeting ground for diverse points of view, both scientific and practical. Students of quality cite treatises on *heroes*, Iacocca and Novak (1984); *gurus*, Oberle (1990); and the *heroic*, Covey (1989). Also cited in the quality literature are thoughts of *passion*, Peters and Austin (1985); *personality*, Maslow (1954) and McGregor (1960); *individual values*, Senge (1990); *chaos*, Peters (1987); and *reckoning*, Halberstam (1987). From competitive theory, there is the "*edge*" movement: *regaining*, Dertouzos, Lester, and Solow (1989); *managing*, Garvin (1988) and Porter (1980, 1985); and *restoring*, Hayes and Wheelwright (1984), Ouchi (1984), and Deming (1982). Then there are the *numbers:* five, Senge (1990), Senge, Kleiner, Roberts, Ross, and Smith (1994), and Kilmann (1984); four, Joiner and Reynard (1994); one, Vogel (1979); and sums, Thurow (1980). The most cited writers who have addressed workplace control are Glasser (1994) and Tichy and Sherman (1993). And, there is the well-known Ralph Nader (1965), who has often reminded us of *nonquality*.

Other interesting studies falling under the quality umbrella deal with the *pursuit of wow* in topsy-turvy times, Peters (1994); the *chase of the Japanese*, Ouchi (1981), and Pascale, Tanner, and Athos (1979); and the *quest of world-class manufacturing*, Ford (1988), Sheridan (1990), Garvin (1983), Hayes, Wheelwright, and Clark (1988), and Reich (1983).

More than just interesting reading, quality and its citations present workplace tools for continual improvement of organizations and society. Quality is determined by organizations' internal as well as external customers. Businesses need to make money, but they must also play an important part in raising the standard of living of everyone. A knowledge of quality is crucial for anybody who needs to deal with conflict to resolve issues. Conflicts within or among organizations or among individuals are frustrating and waste valuable time, energy, and money. For resolving conflicts, quality literature contains key ideas and process strategies. The literature specifies the relationships in models linking various hypothesized effectiveness variables to various managerial efficiency measures. The variables usually describe some combination of the organizational characteristics of doing the right things or doing things right. This work is found in several disciplines, including economics, management, business policy, finance, accounting, international business, sociology, education, hospital administration, engineering, and marketing.

BIBLIOGRAPHIES AND REVIEWS

Reviews of quality-oriented literature have been quite specialized: *control charts*, Montgomery (1980); *determinants of financial performance*, Capon et. al. (1990); *international quality management practices*, American Quality Foundation and Ernst and Young (1991); *job redesign and productivity*, Kopelman (1985); *leadership*, Stogdill (1948); *product quality and worker attitude*, Blau and Roswow (1978); *quality circles*, Konz (1979); *readings in TQM*, Costin (1994); *scientific management*, Bluedorn (1986); *response-surface methodology*, Hill and Hunter (1966); *service industries*, Torbeck (1985) and Cole (1993); *statistical quality control chart techniques*, Vance (1983); and *technological innovation*, Tornatzky, et. al., (1983). A focused review of the reengineering literature was prepared by Nissen (1996). His purpose was to identify and suggest the best practices and integrating lessons learned from the "reengineering" approach to quality. In a recent review of the reengineering and TQM literature, Gadd and Oakland (1996) explore the history of the development, ideals, beliefs, values, knowledge, means of implementation, and techniques involved in the similarities in these two approaches.

Quantitative comparison of quality models is difficult, principally because model specifications and operationalizations of explanatory and dependent variables differ widely. Surely, the quality literature contains knowledge, great knowledge, but it is in uncoordinated bits and pieces. Quality techniques, ranging from simple tools of daily management to complex "process" models (Baldrige), differ widely among studies. Flowing from the business classics ("Fifteen key concepts for managerial success," *Harvard Business Review* 1991) is a tradition that helps quantify specific effects of particular causal variables of key concepts for managerial success. Researchers are, of course, influenced by existing work—particularly in terms of model specification; this influence results in various streams of literature in which a series of results tends to be highly intercorrelated.

Although studies of quality are found in many research traditions, they share the basic approach of "previous citing." Because establishing a truly new quality model is generally infeasible, authors pick and choose particular factors of performance and use citation techniques to verify the existence of theory. This practice results in a comparison of "theories" in a "compare-and-contrast" framework. The challenge for students of quality is determining what was lost in the translation of the most recently cited work.

GENERAL INTERPRETATIVE WORKS

The study of quality has a history but not a pedigree. The distinction is simple. A pedigree suggests a series of causally connected specific works in time; history consists in a temporal ordering of general interpretative works. The citing of names associated with interest in the process of leadership and management is extensive. There is scarcely a major academician, lawyer, psychologist, or scholar who has not been overlooked by those writing and researching the theory and practice of quality in the workplace.

Through the citation indexing process, a liberal sprinkling of multiple-author citations to a wide range of general management is found. Among the most cited *general management* authors, one who is not considered as "quality-oriented," is Ackoff (1970, 1974, 1978, 1981, and 1986). The *production and operations management* literature is boosted by Adam (1972, 1983, 1992), Adam and Swamidass (1989), Adam and Ebert (1982), and Adam, Hershauer, and Ruch (1981 and 1986). Some of the best classics in *organization* are cited through Argyris who has 13 citings from 1955 through 1988. Warren Bennis (1968 through 1995), who also writes on *leadership* is an author who is frequently cited by those writing on quality. Classic contributions on leadership, motivation, and decision making are found in the citings of Vroom (1974), Vroom and Jago (1988), and Vroom and Yetton (1973). Blake and Mouton (1957, 1961, 1962, and 1964) are cited for their work on *group dynamics and managerial grids*.

Among the most prolific *management* writers is Peter Drucker, who admits to finding a new management niche approximately every two years. Drucker's most cited works are 1954, 1964, 1969, 1974, 1979, 1980, 1985, 1986, 1989, and 1992. Drucker writes on management practice, results, discontinuity, purpose and mission, tasks and responsibilities, adventures, turbulent times, innovation and entrepreneurship, results, leadership, politics, non-profit organizations, and postcapitalist society. Almost as prolific is Edward E. Lawler III (1969, 1971, 1973, 1978, 1981, 1983, 1985, 1986, and 1987). Lawler and a variety of his close colleagues, Allan M. Mohrman Jr. (1985, 1987, 1988, 1989), Susan Albers Mohrman (1994), Susan M. Resnick-West (1985 and 1989), Mary Ann Von Glinow (1988 and 1990) and David Nadler (1977, 1979, and 1982), are concerned with *management performance*. Their work is often cited by those studying quality-oriented management. Tichy (1983, 1993) and Tichy and his associates (1982, 1984, 1986, and 1993) are also concerned with management performance, particularly with mastering change.

A cited author in the area of *finance* is Grayson (1967, 1972, 1975, and 1993). A two-minute warning was fired by Grayson and O'Dell (1988). J. Richard Hackman (1984, 1987, and 1989) writes on job characteristics and effective teamwork. He teamed with Edward E.

Lawler III (1971) with a concern for employee reactions to job characteristics. He teamed with Oldman (1975 and 1980) with work on applied psychology where work design was a topic.

Lisa Hammel and a variety of coauthors were cited by quality-oriented writers and researchers for work on *statistics* (1974, 1980, 1983, 1988, 1981, and 1985). Another frequently cited author for work on statistical measurements is Youden (1951, 1959, 1962, 1963, and 1967). George E. P. Box and a number of coauthors are cited for work on operations, quantitative variables, and statistics.

When it comes to *intrinsic motivation*, a philosophy that is very important to W. Edwards Deming, Brian L. Joiner, and Robert E. Kemper and Deborah Codding, is the work of Fredrick Herzberg (1966, 1968, 1979, 1979). He was joined by Mauser and Snyderman (1959) for a classic accomplishment, *The Motivation to Work.* What Fredrick Herzberg did for quality-oriented philosophers with his work in intrinsic motivation, Henry Mintzberg (1973, 1975, 1976, 1978, 1979, 1990) did for the *nature of management*—planning, organizing, leading, and controlling. Mintzberg's structuring of organizations fits quite well with approaches to quality. Quinn (1979, 1980, 1981, and 1987) is also cited for his contributions on *organizational strategy.*

Quality writers and researchers are quite aware of the contributions of Thomas J. Peters and Robert H. Waterman Jr. The renewed quality movement was just getting started when Peters and Waterman (1982) appeared with their study, *In Search of Excellence.* They described the characteristics that best characterized how excellently run companies operate in terms of *leadership, competition, and organization.* Peters followed this work with much cited contributions in 1985, 1987, and 1994. Robert H. Waterman Jr. was cited for his 1987 work, *The Renewal Factor.*

Porter (1980, 1985, 1986, and 1990) is often cited for his work on *competitive strategy.* Although not looked upon favorably by W. Edwards Deming as interpreted by Aguayo (1990), a number of quality philosophers cite Porter. Much to the pleasure of at least Aguayo and Deming is the work of Kohn (1986 and 1990). Aguayo, Deming, Kohn, and Kemper and Codding (1994) favor the concept "competition with" as opposed to Porter's "competition against" approach. The Deming philosophy is very much a win-win approach where many interpret Porter's philosophy as win-lose.

Reich (1983, 1985, 1987, 1991) is cited for his work on American business. He traces the evolution of *macro-business practices* through the 1970s and moves through the quality movement, a movement he attributes to W. Edwards Deming. The plight of the *American worker* is still anchored by the much cited work of Roethlisberger and his associates (1939, 1945). Global economic issues are cited in the work of Thurow (1980, 1983, 1985, 1987, 1990, and 1992).

Various scholars have studied the *industrial civilization* in the organizational setting. These scholars include Ackoff (1975); Mayo (1933, 1946, 1947, and 1977); Reich (1983); Simon (1957 and 1977), and Rokeach (1960). Among the leadership and organization researchers cited by those writing and researching the quality literature are Blake and Mouton (1961), Bennis (1983), and Covey (1989).

THEORETICAL APPROACHES TO QUALITY

A meta study provides one alternative to information summary; such a study quantifies a comparison of results from diverse approaches which are not directly comparable in terms of research technology or model specification. This paper summarizes a meta study of statistical results in the literature on quality[1], TQC, TQM, reengineering, Baldrige, ISO, continuous improvement, zero defects, QFD, and other research classified as quality. In an original study 5,740 citations were reviewed. In this paper the principal items published between 1913 and 1996 are cited. Four hundred, forty-seven citations were eliminated from an original 6,187 because of incomplete and erroneous information.

Quality[1]

Quality[1] was a way of life for Deming (1986, 1993, 1994) and is a way of life for Kemper and Codding (1994). It pervades interpersonal relations, organizational processes, cultural diversity, and, for Pirsig (1974), values. In the quality[1] approach, the quality variables—leadership (doing the right things), management (doing things right), win-lose orientation, organization (centralization/decentralization), assertiveness (concern with one's own outcome), and cooperativeness (concern with the outcomes of others)—are all treated as dependent variables. A sense of what is good is the key to quality[1]. Although quality[1] is considered a formal activity, it is prevalent in informal marital interactions, superior-subordinate relationships, and customer-merchant exchanges most notably as conflict. A growth industry in the United States, conflict has captured the attention of behavioral scholars because of its linkages to ethics, trust, intrinsic motivation, pride in work, joy in the workplace, loyalty, individual and group development, and productivity—all of which are inherently intertwined. Quality[1] cannot occur without trust, loyalty cannot be debated without a common set of ethical behaviors, and pride in work cannot transpire without intrinsic motivation. These events are inherent in Deming's work and are made more visible in the win-win-Win model developed by Kemper and Codding (1994). This type of quality[1] is life itself. Such quality happens for a person at home and at work. A person takes his or her given behaviors to work and is faced with the required behaviors of the organization. What emerges will be value driven by all participants in the workplace. Such a philosophy is also prevalent in Goldratt's (1994) and in Goldratt and Cox's (1992, 1994) works, which will be explored later.

Much of quality[1] is influenced by the life-long work of Deming. Table 6 lists cited materials written about or influenced by the work of W. Edwards Deming. He wrote 34 articles and was cited 85 times in the literature. In 123 publications, Deming is a prominent force. His name appears on 53 titles. He is prominent in industrial organization, education, health care, economics, engineering, and management literature.

Deming (1986, 1993, 1994) was quick to point out that there was no recipe for implementing quality[1]. The best that he could offer was his philosophy and his theory of profound knowledge. Quality[1] people—managers and workers—must have profound knowledge (theory of systems, theory of variation, theory of knowledge, and theory of psychology) of an organization. Only then, he stated, can the organization be managed for quality[1]. According to Deming, an organization is always in transition; that is, constant and continual improvement is the agenda each day.

Deming was characterized by most who met him in his seminars and consulting work as a curmudgeon, and on that basis he was often belittled (Bowles and Hammond 1991, Creech 1993, Gabor 1990, and Walton 1986, 1991). In these instances, what one has to do is separate the person from the philosophy and rely on the knowledge being expounded.

It is important to note that some of the authors of works on Deming were not students of management, leadership, or quality. They were journalists who capitalized on the popularity, or unpopularity, of Deming and the times. The most cited journalists are Dobbins (1990), Gabor (1988, 1990), and Walton (1986, 1990).

Deming's seminars generated a number of often-cited books. Representative of the titles are Aguayo (1990) and Latzko and Saunders

(1995). Aguayo represents an excellent introduction to Deming. Latzko and Saunders' book does well with undergraduates as it is a simulation of Deming's four-day workshops. Deming's teachings engendered many followers, mostly referred to as Deming masters. The most cited and influential of these devotees are Fellers (1994), Joiner Associates (1993), Joiner (1994), Mann (1985), Moen (1989), Neave (1990), Scherkenbach (1986), and Scholtes (1993). Joiner (1994) carries on the work of Deming, with whom Joiner had a close relationship for over three decades. Joiner's *Fourth Generation Management* (1994) provides much help in appreciating the crucial role leadership and management play in achieving improved performance. The book contains excellent notes and a good list of recommendations for future study—Deming oriented.

According to Kemper and Codding (1994), what separates quality[1] from TQC, TQM, reengineering, and all of the other quality movements is its reliance on the behavioral topics of ethics, trust, pride, loyalty, and the scientific approach of variation. Among the citations on ethics are Bennett (1988), Berenbeim (1992), Fine (1993), Hosmer (1991), and Rudelius and Buchholz (1979). Trust is the topic of articles by Farnhm (1989), Ishihara (1990), Pascarella (1993), and Whitney (1993). Pride as a component of quality[1] is cited in Gerhard and Sparrow (1988) and Resnick (1985). For loyalty the citings are Guyon (1980), Matejka (1991), and O'Boyle (1985). Leonard (1991) takes quality[1] to the schools and (1992) to the railroads. Mackey and Mackey (1992) apply Deming to libraries.

Many organizational behaviorists looked upon Deming as "just another statistician," but he surely was much more than that. What most of Deming's detractors did not appreciate, very likely due to their lack of comprehension, was how Deming used the theory of variation in his behavioral model. Deming's work opposed the use of "gut reactions" by managers. Demingites look to the theory of variation as a means to quality[1]. The study of variation allows quality[1] to determine the causes of organizational problems. Most problems are caused by the system, yet most managers blame the worker. If one gains anything from Deming's quality[1] philosophy (Aguayo 1990; Deming 1981-1982, 1982, 1993, 1994; Gabor 1990; Kemper and Codding 1994; Latzko and Saunders 1995; Scherkenbach 1986; and Walton 1990), it is the fact that quality[1] must start at the top because that is where responsibility for designing the system rests. When the system is at fault, it is management's responsibility. In a downsizing activity, it is management that almost certainly should be released, not the workers. Workers can do only what they are trained to do, and training is the responsibility of management. Special causes, those that fall outside established control limits and that infrequently occur despite the existence of a sound system, are often unavoidable; nevertheless, they should be cooperatively studied by management and workers to see if avoidance is feasible. Variation citings include Anderson (1990), Gutt and Gruska (1977), Holmes and Michalek (1982), Messina (1985), Nolan and Provost (1990), Sinibaldi (1983), Sullivan (1984), and Wheeler (1993).

Total Quality Control (TQC)

The systematic, company-wide, continuous-improvement efforts, self-directing work teams, employee-involvement programs, flexible manufacturing, quick changeover, customer focus, supplier integration, and cycle-time reduction components of total-quality management have been practiced in Japan since the late 1940s. Aided by W. Edwards Deming, Joseph M. Juran, and A. V. Feigenbaum, the Japanese perfected the main innovations in continuous improvement—*kaizen*. It was done out of necessity. TQC means quality concerning each of the following: work, service, information, process, division, people, company, and objectives. As developed by the Japanese, TQC treats leadership as an independent variable. All other quality variables—management (doing things right), win-lose orientation, organization (centralization/ decentralization), assertiveness (concern with one's own outcome), and co-operativeness (concern with the outcomes of others)—are treated as dependent variables. The Japanese interpreted this situation to mean "Fix the problem, not the blame."

In surveying the TQC approach, one notes that the important literature is heavily Japanese oriented: Ohno (1988), Ohno and Mito (1988), and Kaoru Ishikawa (1980, 1983, 1985). Ohno created the concept of just in time and the production techniques that are the basis of what is called flexible manufacturing or lean production. He transformed Toyota from a small, near-bankruptcy manufacturer of cars to one of the largest, most-diversified, most-successful vehicular producers in the world. The lack of English translations of his work contributes to the few citations in the literature and an overlooked quality career. Kaoru Ishikawa is one of the most cited TQC writers. He is read by managers who want to increase profits, reduce labor strife, improve customer relations, and achieve defect-free production. Merging the ideas of Deming (various), Juran (various), Crosby (1979,

1984), and Feigenbaum (1961) with his own thoughts and then simplifying them into techniques manageable enough for skilled factory workers to teach to other factory workers, Kaoru Ishikawa developed seven tools used widely in both Japanese and American companies: cause-effect diagrams, flow charts, Pareto charts, run charts, histograms, control charts, and scatter diagrams.

Among the most-cited Japanese contributors to TQC are Asaka and Ozeki (1990), who developed a handbook of quality tools; Imai (1975, 1986), who discussed Japanese business; Karatsu (1988), who wrote of TQC wisdom; Morita, Reingold, and Shimomura (1986), who wrote about Akio Morita and Sony; Ozawa (1982), who described people and productivity in Japan; Shingo (1988), who described the Shingo system for continuous improvement; and Taguchi and Wu (1979), who developed a theory of off-line quality control. Some important Japanese works that are not cited, often because of the date of translation, are Hosotani (1992), who gives an overview of Japanese quality concepts, and Matsumoto (1988), who discusses the unspoken language of Japanese business.

The most-cited American authors, who have capitalized on TQC by researching and writing about the Japanese approach so that it might be adopted by American managers, are Abegglen (1973), Abegglen and Stalk (1985), Ross and Ross (1982), and Schonberger (1982). First, Abegglen investigated the Japanese solution to management/workers and then he collaborated with Stalk with a book on *Kaisha* (1985). Ross and Ross (1982) wrote of Japanese quality circles and productivity. A highly cited work by an American concerning Japanese manufacturing techniques was written by Schonberger (1982). Creveling and Fowlkes (1995) wrote about Taguchi's advanced engineering, but the book is too new for literature citations.

Two of the most-cited Americans who influenced the Japanese in their TQC approach are Feigenbaum (1961) and Shewhard (1931, 1939). Shewhard and his statistics were introduced to the Japanese by Deming. Shewhard developed the science of quality control with its heavy statistical emphasis. Shewhard was an engineer at Bell Laboratories. Feigenbaum, a quality consultant and a former manager of manufacturing operations and quality control at General Electric, coined the term "total quality control." His premise was that quality relates to every function and activity within the organization, not simply manufacturing and engineering. Feigenbaum stated that the four jobs of quality control are: new-design control, incoming-material control, product control, and special-process studies.

The most-cited statistical quality-control works have been contributed by Kume (1985), Duncan (1965), Montgomery (1985), and Ott (1975). Ott discussed process quality control through troubleshooting and interpretation of data.

Total Quality Management (TQM)

Joseph M. Juran is the most-cited TQM guru (see Table 2). Juran (1988) believes that quality has multiple meanings. One meaning is product performance, which results from product features that create product satisfaction and lead customers to buy the product. Another Juran meaning, freedom from deficiencies, creates product dissatisfaction and leads customers to complain. Product satisfaction and product dissatisfaction are not opposites according to Juran. His simple definition of quality is "fitness for use" and he emphasizes that there are many uses and users. Customers, contends Juran, include all who are affected by processes and products, and customers include those who are both internal as well as external to a company. Product includes both goods and services.

Stahl (1995), in a quality-management textbook that is too new to be cited, defines TQM as a systems approach that aims to increase value to the customer by continuously designing and improving organizational processes and systems. He goes on to define processes as, "A group of activities that take an input, add value to it, and provide an output to an internal or external customer." He defines systems as collections of processes and resources. What Americans call TQM the Japanese call TQC. Both Juran's and Stahl's definitions are embodied in the definition given on page ix where TQC was defined. The Japanese like to credit American gurus—such as Deming, Juran, and Feigenbaum—with planting seeds of quality improvement in their country during the late 1940s and 1950s, but for the most part many of the really important TQM innovations in continuous improvement were made in Japan.

The TQM movement is prescription based. As cited in the literature, leadership and centralized decision making are treated as independent variables. Other quality variables—management (doing things right), win-lose orientation, assertiveness (concern with one's own outcome), and cooperativeness (concern with the outcomes of others)—are treated as dependent variables. Management orientation, as opposed to leadership orientation, is what separates quality[1] from TQM. There is no prescription for ethics, trust, pride, joy, loyalty, and intrinsic motivation. Deming's key to quality[1] was not his 14 points; it was his values and theory of knowledge. His 14 points have been improved from year to year by those whom he influenced. This collaborative improvement by others was something that many TQM people missed. Deming preached collaboration; he was also quick to give credit to others for his ideas. His quality is so collaboration oriented that some think they see a bit of communism in his ideas (1993). This idea, of course, is absurd; it stems from those who have mistakenly based their work on what people say about Deming rather than on what Deming actually wrote.

One of the best reference-oriented, new TQM books is Creech (1994), a former four-star general, who used TQM principles to effect the U.S. Air Force's stunning success in the Persian Gulf War. Creech's work is full of citations; however, overgeneralization very likely exists in some of his comments. He said, "I've read just about everything I can find on business management and quality matters—hundreds of books old and new. That research has included reading virtually everything written by the Big Four: Deming, Juran, Feigenbaum, and Crosby." There is no evidence in his citations or his writing to reveal that the preceding quotation is true. If it is true, something was lost in Creech's translation. He developed a decentralized leadership approach to TQM. According to Creech, his five pillars of TQM are based on teams, not functions; his supervisory focus is centered on outputs, not inputs; and his work-accomplishment mindset is on the team's product, not on each person's job. Creech's decentralized orientation " . . . affects every aspect of the management system operation and interaction—not only the structure, but also all facets of organizational character, culture, and climate. It takes the human spirit and human system aspects into full account."

The 1990s have seen the introduction of books that cover numerous fields. Health care is cited in the works of Al-Assaf and Schmele (1993) and Omachonu (1991). In higher education, the most cited is Lewis and Smith (1994); in education in general there are Schmoker and Wilson (1993) and Freeman (1992); and in government there is Carr and Littman (1990). Juran's most-cited works are from 1964, 1981, 1988, 1988, 1989; Juran and Gryna (1980); and Juran, Gryna, and Bingham (1976). Other most-mentioned TQM works with excellent citings are Berry (1991); Costin (1994); Gitlow, Gitlow, Oppenheim, and Oppenheim (1989); Omachonu and Ross (1994); Sashkin and Kiser (1993); and Zabel and Avery (1992).

In the quality literature there are a number of definitions that are a part of or are associated with operational-quality management. As is true with automation, robotics, and computer technologies, these components and their principles will not by themselves yield management quality. These components are beneficial to management when they are combined with other variables, components, processes, and systems. The identification of these components and the most-cited works follow.

Quality—JIT. Just-in-time inventory and production systems are considered the most important single concept of modern industrial work—Bowles and Hammond (1991) and Stahl (1994). The concept of JIT states that materials and components should be made and arrive at a factory, or from one work station to another within a plant, at precisely the moment they are needed for use by an internal or external customer. A JIT system is also referred to as a demand-pull inventory system because each workstation or worker is to have output only when the next workstation or worker on line is ready to receive more input. This arrangement contrasts with the traditional push-inventory system, in which large numbers of parts are made independent of when the next workstation or worker can use them. Among the most-cited works with excellent citings on JIT are Monden (1986), Ohno and Mito (1988), and O'Grady (1988).

Quality—Benchmarking. Competitive benchmarking occurs when a person analyzes what the best competitor or leading companies in the industry are doing to discover the products, processes, services, and practices that satisfy customers' needs. Functional benchmarking results from the study and possible emulation of the best processes and systems in the world, whether in the firm's own industry or in another industry. Picking the best-of-the-best techniques built a new paging device at Motorola, a competitive strategy with a 10-step benchmarking model for Xerox, an improved and a most-popular Taurus for Ford, and a quality standard used in the Baldrige process. The most-often cited, stand-alone works on benchmarking are Camp (1989), Spendolini (1991), and Whiting (1991).

Quality—Empowerment. Simply put, empowerment is sharing with nonmanagerial employees the power and authority to make and implement decisions. It means giving employees the authority and information they need to make wise business decisions and solve problems. Empowerment is a decentralized approach. According to Creech (1994), ". . . it must be at all levels, especially at the front line, so that enthusiastic involvement and common purpose are realities, not slogans." Employees often take pride in the ownership of a problem and their empowerment to find a solution. The basis for empowerment is found in the much-cited work of Fredrick Herzberg (1966, 1968, 1979, 1987) and Herzberg, Mauser, and Snyderman (1959). Herzberg's research tells us that achievement, recognition, work itself, responsibility, and advancement are people satisfiers. The dissatisfiers are company policy, supervision, supervisors, work conditions, and salary. Every writer or researcher on quality, TQC, and TQM lists empowerment as a critical factor. A much-cited writing strictly on empowerment is McKenna (1993).

Quality—Teams. Several types of teams exist in quality organizations. Some customer-relevant teams are cross functional, others are within a discipline. Some teams are permanent, others are temporary. Cross-functional teams consists of at least two members who represent different organizational functions—production, marketing, and finance, for example. A task-force/problem-solving team is a temporary entity that deals with unique problems. A formal team is officially created by the organization; informal teams are not official organizational teams. Instead, they form because they have common interests.

Empowered teams share with managers the power to operate the cross-functional systems designed by managers. In quality organizations, teams flatten the organization with a few layers of managers, thus leading to less-direct supervision of employees. Self-managed work teams have the power to make the operating decisions and to operate the systems designed by managers. These teams plan, set priorities, organize, coordinate with others, measure, take corrective action, solve problems, and deal with personnel issues. Cohesiveness and norms bring about cooperativeness among the teams' members. The team concept supports the basic attitude that the company belongs to each team member, not just management.

The most-cited works on self-managed teams include Brower (1992); Donovan (1986); Glaser (1990); Holpp (1992); Hughes (1991); Orsburn, Moran, Musselwhite, Zenger and Perrin (1990); and Wellins, et. al. (1990). The most-cited, self-standing publications on teamwork include Aubrey and Felkins (1988), Benson (1992), Hackman (1989), Larson and LaFasto (1989), Lee (1990), Lefton and Buzzotta (1987), and Parker (1990).

Team-based plants at GM were the focus of Cherry (1982) and joint teams at Alcoa-Kodak were the subject of Kegarise and Miller (1985). Empowered teams appear in the work of Wellins, Byham, and Wilson (1991). Special-task teams and pride teams are cited in Gabor (1986) and Gerhard and Sparrow (1988). A case for no teams is made by Verespej (1990).

The most-cited handbooks and guides for teams are Dyer (1987); Joiner Associates (1985); Kinlaw, (1991); Marchington (1992); McEachern, Schiff, and Cogan (1992); Mears and Voehl (1994); O'Dell (1989); Poza and Markus (1980); Reddy and Jamison (1988); Scholtes and Joiner Associates (1988); and Sundstrom, Demeuse, and Futrell (1990). Ryan (1992) is cited for his quality-team concept in TQC.

Quality—Quality Circles. What first caught American managers' attention when they became interested in quality was the Japanese concept of quality circles (QC). The idea behind QCs is to have workers meet occasionally to discuss work problems. The workers would then develop ideas about how to solve the problems identified. QCs became popular in Japan during the 1960s and 1970s. According to Sashkin and Kiser (1993), QCs began formally in 1962, and by 1980 there were over 100,000 QCs in operation in Japanese organizations. American firms began using QCs in the mid-1970s; they gained in popularity throughout the 1980s. By 1986 QCs, with mixed results, were so common that *BusinessWeek* listed them as a fad of the 1980s. Failures of QCs were due more to the way the approach was used than to some flaw with the technique itself. QC trainers commonly offer and provide services to "install" QCs. This approach treats QCs as something that can be fastened to an organization, such as an air conditioner that has been attached to a house to provide comfort. Deming (1986, 1993, 1994) said, "A usual stumbling block in [quality] is management's supposition that quality control is something that you install, like . . . a new carpet." This management approach lead to the failure of most QC programs. The quality-circle technique proved to be best used in the context of an organization-wide effort toward quality improvement. Used as such, in an organizational culture designed to support quality, TQC, or TQM, quality circles can be useful and productive. QCs were not a Japanese invention. In the late 1940s at Detroit Edison, Norman R. G. Maier, an American industrial psychologist, introduced an employee-team/problem-solving approach very similar to the QC concept. Despite a variety of successes, the approach that inspired Japanese managers to invent quality circles did not become popular in the United States until after a quarter century. It was then reintroduced as an "exotic" Japanese management technique.

An annotated bibliography of QCs is found in Konz (1979). A cited primer on quality circles was produced by Dailey and Kagerer (1982) and cited guides were produced by Ingle (1982), Robson (1982), Thompson (1982), and Fitzgerald and Murphy (1982). For country success, the following citings are helpful: U.S., Cole and Tachiki (1984), Hanley (1980), and Gryna (1981); Canada, Knight (1983); Japan, Konz (1979); and UK, Morland (1981). For citations that discussed QCs after the QC fad in America see Lawler and Mohrman (1985, 1987) and Meyer and Stott (1986).

Reengineering

Reengineering, Hammer and Champy (1993), is the fundamental rethinking and radical redesign of business processes to achieve dramatic improvements in critical, contemporary measures of performance like cost, quality, service, and speed. This definition contains four key words: *fundamental* (examining why do we do what we do and why we do it that way); *radical* (getting to the root of things, throwing away the old); *dramatic* (achieving quantum leaps in performance); and *process* (organizing activities systematically to create something of value for customers).

Reengineering, much like the Baldrige approach to quality, is process centered. According to Creech (1994), process revisions do not and will not produce the efficiency, boost, and aspiration a company needs. Reengineering as cited in the literature highlights and treats quality variables as independent variables.

Processes are increasingly regarded as the way to organize a firm, rather than by function. Viewing the materials-transformation process in terms of those activities tied to transforming materials into something of value for the customer is a process view. Such a view examines inventory in terms of customer value, not internal economics. Such a view can be the basis of reengineering processes. One of the biggest advantages of concentrating on processes, rather than on functions, is that processes enable the organization to focus on the customer. Many companies have discovered that completely redesigning a process is entirely different from implementing the proposed changes. Though in theory managers want to take out a clean sheet and design a new process from scratch, in practice this approach often leads to great hassle for relatively little additional benefit. Ultimately, all change is social change. Any change requires changes in behavior and inter-actions within and among groups—changes that do not happen overnight.

A focused review of the reengineering literature was prepared by Nissen (1996). His purpose was to identify and suggest the best practices and integrating lessons learned from the "reengineering" approach to quality. In a recent review of the reengineering and TQM literature, Gadd and Oakland (1996) explore the history of the development, ideals, beliefs, values, knowledge, means of implementation, and techniques involved in the similarities in these two approaches. Among the key citations that give an overview of reengineering are: Hammer (1990); Hammer and Champy (1993); Hammer and Stanton (1995); Haylet, Plewa, and Watts (1993); Huff (1992); and Layden (1993).

Baldrige

Another way to attain quality is to review the criteria of the Malcolm Baldrige National Quality Award, American Productivity and Quality Center (1990). Although there have been some concerns about the amount of work required to meet all of the criteria (leadership, information and analysis, strategic quality planning, human-resource development and management, management of process quality, quality and operational results, and customer satisfaction), they have been used by many managers as a guide for managerial and organizational improvement. Some companies require their suppliers—"Baldrige competition keeps suppliers competitive"(1989)—to apply the Baldrige criteria to themselves to improve the suppliers' operations.

Widely praised when it began, Reimann (1990), the Baldrige Award has attracted increasing criticism from Galvin (1991), Zemke (1991), and "The Baldrige boondoggle" (1992). Lines have formed regarding the criteria—including the makeup and weighing of the seven categories—and even over the award itself. Deming (1993) dismisses the Baldrige by saying, "The Baldrige Award does not codify principles of management of quality. It contains nothing about management of quality. The focus is purely on results." Phil Crosby said, "The Baldrige criteria have trivialized the quality crusade, perhaps beyond help." Some critics like the Baldrige just because it generated an awareness of total quality. Creech (1994) notes that quality principles flow from the top down; decisions flow from the bottom up. That implies, says Creech, " . . . the need to have leadership operating from the very bottom of the organization." Then he goes on to say, "The Baldrige criteria allocates (*sic*) only 100 of 1,000 points to leadership.

I believe that if those administering the Baldrige award looked on leadership as I do they would realize that you must look for its presence everywhere in the organization."

Despite some criticism from him, one of the Baldrige's most notable boosters is Robert Galvin (1991), Motorola's former chairman. He presided over the company during a transformation that made it the first company-wide Fortune 500 company to win the Baldrige. He believes that the award should be a national policy and that every company should be considered a candidate. Galvin calculated that if every company in America applied—made the investment that is required to apply—the GNP would grow by a minimum of one half of one percent. Blackburn and Rosen (1993) and Brinksman (1991) believe that the Baldridge provides useful standards for assessing quality.

The critics, however, point out that the Baldrige does not address such areas as financial performance, innovation, long-term planning, or environmental issues.

The Baldrige, Bowles and Hammond (1991), is not a comprehensive business award; instead, it is a quality-*practices* award, Brown (1992). It was never intended to rescue businesses or be the master plan for competitiveness. This extra responsibility has been thrust on it because of its enormous appeal to business and the absence of any other national criteria. As cited in the literature, the Baldrige approach emphasizes quality variables as independent variables. Among the most-cited works on the Baldrige are: George (1992), *The Baldrige Quality System: The Do-It-Yourself Way to Transform Your Business*; Hart (1992), "Using the Baldrige criteria for assessment and continuous improvement"; Kelly (1992), "How the states are playing midwife to baby Baldriges'"; National Institute of Standards and Technology (1994), Malcolm Baldrige Quality Award 1993 award criteria; the National Institute of Standards and Technology (1994); Malcolm Baldrige national quality award 1992 fact sheet.

International Standards Organization (ISO)

ISO is a nongovernmental, voluntary-standards organization with worldwide membership. Its purpose is to develop and promulgate voluntary international standards. The activities take place in many topics and fields. ISO is essentially an organization of organizations—no individuals, companies, or countries are direct members. The ISO series of international quality standards were first published in 1987. Five basic quality-system documents were released: (1) Quality-management and quality-assurance standards; (2) Model for quality assurance in design, development, and production; (3) Model for quality assurance in production, installation and servicing; (4) Model for quality assurance in final inspection and test; and (5) Quality-management and quality-system elements—Part 1: Guidelines.

The ISO quality-system standards are a series of documents that have gained universal acceptance. A universally accepted standard is embraced by the business communities of each member nation. To assure acceptance by businesses, standards are generically written. Each affected business interprets and applies the standard.

ISO is based in Geneva, Switzerland, but its primary standards-development activities are performed by volunteers from the member countries. The United States is represented by the American National Standards Institute (ANSI). ANSI is the designated U.S. voluntary-standards body, and it holds the U.S. position within ISO's membership.

According to Wilson (1995), "Since their introduction to a somewhat questioning user base, these standards have become one of the most significant influences on the advance of the global-quality movement. Now it is quite likely most business organizations with international undertakings or intentions are well aware of these standards. Many organizations are currently attempting to learn more about these documents and their application."

ISO 8402 provides the following definitions for quality system and quality management:

> Quality system—The organizational structure, responsibilities, procedures, and resources needed to implement quality management.
>
> Quality management—All of the management-function activities used (a) in determining quality policy, objectives, and responsibilities, and (b) implementing the activities through quality planning, quality control, quality assurance, and quality improvement within the quality system.

The most-cited exploratory literature on ISO 9000 includes Halligan (1992), Marquardt (1992), Raynor (1993), Southard (1996), Spizizen (1992), and Sprow (1992). ISO tends to emphasize leadership (doing the right things) as an independent variable and management (doing things right) as a dependent variable. Handbooks and guidebooks often cited are ASQC Chemical and Process Industries Division (1992), Bureau of Business Practice (1992), Keeney (1995), Lamprecht (1993, 1994), and Peach (1994). Publications regarding software are Schmauch (1994) and Wilson and LearnerFirst (1994).

Voehl (1993) shows how to adapt ISO 9000 to various business industries and institutions of higher learning. Wilson (1995) presents an eight-step process to successful ISO 9000 implementation with his system approach to quality management. This publication also gives an excellent "who/what/when/where/how?" overview of ISO 9000. MacLean (1993) tells the reader how to document quality for ISO 9000. Morrow (1993) indicates how international agreements increase the clout of ISO 9000. Many ISO publications are now coming on the market and are too recent for literature citing. The current ASQC Quality Press catalog lists 24 new ISO-oriented publications.

Zero Defects

Zero defects has been considered a "crusade" to achieve greater workplace and product quality. Philip Crosby was the principal initiator of the zero-defects movement in the United States. There is evidence in the literature that he did not intend his zero-defects policy to become a crusade. Zero defects is a lofty goal, but if a person understands Deming and his theory of variation, she or he would quickly come to the conclusion that zero defects are impossible. Furthermore, defects caused by the system are beyond the control of the workers. The system is designed by management and the defects are management's responsibility. The best one can do is to find out what caused the defects and then either correct the system or train employees better. A zero-defects policy creates winners and losers. Zero defects became a mental exercise that used people as machines and disregarded the fact that people are people. Nobody wants to be a loser—losers create defects! Such a policy places too little emphasis on treating people as people. The zero-defects approach tends to treat all of the quality variables as independent.

The zero-defects movement has sputtered and faded from the quality scene. In its heyday, the most-cited works were Crosby (1979), where he presented the idea that quality was free, and Crosby (1984), where he talked about hassle-free management. Crosby's message was that quality can be caused by deliberate management action. Crosby preached four absolutes of quality management: (1) quality is defined as conformance to requirements (2) the system for causing quality is prevention (3) the performance standard is zero defects and (4) the measurement of quality is the price of nonconformance. According to Crosby, relationships and quality are two keys to successful leadership. A management team must exercise care to avoid viewing relationships and quality as overhead functions that do not contribute directly to profitability. Crosby provides a 14-step plan for quality improvement: management commitment, quality-improvement teams, measurement, cost of quality, awareness, corrective action, zero-defects planning, employee education, zero-defects day, goal setting, error-cause removal, recognition, quality councils, and do it all again.

Motorola, Rifkin (1991), pursued a zero-defects policy with its Six Sigma quality program. The reader must note, though, that its emphasis was on "virtually no defects." Motorola did not achieve zero defects, but by reducing defects through its Six Sigma effort, it estimated that $500 million was saved in 1990.

Continuous Improvement

There are those students of quality—Bowles and Hammond (1991), Bounds and Dobbins (1991, 1993), Bounds and Dewhirst (1991), Bounds and Pace (1991), Bounds and et. al. (1994), and Goldratt (1984, 1986, 1992, 1994)—who believe that the concept of quality is ambiguous. They prefer continuous improvement as a more descriptive level of commitment required to make things happen. The work of Bowles and Hammond and Goldratt might fit into the quality[1] approach. In the case of Bowles and Hammond, they see something beyond quality—quality is not enough. The last of Bowles and Hammond's ten commandments of continuous improvement is "Quality is not enough." What they seem to mean is that everything can be improved . . . forever. Crosby (1979, 1984) used the phrase "Do it all over again." Kemper and Codding (1994) described a full cycle of ongoing improvement and then told readers to "Do it all over again." They wanted a transformation from a compete-against society to a compete-with society and saw a never-ending process. Deming (1993, 1994) used the term transformation. An individual once transformed, said Deming (1993), will: set an example; be a good listener, but will not compromise; continually teach other people; help people to pull away from their current practices and beliefs; and move into the new philosophy without a feeling of guilt about the past. Deming preferred the word *metanoia* (me•ta•no•ia) as being more suitable than transformation. *Metanoia*, a Greek word, means penitence, repentance, reorientation of one's way of live, and spiritual conversion. Transformation means change of form, shape, or appearance.

Bowles and Hammond (1991) said that American companies can compete, and compete well, if they follow the lessons that make up what they call "The Ten Commandments of Continuous Improvement": (1) put the customer first; (2) innovate constantly; (3) design quality into products and services; (4) improve everything continuously; (5) create and support a safe-work/open-work environment; (6) do not shoot the messenger; (7) stop imitating the Japanese; (8) use time wisely; (9) do not sacrifice long-term improvements for short-term profits; and (10) quality is not enough. Bowles and Hammond cite an impressive number of publications in their work.

Goldratt is included here, not because the title of one of his works includes "Quality is not enough," but because he does not really give a descriptive title to the total of his work. He notes in several of his works that what he is describing is a new overall management philosophy. Obviously, Goldratt has read Deming, but except for one page in *The Race* (1986), Deming is not referenced. Goldratt does little referencing or citing. He has no problem with differentiating among total quality management, JIT, and theory of constraints (TOC). Often, his collective works seem to fit under the TOC title. At other times, his collective works are referred to as "throughput theory." He defines throughput as the rate at which the system generates money through sales now and in the future. His definition of constraint is anything that limits a system from achieving higher performance versus its goal. Goldratt's readers, then, are charged with the task of eliminating constraints on the system. The manager identifies the system's constraints, decides how to exploit the its control, subordinates everything else to exploiting the system's force in priority order, elevates the next restraint, and then, if elevation of the a new limitation does not cause the original pressure to reappear, goes back to Step 1: Identify the system's next constraint. The purpose of all this activity, as stated before, is to generate money through sales now and in the future. Goldratt also places a heavy emphasis on the organi-zational goal of raising the standard of living for everybody now and in the future.

Introduced in 1984, *The Goal* is a management textbook written in the format of a love story. It was successful beyond Goldratt's wildest dream. In 1994 Goldratt continued the story about Alex Rogo with *It's*

Not Luck. Much as Deming does, Goldratt strongly implies that real people strive to put quality in their entire lives, not just their work lives. Quality is life. At work, as in life, management seeks to strengthen the organization or system. In TOC, an analogy is drawn between a system and a chain. If you want to improve the strength of a chain, you have several alternatives: Concentrate on strengthening the strongest link, concentrate on strengthening the largest link, apply effort uniformly over all the links, or attempt to identify the weakest link and then concentrate efforts on strengthening that single link. Goldratt and his followers at his institute suggest that management should work at the last alternative. First, management must identify the weakest link, which is a constraint. Then, the weakest link should set the pace for the entire system. If this process is not done, a larger load placed on the weakest link can break the chain. Next, management concentrates its improvement efforts on the weakest link. Finally, if the improvement efforts are successful, eventually the weakest link will improve to the point where it is no longer the weakest link. Any further efforts to improve the former weakest link will provide little or no benefit. At this point, management must identify a new weakest link and shift efforts to improve it.

Goldratt and Fox's (1986) most important contribution to quality may have been in their work on inventory. There is no throughput until a product or service is sold. If everything you produce is still in inventory, the company is not making money—it is headed toward bankruptcy. Collectively, the message from Goldratt is strive for continuous improvement, make more money now and in the future, and raise the standard of living of everyone now and in the future.

Bounds and his colleagues may well be on a paradigm-shift crusade. Much as with Bowles and Hammond (1991), Bounds sees beyond quality. Bounds' work is orientated toward doing things right, rather than toward leadership, which is doing the right things.

Quality Function Deployment (QFD)

QFD—Akao, Yoji and Tetsuichi Asaka (1990)—is used to ensure that the design of new products and services is based on customer criteria. It was developed by Dr. Yoji Akao, a professor of industrial engineering at Tamagawa University, around 1966 and was first systematized at Mitsubishi's Kobe shipyards in the mid-1970s. Some researchers credit Genichi Taguchi with the development of the first QFD computer model and its first use at Kobe. QFD starts with customer criteria, translates them into product or service requirements, and then translates them into product- or service-requirement measures. It is a customer-driven system that attempts to achieve early coupling among the requirements of the customer, marketing, and design engin-eering. QFD actually considers a product as a collection of attributes to fulfill customer-value requirements, (Stahl 1994).

Creech (1994) notes that QFD requires complex computer modeling techniques, astute methods of devising the interactive matrices that portray the integration aspects, large data bases, and extensive computer-processing capability. QFD is designed to provide insight, focus, and coherence to the QFD cycle. QFD integrates the three dimensions of (1) company-wide quality; (2) focus on customer requirements; and (3) translation of quality perceptions into product characteristics and then into the manufacturing process. QFD unfolds in steps or phases: (1) do product planning; (2) prioritize and weight the relative importance that customers have assigned to each characteristic; (3) know how products compare through competitive evaluation; (4) do the design process in which customer product characteristics meet the measurable engineering characteristics; (5) do a redesign by comparing the strengths of relationships between engineering characteristics and customer characteristics; (6) do a redesign to judge potential trade-offs between engineering and customer characteristics; (7) do process planning by taking the output from the design process where the key processes (cutting, stamping, welding, painting, assembly, etc.) are determined; and (8) perform process control in which the output from Step 7 goes to process control, where the necessary process flows and controls are designed, Omachonu and Ross (1994).

Bowles and Hammond (1991) point out that the Saturn plant makes extensive use of QFD to engineer in features identified as customer requirements. For example, engineers use the process to identify 14,000 variables that can be controlled in the manufacture of a transmission; they then narrow their search for improvements to the 200 that are most important to customers. To help in the process, the company keeps Honda and Acura test vehicles in the plant so workers and engineers can stay in close touch with the products they are trying to beat.

Outside the exploratory citations noted above, the most-cited works of QFD are: Asaka and Ozeki (1990), Band (1991), and King (1987).

KEY SOURCES OF QUALITY LITERATURE

Abegglen (1973)
Abegglen and Stalk (1985)
Aguayo (1990)
Akao and Asaka (1990)
Al-Assaf and Schmele (1993)
American Quality Foundation (1991)
Anderson (1990)
Asaka and Ozeki (1990)
ASQC Chemical and Process (1992)
Band (1991)
Baranson (1981)
Barry (1988)
Bennett (1988)
Benson (1988)
Berenbeim (1992)
Berry (1991)
Blackburn and Rosen (1993)
Bluedorn (1986)
Bounds and Dobbins (1991)
Bounds and Dobbins (1993)
Bounds and Dewhirst (1991)
Bounds and Pace (1991)
Bounds and et. al. (1994)
Bowles and Hammond (1991)
Brinksman (1991)
Brower (1992)
Brown (1992)
Bureau of Business Practice (1992)
Burr (1990)
Camp (1989)
Capon, Farley, and Hoenig (1990)
Carr and Littman (1990)
Cherry (1982)
Coate (1990)
Cole (1981)
Cole (1993)
Costin (1994)
Covey (1989)
Creech (1994)
Creveling and Fowlkes (1995)
Crosby (1979)
Crosby (1984)
Daily and Kagerer (1982)
Deming (1956)
Deming (1981-1982)
Deming (1982)
Deming (1986)
Deming (1993)
Deming (1994)
DeMott (1992)
Dertouzos, Lester, and Solow (1989)
Dobbins (1990)
Dome (1993)
Dome, Culver, and Rawcliffe (1994)
Duncan (1965)
Dyer (1987)
European Foundation for Quality Management (1994)
Farnham (1989)
Feigenbaum (1961)
Feigenbaum (1994)
Fellers (1994)
Fine (1993)
Fitzgerald (1982)
Ford (1988)
Freeman (1992)
Gabor, A. (1988)
Gabor, A. (1990)
Gabor, C. (1986)
Gadd and Oakland (1996)
Galvin (1991)
Garvin (1983)
Garvin (1988)
Garvin (1991)
George (1992)
Gerhard and Sparrow (1988)
Gilmore (1990)
Gitlow, Gitlow, Oppenheim, and Oppenheim (1989)
Glaser (1990)
Glasser (1994)
Goal QPC Research Report (1994)
Goff, Shbeckley, and Hastings (1992)
Goldratt (1994)
Goldratt and Cox (1984)
Goldratt and Cox (1992)
Goldratt and Fox (1986)
Gryna (1981)
Gutt and Gruska (1977)
Guyon (1980)
Hackman (1987)
Hackman (1989)
Halberstam (1987)
Halligan (1992)

Hammer (1990)
Hammer and Champy (1993)
Hammer and Stanton (1995)
Hanley (1980)
Hart (1992)
Hayes and Wheelwright (1984)
Hayes, Wheelwright, and Clark (1988)
Haylet and Watts (1993)
Herzberg (1966)
Herzberg (1968)
Herzberg (1979)
Herzberg (1987)
Herzberg, Mauser, and Snyderman (1959)
Hill and Hunter (1966)
Holmes and Michalek (1982)
Holpp (1992)
Hosmer (1991)
Hosotani (1992)
Huff (1992)
Hughes (1991)
Iacocca and Novak (1984)
Imai (1986)
Ingle (1982)
Ishikawa (1980)
Ishikawa (1983)
Ishikawa (1985)
Joiner Associates (1993)
Joiner and Reynard (1994)
Juran Institute (1989)
Juran (1964)
Juran (1981)
Juran (1986)
Juran (1988)
Juran (1988)
Juran (1989)
Juran (1995)
Juran and Gryna (1980)
Juran, Gryna, and Bingham (1976)
Kamata (1982)
Karatsu (1988)
Keeney (1995)
Kegarise and Miller (1985)
Kelly (1992)
Kemper and Codding (1994) (1994)
Kilmann (1984)
King (1987)
Kinlaw (1991)
Knakal (1992)
Knight (1983)
Kohn (1986)
Konz (1979) (1979)
Kopelman (1985)
Koska (1990)
Kume (1985)
Kusaba (1981)
Lamprecht (1993)
Lamprecht, (1994)
Lareau (1991)
Larson and LaFasto (1989)
Latzko and Saunders (1995)
Lawler (1986)
Lawler and Mohrman (1985)
Lawler and Mohrman (1987)
Layden (1993)
Lee (1990)
Lefton and Buzzotta (1987)
Leonard (1992)
Lewis and Smith (1994)
Mackey and Mackey (1992)
MacLean (1993)
Malec (1992)
Mann (1985)
Marchese (1991)
Marchington (1992)
Marquardt (1992)
Maskery (1991)
Maslow (1954)
Matejka (1991)
Matsumoto (1988)
McEachern, Schiff, and Cogan (1992)
McGregor (1960)
McKenna (1993)
McNeil (1992) (1992)
Mears and Voehl (1994)
Messina (1985)
Meyer and Stott (1986)
Mizuno (1979)
Moen (1989)
Monden (1985)
Monden (1986)
Montgomery (1980)
Montgomery (1985)
Moran (1991)
Morita, Reingold, and Shimomura (1986)
Morland (1981)
Morrow (1993)

Nader (1965)
National Institute of Standards and Technology (1994) (1994)
Neave (1990)
Nemoto (1987)
Nissen (1996)
Nolan and Provost (1990)
Oberle (1990)
O'Boyle (1985)
O'Dell (1989)
Ogawa (1984)
O'Grady (1988)
Ohno (1988)
Ohno and Mito (1988)
Omachonu (1991)
Omachonu and Ross (1994)
Orsburn, Moran, Musselwhite, Zenger, and Perrin (1990)
Ott (1975)
Ouchi (1981)
Ouchi (1984)
Ozawa (1982)
Parker (1990)
Pascale and Athos (1979)
Pascarella (1993)
Patchin and Cunningham (1983)
Peach (1994)
Peters, D. (1992)
Peters (1987)
Peters (1994)
Peters and Austin (1985)
Peters and Waterman (1982)
Pirsig (1974)
Porter (1980)
Porter (1985)
Power (1992)
Poza and Markus (1980)
Raynor (1993)
Reddy and Jamison (1988)
Reich (1983)
Reimann (1990)
Rendall (1981)
Resnick-West (1985)
Rifkin (1991)
Roberts (1994)
Robson (1982)
Ross and Ross (1982)
Rudelius and Buchholz (1979)
Ryan (1992)
Sarazen (1990)
Saskin and Kiser (1993)
Sayle (1991)
Scherkenbach (1986)
Schmauch (1994)
Schmoker and Wilson (1993)
Scholtes (1993)
Scholtes and other Joiner Associates (1988)
Schonberger (1982)
Semmer (1990)
Senge (1990)
Senge (1992)
Senge, Kleiner, Roberts, Ross, and Smith (1994)
Shainin (1990)
Sheridan (1990)
Shewhard (1931)
Shewhard (1939)
Shingo (1988)
Sholtes (1988)
Sinibaldi (1983)
Southard (1996)
Spendolini (1991)
Spizizen (1992)
Sprow (1992)
Stahl (1994)
Stogdill (1948)
Sullivan (1984)
Sundstrom, Demeuse, and Futrell (1990)
Taguchi (1978)
Taguchi (1986)
Thompson (1982)
Thurow (1980)
Tichy and Sherman (1983)
Torbeck (1985)
Tornatzky, Eveland, Boylan, Hetzner, Johnson, Roitman, and Schneider (1983)
Vance (1983)
Verespej (1990)
Voehl (1993)
Voehl (1993)
Vogel (1979)
Walton (1986)
Walton (1990)
Waxler and Higginson (1994)
Wellins (1990)
Wellins, Byham, and Wilson (1991)
Wheeler (1993)
Whiting (1991)
Whitney (1993)
Wilson (1995)
Wilson and LearnerFirst (1994)
Yucht (1992)
Zabel and Avery (1992)
Zemke (1991)

MOST-CITED AUTHORS

Abegglen, James C. [4] {10}
Abernathy, William J. [8] {12}
Ackoff, Russell L. [7] {9}
Adam, Everett E., Jr. [7] {10}
Addelman, Sidney [4] {4}
Akao, Yoji [3] {4}
Albrecht, Karl [6] {7}
American Society for Quality Control [7] {7}
Amsden, Davida M., and Robert T. Amsden (Eds.). [5] {6}
Amsden, Robert T. [4] {5}
Argyris, Chris [14] {24}
Aubrey, Charles A., III, [5] {7}
Bajaria, H. J. [7] {8}
Baker, E. M. [3] {3}
Balkin, D. B. [4] {4}
Barrier, Michael [6] {13}
Beer, Michael [5] {5}
Bennett, Amanda [5] {5}
Bennis, Warren G. [15] {21}
Benson, Tracy E. [5] {10}
Berger, R. L. [4] {5}
Bicking, Charles A. [8] {9}
Bingham, R. S., Jr. [13] {13}
Blake, Robert R., and Jane S. Mouton [5] {6}
Blau, Peter M. [3] {3}
Bounds, G. M. [7] {11}
Bowles, Jerry G. [8] {11}
Box, George E. P. [22] {25}
Buffa, E. S. [4] {8}
Burck, Charles G. [4] {7}
Burr, John T. [5] {5}
Buzzell, Robert D. [6] {13}
Carothers, G. Harlan, Jr. [4] {4}
Cartwright, Dorwin [3] {3}
Caves R. E. [3] {3}
Cleland, David I. [5] {5}
Cole, Robert E. [20] {28}
Crosby, Philip B. [13] {41}
Cuthbert, Daniel [6] {6}
Daft, Richard L. [5] {5}
Davies, Owen L. [6] {7}
Day, Charles R., Jr. [5] {9}
Deming, William Edwards [34] {85}
Dewar, Donald L. [5] {5}
Dodge, H. F. [18] {22}
Donovan, J. Michael [9] {9}
Dowling, William F. [4] {5}
Drucker, Peter F. [22] {73}
Duncan, Acheson J. [4] {8}
Egermayer, F. [4] {8}
Eisenhardt, K. M. [6] {7}
Eubanks, Paula [4] {7}
Feigenbaum, Armand V. [11} {18}
Fisher, Ronald A. [5] {6}
Freedman, Jonathan L. [3] {3}
Fuchsberg, G. [5] {7}
Fukada, R. [4] {7}
Gabor, Andrea [6] {16}
Galbraith, J. R. [7] {10}
Gale, Bradley T. [6] {6}
Gardner, John W. [8] {10}
Garvin, David A. [6] {22}
Gibson, Price [5] {5}
Gitlow, H. [9] {17}
Glichev, A. V. [5] {8}
Godfrey, A. Blanton [5] {6}
Goldratt, Eliyahu M. [21] {28}
Gomez-Mejia, L. R. [5] {5}
Grant, E. L. [4] {9}
Groocock, J. M. [10] {12}
Gryna, Frank M., Jr. [6] {8}
Hackman, J. Richard [10] {14}
Hagan, J. T. [3] {3}
Hahn, G. J. [6] {8}
Halberstam, David [5] {8}
Hald, A. [4] {6}
Hammel, Lisa [8] {8}
Hammer, Michael [3] {5}
Harrington, H. James [7] {11}
Hayes, Glenn E. [7] {9}
Hayes, R. H. [9] {37}
Herzberg, Fredrick [5] {12}
Heskett, James L. [3] {4}
Hill, Hubert M. [4] {4}
Hoerr, J. [8] {14}
Holpp, Lawrence [3] {6}
Holusha, John [6] {9}
Horton, Thomas R. [3] {3}
Hunter, J. Stuart [5] {5}
Imai, Masaaki [9] {18}
Ingle, Sud [3] {4}

Ishikawa, Kaoru [20] {55}
Johnson, C. [3] {4}
Johnson, H. Thomas [3] {7}
Joiner Associates [3] {3}
Joiner, Brian L. [1] {2}
Joiner, Charles W. [2] {2}
Juran Institute [3] {3}
Juran, Joseph M. [53] {120}
Kackar, Raghu N. [4] {7}
Kanter, R. M. [6] {9}
Karabatsos, Nancy [5] {5}
Karatsu, Hajime [4] {6}
Kemper, Robert E. [5] {5}
Kendrick, J. W. [6] {8}
Klein, J. A. [4] {4}
Kondo, Y. [5] {5}
Konz, Stephen A. [4] {4}
Kotter, John P. [5] {6}
Kume, Hitoshi [5] {9}
Latzko, William J. [7] {7}
Lawler, Edward E., III. [21] {35}
Lawrence, Paul R. [6] {2}
Lenz, John [7] {7}
Levinson, Harry [3] {3}
Levitt, Theodore [7] {17}
Lucas, J. M. [5] {5}
Maccoby, Michael [5] {6}
Maier, Norman R. [4] {4}
Main, Jeremy [8] {12}
March, James G. [4] {8}
Martin, J. [5] {5}
Mayo, Elton [4] {4}
McGregor, Douglas [5] {11}
Messina, William S. [10] {11}
Metzger, B. [3] {4}
Miller, Lawrence M. [4] {4}
Mintzberg, Henry [11] {18}
Mizuno, S. [5] {7}
Mohrman, A. M., Jr. [7] {8}
Monden, Yasuhiro [6] {9}
Montgomery, D. C. [6] {11}
Nadler, David A. [4] {5}
Ohno, Taiichi [2] {5}
Ott, Ellis R. [7] {14}
Ouchi, William G. [4] {15}
Pascale, Richard Tanner [4] {14}
Pascarella, Perry [3] {4}
Peters, Thomas J. [11] {37}
Phadke, Madhav S. [6] {6}
Plossl, G. W. [7] {13}
Port, Otis [6] {10}
Porter, Michael E. [8] {19}
Pyzdek, Thomas [5] {7}
Nelson, L. S. [9] {13}
Ogilvy, David [4] {5}
Ohmae, Kenichi [4] {9}
Quinn, James Brian [6] {14}
Rehder, Robert R. [4] {5}
Reich, Robert B. [5] {12}
Ross, Joel E. [6] {9}
Roth, Williams, Jr. [16] {16}
Rubenstein, Sydney P. [4] {4}
Ryan, John M. [6] {6}
Schein, Edgar Henry [5] {5}
Scherkenbach, William W. [5] {10}
Schilling, Edward G. [10] {11}
Scholtes, Peter R. [4] {7}
Schonberger, Richard J. [10] {23}
Schoonhoven, C. B. [6] {6}
Schumacher, R. B. F. [4] {5}
Senge, Peter M. [4] {8}
Shainin, Dorian [4] {4}
Sheridan, John H. [4] {6}
Shetty, V. K. [8] {10}
Shewhart, William A. [2] {17}
Shingo, Shigeo [4] {8}
Simon, Herbert A. [4] {4}
Stahl, Michael J. [7] {7}
Sullivan, L. P. [5] {7}
Taguchi, Genichi [8] {14}
Takeuchi, H. [3] {7}
Taylor, Frederick Winslow [6] {10}
Thurow, Lester C. [8] {17}
Tichy, Noel M. [7] {8}
Tippett, L. H. C. [5] {6}
Tribus, Myron [5] {6}
Tsurumi, Yoshi [3] {3}
Tuchman, Barbara W. [3] {4}
Ungson, G. R. [4] {5}
Uttal, Brothers [6] {8}
Voehl, Frank W. [5] {6}
Vogel, E. F. [4] {7}
Von Glinow, M. A. [3] {4}
Walsh, L. [6] {6}
Walton, Mary [4] {11}
Walton, Richard E. [7] {14}
Wight, Oliver W. [4] {7}
Zemke, Ronald E. [8] {10}

PROFESSIONAL ASSOCIATIONS AND SOCIETIES

Academy of Management
Academy of Marketing
Administrative Management Society Foundation
Alban Institute
American Association for Higher Education
American Association of School Administrators
American Management Association (AMACOM) (26)
American Chemical Society
American Dietetic Association
American Hospital Association
American Institute of Industrial Engineers (AIIE)
American Medical Association
American National Standards Institute
American Planning Association
American Psychological Association
American Society for Quality Control (ASQC) (253)
American Society for Testing and Materials (11)
American Society for Training and Development
American Society of Horticulture
American Society of Hospital Pharmacists
American Society of Mechanical Engineers
American Society of Training Directors
American Statistical Association (14)
Asian Productivity Organization (7)
Association for Manufacturing Excellence
The Association for Overseas Technical Scholarship
Association for Supervision and Curriculum Development
Association of Official Analytical Chemists
Association for Quality and Participation
British Institute of Management
Canadian Ceramic Society
Eastern Academy of Management
Goal/QPC (9)
Ohio Quality and Productivity Form (5)
International Association for Quality Control (21)
International Society for Educational Information
Institute of Electrical and Electronics Engineers (IEEE) (59)
IEEE Computer Society
Industrial Society
Industrial Technology Institute
Institute of Business Technology
Institute of Industrial Engineers
Institute of Mathematical Statistics
Institute of Radio Engineers
Institute of Statistical Mathematics
International Association of Quality Circles (19)
Japan Management Association
Japanese Society for Quality Control
Japanese Standards Association
National Academy of Sciences
National Association of Purchasing Agents
National Science Teachers Association
National Society for Professional Engineers
Newspaper Enterprise Association
Operational Research Society
Pacific Sociological Association
Profit Sharing Research Foundation
Purchasing Management Association
Quality Technical Associates
Quality Circle Institute
Rochester Quality Control Conference
Royal Statistical Society (11)
Society of American Value Engineers (SAVE)
Society of Automotive Engineers
Society of Manufacturing Engineers
The Strategic Planning Institute
Technical Association of the Pulp and Paper Industry
Union of Japanese Scientists and Engineers (JUSE) (23)
Western Academy of Management
Work in America Institute

PUBLISHERS

Academic Press
Addison-Wesley
Admiral Corporation
Alamo Learning Systems
Alfred A. Knopf
Allyn and Bacon
AMACOM/American Management Association
American Sciences Press
Arno Press
Arthur Andersen and Company
ASQC Quality Press
Atheneum
Auerbach Publishers
Avon Books
Ballinger
Bank Marketing
Bantam Books
Barrett Management Services
Basic Books
Basil Blackwell
Berkley
Berrett-Koehler
Boston Publishing Company
BPI
Brooks/Cole
Business One Irwin
Carol Publishing
CBI Publishing Company
CEE Press
Chobunsha
Clarkson N. Potter
Collier Macmillian
Columbia University Press
Conference Board
Coopers and Lybrand
Delmar Publishing
Development Dimensions International, Association for Quality and Participation
Dodd Mead
Dorsey Press
Doubleday
Dover
Dow Jones-Irwin
Dryden Press
Duxbury Press
E. P. Dutton
Engineering Press
Enterprise Australia Publications
Ernst and Young
Free
Free Press
Freeman, W. J.
G. W. Plossl and Company
George Washington University, Department of Agriculture
Goodyear
Gower Press
Grosset and Dunlop
Greenwood Press
Grid
Grossman
Gulf Publishing
Hafner Publishing Company
Harper and Brothers
Harper and Row
Harper Business
Harper Colophon Books
HarperCollins
Harvard Business School Press
Harvard Business School Working Paper
Harvard University Press
Hitchcock Publishing
Hive Publishing
Holden-Day
Holt, Rinehart and Winston
Houghton Mifflin
Howard Wilford Bell
Human Relations
ICS Press
Independent Sector
Industrial Engineering and Management Press
Irwin
Jacobs Engineering Group
John Wiley
Johns Hopkins Press
Johns Hopkins University Press
Joiner Associates
Jossey-Bass
Juran Institute
JUSE Press

Kodansha International
Kogan Page Limited
Kraus International Publications
Leadership Press, The
Lexington Books
Little Brown
Los Angles Press
Macmillan
Manufacturing Productivity Center
Marcel Dekker
McGraw-Hill
Meieki Nakamura Ku
Mentor Books
Mercury Press
MIT, Center for Advanced Engineering Study
MIT Press
National Academy of Sciences
New American Library
New Win Publishing
Nichols Publishing
Nippon Kagaku Gijutsu Remmei
North Atlantic Treaty Organization
North River Press
Office of Naval Operations, Total Quality Leadership
Ogilvy and Mather
Oliver and Boyd
OR and C.
Organization Design and Development
Oxford University Press
Pan Books
Pantheon Books
Penn Well Books
Pergamon Press
Perigee Books
Pfeiffer and Company
Phi Delta Kappa Educational Foundation
Pitman
Porter Sargent
Praeger
Prague University Press
Prentice-Hall
Prestwick Books
Princeton University Press
Productivity Press
Putnam
PWS-Kent
Quality America
Quality and Reliability
Quality Resources
Quality Technical Associates
Quorum Books
Rand McNally
Random House
Reston Publishing Company
Rinehart and Winston
Row, Peterson and Company
Sage
Science Research Associates
Simon and Schuster
Simul Press
SPC Press
St. Lucie Press
St. Martin's Press
Stanford University Press
Stechert-Hafner
Strategy Associates
3A Corporation
Time Books
Truman Talley Books
U.S. Government Printing Office
University Associates
University of California Press
University of Chicago Press
University of Colorado Press
University of Illinois
University of Iowa Press
University of Michigan, Center for Japanese Studies
University of Missouri, Research Center, College of Business and Public Administration
University of Michigan Press
University of Pennsylvania Press
University of Southern California
Van-Nostrand Reinhold
Vintage Books
W. W. Norton
Warner Books
West Publishing
Western Electric
Whirlpool Corporation
William Morrow
World Publishing Company
Yale University Press
Xerox Corporation

PERIODICAL SOURCES

Academy of Management Executive
Academy of Management Journal (20)
Academy of Management Review
Across the Board
Administrative Science Quarterly (26)
American Banker
American Machinist
American Psychologist
American Society of Training Directors Journal
American Statistician
Ann Arbor Observer
Annals of Eugenics
Annals of Mathematical Statistics
Annual Review of Psychology
Antitrust Bulletin
APICS Journal
APICS Special Report
Applied Statistics
ASIA Magazine
ASQC Annual Congress Proceedings
ASQC Annual Technical Congress Quarterly Transactions (125)
AT&T Technical Journal
Automotive News
Bell System Technical Journal
Bell Telephone Laboratories
Biometrics (13)
Biometrika
Business and Society Review
Business Horizons (15)
Business Journal
Business Marketing
BusinessWeek (105)
California Management Review (20)
Chemical Purchasing
Chemical Week
Chief Executive
Columbia Journal of World Business
Common Statistics—Theory and Methods
Control and Applied Statistics
CRSO Working Paper
Datamation
Decision Sciences
The Dial
The Economist
Electronic Business
EOQC Quality
Executive Excellence
Executive Excellence
Factory Management and Maintenance
Financier
FMS Magazine
Fortune (134)
Harvard Business Review (172)
Hinshitsu Kanri Statistical Quality Control
Hospitals
HR Focus
The Human Element
Human Resource Management
Human Resources Policies and Practices
IAQC Conference Transactions (21)
IBM Technical Report
Inc.
Industrial Engineering (35)
Industrial Management and Data Systems
Industrial Management
Industrial Quality Control (27)
Industrial Relations
Industry Week (45)
Institutional Distribution
Interfaces
International Management
International Review of Economics and Business
The Japan Economic Journal
Japan Labor Bulletin
The Japan Times Weekly
Journal for Quality and Participation (7)
The Journal of Applied Behavioral Science
Journal of Applied Psychology
Journal of Business Strategy
Journal of Business
Journal of Commerce and Commercial
Journal of Contemporary Business
Journal of Cost Management
Journal of General Management
Journal of Industrial Economics

Journal of Management Studies
Journal of Management
Journal of Marketing
Journal of Nursing Administration
Journal of Occupational Behavior
Journal of Operations Management
Journal of Personality and Social Psychology
Journal of Quality Technology (72)
Journal of Social Issues
Journal of Textile Institute Transactions
Journal of the American Statistical Association
Journal of the Canadian Ceramic Society
Journal of the EOQC
Journal of the Institute of Quality Assurance
Journal of the Japanese Society for Quality Control
Journal of the Royal Statistical Society
The Juran Report
Letter
Library Journal
M and O
Machine Design
Management Accounting
Management Decision (UK)
Management Review (41)
Management Science (23)
Manufacturing Engineering
Materials Research and Standards
Mechanical Engineering
Modern Healthcare
Modern Materials Handling
National Productivity Review (35)
Nation's Business
New Management
New Republic
New York Times
Newsletter (Plossl)
Organizational Behavior and Human Performance
Organizational Dynamics (31)
Pacific Basin Quarterly
Paperboard Packaging
Performance Management
Personnel Administrator
Personnel Journal
Personnel Psychology
Personnel (19)
Planning Review
Professional Engineer
Public Utilities Fortnightly
Pulp and Paper International
Quality Assurance
Quality Circles Journal (9)
The Quality Executive
Quality in Manufacturing
Quality Magazine
Quality Management and Engineering
Quality Management Journal
Quality Progress (70)
Quality Review Bulletin
Quality Review
Quality vs Progress
Quality (21)
Quarterly Journal of Economics
RCA Engineer
Reports of Statistical Applications and Research
Research Series
Research-Technology Management
RQ
SAM Advanced Management Journal
Science
Simulation Magazine
Sloan Management Review (33)
Small Business Reports
South Carolina Business Journal
Special Technical Publication
Standardization
Strategic Management Journal (11)
Supervisory Management
Supply House Times
Survey of Business
TAPPI
Target
Technical Report (University of Wisconsin)
Technology Review
Technometrics (18)
Technowledge
The Theory of Constraints Journal (13)
Tooling and Production
Topics in Total Compensation
Toyota Quarterly Review
Training and Development Journal
Training (21)
U.S. News and World Report
United Press International
Wall Street Journal (66)

WORKS ABOUT AND WORKS BASED ON THE PHILOSOPHY OF W. EDWARDS DEMING

Aguayo, Rafael (1990) (*4)
American Productivity and Quality Center (1990)
Austin, Nancy K. (1991)
Baker, E. M., and H. L. M. Artinian (1985)
Broadhead, James L. (1991)
Butterfield, Ronald (1991)
Deming's demons: The management guru thinks U. S. corporations are crushing their worker incentive (1990)
Dobbins, Lloyd (1990) (*4)
Duncan, Jack W., and Joseph G. Van Matre (1990) (*3)
Fellers, Gary P. (1994)
Ferguson, Gary (1990)
Gabor, Andrea (1988)
Gabor, Andrea (1988) (*6)
Gabor, Andrea (1989)
Gabor, Andrea (1990) (*5)
Gillem, T. (1988)
Gitlow, H. (1987) (*2)
Gitlow, H., and S. Gitlow (1987) (*2)
Hodgeson, Alan (1987) (*3)
Holt, Maurice (1993) (*3)
Joiner Associates (1990)
Joiner Associates (1993)
Joiner, Brian L., and Marie Gaudard (1990)
Joiner, Brian L., and Sue Reynard (1994)
Kemper, Robert E., and Deborah Codding (1994)
Killian, Ceil S. (1988) (*2)
Killian, Ceil S. (1992) (*2)
Kosaky, Yoshida (1989) (*2)
Koska, Mary T. (1990) (*4)
Latzko, William J. (1982)
Latzko, William J., and David M. Saunders (1995)
Leonard, James F. (1991)
Lerz, William H. (1992) (*2)
Maccoby, Michael (1990)
Mackey, Terry and Kitty Mackey (1992) (*2)
Mann, Nancy R. (1984)
Mann, Nancy R. (1985) (*5)
March, Artemis (1986) (*2)
Maskery, Mary Ann (1991)
Moen, Ronald D. (1989)
Neave, Henry R. (1990) (*4)
Pickard, Jane (1992)
Salkin, Stephanie and William Edwards Deming (1992) (*2)
Scherkenbach, William W. (1986) (*7)
Scherkenbach, William W. (1986) (*3)
Scherkenbach, William W. (1986) (*3)
Scherkenbach, William W. (1991) (*3)
Scholtes, Peter R. (1987)
Scholtes, Peter R. (1993)
Scholtes, Peter R. and Joiner Associates (1988)
Tetzeli, Rick (1993)
Walton, Mary (1986) (*5)
Walton, Mary (1986) (*3)
Walton, Mary (1990) (*6)
Walton, Mary (1991)
Williams, Robert (1991)
Yoshida, Kosaku (1989)

KEY: (*4) = Number of citings

IMPLICATIONS FOR LEADERS AND MANAGERS

Leaders and managers are understandably curious about the new paradigms of business. For example, consider the following questions:

> Do external focus and flexible culture affect earnings? If so, by how much?
> What should a leader know about the new global economy?
> What should be done to make more money now and in the future and to improve the standard of living of everyone now and in the future?
> Employee empowerment, cooperation, harmony, trust, and honesty affect earnings, but by how much?

Leaders are frustrated with debates over particular approaches to quality, as well as with the fact that no one model is likely to deal with the exact situation leaders face.

By assessing the evidence provided by this meta study in which the many detailed characteristics of particular approaches to quality are at least partially controlled statistically, a set of guidelines is developed to aid leaders practice which models "generally" hold true for most situations. With much qualification, therefore, I present the following observations:

- No matter how good the process is, quality is not achieved unless the right things are done for internal and external customers.
- Empowering people is helpful. Unfortunately, many leaders do not have a clear picture of whether decentralizing decision making to gain loyalty is a good idea.
- By themselves, JIT, benchmarking, empowerment, teams, quality circles, and cutting-edge technology do not result in quality.
- An environment that does not create trust and that does not allow a person to take pride in her or his work and have joy in the workplace will not foster loyalty, will not result in individual and group growth and development, will not allow the organization to make more money now and in the future, and will not allow people to raise their standard of living now and in the future.
- High-quality products and services enhance performance; excessive control can hurt performance. Firing anyone without knowing whether the system is the cause of a downturn or whether special causes are the cause of a downturn should be

made with caution.

- Any environment that creates winners and losers will eventually destroy its people or prompt "the losers" to get even—violence in the workplace.
- A product or service that is "not broken" (one that is okay, satisfactory, or all right) should nevertheless be fixed. The results indicate that the determinants of success involve continuous improvement. Furthermore, results hint at the presence of strong interactive effects among all parts of the system.
- Leaders need to understand systems, variation, psychology, prediction, and organizational constraints if they are to create an environment where loyalty, individual and group growth and development, and productivity prosper.
- Quality is not an "add on."
- Quality[1] is a way of life.
- Managers do not motivate anyone. Motivation comes from within. The best managers can do is to create an environment where every individual wins.
- In conflicts, communica*tion* is free, negotia*tion* resolves conflicts and is also free, media*tion* brings in a third party and adds to the cost of doing business, arbitra*tion* requires a third party who increases the cost and creates winners and losers, litiga*tion* creates a winner and a loser and adds much cost to doing business, and retalia*tion* makes a winner and a loser and allows losers to get even—and maybe get someone seriously injured or killed!
- All change requires social change.

Although the foregoing remarks hold true for the majority of situations, they should be viewed with caution, as there is documented variation in the magnitude of a given effect in different contexts.

IMPLICATIONS FOR RESEARCH PRACTICE AND FUTURE RESEARCH

This meta study opens a variety of research issues that lurk beneath the surface of the quality literature. Internal and external customers, scientific observation, and long-term improvement form the basis of leadership philosophy. The results present a perplexing array of possible causal variables—far more than are likely to be specified in any single study. A meta study provides one route for integrating the results of effects of these many factors, even when they are not explicitly studied together. In fact, given the large number of potential explanatory factors and limited data bases, further meta analysis may be the only feasible way to sort through alternative explanations in the existing literature.

Some explanatory variables (quality circles, empowerment, benchmarking, process control, and teams) have been studied so extensively that one wonders if more research effort is really needed; on the other hand, other variables (trust, ethics, intrinsic motivation, pride and joy in work, loyalty, and decentralization of decision making) have been neglected. Examination of the little-studied factors in the approach called quality would provide a more comprehensive understanding of performance relationships and provide for better integration of the quality field. Meta analysis provides one method of achieving integration; more creatively designed studies would provide an additional and a richer approach.

Many more significant positive than significant negative relationships in doing things right were found. It is suspected that a bias operates toward seeking variables related to good-process performance. However, there is value in theory development and empirical testing involving variables that lead to poor management and leadership performance; not simply those involving control. There is evidence that a theory of poor quality would not simply be a symmetric mirror of a theory seeking to explain good quality.

One result of this meta study is that the level of analysis (quality[1] vs. TQC vs. TQM vs. reengineering vs. continuous improvement vs. Baldridge vs. ISO vs. zero defects vs. QFD) along with other contextual factors—such as systems, psychology, prediction, constraints, and variation—highlight collaboration specification and win-lose matters. When any factor makes a qualitative difference in interpretation of results, an individual study may surface. Surely, new methodologies are needed to deal with special classes of problems found in quality performance: loyalty, trust, intrinsic motivation, individual and group growth and development, and fear.

This meta study identifies the need for five particular types of research:

- The field is badly in need of more work on trust. In particular, there are few integrated studies that consider the nature of mutual faith in the intentions and behaviors of others in the workplace. Trust is a cycle that includes observation on treatment of people and leads to new prediction.

- There is a dearth of genuinely dynamic analysis that tracks intrinsic motivation that causes loyalty and job satisfaction. This restriction limits investigation of the nature of pride and joy in the workplace. We need more work on how successful workers become successful, on how unsuccessful workers stay unsuccessful, and on how successful workers become unsuccessful.
- Much quality research appears to have been done with competition-against rather than with competition-with explanations. This occurrence is partly caused by lack of data that would make such analysis infeasible. Very useful to have available would be a comprehensive data base that systematically links over time key elements of collaboration, accommodation, avoidance, compromise, and one-win competition at the organizational level.
- Very little bona fide and vibrant inquiry exists as to the positive and negative role of fear in the workplace leading to various optimal combinations of winning, security, joy, and pride. Work on interaction of efforts to meet numerical objectives in many American production lines and offices may prevent innovation and improvement. Information is badly needed if the goal of analysis is to move toward optimal allocation of resources among controllable variables.
- Much research is needed to verify the relationship between process orientation and organizational performance.

CONCLUSIONS AND RECOMMENDATIONS

Based on the material presented in this paper, one conclusion is that the quality literature can be divided into at least nine schools of thought: quality[1], TQC, TQM, reengineering, Baldrige, ISO, zero defects, continuous improvement, and QFD. Quality[1], TQC, and continuous improvement are leadership based (doing the right things); on the other hand, TQM is management based (doing things right). TQM has a doing-the-right-things-for-customers beginning and then follows with a strong doing-right-things-by-employees orientation. Reengineering, Baldrige, ISO, and zero defects are also management based.

Three additional conclusions are that the literature on quality approaches and classifications lacks scholarship, making it difficult to track the dependent and independent variables used, that the definitions given by various popular authors are generally incompatible and often contradictory, and that the new approaches to quality are well founded in bits and pieces of classical leadership and management theory. Nevertheless, the important papers, the important approaches and classifications, and the present state of quality knowledge have been identified.

The preceding conclusions lead to some recommendations for people interested in learning about quality; for managers, supervisors, and their subordinates who practice leadership and management routinely; for researchers investigating quality; and for students seeking an imaginative area for interesting study and research. The recommendations are that such individuals, minimally, should become familiar with the following:

- **Principal researchers, practitioners, and writers**—Philip B. Crosby, William Edwards Deming, Peter F. Drucker, Eliyahu M. Goldratt, R. H. Hayes, Kaoru Ishikawa, Joseph M. Juran, Edward E. Lawler, Thomas J. Peters, and Richard J. Schonberger (see pages 25-29 and page 35).
- **Publishers**—Addison-Wesley, ASQC Quality Press, Ballinger, Bantam Books, Free Press, Harper and Row, Harvard University Press, Holt, Rinehart and Winston, Houghton Mifflin, Irwin, John Wiley, Jossey-Bass, JUSE Press, Lexington Books, Macmillan, McGraw-Hill, MIT Press, Prentice-Hall, Productivity Press, Quorum Books, Random House, Holt Rinehart and Winston, Simon and Schuster, University of California Press, and West Publishing. (see pages 31-32).
- **Periodical sources**—*ASQC Annual Technical Quality Congress Transactions*, *BusinessWeek*, *Fortune*, *Harvard Business Review*, *Industrial Engineering*, *Industrial Quarterly Control*, *Industry Week*, *Technometrics*, *Journal of Quality Technology*, *Management Review*, *Organizational Dynamics*, *Quality Progress*, and *The Wall Street Journal* (see pages 33-34).
- **Associations** and **societies**—American Management Association, American Society for Quality Control, American Statistical Association, the Asian Productivity Organization, the International Association for Quality Control, International Association of Quality Circles, and the Union of Japanese Scientists and Engineers (see page 30).
- **The new writings and other developments** that will certainly appear on quality[1], TQC, TQM, reengineering, Baldrige, ISO, zero defects, continuous improvement, and QFD.

CITATIONS

Bold face entries represent the most important citations on the subject. For a guide to number of citations and entry order, please see the "Citation Style Configurations" chapter, pages xv-xvii.

AAHE. (1993) *Statewide Leadership of CQI Higher Education.* (Session 36). Chicago, IL: American Association for Higher Education.

Abegglen, James C. (1973) *Management and Worker: The Japanese Solution.* Tokyo: Kodansha International. (*5)

Abegglen, James C. (1983) How to defend your business against Japan. *BusinessWeek.* (August 15) 33.

Abegglen, James C. (1984) *The Strategy of Japanese Business.* Cambridge, MA: Ballinger.

Abegglen, James C., and George Stalk Jr. (1985) *Kaisha: The Japanese Corporation.* New York: Basic Books. (*6)

Abell, Derek F., and S. Hammond. (1979) *Strategic Market Planning: Problems and Analytical Approaches.* Englewood Cliffs, NJ: Prentice-Hall.

Abernathy, William J. (1978) Patterns of industrial innovation. *Technology Review.* (June) 40-47.

Abernathy, William J. (1978) *The Productivity Dilemma: Roadblock to Innovation in the Automobile Industry.* Baltimore, MD: Johns Hopkins Press. (*3)

Abernathy, William J., and Kim B. Clark. (1982) Notes on a trip to Japan: Concepts and interpretations. In Robert E. Cole (Ed.) *Industry at the Crossroads.* Ann Arbor, MI: University of Michigan, Center for Japanese Studies.

Abernathy, William J., Kim B. Clark, and Alan B. Kantrow. (1981) The new industrial competition. *Harvard Business Review.* 59, (September-October) 68-81.

Abernathy, William J., Kim B. Clark, and Alan B. Kantrow. (1983) *Industrial Renaissance: Producing a Competitive Future for America.* New York: Basic Books. (*3)

Abernathy, William J., and John E. Corcoran. (1983) Relearning from the old masters: Lessons of the American system of manufacturing. *Journal of Operations Management.* 3, (August) 155-168. (*2)

Abernathy, William J., and R. H. Hayes. (1980) Managing our way to economic decline. *Harvard Business Review.* 58, (July-August) 68-81.

Abou-Zeid, R. Mohammad. (1975) Group technology. *Industrial Engineering.* 7, (April) 32-39.

Aboud, George M., Sr. (1980) DOD procurement quality requirements (ASPR). *ASQC Annual Technical Quality Congress Transactions.* Milwaukee, WI: ASQC Quality Press, 771-782.

Abrams, Bill. (1981) P and G may give Crest a new look after failing to brush off rivals. *Wall Street Journal.* (January 8) 21. (*2)

Achatz, R., and D. J. Parrish. (1987) Host computer controls FMS at all levels. *FMS Magazine.* 5, (January) 21-25.

Ackoff, L. (1971) Towards a system of systems concepts. *Management Science.* 17, (January) 661-673.

Ackoff, Russell L. (1970) *A Concept of Corporate Planning.* New York: John Wiley.

Ackoff, Russell L. (1974) *Redesigning the Future.* New York: John Wiley. (*2)

Ackoff, Russell L. (1978) *The Art of Problem Solving.* New York: John Wiley. (*2)

Ackoff, Russell L. (1981) *Creating the Corporate Future.* New York: John Wiley. (*2)

Ackoff, Russell L. (1986) *Management in Small Doses*. New York: John Wiley.

Ackoff, Russell L. (1986) The mismatch between educational systems and the requirements for successful management. *Wharton Alumni Magazine*. (Spring) 16-18.

Ackoff, Russell L., and R. Snow. (1985) *Revitalizing Western Economies*. San Francisco, CA: Jossey-Bass.

Adam, Everett E., Jr. (1972) An analysis of the change in performance quality employing operant conditioning procedures. *Journal of Applied Psychology*. 56, (December) 480-86.

Adam, Everett E., Jr. (1983) Towards a topology of production and operations management systems. *Academy of Management Review*. 365-375. (*2)

Adam, Everett E., Jr. (1992) Quality improvement as an operations strategy. *Industrial Management and Data Systems*. 92, (July-August) 3. (*2)

Adam, Everett E., Jr., and Ronald J. Ebert. (1982) *Production and Operations Management: Concepts, Models, and Behavior*. Englewood Cliffs, NJ: Prentice-Hall. (*2)

Adam, Everett E., Jr., J. C. Hershauer, and W. A. Ruch. (1981) *Productivity and Quality-Measurement as a Basis for Improvement*. Englewood Cliffs, NJ: Prentice-Hall.

Adam, Everett E., Jr., J. C. Hershauer, and W. A. Ruch. (1986) *Productivity and Quality: Measurement as a Basis for Improvement*. Columbia, MO: Research Center, College of Business and Public Administration, University of Missouri.

Adam, Everett E., Jr. and Paul M. Swamidass. (1989) Assessing operations management from a strategic perspective. *Journal of Management*. 15, 181-203.

Adamek, Kenneth C. (1979) Automated collective analysis of scrap and rework. *ASQC Annual Technical Quality Congress Transactions.* Milwaukee, WI: ASQC Quality Press, 190-199.

Adams, H. W. (1975) Solution as problems: The case of productivity. *Public Productivity Review.* 1, (September) 36-43.

Adams, J. (1993) Toward an understanding of inequity. *Journal of Abnormal and Social Psychology.* (67) 5, 422-436.

Adams, J. S. (1963) Wage inequities, productivity and work quality. *Industrial Relations.* 3, (October) 9-16.

Adams, M. (1992) TQM: OD's role in implementing value-based strategies. In C. N. Jackson and M. R. Manning (Eds.) *Intervening in Client Organizations.* Organizational Development Annual, IV. Alexandria, VA: American Society for Training and Development.

Addelman, Sidney. (1961) Irregular fractions of the 2^n factorial experiments. *Technometrics.* 3, (April) 479-496.

Addelman, Sidney. (1962) Symmetrical and asymmetrical fractional factorial plans. *Technometrics.* 4, (January) 47-58.

Addelman, Sidney. (1963) Techniques for constructing fractional replicate plans. *Journal of the American Statistical Association.* 58, (301) 45-71.

Addelman, Sidney. (1969) Sequences of two-level fractional factorial plans. *Technometrics.* 11, (March) 477-509.

Adebayo, J. L. S. (1993) Business process reengineering: The case of the National and Provincial Building Society. Unpublished Master's thesis, University of Bradford.

Adler, Mortimer. (1982) *The Paideia Proposal: An Educational Manifesto.* New York: Collier Macmillan.

Adler, N. J. (1991) *International Dimensions of Organizational Behavior.* Second edition. Boston, MA: PWS-Kent.

Adler, P. S. (1986) New technologies, new skills. *California Management Review.* 29, (Fall) 9-28.

Admiral Corporation. (1976) *Supplier Quality Control Manual.* Galesburg, IL: Admiral Corporation.

Advisory Group on Reliability of Electronic Equipment (1957) *Reliability of Military Electronic Equipment.* Office of the Assistant Secretary of Defense (R and D). Washington, DC: U.S. Government Printing Office.

Advisory Group on Reliability of Electronic Equipment (1958) *Reliability of Military Electronic Equipment.* Office of the Assistant Secretary of Defense (R and D). Washington, DC: U.S. Government Printing Office.

Aeh, Richard K. (1990) Focus on the process. *Journal of Systems Management.* 41, (November) 20.

Affourtit, B. B. (1986) Statistical process control (SPC): The implementation of common misconceptions. *ASQC Annual Technical Quality Congress Transactions.* Milwaukee, WI: ASQC Quality Press, 440-445.

AFSC Chief Randolph cites value of CPAR. (1989) *Defense Daily.* (February 2) 167. (*2)

Aggarwal, Sumer C. (1985) MRP, JIT, OPT, FMS? *Harvard Business Review.* 63, (September-October) 8-16. (*2)

Aguayo, Rafael. (1990) *Dr. Deming: The Man Who Taught the Japanese About Quality.* New York: Carol Publishing. (*4)

Aharony, I., and S. Strasser. (1993) Patient satisfaction: What we know about and what we still need to explore. *Medical Care Review.* 50, 49-79.

Aiba, K. (1966) Significance of quality designing. *Hinshitsu Kanri.* 17, (July) 88-89.

Aiken, M., and J. Hage. (1968) Organizational interdependence and intraorganizational structure. *American Sociological Review*. 33, 912-919.

Ailleret, Pierre. (1977) The importance and probable evolution of standardization. *Standardization News*. 5, 8-11.

Ainsworth, L. (1980) The use of signal-detection theory in the analysis of industrial inspection. *Quality Assurance*. 6, (September) 63-68.

Akao, Yoji and Hoshin Kanri. (1991) *Policy Deployment for Successful TQM*. Cambridge, MA: Productivity Press.

Akao, Yoji and Tetsuichi Asaka (Eds.). (1990) *Quality Function Deployment: Integrating Customer Requirements into Product Design*. Cambridge, MA: Productivity Press. (*3)

Al-Assaf, A. F., and June A. Schmele. (1993) *Total Quality in Healthcare*. Delray Beach, FL: St. Lucie Press.

Alaimo, A. P. (1969) A total inspection system. *ASQC Annual Technical Quality Congress Transactions*. Milwaukee, WI: ASQC Quality Press, 71-78.

Albert, K. J. (1983) *The Strategic Management Handbook*. New York: McGraw-Hill.

Albrecht, A., and J. Gaffney (1983) Software function, source lines of code, and development effort prediction. *IEEE Transactions on Software Engineering*. SE-9, (No. 6) 639-647.

Albrecht, Karl. (1983) *Organization Development: A Total Systems Approach to Positive Change*. Englewood Cliffs, NJ: Prentice-Hall.

Albrecht, Karl. (1985) *Service America: Doing Business in the New Economy*. Homewood, IL: Dow Jones-Irwin.

Albrecht, Karl. (1988) *At America's Service: How Corporations Can Revolutionize the Way they Treat Their Customers*. Homewood, IL: Dow Jones-Irwin.

Albrecht, Karl. (1990) *Service Within: Solving the Middle Management Leadership Crisis*. Homewood, IL: Dow Jones-Irwin.

Albrecht, Karl. (1993) Hospitals need kinder, gentler, TQM. *Modern Healthcare*. 23, (January) 29. (*2)

Albrecht, Karl and Ron Zemke. (1990) *Service America: Doing Business in the New Economy*. New York: Warner Books.

Albus, J. S., and Michael L. Fitzgerald. (1982) *An Architecture for Real-Time Sensory-Interactive Control Robots*. New York: International Federation of Automatic Control (FAC).

Alderfer, C. P. (1972) *Existence, Relatedness, Growth: Human Needs in Organizational Settings*. New York: Free Press.

Aldrich, H., and D. A. Whetton. (1981) Organization-sets, action-sets and networks: Making the most of simplicity. In Paul C. Nystrom and William H. Starbuck (Eds.) *Handbook of Organization. Design Volume 1*. New York: Oxford University Press, 385-408.

Aleo, Joseph P., Jr. (1992) Redefining the manufacturer-supplier relationship. *Journal of Business Strategy*, (September/October) 10-14.

Alexander, C. Philip. (1981) Learning from the Japanese. *Personal Journal*. 60, (August) 19.

Alexander, Kenneth. (1987) The worker, the union and the democratic workplace. *The American Journal of Economics and Sociology*. (October) 25-29.

Alexander, Tom. (1985) Cray's way of staying super-duper. *Fortune*. (March 15) 76.

Alinsky, S. (1971) *Rules for Radicals*. New York: Random House.

Allan, Elyse. (1990) Measuring quality costs: A shifting perspective. *Presentation*. (April 2) 17-18.

Allan, Elyse. (1991) Measuring quality costs: A shifting perspective. In *Global Perspectives on Total Quality*. New York: The Conference Board, 35-44.

Allen, C. W. (1984) A case history of introducing CAD into a large aerospace company. In P. Arthur (Ed.) *CAD/CAM in Education and Training*. London, UK: Kogan Page.

Allen, G. C. (1981) *The Japanese Economy*. New York: St. Martin's Press.

Allen, L. A. (1958) *Management and Organization*. New York: McGraw-Hill.

Allen, P. E. (1959) Evaluating inspection costs. *ASQC Annual Technical Quality Congress Transactions*. Milwaukee, WI: ASQC Quality Press, 585-596.

Allen, T. J. (1967) Communications in the research and development laboratory. *Technology Review*. (October-November) 17-19. (*3)

Allen, T. J., and S. I. Cohen. (1969) Information flow in research and development laboratories. *Administrative Science Quarterly*. 14, (March) 12-19.

Allen, T. J., D. M. S. Lee, and M. Tushman. (1980) R and D performance as a function of internal communication, project management and the nature of work. *IEEE Transactions on Engineering Management*. 27, 2-12.

Allen, Woody. (1971) *Getting Even*. New York: Random House.

Allender, Hans D. (1992) Total quality management: A primer on a new management paradigm. *The Quality Observer*. (February) 22-24.

Allender, Hans D. (1992) Using quality circles to develop an action plan required for leading organizations. *Industrial Management*. 34, (September-October) 8.

Allio, Robert J. (1984) Executive retraining: The obsolete MBA. *Business and Society Review*. (Summer) 42-44.

Allor, Phillip. (1988) Target for excellence. *Quality*. (September) 18-19.

Alster, Norm. (1989) What flexible workers can do. *Fortune*. (February 13) 46-47.

Alston, J. P. (1983) Three principles of Japanese management. *Personnel Journal*. 62, (September) 758-763.

Altschuler, A., M. Anderson, D. Jones, Daniel Roos, and J. Womack. (1984) *The Future of the Automobile: The Report of MIT's Automobile Program*. Cambridge, MA: MIT Press. (*2)

Aly, Nael A., Venetta J. Maytubby, and Ahmad K. Elshennawy. (1990) Total quality management: An approach and a case study. *Computers and Industrial Engineering*. (Issues 1-4) 111-116.

Ambrosia, John. (1993) Trentwood: A study in modern maturity. *Iron Age*. 9, (February) 32. (*2)

Ambrosino, G., J. Green, L. Kein and M. Lyons. (1988) Entrepreneurial needs assessment: A review of Massachusetts smaller businesses, a study cosponsored by Arthur Young and Company and the U.S. Small Business Administration and implementation of computer integrated manufacturing (CIM) in the aircraft industry. Working Paper. College of Business Administration, Georgia State University, Atlanta, GA.

American Management Association. (1991) *Blueprints for Service Quality: The Federal Express Approach*. New York: American Management Association Membership Publications Division.

American National Standards Institute. (1978) *Quality Systems Terminology*. American National Standard A-3. Milwaukee, WI: ASQC Quality Press.

American National Standards Institute. (1980) *Sampling Procedures and Tables for Inspection by Attributes*. Milwaukee, WI: ASQC Quality Press. (*2)

American National Standards Institute. (1985) *Guides for Quality Control*. New York: ANSI.

American National Standards Institute. (1985) *Guide for Quality Control Charts; Control Chart Method for Analyzing Data; Control Chart Method of Controlling Quality during Production.* Milwaukee, WI: ASQC Quality Press.

American National Standards Institute. (1986) An attribute skip-lot sampling program. *Quality Progress*. 19, (March) 99.

American Productivity and Quality Center. (1989) Hewlett-Packard examines manufacturing excellence beyond its backyard. *Letter*. (July) 1, 6-7.

American Productivity and Quality Center. (1990) Florida utility becomes first overseas company to win Japan's Deming Prize. *Letter*. (March) 1, 7.

American Productivity and Quality Center. (1990) Roger Milliken outlines Baldrige-winning philosophy. *Letter*. (December) 1, 6.

American quality efforts receive report card. (1992) *Machine Design*. (June 11) 16. (*2)

American Quality Foundation and Ernst and Young. (1991) *International Quality Study: The Definitive Study of the Best International Quality Management Practices*. Cleveland, OH: Ernst and Young.

American Society for Quality Control. (1968) *General Requirements for a Quality Program*. (ASQC Standard C1-1968). Milwaukee, WI: ASQC Quality Press.

American Society for Quality Control. (1976) *Procurement Quality Control: A Handbook of Recommended Practices*. Second edition. Milwaukee, WI: ASQC Quality Press.

American Society for Quality Control. (1977) *Guide for Reducing Quality Costs*. Milwaukee, WI: ASQC Quality Press.

American Society for Quality Control. (1977) *How to Conduct a Supplier Survey*. Milwaukee, WI: ASQC Quality Press.

American Society for Quality Control. (1979) *Generic Guidelines for Quality Systems*. (ANSI/ASQC Z1.15-1979) Milwaukee, WI: ASQC Quality Press.

American Society for Quality Control. (1980) *Consumer Attitudes on Quality in the United States, 1980*. Milwaukee, WI: ASQC Quality Press.

American Society for Quality Control. (1980) *Guide for Managing Vendor Quality Costs*. Milwaukee, WI: ASQC Quality Press.

American Society for Quality Control. (1983) *Glossary and Tables for Statistical Quality Control*. Milwaukee, WI: ASQC Quality Press.

American Society for Quality Control. (1986) *Principles of Quality Costs*. Milwaukee, WI: ASQC Quality Press.

American Society for Quality Control. (1987) QA/QC software directory. *Quality Progress*. 20, (March) 33-66.

American Society for Quality Control. (1989) *The Hare and the Tortoise Revisited: The Businessman's Guide to Continuous Quality Improvement*. Milwaukee, WI: ASQC Quality Press.

American Society for Testing and Materials. (1976) *Moisture Content Determination: Oven Drying Method D 644*. Philadelphia, PA: ASTM.

American Society for Testing and Materials, Committee E-11 on Statistical Methods. (1976) *ASTM Manual on Presentation of Data and Control Chart Analysis STP 15D*. Fourth revision. Philadelphia, PA: ASTM.

American Society of Hospital Pharmacists. (1980) *ASHP Guidelines on Hospital Drug Administration and Control*. Washington, DC: ASHP.

American Telephone and Telegraph. (1984) *Statistical Quality Control Handbook.* Charlotte, NC: Delmar Printing Company.

America's best plants: Corning; Dana; Ford; Motorola; Texas Instruments; Xerox. (1990) *Industry Week.* (October 15) 28-62.

America's search for quality. (1983) Benton Habor, MI: Whirlpool Corporation.

Amerine, M. A., E. B. Roessler, and F. Filipello. (1959) Modern sensory methods of evaluating wines. *Hilgardia.* 28, 477.

Ammer, D. S. (1969) Materials management as a profit center. *Harvard Business Review.* 47, (January-February) 72-82.

Ammer, D. S. (1980) *Materials Management and Purchasing.* Homewood, IL: Irwin.

Amsden, Davida M., and Robert T. Amsden (Eds.). (1976) *Q.C. Circles: Applications, Tools, and Theory.* Milwaukee, WI: ASQC Quality Press. (*2)

Amsden, Davida M., and Robert T. Amsden (Eds.). (1978) *Problem-Solving Comparisons: QC Circles, KT, ZD and others.* Milwaukee, WI: ASQC Quality Press, 41-46.

Amsden, Davida M., and Robert T. Amsden (Eds.). (1978) Statistics applied to and by QC circles. *ASQC Annual Technical Quality Congress Transactions.* Milwaukee, WI: ASQC Quality Press, 201-206.

Amsden, Davida M., and Robert T. Amsden (Eds.). (1979) The research aspects of QC circles. *ASQC Annual Technical Quality Congress Transactions.* Milwaukee, WI: ASQC Quality Press.

Amsden, Davida M., and Robert T. Amsden (Eds.). (1980) Results of research on QC circles. *ASQC Annual Technical Quality Congress Transactions.* Milwaukee, WI: ASQC Quality Press.

Amsden, Robert T. (1981) A look at QC circles. In H. J. Bajaria (Ed.) *Quality Assurance: Methods, Management and Motivation.* Dearborn, MI: Society of Manufacturing Engineers, 225-230.

Amsden, Robert T., and Davida M. Amsden. (1980) A look at QC circles. *Tooling and Production.* (June) 23-25.

Amsden, Robert T., Howard E. Bulter, and Davida M. Amsden. (1986) *SPC Simplified: Practical Steps to Quality.* New York: Kraus International Publications. (*2)

Amsden, Robert T., Howard E. Butler, and Davida M. Amsden. (1989) *SPC Simplified: Practical Steps to Quality.* White Plains, NY: Quality Resources.

Amster, S. J., and J. H. Hooper. (1986) Statistical methods for reliability improvement. *AT and T Technical Journal.* 65, (March-April) 69-76.

Amster, S. J., and J. H. Hooper. (1983) Accelerated life tests with measured degradation data and growth curve models. American Statistical Association Annual Meeting, Program and Abstracts.

Amster, S. J., G. G. Brush, and B. Saperstein. (1982) Planning and conducting field tracking studies. *Bell System Technical Journal.* 61, (September) 2333-2364.

Ancona, D. G., and D. Caldwell. (1990) Improving the performance of new product teams. *Research Technology Management.* (March-April) 25-29.

Anderson, C. S., and A. Kleingartner. (1987) Human resources management in high technology firms and the impact of professionalism. In A. Kleingartner and C. S. Anderson. (Eds.) *Human Resources Management in High Technology Firms.* Lexington, MA: D. C. Heath.

Anderson, Craig A., and Robin D. Daigh, (1991) Quality mind-set overcomes barriers to success. *Healthcare Financial Management.* 45, (February) 20-22.

Anderson, D. A and A. M. Thomas. (1978) Resolution IV fractional factorial designs for the general asymmetrical factorial. *Communications in Statistics.* A8, 931-943.

Anderson, Dave. (1982) When three meant six. *New York Times.* (December) 27, C1, C3.

Anderson, David R., Dennis J. Sweeney, and Thomas A. Williams. (1989) *Quantitative Methods for Business.* St. Paul, MN: West Publishing.

Anderson, Doug. (1991) How to use cost of quality data. In *Global Perspectives on Total Quality.* New York: The Conference Board, 37.

Anderson, H. (1991) The open corporation: Reengineering for the client/server revolution. *Forbes.* (October) 131-140.

Anderson, Larry H. (1990) Controlling process variation is key to manufacturing success. *Quality Progress.* 23, (August) 91-93.

Anderson, M., and R. Lieva. (1986) *Quantitative Management: An Introduction.* Boston, MA: PWS-Kent.

Anderson, P. (1982) Marketing, strategic planning and the theory of the firm. *Journal of Marketing.* 42, (Spring) 15-26.

Anderson, R. T., and T. L. Martin. (1982) *Guidebook for Management of Software.* Lockport, VA: Quality Technical Associates.

Anderson, Richard E. (1993) HRD's role in concurrent engineering. *Training and Development Journal.* 47, (June) 49-54.

Andrade, Joanne and Helen Ryley. (1992) A quality approach to writing assessment. *Educational Leadership.* 50, (November) 52-54.

Andreasen, Alan R., and Arthur Best. (1977) Consumers complain: Does business respond? *Harvard Business Review.* 55, (July-August) 121.

Andrews, D. C., and S. K. Stalick. (1994) *Business Reengineering: The Survival Guide*. New York: Yourdon Press.

Andrews, Kenneth R. (1968) Introduction to the anniversary edition. In Chester I. Barnard (Ed.) *The Functions of the Executive*. Cambridge, MA: Harvard University Press.

Andrews, Kenneth R. (1971) *The Concept of Corporate Strategy*. Homewood, IL: Dow Jones-Irwin.

Andrews, Kenneth R. (1982) Rigid rules will not make good boards. *Harvard Business Review*. 60, (November-December) 34-40.

Andrews, R. (1957) Is management training effective? *Harvard Business Review*. 35, (January-March) 56-61.

Andrews, S. L. (1990) QA vs. QI: The changing role of quality in health care. *Journal of Quality Assurance*. 38, (January) 14-15.

Andrews, Walter. (1988) Pentagon adopts Japanese production techniques. *United Press International*. (August) 17-26. (*3)

Ansari, Shahid L. (1977) An integrated approach to control systems design. *Accounting Organizations and Society*. 2, 101-112.

Ansari, Shahid L. (1986) Survey identifies critical factors in successful implementation of just-in-time purchasing techniques. *Industrial Engineering*. 18, (October) 44-50.

Ansari, Shahid L. (1987) The potential benefits of just-in-time purchasing for U.S. *Manufacturing Production and Inventory Management*. 28, 30-36.

Anscombe, F. J. (1948) The transformation of poisson, binomial, and negative binomial data. *Biometrika*. 35, 246-254.

Ansoff, II. Igor. (1965) *Corporate Strategy*. New York: McGraw-Hill.

Ansoff, H. Igor. (1974) Corporate structure present and future. Vanderbilt University Working Paper. (February) 17.

Anthes, Gary H. (1993) ISO standard attracts U.S. interest. *Computerworld.* (April 26) 109.

Anthony, Robert N., John Deardon, and Norton M. Bedford. (1984) *Management Control Systems*. Homewood, IL: Irwin.

Antilla, Susan. (1981) East meets west: The quality circle. *Working Woman*. 88, (October) 91.

Anzai, Y., and Herbert A. Simon. (1979) The theory of learning by doing. *Psychological Review.* 86, 124-140.

Aoki, Satoshi. (1980) *The Crisis of Nissan Group.* Tokyo: Chobunsha.

Aoki, Satoshi. (1981) *Secret of Nissan S-Organization.* Tokyo: Chobunsha.

Aonuma, Yoshimatsu. (1980) The Japanese and the organization. *Toyota Quarterly Review.* 9, (Spring) 9-19.

Apcar, M. (1985) Middle managers and supervisors resist moves to more participatory management. *Wall Street Journal*. (September, 16) 31-34.

ARA Services Inc. (1980) *ARA Performance Incentive Operational Manual.* Philadelphia, PA: ARA Services, 145-187.

Archibald, Russell D. (1976) *Managing High-Technology Programs and Projects*. New York: John Wiley.

Ardalan, Alizeza, Jack Hammesfahr, and James Pope. (1992) Total quality control: The repair facility. *Industrial Management and Data Systems*. 92, (December) 7. (*2)

Ardolini, C., and J. Hohenstien. (1974) Measuring productivity in the federal government. *Monthly Labor Review.* 97, (November) 13-20.

Argyris, Chris. (1953) Human problems with budgets. *Harvard Business Review*. 31, (January-February) 61-64.

Argyris, Chris. (1957) *Personality and Organization.* New York: Harper and Row. (*4)

Argyris, Chris. (1962) *Interpersonal Competence and Organizational Effectiveness.* New York: Dorsey Press. (*3)

Argyris, Chris. (1967) Today's problems with tomorrow's organizations. *Journal of Management Studies.* (February) 34-40. (*2)

Argyris, Chris. (1971) *Management and Organization Development.* New York: McGraw-Hill.

Argyris, Chris. (1976) *Increasing Leadership Effectiveness.* New York: John Wiley.

Argyris, Chris. (1976) Theories of action that inhibit individual learning. *American Psychologist.* 31, (June) 638-654.

Argyris, Chris. (1978) *Organizational Learning: A Theory of Action Perspective.* Reading, MA: Addison-Wesley.

Argyris, Chris. (1985) *Strategy, Change, and Defensive Routines.* Boston, MA: Pitman.

Argyris, Chris. (1988) *Reasoning, Learning and Action.* San Francisco, CA: Jossey-Bass. (*2)

Argyris, Chris. (1990) *Overcoming Organizational Defenses.* Englewood Cliffs, NJ: Prentice-Hall. (*4)

Argyris, Chris, R. Putnam, and D. M. Smith. (1988) *Action Science.* San Francisco, CA: Jossey-Bass.

Argyris, Chris., and D. Schon. (1978) *Organizational Learning: A Theory of Action Perspective.* Reading, MA: Addison-Wesley.

ARINC Research Corporation. (1962) *Reliability Theory and Practice.* Washington, DC: ARINC.

Armitage, H., and R. Grant. (1993) Activity-based management information: TQM's missing link. *CMA—The Management Accounting Magazine*. 67, (March) 7.

Armstrong, J. S. (1982) The value of formal planning for strategic decisions. *Strategic Management Journal*. 3, (March-April) 197-221

Armstrong, J. S. (1985) Changing management control strategies: The role of competition between accountancy and other organizational professions. *Harvard Business Review*. 63, (November-December) 115-122.

Arnitz, William E. (1981) GIDEP can improve productivity through information exchange. *Proceedings, Annual Reliability and Maintainability Symposium*. New York: IEEE, 128-131.

Arnold, M. B. (1960) *Emotion and Personality: Psychological Aspects*. New York: Columbia University Press. (*2)

Arnold, T. (1935) *The Symbols of Government*. New Haven, CT: Yale University Press.

Aronson, E. (1980) *The Social Animal*. San Francisco, CA: W. J. Freeman.

Arrington, Lance. (1990) Training and commitment: Two keys to quality. *Chief Executive*. (September) 72-73.

Arrow, Kenneth J. (1974) *The Limits of the Organization*. New York: W. W. Norton.

Artamonov, V. P. (1977) *Quality of Work*. Moscow: Gosstandart. (*2)

Artes, A. E. (1977) Upgrading of specialists in products quality control through VISM. Proceedings, ETC Seminar. Odessa, TX: ETC. (*2)

Arthur Anderson. (1961) *Operations Research in the Firm*. Chicago, IL: Arthur Anderson and Company.

Artificial intelligence is here. (1984) *BusinessWeek*. (July 9) 57.

Artzt, Edwin L. (1992) Developing the next generation of quality leaders. *Quality Progress*. 25, (October) 25-27.

Arvey, R., and J. Campion. (1982) The employment interview: A summary and review of recent research. *Personnel Psychology*. 35, (February) 281-322.

As IBM losses mount, so do the complaints about company perks. (1993) *Wall Street Journal*. (October 27) A.

Asaka, Tetsuichi and Kazuo Ozeki (Eds.). (1990) *Handbook of Quality Tools: The Japanese Approach*. Cambridge, MA and Norwalk, CT: Productivity Press. (*4)

ASD's quality assurance program rates in top 10. (1984) Assembly engineering. *Newsline*. (August) 6.

Asher, J. M. (1988) Cost of quality in service industries. *International Journal of Quality and Reliability Management (UK)*. 5, (Issue 5) 38-46.

Ashkenas, D., and Todd D. Jick. (1982) Productivity and QWL success without ideal conditions. *National Productivity Review*. 1, (August) 381-388.

Ashkenas, Ronald and Robert Schaffer. (1992) The lemmings who love total quality. *New York Times*. (May 3) F13.

Ashmore, G. Michael. (1989) Applying expert systems to business strategy. *Journal of Business Strategy*. (September-October) 46-49. (*2)

Asimov, Isaac. (1987) *Would you Believe*? New York: Grosset and Dunlap. (*2)

Ashby, W. Ross. (1956) *An Introduction to Cybernetics*. New York: John Wiley.

Assael, H. (1985) *Marketing Management*. Boston, MA: PWS-Kent.

At Emery Air Freight: Positive reinforcement boosts performance. (1973) *Organizational Dynamics.* 1, (Winter) 41-50.

AT&T (1988) *SQC Troubleshooter User Manual.* Indianapolis, IN: AT & T.

AT&T (1989) *A History of Quality and Assurance at AT & T, 1920-1970.* Indianapolis, IN: AT & T Customer Information Center.

AT&T Corporate Quality Office (1995) *Using ISO 9000 to Improve Business Processes.* Indianapolis, IN: AT & T.

AT&T Technologies and Bonnie B. Small (Ed.), (1956) *Statistical Quality Control Handbook.* Indianapolis, IN: Western Electric Company.

AT&T's hard bargain: A watershed for the industry? (1986) *BusinessWeek.* (June) 37.

Atanasov, A. (1977) Initial criteria and basic factors underlying the level of postgraduate education and training of QC specialists. Proceedings, ETC Seminar. Odessa, TX: ETC. (*2)

Atchison, Thomas A. (1992) TQM: The questionable movement? *Healthcare Financial Management.* 46, (March) 15.

Atkinson, A. C., and William G. Hunter. (1968) Design of experiments for parameter estimation. *Technometrics.* 11, (May) 271-290.

Atkinson, P. E. (1990) *Creating Culture Change: The Key to Successful Total Quality Management.* Bedford, UK: IFS Ltd.

Attwood, Dennis J. (1996) *The Office Relocation Sourcebook: A Guide to Managing Staff Throughout the Move.* New York: John Wiley.

Attwood, J. S., R. Coleman and J. L. Singer. (1969) Automated instruction for vigilance training. *Journal of Applied Psychology.* 53, (February) 218-223.

Aubrey, Charles A., III. (1985) *Quality Management in Financial Services*. Milwaukee, WI: ASQC Quality Press.

Aubrey, Charles A., III, and Lawrence Eldridge. (1981) Banking on high quality. *Quality Progress*. 14, (December) 14-19. (*2)

Aubrey, Charles A., III, and Patricia K. Felkins. (1988) *Teamwork: Involving People in Quality and Productivity Improvement*. Milwaukee, WI: ASQC Quality Press. (*2)

Aubrey, Charles A., III, and Wendy Carol Fend. (1982) Management, professional and clerical quality circles. *ASQC Annual Technical Quality Congress Transactions*. Milwaukee, WI: ASQC Press, 54-61. (*2)

Aubrey, Charles A., III, and D. A. Zimbler. (1982) A banking quality cost model: Its uses and results. *ASQC Annual Technical Quality Congress Transactions*. Milwaukee, WI: ASQC Quality Press, 195-201.

Auerbach, Jerrold. (1983) *Justiace Without Law?* New York: Oxford University Press.

Auld, D. A and R. E. Baxter. (1983) *The American Dictionary of Economics*. New York: Facts On File.

Aust, L. B., M. C. Gacula, S. C. Beard, and R. W. Washam, II. (1985) Degree of difference test method in sensory evaluation of heterogeneous product types. *Food Science*. 50, 511.

Austin, Nancy K. (1991) Dr. Deming and the "Q" factor. *Working Women*. 16, (September) 9.

Austin, Nancy K. (1993) Quality-speaks: A manager's glossary. *Working Woman*. 18, (March) 26. (*3)

Austin, Nancy K. (1993) The lowdown on quality. *Working Woman*. 18, (March) 22. (*3)

Automotive Industry Action Group. (1991) *Fundamental Statistical Process Control*. Southfield, MI: Automotive Industry Action Group.

Availability. (1981) *Caterpillar Annual Report.* 14.

Avedisian, Joyce, Ron Cowin Ferguson, and Bill Roth. (1986) Beyond crisis management. *Pulp and Paper International.* 60, (February) 33-36.

Axelrod, Robert. (1983) *The Evolution of Cooperation.* New York: Basic Books.

Axland, Suzanne. (1991) Looking for a quality education? *Quality Progress.* 24, (October) 31-34.

Axland, Suzanne. (1992) A higher degree of quality. *Quality Progress.* 25, (October) 33-38, 41-61.

Axline, Larry L. (1991) TQM: A look in the mirror. *Management Review.* 80, (July) 64.

Ayers, R. U. (1984) *The Next Industrial Revolution.* Cambridge, MA: Ballinger.

Azadivar, F. (1984) *Design and Engineering of Production Systems.* San Jose, CA: Engineering Press.

Azgaldov, G. G. (1977) *Theory and Practice of Estimation of Product Quality.* Moscow: Ekonomika. (*2)

Azumi, Koya and Charles McMillan. (1976) Worker sentiment in the Japanese factory: Its organizational determinants. In Lewis Austin (Ed.) *Japan: The Paradox.* New Haven: Yale University Press.

Baatz, E. B. (1992) What is return on quality, and why should you care. *Electronic Business.* 18, (October) 60.

Babbage, C. (1832) *On the Economy of Machinery and Manufactures.* Second edition. London, UK: Charles Knight.

Babbit, Robert C. (1981) One company's approach to quality circles. *Quality Progress.* 14, (October) 28-29.

Babcombe, P. (1970) Quality control for the very small batch. *Quality Engineer*. 34, (January-February) 19-22.

Bacas, Harry. (1987) Make it right for the customer. *Nation's Business*. 75, (November) 50.

Bacharach, S. B. (1989) Organizational theories: Some criteria for evaluation. *Academy of Management Review*. (April) 496-515.

Back in 1890: Serving customers worldwide. (1980) *Johnson and Johnson 1980 Annual Report*. 20.

Backlash isn't just against Japan. (1992) *BusinessWeek*. (February 10) 30.

Bacon, Donald C. (1989) How the Baldridge winners did it. *Nation's Business*. 77, (January) 32.

Bacon, Donald C. (1990) A pursuit of excellence. *Nation's Business*. 78 (January) 27-28.

Bader, M. E. (1980) Quality assurance and quality control. Part 1: Specifications. *Chemical Engineering*. 83, (February) 11, 92-96.

Bader, M. E. (1983) *Practical Quality Management in the Chemical Process Industry*. New York: Marcel Dekker.

Badovick, G. J., and S. E. Beatty. (1987) Shared organizational values: Measurement and impact upon strategic marketing implementation. *Academy of Marketing Science*. 15, (Spring) 19-26.

Baets, W. (1993) IT for organisational learning: Beyond business process engineering. *Business Change and Reengineering*. 2, (No. 2) 32-40.

Bahis, Jane Easter. (1992) Managing for total quality: Practitioners must inspire employee involvement. *Public Relations Journal*. 48, (April) 16-20. (*3)

Baida, Peter. (1990) *Poor Richard's Legacy: American Business Values From Benjamin Franklin to Donald Trump*. New York: William Morrow.

Bailey, E. E., D. R. Graham, and D. P. Kaplan. (1986) *Deregulating the Airlines*. Cambridge, MA: MIT Press.

Bailey, J. (1993) Why customers trash the garbage man. *Wall Street Journal*. (March 17) 81A, 81B.

Bailey, R. A., and R. A. Gilbert. (1982) Strife testing. *Quality*. (November) 53-55.

Baily, P. (1977) *Purchasing Principles and Techniques*. Third edition. London, UK: Pitman.

Baily, R. W. (1982) *Human Performance Engineering: A Guide for System Designers*. Englewood Cliffs, NJ: Prentice-Hall.

Bailyn, L. (1985) Autonomy in the Industrial Rand lab. *Human Resource Management*. 24, (Spring/Summer) 129-146.

Bain, D. (1982) *The Productivity Prescription*. New York: McGraw-Hill.

Bainbridge, John. (1972) *The Super-Americans*. New York: Holt, Rinehart and Winston.

Bainbridge, T. R. (1965) Staggered, nested designs for estimating variance components. *Industrial Quality Control*. 22, (January) 12-20.

Baird, Lloyd and Llan Meshoulam. (1992) Getting payoff from investment in human resource management. *Journal of Business*. 35, (January) 68.

Bajaria, H. J. (1979) Motivating line engineers for reliability, Part I. *ASQC Annual Technical Quality Congress Transactions*. Milwaukee, WI: ASQC Quality Press, 767-773.

Bajaria, H. J. (1980) Motivating line engineers for reliability, Part II. *ASQC Annual Technical Quality Congress Transactions*. Milwaukee, WI: ASQC Quality Press, 168-176.

Bajaria, H. J. (1983) *Integration of Reliability, Maintainability and Quality Parameters in Design*. Warrendale, PA: Society of Automotive Engineers.

Bajaria, H. J. (1985) *AT and T Statistical Quality Control Handbook*. Chicago, IL: Western Electric.

Bajaria, H. J. (1991) *Quality Assurance: Methods, Management and Motivation*. Dearborn, MI: Society of Manufacturing Engineers. (*3)

Bajaria, H. J. (1991) Quality focused automation. *Tooling and Production*. (March) 25-26.

Baker, E. M. (1975) Signal detection theory analysis of quality control inspector performance. *Journal of Quality Technology*. 7, (April) 62-71.

Baker, E. M. (1982) Managing for quality through employee involvement. *ASQC Annual Technical Quality Congress Transactions*. Milwaukee, WI: ASQC Quality Press, 282-284.

Baker, E. M., and H. L. M. Artinian. (1985) The Deming philosophy of continuing improvement in a service organization: The case of Windsor Export Supply. *Quality Progress*. 18, (June) 61-69.

Baker, E. M., and J. R. Schuck. (1975) Theoretical note: Use of signal detection theory to clarify problems of evaluating performance in industry. *Organization Behavior and Human Performance*. 13, 307-317.

Baker, R. A. (1968) Limitation of present objective techniques in sensory characterization. *Correlation of Subjective-Objective Methods in the Study of Odors and Taste*. Philadelphia, PA: American Society for Testing and Materials.

Baker, William M. (1994) Understanding activity-based costing. *Industrial Management*. 36, (March/April) 28-30.

Bakewell, K. G. B. (1970) *How to Find Out: Management and Productivity.* New York: Pergamon Press.

Bakke, E. (1950) *Bonds of Organization.* New York: Harper and Row.

Balakrishnan, S., and M. P. Koza. (1988) The emergence of supernationals in global industry. In L. R. Gomez-Mejia and M. W. Lawless (Eds.) *Conference Proceedings Managing the High Technology Firm.* Boulder, CO: University of Colorado Press, 391-395.

The Baldrige boondoggle. (1992) *Machine Design.* (August 6) 25-29.

Baldrige competition keeps suppliers competitive. (1989) *Technowledge.* 3, (October) 3. (*2)

Baldwin, David and David Gromes. (1983) EI at Canton Forge. *Work Life Review.* 2, (March) 17-21.

Baligia, B. R., and Alfred M. Jaeger. (1984) Multinational corporations: Control systems and delegation issues. *Journal of International Business Studies.* (Fall) 25-40.

Balkin, D. B. (1987). Compensation strategies for research and development staff. *Topics in Total Compensation.* 2, (Winter) 207-215.

Balkin, D. B., and L. R. Gomez-Mejia. (1984) Determinants of R and D compensation strategies in the high tech industry. *Personnel Psychology.* 37, (June) 635-650.

Balkin, D. B., and L. R. Gomez-Mejia. (1985) Compensation practices in high technology industries. *Personnel Administrator.* (June) 111-118, 122-124.

Balkin, D. B., and L. R. Gomez-Mejia. (1987) Toward a contingency theory compensation strategy. *Strategic Management Journal.* 8, (January-February) 169-182.

Ball, L. W. (1974) Complex systems. In *Quality Control Handbook.* Third edition. New York: McGraw-Hill.

Ball, Robert A. (1980) Europe outgrows management American style. *Fortune.* (October 15) 147-148. (*2)

Ball, Robert A., and Stephen P. Barney. (1982) *Quality Circle Project Manual.* Rawsonville, MS: UAW-Ford Employee Involvement.

Ballard, D. H., and C. M. Brown. (1982) *Computer Vision.* Englewood Cliffs, NJ: Prentice-Hall.

Ballen, Kate. (1989) The new look of capital spending. *Fortune.* (March 13) 115-120.

Ballou, D. P., and H. L. Pazer. (1982) The impact of inspector fallibility on the inspection policy in serial production systems. *Management Science.* 28, (April) 387-399.

Band, William A. (1989) Marketers need to understand the high cost of poor quality. *Sales and Marketing Management in Canada.* (November) 56-59.

Band, William A. (1991) *Creating Value for Customers: Designing and Implementing a Total Corporate Strategy.* New York: John Wiley. (*2)

Bando, Satoshi. (1981) Qualitative change in the labor movement. *Japan Echo.* 8, (Spring) 30-37.

Bandura, A. (1977) Self-efficacy: Toward a unifying theory of behavioral change. *Psychological Review.* 84, 191-215.

Bank of Boston, Economics Department. (1988) Summary of Findings of Bank of Boston Survey on Exporting by Young High Tech Companies. Boston, MA: Bank of Boston.

Banks, J. (1989) *Principles of Quality Control.* New York: John Wiley. (*2)

Banks, J., and J. S. Carson, II. (1984) *Discrete Event Simulation.* Englewood Cliffs, NJ: Prentice-Hall.

Barankin, Edward W. (1964) Probability and the east. *Annals of the Institute of Statistical Mathematics* (Tokyo) 16, 216.

Baranson, J. (1981) *The Japanese Challenge to U.S. Industry.* Lexington, MA: Lexington Books.

Barasia, Cyril and Ramesh Barasia. (1977) A support system life cycle cost model. *Proceedings, Annual Reliability and Maintainability Symposium.* New York: IEEE, 297-302.

Barasia, R. K., and T. D. Kiang. (1978) Development of a life cycle management cost model. *Proceedings, Annual Reliability and Maintainability Symposium.* New York: IEEE, 254-260.

Barbeson, R. A. (1970) Picking optimization methods. *Chemical Engineering.* 77, 32-142.

Barge, Bruce. (1992) Total quality: A risk management opportunity. *National Underwriter.* 96, (February) 17. (*2)

Barker, Kenneth N. (1961) *A Study of the Problem of Detecting Medication Errors in a Hospital.* Gainesville, FL: University of Florida.

Barker, Kenneth N. (1969) The effects of an experimental medication system on medication errors and costs. *American Journal of Hospital Pharmacy.* (June-July) 324-333.

Barker, Kenneth N., and W. McConnell. (1962) How to detect medication errors. *Medical Hospital.* (July) 95-105.

Barker, Kenneth N., W. W. Kimbrough, and W. M. Heller. (1966) *A Study of Medication Errors in a Hospital.* Oxford, MS: University of Mississippi Press.

Barker, T. J. (1985) *Quality by Experimental Design.* New York: Marcel Dekker.

Barker, Thomas B. (1986) Quality engineering by design: Taguchi's philosophy. *Quality Progress.* 19, (December) 24-30.

Barley, S. R. (1983) Semeiotics and the study of occupational and organizational cultures. *Administrative Science Quarterly.* 28, (April) 393-413.

Barlow, Richard E., and Frank Proschan. (1975) *Statistical Theory of Reliability.* New York: Holt, Rinehart and Winston.

Barmash, Isadore. (1976) *For the Good of the Company: Work and Interplay in a Major American Corporation.* New York:

Barnard, Chester I. (1968) *The Functions of the Executive.* Cambridge: Harvard University Press. (*5)

Barnard, George A. (1954) Sampling inspection and statistical decisions. *Journal of the Royal Statistical Society.* 16, (Series B) 151-171.

Barnard, John. (1983) *Walter Reuther and the Rise of the Auto World.* Boston, MA: Little, Brown.

Barnes, R. M. (1980) *Motion and Time Study: Design and Measurement of Work.* New York: John Wiley.

Barnet, Richard J. (1984) *The Alliance.* New York: Simon and Schuster.

Barnett, C. (1986) *The Pride and the Fall.* New York: Free Press.

Barnett, E. H. (1960) Introduction to evolutionary operation. *Industrial and Engineering Chemistry.* 52, 500-503.

Barnett, J. L. (1994) Process visualization: Getting the vision right is key. *Information Systems Management.* (Spring) 14-23.

Barney, J. B. (1986) Organizational culture: Can it be a source of sustained competitive advantage? *Academy of Management Review.* (February) 656-665.

Barney, Stephen P. (1982) Quality circles: Adapting materials and training to organizational needs. *Quality Progress.* 15, (December) 31-34.

Barnouw, V. (1979) *Culture and Personality.* Homewood, IL: Dorsey Press.

Barr, Donald R. (1969) Using confidence intervals to test hypotheses. *Journal of Quality Technology.* 1, (February) 256-258.

Barra, Ralph J. (1983) *Putting Quality Circle to Work: A Practical Strategy for Boosting Productivity and Profits.* New York: McGraw-Hill. (*2)

Barrier, Michael. (1992) Doing well what comes naturally. *Nation's Business.* 80, (September) 25. (*2)

Barrier, Michael. (1992) Seeking and finding, the quality leaders. *Nation's Business.* 80, (September) 36. (*2)

Barrier, Michael. (1992) Small firms put quality first. *Nation's Business.* 80, (May) 22. (*2)

Barrier, Michael. (1992) Spreading the word: Quality. *Nation's Business.* 80, (August) 56. (*2)

Barrier, Michael. (1992) When 'just in time' just isn't enough. *Nation's Business.* 80, (November) 30. (*2)

Barrier, Michael. (1993) Where 'quality' is a language. *Nation's Business.* 81, (January) 57. (*3)

Barron, C. (1977) British 3M's multiple management. *Management Today.* (March) 56-57. (*4)

Barron, D. W. (1971) *Computer Operating Systems.* New York: Chapman and Hall.

Barry, Dave. (1992) *Dave Barry Does Japan.* New York: Random House.

Barry, Gerald J. (1988) Stay tuned. *The Quality Review.* (Spring) 34-39.

Barry, E. N. (1959) Work simplification applied to inspection. *Industrial Quality Control.* 15, (May) 56-58; also (June) 19-20.

Barry, Thomas J. (1988) Quality Circles: Proceed with Caution. Milwaukee, WI: ASQC Quality Press.

Barry, Thomas J. (1994) *Excellence Is a Habit: How to Avoid Quality Burnout.* Milwaukee, WI: ASQC Quality Press.

Barsh, L., and Y. Henderson. *The Road: Indian Tribes and Political Liberty.* Berkeley, CA: University of California Press.

Bartee, T. C. (1972) *Digital Computer Fundamentals.* New York: McGraw-Hill.

Barth, Roland. (1991) *Improving Schools from Within.* San Francisco, CA: Jossey-Bass.

Bartlett, C. A., and Sumantra Ghoshal. (1990) Matrix management: Not a structure, a frame of mind. *Harvard Business Review.* 78, (July-August) 138-145.

Bashein, B. J., M. L. Markus, and P. Riley. (1994) Preconditions for BPR success: And how to prevent failures. *Information Systems Management.* (Spring) 7-13.

Bass, B. M. (1985) Leadership: Good, better, best. *Organizational Dynamics.* 13, (Winter) 26-40

Bass, B. M., and G. V. Barrett. (1981) *People, Work and Organizations.* Boston, MA: Allyn and Bacon.

Basset, Edward. (1990) Diamond is forever. *New England Business.* 12, (October 8) 40-44.

Batalden, P. B. (1991) Organizationwide quality improvement in healthcare. *Topics in Health Records Management.* 11, 1-12. (*2)

Batalden, P. B., and E. D. Buchanan. (1989) *Providing Quality Care: The Challenge to Clinicians.* Philadelphia, PA: American College of Physicians.

Batalden, P. B., and T. Gillem. (1988) *Hospitalwide Quality Improvement Storytelling.* Nashville, TN: Hospital Corporation of America.

Baten, W. D. (1956) An analysis of variance applied to screw machines. *Industrial Quality Control.* 12, (April) 25-28.

Bateson, Gregory. (1980) *Mind and Nature: A Necessary Unity.* New York: Bantam Books. (*2)

Batson, H. C. (1956) Applications of factorial chi-squared analysis to experiments in chemistry. *ASQC Annual Technical Quality Congress Transactions.* Milwaukee, WI: ASQC Quality Press, 9-23.

Batt, W. L., Jr., and E. Weinberg. (1978) Labor-management cooperation today. *Harvard Business Review.* 56, (January-February) 96-104.

Baum, Herbert M. (1990) White-collar quality comes of age. *Journal of Business Strategy.* (March/April) 34-37.

Bauman, H. E., and C. Taubert. (1984) Why quality assurance is necessary and important to plant management. *Food Technology.* 38, 101.

Baumgardner, M. (1981) Productivity improvement for office systems. *Journal of Systems Management.* 32, (August) 12-15.

Baumgartel. (1956) Leadership, motivations and attitudes in research laboratories. *Journal of Social Issues.* 12 (February) 15-16.

Baxes, G. A. (1984) *Digital Image Processing.* Englewood Cliffs, NJ: Prentice-Hall.

Bazarro, L. A. (1976) Networking computers for process control. *Chemical Engineering.* 83, (December) 151-156.

Bazerman, M. (1988) *Judgment in Managerial Decision Making.* New York: John Wiley.

Beacon Press, Inc. (1989) *How Grocery Buyers Rate the Various Food Chains in Metropolitan Richmond.* Richmond, VA: Beacon Press.

Beal, Robert. (1991) The lessons of Zytec. *St. Paul Pioneer Press.* (October) 1.

Bean, E., C. Ordowich, and W. A. Wesley. (1985-1986) Including the supervisor in employee involvement effort. *National Productivity Review.* 4, (Winter) 64-77. (*2)

Bean, L. (1987) Where the customer is still king. *Time.* (February) 56-57. (*2)

Beardsley, J. F. (1976) Training is the heart of the Lockheed QC circle program. *ASQC Annual Technical Quality Congress Transactions.* Milwaukee, WI: ASQC Quality Press, 80-85.

Beardsley, J. F. (1980) Ingredients of successful quality circles. IAQC Second Annual Conference Transactions. Cincinnati, OH: International Association of Quality Circles.

Beardsley, J. F. (1982) *Quality Circles.* Midwest City, OK: International Association of Quality Circles.

Beasley, Norman. (1947) *Knudsen.* New York: McGraw-Hill.

Beattie, D. W. (1962) Continuous acceptance sampling procedure based upon a cumulative sum chart for the number of detectives. *Applied Statistics.* 11, (November) 137-147.

Beck, A., and E. Hill. (1972) *A Practical Approach to Organization Development Through MBO.* Reading, MA: Addison-Wesley.

Becker, Ernest. (1973) *The Denial of Death.* New York: Free Press.

Becker, Ernest. (1975) *Escape from Evil.* New York: Free Press.

Becker, Selwyn. (1993) TQM does work: Ten reasons why misguided attempts fail. *Management Review*. 82, (May) 30-33.

Beckhard, Richard. (1969) *Organizational Development: Strategies and Models*. Reading, MA: Addison-Wesley. (*2)

Beckhard, Richard and R. T. Harris. (1987) *Organizational Transitions: Managing Complex Change*. Second edition. Reading, MA: Addison-Wesley. (*3)

Bedworth, D. D., and J. E. Bailey. (1982) *Integrated Production Control System*. New York: John Wiley.

Beebe, W. T. (1978) The gold winner. *Financial World*. (March) 21. (*2)

Beeck, W. O. (1985) Quality and value analysis-engineering, the ideal marriage. *Proceedings of the Conference of Quality and Development*. Berne: European Organization for Quality Control. 3, 299-312.

Beels, G. J. (1985) ESD-Enemy #1. *Quality Progress*. 24, (September) 14-18.

Beene, K. D., and P. Sheats. (1948) Functional roles of group members. *Journal of Social Issues*. 4, 41-49.

Beer, J. J. (1959) *The Emergence of the German Dye Industry*. Urbana: University of Illinois Press.

Beer, Michael. (1980) *Organizational Change and Development: A Systems View*. Santa Monica, CA: Goodyear.

Beer, Michael. (1988) The Critical path for change: Key to success and failure in six companies. In R. J. Kilmann, T. J. Covin, and Associates (Eds.) *Corporate Transformation: Revitalizing Organizations for a Competitive World*. San Francisco, CA: Jossey-Bass, 17-45.

Beer, Michael, and R. A. Ruh. (1976) Employee growth thru performance management: Systems used at Corning glass works. *Harvard Business Review.* 54, (July-August) 59-66.

Beer, Michael, Russell A. Eisenstat, and Bert Spector. (1990) *The Critical Path to Corporate Renewal.* Cambridge, MA: Harvard Business School Press.

Beer, Michael, Russell A. Eisenstat, and Bert Spector. (1990) Why change programs don't produce change. *Harvard Business Review.* 78, (November-December) 158-166.

Begon, Michael, J. L. Harper, and C. R. Townsend. (1986) *Ecology: Individuals, Populations, and Communities.* Sunderland, MA: Sinauer Associates.

Beischel, Mark E. (1990) Improving production with process value analysis: The foundation for activity-based costing. *Jorunal of Accontancy.* (September) 53-57.

Belbin, R. M. (1970) *Quality Calamities and their Management Implications.* (OPN8) London, UK: British Institute of Management.

Belcher, D. W. (1955) *Wage and Salary Administration.* Englewood Cliffs, NJ: Prentice-Hall.

Bell, C. R. (1991) Empowerment is not a gift. *Training.* 28, (December) 98.

Bell, Daniel. (1973) *The Coming of Post-Industrial Society: A Venture in Social Forecasting.* New York: Basic Books.

Bell, Daniel. (1978) *The Cultural Contradictions of Capitalism.* New York: Basic Books.

Bell, G. (1984) The mini and micro industries. *IEEE Transactions on Computing.* (October) 11-14.

Bell, L. Ferris (1983) Quality verification of manufacturing planning. *ASQC Annual Technical Quality Congress Transactions.* Milwaukee, WI: ASQC Quality Press, 70-75.

Bell, L. Ferris and Richard H. Nicholson. (1981) Tailoring quality systems for program requirements. *ASQC Annual Technical Quality Congress Transactions*. Milwaukee, WI: ASQC Quality Press, 263-278.

Bellah, Robert N., et al. (1986) *Habits of the Heart: Individualism and Commitment in American Life*. New York: Harper and Row.

Bellis-Jones, R. and N. Develin. (1992) Activity-based cost management. *Accountants' Digest*. (Spring) 1-36.

Bellman, G. M. (1985) *The Quest for Staff Leadership*. Glenview, IL: Scott Foreman and Company.

Belous, R. (1987) High technology labor markets: Projections and policy implications. In A. Kleingartner and C. S. Anderson (Eds.) *Human Resource Management in High Technology Firms*. Lexington, MA: Lexington Books, 24-45. (*2)

Bemesderfer, John L. (1979) Approving a process for production. *Journal of Quality Technology*. 11, (January) 1-12. (*2)

Bemowski, Karen. (1991) Restoring the pillars of higher education. *Quality Progress*. 24, (October) 37-42.

Bender, Ann. (1975) Statistical tolerancing as it relates to quality control and the designer. *Automotive Division Newsletter of ASQC*. (April) 12.

Bendix, R. (1956) *Work and Authority in Industry*. New York: John Wiley.

Benedict, Ruth. (1946) *The Chrysanthemum and the Sword: Patterns of Japanese Culture*. New York: New American Library.

Benedict, Ruth. (1946) *Patterns of Culture*. New York: Mentor Books, New American Library of World Literature.

Benedict, Ruth. (1967) *The Chrysanthemum and the Sword: Patterns of Japanese Culture*. Reprint. New York: New American Library.

Benjamin, Robert I., John F. Rockart, Michael F. Morton, Michael F. Scott and John Wyman. (1984) Information technology: A strategic opportunity. *Sloan Management Review*. 25, (Spring) 3-10.

Benner, Susan. (1980) He gave key people a reason to stay with the company. *Inc.* (September) 46. (*2)

Bennett, Amanda. (1981) GM's Smith wants leaner firm, more rivalry among its divisions. *Wall Street Journal.* (May 21) 43.

Bennett, Amanda. (1988) Ethics codes spread despite skepticism. *Wall Street Journal.* (July 15) 17.

Bennett, Amanda. (1989) Business takes out its trimming shears. *Wall Street Journal.* (October) 1, 4.

Bennett, Amanda. (1990) *The Death of the Organization Man.* New York: William Morrow.

Bennett, Amanda and J. Solomon. (1989) Quality award becoming job 1 for U.S. companies? *Wall Street Journal.* (November 4) 15-18.

Bennett, Carl A., and Norman L. Franklin. (1954) *Statistical Analysis in Chemistry and the Chemical Industry.* New York: John Wiley.

Bennett, Harry and Paul Marcus. (1951) *We Never Call Him Henry.* New York: Fawcett.

Bennett, J. W., and Ishino Ieao. (1963) Paternalistic economic organizations and Japanese society. In *Paternalism in the Japanese Economy.* Minneapolis, MN: University of Minnesota, 46-65.

Bennis, Warren G. (1956) A theory of group development. *Human Relations.* 9, (May) 277-300.

Bennis, Warren G. (1959) Leadership theory and administrative behavior. *Administrative Science Quarterly.* 4, (March) 31-34.

Bennis, Warren G. (1963) A new role for the behavioral sciences: Effecting organizational change. *Administrative Science Quarterly.* 8, (May) 125-165.

Bennis, Warren G. (1968) Good managers and good leaders. *Across the Board.* 21, (October) 7-11.

Bennis, Warren G. (1968) The temporary society. In Warren G. Bennis and Philip E. Slater (Ed.) *The Temporary Society.* New York: Harper and Row. (*2)

Bennis, Warren G. (1969) *Organization Development: Nature and Origins.* Reading, MA: Addison-Wesley.

Bennis, Warren G. (1976) *The Unconscious Conspiracy: Why Leaders Can't Lead.* New York: AMACOM.

Bennis, Warren G. (1983) The art form of leadership. In Suresh Scrivastva and Associates. (Eds.) *The Executive Mind: New Insights on Managerial Thought and Action.* San Francisco, CA: Jossey-Bass.

Bennis, Warren G. (1989) *On Becoming a Leader.* Reading, MA: Addison-Wesley. (*3)

Bennis, Warren G. (1989) *Why Leaders Can't Lead: The Unconscious Conspiracy Continues.* San Francisco, CA: Jossey-Bass.

Bennis, Warren G., and Bert Nanus. (1985) *Leaders: The Strategies for Taking Charge.* New York: Harper and Row. (*5)

Bennis, Warren G., and Philip J. Slater. (1968) *The Temporary Society.* New York: Harper and Row.

Bennis, Warren G., et al. (1973) *Interpersonal Dynamics.* Homewood, IL: Dorsey Press.

Bennis, Warren G., R. Benne, and K. E. Corey. (1976) *The Planning of Change.* Second edition. New York: Holt, Rinehart and Winston.

Bensman, David. (1987) *Quality Education in the Inner City: The Story of Central Park East Schools.* New York: Central Park East School. (*2)

Benson, H. (1975) *The Relaxation Response.* New York: William Morrow.

Benson, J. (1975) The interorganizational network as a political economy. *Administrative Science Quarterly.* 20, (July) 229-249.

Benson, Tracy E. (1991) The gestalt at the quality management: The concept continues to elude many who have some of the pieces but haven't yet put them together. *Industry Week.* (July) 30.

Benson, Tracy E. (1992) IQSSM: Quality is not what you think it is. *Industry Week.* (October 5) 22. (*2)

Benson, Tracy E. (1992) IQSSM: When less is more. *Industry Week.* (September 7) 68-77. (*3)

Benson, Tracy E. (1992) Quality and teamwork gets a leg up. *Industry Week.* (April 6) 66. (*2)

Benson, Tracy E. (1993) TQM: A child takes a first few faltering steps. *Industry Week.* (April 5) 16. (*3)

Benston, George J. (1980) *Conglomerate Mergers: Causes, Consequences and Remedies.* Washington, DC: American Enterprise Institute for Public Policy Research.

Benveniste, G. (1987) *Professionalizing the Organization.* San Francisco, CA: Jossey Bass.

Berenbeim, Ronald E. (1986) *Company Programs to Ease the Impact of Shutdowns.* New York: The Conference Board.

Berenbeim, Ronald E. (1992) The corporate ethics test. *Business and Society Review.* (Spring) 77-80.

Berger, P. L. (1986) *The Capitalist Revolution.* New York: Basic Books. (*2)

Berger, Robert L. (1984) Looking for software. Directory of software for QA or QC. *Quality Progress.* 17, (March) 28-30. (*2)

Berger, Robert L., and Larry C. Jenkins. (1984) Electronic equipment thermal management. *Proceedings Annual Reliability and Maintainability Symposium.* New York, IEEE, 17-22.

Berger, Robert L., and M. Hale. (1980) Programmable calculators in quality control: Tutorial. *ASQC Annual Technical Quality Congress Transactions*. Milwaukee, WI: ASQC Quality Press, 1-10.

Berger, Roger W., and Thomas H. Hart. (1986) *Statistical Process Control: A Guide for Implementation*. Milwaukee, WI: ASQC Quality Press. (*2)

Berger, S., and S. Sudman. (1991) Making total quality management work. *Healthcare Executive*. (August) 10-12.

Bergsten, F. (1987) Economic imbalances and world politics. *Foreign Affairs*. (Spring) 772. (*2)

Bergstrom, Robin P. (1984) Taking stock in FMS . . . Users speak up. *Manufacturing Engineering*. (June) 48-55.

Berkowitz, L. (1953) Sharing leadership in small decision-making groups. *Journal of Abnormal and Social Psychology*. 48, 231-238.

Berman, D. L., and H. Mase. (1983) The key to the productivity dilemma: The performance manager. *Human Resource Management*. 22, (Spring/Summer) 275-286.

Berman, Harvey S. (1983) International certification for electronic components. *Quality progress*. 16, (November) 12-15.

Bernal, J. D. (1953) *Science and Industry in the Nineteenth Century*. London, UK: Routledge and Kegan Paul.

Bernard, J. E. (1971) *The Scientific and Industrial Revolutions*. Cambridge, MA: MIT.

Berne, E. (1964) *Games People Play*. New York: Grove Press.

Bernstein, Aaron. (1986) Productivity—not pay cuts—will keep union members working. *BusinessWeek*. (August 25) 32, 48.

Bernstein, Aaron. (1991) Busting unions can backfire on the bottom line. *BusinessWeek*. (March 18) 21-22.

Bernstein, Aaron. (1991) Quality is becoming job one in the office, too. *BusinessWeek.* (April 29) 54-56.

Bernstein, Amy (1984) A case for quality. *Business Computer Systems.* (March) 58-58.

Berry, Leonard L., Valarie A. Zeithami, and A. Parasuraman. (1985) Quality counts in services, too. *Business Horizons.* 28, (May-June) 44-52.

Berry, Thomas H. (1991) *Managing the Total Quality Transformation.* New York: McGraw-Hill.

Bertalanffy, von L. (1971) *General Systems Theory.* Harmondsworth, Middlesex: Penguin Books.

Berwick, Donald M. (1988) Continuous improvement as an ideal in health care. *New England Journal of Medicine.* 320, 53-56.

Berwick, Donald M., A. Blanton Godfrey, and Jane Roessner. (1991) *Curing Healthcare: New Strategies for Quality Improvement.* San Francisco, CA: Jossey-Bass.

Best, Arthur. (1981) *When Consumers Complain.* New York: Columbia University Press.

Best, M. (1990) *The New Competition.* Cambridge, MA: Harvard University Press. (*2)

Besterfield, D. H. (1986) *Quality Control.* Second edition. Englewood Cliffs, NJ: Prentice-Hall. (*2)

Betker, Harry A. (1983) Quality improvement program: Reducing solder defects on printed circuit board assembly. *The Juran Report.* (November) 53-58.

Betker, Harry A. (1985) Quality improvement program project to identify and correct all known problems on an electro-mechanical detection device. *The Juran Report.* (Winter) 70-76.

Betker, Harry A. (1985) Storyboarding: It's no Mickey Mouse technique. *The Juran Report.* (Summer) 25-30.

Bettelheim, Bruno. (1976) *On the Uses of Enchantment: The Meaning and Importance of Fairy Tales.* New York: Alfred A. Knopf. (*2)

Bettelheim, Bruno and Karen Zelan. (1981) Why children don't like to read. *Atlantic.* (November) 27.

Betting on the 21st century jet. (1992) *Fortune,* (April 20) 102.

Betting to win on the Baldie winners. (1993) *BusinessWeek* (October 18) 8.

Betts, Frank. (1992) How systems thinking applies to education. *Educational Leadership.* (November) 38-41.

Bevans, John Patrick. (1982) First, choose an FMS simulator. *American Machinist.* 43-145.

Bewley, W. W. (1982) America's productivity decline: Fact or fiction? *Financial Executive.* 50, (April) 31-35.

Bhagwati, F. J. (1988) *Protectionism.* Cambridge, MA: Massachusetts Institute of Technology.

Bhote, Keki R. (1985) CWQC: A new horizon for American management. *ASQC Technical Annual Quality Congress Transactions.* Milwaukee, WI: ASQC Quality Press, 552-557.

Bhote, Keki R. (1987) *Supplier Management.* New York: American Management Association.

Bhote, Keki R. (1988) *World Class Quality: Design of Experiments Made Easier, More Cost Effective Than SPC.* New York: American Management Association. (*2)

Bibeault, Donald B. (1982) *Corporate Turnaround.* New York: McGraw-Hill.

Bicking, Charles A. (1954) Some uses of statistics in the planning of experiments. *Industrial Quality Control.* 10, (January) 23-31.

Bicking, Charles A. (1957) A statistical approach to the study of test precision, I, defining precision standards. *TAPPI.* 3, (March) 191-192.

Bicking, Charles A. (1958) The technical aspects of quality control. *Industrial Quality Control.* 14, (March) 7. (*3)

Bicking, Charles A. (1967) The sampling of bulk material. *Materials Research and Standards.* (March) 95-116.

Bicking, Charles A. (1979) Precision in the routine performance of standard tests. *Standardization.* 9, (January) 13.

Bicking, Charles A., Richard S. Bingham Jr., and R. L. Weiss. (1963) Automatic data logging for experimentation and quality control. *Industrial Quality Control.* 19, (December) 12-16.

Bicking, Charles A., T. A. Donovan, T. W. Sosnowski, and C. M. Bicking. (1967) *Bibliography on Precision Bulk Sampling and Related Applications of Statistics: Supplement.* San Francisco, CA: Technical Association of the Pulp and Paper Industry.

Bieber, Owen. (1982) UAW views circles: Not bad at all. *Quality Circles Journal.* 5, (August) 6.

Bierman, H., Jr., L. E. Fouraker, and R. K. Jaedicke. (1961) *Quantitative Analysis for Business Decisions.* Homewood, IL: Irwin.

Bierne, Mike. (1993) Garvey keeps North Star on the quality path. *American Metal Market.* 101, (February 18) 14A. (*2)

Bingaman, Ron and F. Alton Doody. (1988) *Reinventing the Wheels: Ford's Spectacular Comeback.* Cambridge, MA: Ballinger. (*3)

Bingham, John E., and Garth W. Davies. (1978) *A Handbook of Systems Analysis.* London, UK: Macmillan.

Bingham, R. D., and L. L. Vertz. (1983) The social structure of an academic discipline: Networks and social prestige in political science. *Social Science Quarterly*. 64, 275-287.

Bingham, Richard S., Jr. (1957) An application of continuous sampling plans for chemical acceptance and control. *Industrial Quality Control*. 13, (May) 8-11.

Bingham, Richard S., Jr. (1957) Control charts in multi-stage batch processes. *Industrial Quality Control*. 13, (July) 21-26.

Bingham, Richard S., Jr. (1957) Practical chemical process control. *Industrial Quality Control*. 13, (May) 46-56.

Bingham, Richard S., Jr. (1961) Ten minutes with top management. *Industrial Quality Control*. 18, (October) 5-8.

Bingham, Richard S., Jr. (1962) Chalk dust and chemicals: S.Q.C. training for the chemical industry. *Industrial Quality Control*. 18, (April) 15-18.

Bingham, Richard S., Jr. (1962) Quality control applications in the coated abrasive industry. *Industrial Quality Control*. 19, (November) 5-12.

Bingham, Richard S., Jr. (1962) Tolerance limits and process capability studies. *Industrial Quality Control*. 18, (August) 36-40.

Bingham, Richard S., Jr. (1963) EVOP for systematic improvement. *Industrial Quality Control*. 20, (March) 17-23.

Bingham, Richard S., Jr. (1965) A program for controlling incoming chemical quality. *Chemical Purchasing*. 1, (January-February) 14-16.

Bingham, Richard S., Jr., and J. L. Gioele. (1959) Statistical methods for ceramic process control and experiment planning. *Journal of the Canadian Ceramic Society*. 28, (June) 49.

Bingham, Richard S., Jr., and J. L. Gioele. (1961) Statistical methods for ceramic process control and experiment planning (Addendum). *Journal of the Canadian Ceramic Society*. 30, (July) 135.

Bingham, Richard S., Jr., J. L. Gioele, and V. B. Shelburne. (1959) *Studies in Ore Car and Abrasive Grain Sampling Variation.* ASTM Special Technical Publication 242. (May) 45-56.

Bingham, Richard S., Jr., and A. H. Jaehn. (1986) What management expects from quality control testing program. *TAPPI.* 69, (June) 38-42.

Binstock, S. L. (1977) Quality control in combat training. *Quality Progress.* 10, (May) 10-12.

Binstock, S. L. (1981) Americans express dissatisfaction with quality of U.S. goods. *Quality Progress.* 14, (January) 12-14. (*2)

Birch, D. L., and S. J. MacCacken. (1984) The role played by high-technology firms in job creation. MIT Program on Neighborhood and Regional Change. Cambridge, MA: MIT Press.

Bird, Allan. (1982) A comparison of Japanese and western management. *Management Japan.* 15, (Autumn) 21-24.

Birnbaum, P. H. (1988) Coping with environmental and market forces impacting high technology industry in the 1990s. In L. R. Gomez-Mejia and M. W. Lawless (Eds.) *Conference Proceedings Managing the High Technology Firm.* Boulder, CO: University of Press, 293-299.

Bisognano, M. (1993) Continuous quality improvement in health care. *Managed Care Quarterly.* 1, (No. 2) 53-54.

Bitner, Mary Jo, Bernard H. Booms, and Mary Stanfield Tetreault. (1990) The service encounter: Diagnosing favorable and unfavorable incidents. *Journal of Marketing.* 50, (January) 71-84.

Bittel, L. R., and J. E. Ramsey. (1982) The limited, traditional world of supervisors. *Harvard Business Review.* 60, (July-August) 26-31.

Bjorklund, O. (1981) Life cycle costs: An analysis tool for design, marketing and service. *Q-Bulletin of Alfa-Laval.*

Blache, Klaus, et al. (1988) Process control and people at General Motors' Delta Engine Plant. *IE*. (March) 17-19.

Black, J. T. (1983) Cellular manufacturing systems reduce setup time small lot production economical. *Industrial Engineering*. 15, (November) 36-48.

Blackburn, Joseph D. (1991) *Time Based Competition: The Next Battleground in American Manufacturing*. Homewood, IL: Business One Irwin. (*2)

Blackburn, R., and B. Rosen. (1993) Total quality and human resource management: Lessons learned from Baldrige award-winning companies. *Academy of Management Executive*. 7, (August) 5, 49, 56.

Blacker, F. H. M., and C. A. Brown. (1980) *Whatever Happened to Shell's New Philosophy of Management?* Westmead, UK: Saxon House.

Blacker, Stanley. (1990) Data quality and the environment. *Quality*. (April) 38-42.

Blake, Gary. (1995) Ten tips on writing for ISO 9000. *Quality Digest*. (August) 50-51.

Blake, Robert R., and Jane S. Mouton. (1957) The dynamics of influence and concern. *International Journal of Social Psychiatry*. 2, 263-65.

Blake, Robert R., and Jane S. Mouton. (1961) *Group Dynamics: Key to Decision Making*. Houston, TX: Gulf Publishing.

Blake, Robert R., and Jane S. Mouton. (1962) The developing revolution in management practices. *American Society of Training Directors Journal*. 16, (June) 29-52.

Blake, Robert R., and Jane S. Mouton. (1964) *The Managerial Grid*. Houston, TX: Gulf Publishing. (*2)

Blake, Robert R., and Jane S. Mouton. (1985) *The Managerial Grid III*. Houston, TX: Gulf Publishing.

Blake, Robert R., Jane S. Mouton, L. L. Barnes, and L. E. Greiner. (1964) Breakthrough in organization development. *Harvard Business Review*. 42, (January-February) 88-96.

Blalock, H. M., Jr. (1972) *Social Statistics*. New York: McGraw-Hill.

Blanchard, Benjamin S., and Walter J. Fabrycky. (1981) *Systems Engineering and Analysis*. Englewood Cliffs, NJ: Prentice-Hall.

Blankenship, A. B., and George Edward Breen. (1993) *State-of-the-Art Marketing Research*. Lincolnwood, IL: NTC Business Books.

Blankenstein, Alan M. (1992) Lessons from enlightened corporations. *Educational Leadership*. 49, (Issue 6, March) 71-75.

Blau, G., and M. Rosow. (1978) Trends in product quality and worker attitude: Highlights of the literature. *Studies in Productivity*. (Number 3) Scarsdale, NY: Work in America Institute.

Blau, Peter M. (1955) *The Dynamics of Bureaucracy*. Chicago, IL: University of Chicago Press.

Blau, Peter M. (1964) *Exchange and Power in Social Life*. New York: John Wiley.

Blau, Peter M. (1976) Social exchange in collectivities. In W. M. Evan (Ed.) *Interorganizational Relations*. Pittsburgh, PA: University of Pennsylvania Press.

Blaufuss, Jo. (1972) Metric memo. *Quality Management and Engineering*. (June) 40.

Blaylock, Bruce and L. Reese. (1984) Cognitive style and the usefulness of information. *Decision Sciences*. 15, (Winter) 74-91.

Bleakley, Fred R. (1993) The best laid plans—many companies try management fads only to see them flop. *Wall Street Journal.* (July 6) A1.

Blines, D. (1990) Semi-autonomous team in the zoo. *The Journal for Quality and Participation,* (July-August) 93-95.

Bliss, C. J. (1975) *Capital Theory and the Distribution of Income.* Amsterdam: North-Holland.

Block, Peter. (1981) *Flawless Consulting.* San Diego, CA: University Associates. (*2)

Block, Peter. (1987) *The Empowered Manager: Positive Political Skills at Work.* San Francisco, CA: Jossey-Bass. (*2)

Blodgett, Bonnie. (1992) The private hell of public education. *Lear's Magazine* (April) 10-12.

Bloom, G. F. (1971) Productivity: Weak link in our economy. *Harvard Business Review.* 49, (January-February) 4-14.

Bloom, G. F. (1972) The role of management on labor productivity. *Industrial Management.* 14, (November) 10-13.

Bloom, J. L., and S. Asa. (1981) Tsukuba Science City: Japan tries planned innovation. *Science.* 27, (May) 1239-1247.

Bluedorn, A. (1986) Review of scientific management by F. W. Taylor. *Academy of Management Review.* (April) 443-447.

Bluestone, B., and B. Harrison. (1982) *The DeIndustrialization of America.* New York: Basic Books.

Bluestone, Irving. (1977) Creating a new world of work. *International Labour Review.* 115, (January) 1-10.

Bluestone, Irving. (1996) Unions and quality professionals need to work together to avoid tragedy. *Quality Progress.* (July) 54-55.

Blumberg, Melvin and Donald Gerwin. (1982) *Coping with Advanced Manufacturing Technology*. Milwaukee, WI: University of Wisconsin.

Blumberg, Paul. (1969) *Industrial Democracy: The Sociology of Participation*. New York: Schocken Books.

Blume, Stuart S. (1980) A managerial view of research. *Scientific Productivity*. (January 4) 48-49. (*2)

Blumenthal, Marjory and Jim Dray. (1985) The automated factory. *Vision and Technology Review*. 88, (January) 30-37.

Bly, Robert. (1990) *Iron John*. Reading, MA: Addison-Wesley.

Boardman, J. (1985) The statistician's role in quality improvement. *Amstat News*. (March) 5-8.

Bobbe, R. A., and R. H. Schaffer. (1983) Productivity improvement: Manage it or buy it? *Business Horizons*. 26, (March-April) 62-69.

Bobis, A. H., and L. Andersen. (1970) An approach for economic discrimination between alternative chemical syntheses. *Technometrics*. 12, (August) 439-456.

Bodyfelt, F. W., J. Tobias, and G. M. Trout. (1988) *The Sensory Evaluation of Dairy Products*. New York: Van Nostrand Reinhold.

Boehm, G. (1963) "Reliability" engineering. *Fortune*. (April 15) 124-27, 181-82.

Boeing's dominance of aircraft industry runs into bumpiness. *Wall Street Journal*. (July 10) A1.

Bohl, M. (1971) *Flowcharting Techniques*. Washington DC: Science Research Associates.

Bohm, David. (1965) *The Special Theory of Relativity*. New York: W. A. Benjamin.

Boje, D. M., and R. D. Winsor. (1993) The resurrection of Taylorism: Total quality management's hidden agenda. *Journal of Organisational Change Management*. 6, (No. 4) 57-70.

Bolles, Richard. (1972) *What Color Is Your Parachute?* New York: Ten Speed Press.

Bond, Helen. (1990) Innovative management. *Dallas Business Journal*. (July 2) 17-20.

Bond, T. P. (1983) Basics of an MRB. *Quality*. (November) 48.

Bone, Diane and Rick Griggs. *Quality at Work*. Los Altos: Crisp Publications.

Bonetto, R. et. al. (1985) Simulation of an FMS: The Citroen factory. *Advances in Production Management Systems*. (June) 41-58.

Bonoma, T. V. (1982) Major sales: Who really does the buying? *Harvard Business Review*. 60, (May-June) 113.

Bonoma, T. V. (1985) *The Marketing Edge: Making Strategies Work*. New York: Free Press.

Bonser, Charles F. (1992) Total quality education? *Public Administration Review*. 52, (Issue 5, September/October) 504-512. (*2)

Bonstingal, John Jay. (1992) *Schools of Quality*. New York: Free Press.

Bonstingal, John Jay. (1992) The quality revolution in education. *Educational Leadership*. (November) 4-9.

Bookman, Bob. (1992) Energizing TQM with right-brain thinking. *Training*. 29, (August) 62. (*2)

Booth, W. E. (1987) Stem and leaf displays. *Quality*. (March) 62-64.

Boothe, R. (1990) Who defines quality in service industries? *Quality Progress*. 23, (February) 65-67.

Boreman, E. G. (1969) *Discussion and Group Methods: Theory and Practice.* New York: Harper and Row.

Bos, H. C. (1977) *The Use of Appropriate Technology: A Survey of Equality of Opportunity within and among Nations.* New York: Praeger.

Bothwell, L. (1983) *The Art of Leadership.* Englewood, Cliffs, NJ: Prentice-Hall.

Boudreault, Art. (1975) Component integrity-A key factor in optimum design. *Quality.* (June) 20-22.

Boulding, K. I. (1953) *The Organizational Revolution.* New York: Harper and Row.

Boulding, Kenneth E. (1966) General systems theory: The skeleton of science. *Management Science.* 12, (April) 31-40.

Boulding, Kenneth E. (1978) *General Systems Theory: The Skeleton of Science.* New York: Bradburn. (*2)

Boulton, W. (1993) *Resource Guide for Management of Innovation and Technology.* St. Louis: A joint publication of the American Assembly of Collegiate Schools of Business, the National Consortium for Technology in Business and the Thomas Walter Center for Technology Management at Auburn University.

Bounds, G. M., and G. H. Carothers. (1991) The role of middle management in improving competitiveness. In Michael J. Stahl and G. M. Bounds (Eds.) *Competing Globally Through Customer Value: The Management of Strategic Suprasystems.* Westport, CT: Quorum Books, 146-188. (*2)

Bounds, G. M., and H. D. Dewhirst. (1991) Assessing progress in managing for customer value. In Michael J. Stahl and G. M. Bounds. *Competing Globally through Customer Value: The Management of Strategic Suprasystems.* New York: Quorum Books, 307-339.

Bounds, G. M., and Gregory H. Dobbins. (1991) The manager's job: A paradigm shift to a new agenda. In Michael J. Stahl and G. M. Bounds. *Competing Globally Through Customer Value.* Westport, CT: Quorum Books, 117-145. (*2)

Bounds, G. M., and Gregory H. Dobbins. (1993) Changing the managerial agenda. *Journal of General Management.* 18, (Spring) 77-93. (*2)

Bounds, G. M., and L. A. Pace. (1991) Human resource management for competitive capability. In Michael J. Stahl and G. M. Bounds. *Competing Globally through Customer Value: The Management of Strategic Suprasystems.* New York: Quorum Books.

Bounds, G. M., J. M. Reeve, and K. C. Gilbert. (1991) Managerial performance measurement. In Michael J. Stahl and G. M. Bounds. *Competing Globally Through Customer Value: The Management of Strategic Suprasystems.* New York: Quorum Books, 369-370.

Bounds, G. M., et. al. (1994) *Beyond Total Quality Management Toward the Emerging Paradigm.* New York: McGraw-Hill.

Bourgeois, L. J., and K. M. Eisenhardt. (1987) Strategic decision processes in Silicon Valley: The anatomy of the living dead. *California Management Review.* 30, (Fall) 143-159. (*2)

Bourgeois, L. J., and K. M. Eisenhardt. (1988) Strategic decision processes in high velocity environments: Four cases in the microcomputer industry. *Management Science.* 34, (Spring) 816-835.

Bowen, David E., and Edward E. Lawler III. (1992) Total quality oriented human resources management. *Organizational Dynamics.* 20, (Spring) 29-41. (*3)

Bowen, William. (1981) Lessons from behind the Kimo number. *Fortune.* (June 15) 247-250.

Bower, Joseph L. (1974) *Managing the Resource Allocation Process.* Boston, MA: Harvard University Press.

Bower, Joseph L. (1983) *The Two Faces of Management.* Boston, MA: Houghton Mifflin. (*3)

Bower, Joseph L., et al. (1991) *Business Policy: Text and Cases.* Seventh edition, Homewood, IL: Irwin.

Bowers, D. G. (1966) Predicting organizational effectiveness with a four-factor theory of leadership. *Administrative Science Quarterly.* 11, (August) 238-263.

Bowers, D. G. (1973) OD techniques and their results in 23 organizations: The Michigan ICL study. *The Journal of Applied Behavior Science.* 9, (April) 21-23. (*2)

Bowers, D. G., and J. L. Franklin. (1972) Survey-guided development: Using human resources measurement in organizational change. *Journal of Contemporary Business.* 1, 43-55.

Bowers, Virgil L. (1978) Procurement quality assurance of PC boards. *ASQC Annual Technical Quality Congress Transactions.* Milwaukee, WI: ASQC Quality Press, 62-69.

Bowker, Albert H., and H. P. Goode. (1952) *Sampling Inspection by Variables.* New York: McGraw-Hill.

Bowker, Albert H., and Gerald J. Lieberman. (1972) *Engineering Statistics.* Englewood Cliffs NJ: Prentice-Hall. (*2)

Bowles, Jerry G. (1985) The renaissance of American quality. *Fortune.* (October 14) First annual quality improvement section.

Bowles, Jerry G. (1986) The quality imperative. *Fortune.* (September 29) Second annual quality improvement section.

Bowles, Jerry G. (1987) Quality: The competitive advantage. *Fortune.* (September 28) Third annual quality improvement section.

Bowles, Jerry G. (1988) Beyond customer satisfaction through quality improvement. *Fortune.* (September 24) Fourth annual quality improvement section. (*2)

Bowles, Jerry G. (1989) The race to quality improvement. *Fortune.* (September 25) Fifth annual quality improvement section.

Bowles, Jerry G. (1990) The human side of quality. *Fortune.* (September 24) Sixth annual quality improvement section.

Bowles, Jerry G. (1992) Quality '92: Leading the whole world-class company. *Fortune.* (September 21) 159. (*2)

Bowles, Jerry G., and Joshua Hammond. (1991) *Beyond Quality: New Standards of Total Performance That Can Change the Future of Corporate America.* New York: Berkeley. (*2)

Bowles, Samuel and Herbert Gintis. (1976) *Schooling in Capitalist America: Educational Reform and the Contradictions of Economic Life.* New York: Basic Books.

Bowman, E. H., and R. B. Fetter. (1957) *Analysis for Production Management.* Homewood, IL: Irwin.

Bowsher, Jack E. (1989) *Educating America.* New York: John Wiley.

Box, George E. P. (1954) Exploration and exploitation of response surfaces. *Biometrics.* 10, (March) 27-30.

Box, George E. P. (1957) Evolutionary operation: A method for increasing industrial productivity. *Applied Statistics.* 6, 81-101.

Box, George E. P. (1966) A simple system of evolutionary operation subject to empirical feedback. *Technometrics.* 9, (January) 10-26.

Box, George E. P., and D. W. Behnken. (1960) Some new three level designs for the study of quantitative variables. *Technometrics.* 2, (March) 477-482.

Box, George E. P., and D. R. Cox. (1964) An analysis of transformations. *Journal of the Royal Statistical Society.* 26, (March) 211.

Box, George E. P., and Norman R. Draper. (1969) *Evolutionary Operation*. New York: John Wiley.

Box, George E. P., and Norman R. Draper. (1969) Isn't my process too variable for EVOP? *Technometrics*. 10, (May) 439-444.

Box, George E. P., and Norman R. Draper. (1987) *Empirical Model Building with Response Surfaces*. New York: John Wiley.

Box, George E. P., and J. Stuart Hunter. (1959) Condensed calculation for evolutionary operation programs. *Technometrics*. 1, (April) 77-95.

Box, George E. P., and J. Stuart Hunter. (1961) The 2k-P fractional factorial designs: Part I. *Technometrics*. 3, (August) 41-48. (*2)

Box, George E. P., J. Stuart Hunter, and William G. Hunter. (1978) *Statistics for Experiments*. New York: John Wiley. (*2)
+
Box, George E. P., and William G. Hunter. (1978) *Statistics for Experimenters-An Introduction to Design, Data Analysis and Model Building*. New York: John Wiley. (*2)

Box, George E. P., and G. M. Jenkins. (1962) Some statistical aspects of adaptive optimization and control. *Journal of the Royal Statistical Society*. 2, (May) 297-333.

Box, George E. P., and G. M. Jenkins. (1970) *Time Series Analysis, Forecasting and Control*. San Francisco, CA: Holden-Day.

Box, George E. P., and George C. Tiao. (1973) *Bayesian Inference in Statistical Analysis*. Reading MA: Addison-Wesley.

Box, George E. P., and P. W. Tidwell. (1962) Transformation of the independent variable. *Technometrics*. 4, (June) 531.

Box, George E. P., and K. B. Wilson. (1951) On the experimental attainment of optimum conditions. *Journal of the Royal Statistical Society*. 13, (June) 1.

Box, George E. P., and H. P. Youle. (1955) The exploration and exploitation of response surfaces: An example of the link between the fitted surface and the basic mechanism of the system. *Biometrics*. 11, (February) 287.

Box, George E. P., and H. P. Youle. (1955) The exploration and exploitation of response surfaces II. An example of the link between the fitted surface and the basic mechanism of the system. *Biometrics*. 11, (May) 287-323.

Boyett, Joseph H., and Henry P. Conn. (1991) *Workplace 2000: The Revolution Reshaping American Business*. New York: E. P. Dutton.

Boykin, Raymond and Reuben R. Levary. (1985) An interactive decision support system for analyzing ship voyage alternative. *Interfaces*. 15, (March-April) 81-84.

Boynton, Andrew C., and Robert W. Zmud. (1984) An assessment of critical success factors. *Sloan Management Review*. 25, (Summer) 17-27.

Brach, J. P., Jr., and L. J. Phaller. (1980) Integrated test—A must for reliability achievement. *Proceedings, Annual Reliability and Maintainability Symposium*. New York: IEEE, 242-247.

Braddon, R. (1983) *Japan Against the World: 1941-2041*. New York: Stein and Day.

Braddon, R. (1983) *The Other 100 Years War*. London, UK: Collins.

Bradford, D. L., and A. R. Cohen. (1984) *Managing for Excellence*. New York: John Wiley. (*3)

Bradford, L. P., J. R. Gibb, and K. P. Benne. (1964) *T-Group Therapy and the Laboratory Method*. New York: John Wiley. (*2)

Brady, J. M. (1981) *Computer Vision*. New York: North-Holland.

Brainard, E. H. (1966) Just how good are vendor surveys? *Journal of Quality Assurance*. 14, (August) 22-25. (*2)

Branco, George J., and Robert S. Willoughby. (1987) Extending quality improvement to suppliers. *Proceedings, Fourth Annual Conference on Quality Improvement*. Piqua, OH: Ohio Quality and Productivity Form, 21-34.

Brandt, D. A. (1963) When the swallows come home. *ASQC Annual Technical Quality Congress Transactions*. Milwaukee, WI: ASQC Quality Press, 176.

Brandt, Ron. (1992) The quality movement's challenge to education. *Leadership*. 49, (March) 23-26.

Brassard, Michael. (1988) Key points in management by planning. Presented at the Fifth Annual Goal/QPC Conference. Methuen, Massachusetts.

Brassard, Michael. (1988) *The Memory Jogger*. Methuen, MA: Goal/QPC.

Brassard, Michael. (1989) *The Memory Jogger Plus+: Featuring the Seven Management and Planning Tools*. Methuen, MA: Goal/QPC.

Braudel, F. (1985) *The Perspective of the World.* London, UK: Fontana Press.

Braverman, Jerome D. (1981) *Fundamentals of Statistical Quality Control*. Reston, VA: Reston Publishing Company.

Break-even analysis: Analyzing the relationship between costs and revenues. (1986) *Small Business Report*. (August) 22-24.

Brennan, J. (1972) *Operational Research in Industrial Systems.* London, UK: English Universities Press.

Brethower, D. M. (1982) The total performance system. *Industrial Behavior Modification: A Management Handbook.* New York: Pergamon Press, 340-369.

Brewer, Henry F., and Richard J. Zaworski. (1981) Initiation of a supplier surveillance program. *ASQC Annual Technical Quality*

Congress Transactions. Milwaukee, WI: ASQC Quality Press, 992-995.

Brezonick, Mike. (1992) Understanding ISO 9000. *Diesel Progress Engines and Drives*. 58, (September) 12. (*2)

Bridge, David H. (1987) Managing quality improvement. In M. Sepehri (Ed.) *Quest for Quality: Managing the Total System*. Norcross, New York: Institute of Industrial Engineers, 66-74.

Bridgman, P. W. (1928) *The Logic of Modern Physics*. New York: Macmillan.

Bridgman, P. W. (1980) *Reflections of a Physicist*. New York: Arno Press. (*2)

Briefs, U., C. Ciborra, and L. Schnieder. (1983) *Systems Design For, With, and By The Users*. Amsterdam: North-Holland.

Bright, D. S. (1985) *Gearing Up for the Fast Lane*. New York: Random House.

Brinkley, David. (1988) *Washington Goes to War*. New York: Alfred A. Knopf.

Brinksman, Keith. (1991) Banking and the Baldrige Award. *Bank Marketing*. (April) 30-32.

Brisley, C. L. (1952) How you can put work sampling to work. *Factory*. 110, (July) 84-89.

British Standards Institution. (1981) *Handbook 22: Quality Assurance*. London, UK: BSI.

British Standards Institution. (1982) *Sectional List of British Standards SL BSI*. London, UK: BSI.

Broadbent, D. E. (1986) The clinical impact of job design. *British Journal of Clinical Psychology*. 24, (Winter) 33-44.

Broadhead, James L. (1991) The post-Deming diet: Dismantling a quality bureaucracy. *Training*. 28, (February) 28, 41-43.

Brocka, B. (1985) How to buy high quality software. *Quality Progress*. 18, (March) 28-31.

Brodie, Michael. (1985) Can GM manage it all? *Fortune*. (July 9) 26.

Brodie, Michael. (1987) Helping workers to work smarter. *Fortune*. (June 8) 87. (*2)

Bromwich, M., and A. G. Hopwood. (1986) *Research and Current Issues in Management Accounting*. London, UK: Pitman.

Bronson, Gail. (1981) Colgate works hard to become the firm it was a decade ago. *Wall Street Journal*. (November) 1, 8.

Brook, R., and A. Avery. (1975) *Quality Assurance Mechanism in the U.S.: From There to Where?* Santa Monica, Calif.: Rand Corporation.

Brooke, Keith A. (1982) QC circles success depends on management readiness to support workers' involvement. *Industrial Engineering*. 14, (January) 76-79.

Brookfield, S. D. (1987) *Developing Critical Thinkers*. San Francisco, CA: Jossey-Bass.

Brooks, Frederick P., Jr. (1978) *The Mythical Man-Month: Essays on Software Engineering*. Reading, MA: Addison-Wesley. (*2)

Brooks, John. (1969) *Once in Golconda*. New York: Harper and Row.

Brooks, John. (1973) *The Go-Go Years*. New York: Weybright and Talley.

Bross, Irving. (1953) *Design for Decision*. New York: Macmillan.

Brower, Michael J. (1992) Implementing TQM with self-directed teams. In Harry Ivan Costin (Ed.) *Readings in Total Quality Management.* (1994) Fort Worth, TX: Dryden Press, 403-420.

Brower, Michael J. (1992) The paradigm shifts required to apply TQM and teams in higher education. In Harry Ivan Costin (Ed.) *Readings in Total Quality Management.* (1994) Fort Worth, TX: Dryden Press, 485-497.

Brown, A. (1947) *Organization of Industry.* Englewood Cliffs, NJ: Prentice-Hall.

Brown, Arthur W. (1974) Procurement engineering. *ASQC Annual Technical Quality Congress Transactions.* Milwaukee, WI: 161-168.

Brown, B. G. (1992) *Baldrige Award Winning Quality: How to Interpret the Malcolm Baldrige Award.* White Plains, NY: Quality Resources. Milwaukee, WI: ASQC Quality Press.

Brown, C., and M. Reich. (1989) When does union-management cooperation work? A look at NUMMI and GM-Van Nuys. *California Management Review.* 31, (Spring) 26-44.

Brown, Carolyn. (1992) Quality pays off. *Black Enterprise.* 22, (June) 281. (*2)

Brown, Dale S. (1993) Quality through equality: Using TQM to hire and retain workers with disabilities. *Industrial Engineering.* 25, (January) 60. (*2)

Brown, F. B. (1984) *Crisis in Secondary Education.* Englewood Cliffs, NJ: Prentice-Hall.

Brown, F. X., and R. W. Kane. (1978) Quality cost and profit performance. *ASQC Annual Technical Quality Congress Transactions.* Milwaukee, WI: ASQC Quality Press, 505-514.

Brown, H. (1991) The first Baldrige-based community quality award journal for quality and participation. *Wall Street Journal.* (September 15) 86-87.

Brown, J. A. (1954) *The Social Psychology of Industry.* Baltimore, MD: Penguin Books.

Brown, Mark Graham. (1990) How to guarantee poor quality service. *Journal for Quality and Participation.* (December) 6-11.

Brown, Mark Graham. (1994) *How to Interpret the Malcolm Baldrige Award Criteria.* Fifth edition. Milwaukee, WI: ASQC Quality Press.

Brown, N. Raymond, Jr. (1966) Zero defects the easy way with target area control. *Modern Machine Shop.* (July) 16.

Brown, P. B. (1990) The real cost of customer service. *Inc.* (September) 49-60. (*2)

Brown, R. G. (1963) *Smoothing, Forecasting, and Prediction of Discrete Time Series.* Englewood Cliffs, NJ: Prentice-Hall.

Brown, R. G. (1967) *Decision Rules for Inventory Management.* New York: Holt, Rinehart and Winston.

Brown, R. H. (1976) Social theory as metaphor. *Theory and Society.* (Vol. 3) 169-197.

Brown, S. (1993) Launching a change program is easy. *Industry Week.* (April 4) 50.

Brown, S. (1993) Quality through equality: Using TQM to hire and retain workers with disabilities. *Industrial Engineering.* 25, (January) 60.

Brown, Tom. (1992) Are you vision-driven? Part II, *Industry Week.* (June 1) 11.

Brown, Tom. (1992) Is your company vision-driven? *Industry Week.* (May 18) 11.

Brown, Tom. (1992) Why teams go ‘bust’. *Industry Week.* (March 2) 17-20.

Brown, Tom. (1993) Launching a change program is easy. *Industry Week.* (April 19) 50. (*2)

Brown, V. L. (1982) *Human Intimacy: Illusion and Reality.* Salt Lake City, UT: Parliament Publishers.

Brown, W. (1987) Contract talks could retool the auto industry. *Washington Post.* (July 19) H1. (*3)

Brown, W. (1988) The making of the all-new Thunderbird. *Washington Post Magazine.* (November) 43-67. (*2)

Brown, W., and Frank Swoboda. (1992) Saturn's design turns on a dime. *Washington Post.* (July 6) H1.

Brownell, Peter. (1983) Leadership style, budgetary participation and managerial behavior. *Accounting Organizations and Society.* 8, 307-321.

Browning, J. (1990) The ubiquitous machine. *The Economist.* (June 16) 5.

Bruce-Briggs, B. (1982) The dangerous folly called theory Z. *Fortune.* (May 15) 31-34. (*2)

Bruhn, W. (1979) Sensory testing and analysis in quality control. *Dragaco Report.* (September) 207.

Bruner, Jerome S. (1973) *On Knowing: Essays for the Left Hand.* New York: Atheneum. (*2)

Bruner, Jerome S. (1979) *On Knowing: Essays for the Left Hand.* Cambridge, MA: Harvard University Press.

Brunet, Lucie. (1981) Quality circles: Can they improve QWL. *The Canadian Scene.* 4, 1-2.

Brunetti, Wayne. (1986) Policy development—a corporate roadmap. *The Juran Report.* 8, (Winter) 20-29.

Brunetti, Wayne. (1987) Policy deployment—a corporate roadmap. *Proceedings, Fourth Annual Conference on Quality Improvement.* Piqua, OH: Ohio Quality and Productivity Forum, 51-78.

Brunswik, E. (1952) *The Conceptual Framework of Psychology.* Chicago, IL: University of Chicago Press.

Bruzzese, Anita. (1991) What business schools aren't teaching. *Incentive.* 165, (Issue 3, March) 29-31.

Bryan, N. S. (1981) Contracting for life cycle cost to improve system affordability. *Proceedings, Annual Reliability and Maintainability Symposium.* New York: IEEE, 342-345.

Bryant, Stephen and Joseph Kearns. (1982) Workers' brains as well as their bodies: Quality circles in a federal facility. *Public Administration Review.* 42, (March-April) 144-150.

Bryson, B. (1990) *The Mother Tongue: English and How It Got That Way.* New York: William Morrow.

Buback, Kenneth and Jaroslav Dutkewych. (1982) Quality circles in health care: The Henry Ford hospital experience. IAQC Fourth Annual Conference Transactions. Cincinnati, OH: International Association of Quality Circles.

Buchanan, D., and D. Bobby. (1983) Advanced technology and the quality of working life: The effects of computerized controls on biscuit-making operators. *Journal of Occupational Psychology.* 56, 109-119.

Buchanan, D., and D. Bobby. (1983) Organizations in the computer age: Technological imperatives and strategic choice. *Journal of Occupational Psychology.* 56, 70-83.

Buchanen, Scott. (1948) *The Portable Plato.* New York: Viking Press.

Buckley, John W. (1971) Goal-process system interaction in management: Correcting the imbalance. *Business Horizons.* 14, (December) 81-89. (*2)

Buckley, W. F. (1983) *Overdrive.* Garden City, NY: Doubleday.

Bucklow, Maxine. (1973) *A New Role for the Work Group*. Chicago, IL: University of Chicago Press.

Buckrop, R. L. (1976) Nondestructive testing overview. *Quality Progress*. 9, (June) 26-29.

Buffa, E. S. (1973) *Modern Production Management.* New York: John Wiley. (*2)

Buffa, E. S. (1984) *Meeting the Competitive Challenge: Manufacturing Strategy of U.S. Companies*. Homewood, IL: Dow Jones-Irwin. (*4)

Buffa, E. S., and H. Taubert. (1972) *Production Inventory Systems, Planning and Control.* Homewood, IL: Irwin.

Bulkeley, W. M. (1987) Two computer firms with clashing styles fight for market niche. *Wall Street Journal.* 6, (July) 1.

Bulkeley, W. M. (1987) The right mix: New software makes the choice much easier. *Wall Street Journal.* (March 27) 25.

Bull, M. J. (1992) QA: Professional accountability via CQI. In C. G. Meisenheimer. *Improving Quality: A Guide to Effective Programs*. Gaithersburg, MD: Aspen.

Bullock, R. J., and Edward E. Lawler III. (1984) Gainsharing: A few questions and fewer answers. *Human Resource Management*. 23, (Winter) 23-40. (*3)

Bullock, R. J., and P. F. Bullock. (1982) Gainsharing and Rubik's cube: Solving system problems. *National Productivity Review*. 2, (January) 396-407.

Buono, A. F., J. L. Bowditch and J. W. Lewis III. (1985) When cultures collide: The anatomy of a merger. *Human Relations*. 38, (May) 477-500.

Burbridge, J. L. (1971) *Production Planning.* London, UK: William Heinemann.

Burch, S. W. (1983) The aging U.S. auto stock: Implications for demand. *Business Economics.* (May) 22-26.

Burck, Charles G. (1978) How GM turned itself around. *Fortune.* (January 1) 25-26. (*2)

Burck, Charles G. (1980) A comeback decade for the American car. *Fortune.* (June 1) 63. (*2)

Burck, Charles G. (1981) What happens when workers manage themselves. *Fortune.* (July 18) 68.

Burck, Charles G. (1981) What's in it for the unions. *Fortune.* (August 24) 88-92. (*2)

Burck, Gil. (1940) International business machines. *Fortune.* (January 15) 41. (*2)

Burgam, Patrick. (1984) FMS control: Covering all the angles. *CAD/CAM Technology.* 11-14.

Burgelman, R. A., and M. Madique. (1988) *Strategic Management of Technology and Innovation.* Chicago, IL: Irwin.

Burgelman, R. A., T. J. Kosnik, and M. Van den Poel. (1987) The innovative capabilities audit framework. In R. A. Burgelman and M. Madique (Eds.) *Strategic Management of Technology and Innovation.* Homewood, IL: Irwin

Burgess, John A. (1983) Quality assurance in testing. *Quality.* (January) 36-37.

Burgess, John A. (1984) *Design Assurance for Engineers.* New York: Marcel Dekker.

Burgess, John A. (1985) Design reviews for all seasons. *ASQC Annual Technical Quality Congress Transactions.* Milwaukee, WI: ASQC Quality Press, 451-455.

Burington, R. S and D. C. May. (1970) *Handbook of Probability and Statistics with Tables,* New York: McGraw-Hill.

Burke, G. and J. Peppard. (1993) Business process redesign: Research directions. *Business Change and Reengineering.* 1, (No. 1) 43-47.

Burkett, Larry. (1990) *Business by the Book: The Complete Guide of Biblical Principles for Business Men and Women.* Expanded edition. Nashville, TN: Thomas Nelson Publishers.

Burlingame, Roger. (1946) *Engines of Democracy.* New York: Scribners.

Burlingame, Roger. (1955) *Henry Ford: A Great Life in Brief.* New York: Alfred A. Knopf.

Burns, J. M. (1978) *Leadership.* New York: Harper and Row. (*2)

Burns, M. J., and R. B. Woodruff. (1990) Value: An integrative perspective. *American Psychological Association Proceedings*, 10-24.

Burns, T., and G. Stalker. (1961) *The Management of Innovation.* London, UK: Tavistock Publications. (*4)

Burr, Irving W. (1953) *Engineering Statistics and Quality Control.* New York: McGraw-Hill. (*2)

Burr, Irving W. (1967) Specifying the desired distribution rather than maximum and minimum limits. *Industrial Quality Control.* 24, (February) 94-101.

Burr, Irving W. (1976) *Statistical Quality Control Methods.* New York: Marcel Dekker. (*3)

Burr, John T. (1987) Overcoming resistance to audits. *Quality Progress.* 20, (January) 15-18.

Burr, John T. (1989) *SPC Tools for Operators.* Milwaukee, WI: ASQC Quality Press.

Burr, John T. (1990) Going with the flow (chart). In Harry Ivan Costin (Ed.) *Readings in Total Quality Management.* (1994) Fort Worth, TX: Dryden Press, 171-175.

Burr, John T. (1990) Pareto charts. In Harry Ivan Costin (Ed.) *Readings in Total Quality Management.* (1994) Fort Worth, TX: Dryden Press, 217-221.

Burr, John T. (1990) Scatter diagrams. In Harry Ivan Costin (Ed.) *Readings in Total Quality Management*. (1994) Fort Worth, TX: Dryden Press, 223-227.

Burrell, Claude W., and L. W. Ellsworth. (1982) *Quality Data Processing: The Profit potential in the 80's.* Tenafly, NJ: Burrell-Ellsworth Associates.

Burris, Beverly H. (1989) Technocratic organization and control. *Organization Studies*. 10, 1-22.

Burrows, Peter. (1990) Commitment to quality: Five lessons you can learn from award entrants. *Electronic Business*. 16, (October 15) 56-58.

Bursk, C. (1954) *The Management Team*. Cambridge, MA: Harvard University Press.

Burt, R. (1980) Cooptive corporate actor networks: Are consideration of interlocking directorates involving American manufacturing. *Administrative Science Quarterly*. 25, (September) 557-582.

Burtenshaw, O. L., and N. A. Klein. (1969) Let's put quality control in its place. *ASQC Annual Technical Quality Congress Transactions*. Milwaukee, WI: ASQC Quality Press, 417-418.

Bushe, Gervase R. (1988) Cultural contradictions of statistical process control in American manufacturing corporations. *Journal of Management*. (March) 19-31.

Bushnell, David S., and Michael B. Halus. (1992) TQM in the public sector: Strategies for quality service. *National Productivity Review.* 11, (Summer) 355. (*2)

Business bulletin. (1993) *Wall Street Journal.* (February 4) A1.

Business fads: What's in—and out. (1986) *BusinessWeek.* (January 20) 27.

Business Roundtable. (1978) *Cost of Government Regulation Study for the Business Roundtable.* New York.

Buss, D. D. (1986) GM radically shifts its strategy to match output, sales. *Wall Street Journal.* (December 19) 6. (*3)

Buss, Dale and Melinda Grenier Guiles. (1986) GM slows big drive for Saturn to produce small car in five years. *Wall Street Journal.* (October 30) 25-28. (*3)

Bussell, D. (1983) Is vertical integration profitable? *Harvard Business Review.* 61, (January-February) 92-102.

Buterbaugh, Laura. (1992) TQM: The quality-care revolution. *Medical World News.* 33, (June) 17.

Butler, C., and G. R. Bryce. (1986) Implementing SPC with Signetics production personnel. *Quality Progress.* 19, (April) 24-27.

Butman, John. (1993) *Flying Fox: A Business Adventure in Teams and Teamwork.* Milwaukee, WI: ASQC Quality Press.

Butterfield, Ronald. (1990) *Quality Service Pure and Simple.* Milwaukee, WI: ASQC Quality Press.

Butterfield, Ronald. (1991) Deming's 14 points applied to service. *Training: The Magazine of Human Resources Development.* 28, (March) 50.

Buzzell, Robert D. (1981) Are there natural structures? *Journal of Marketing.* 45, (Winter) 42-51.

Buzzell, Robert D., and Bradley T. Gale. (1987) *The PIMS Principles: Linking Strategy to Performance.* New York: Free Press. (*7)

Buzzell, Robert D., Bradley T. Gale, and R. G. M. Sultan. (1975) Market share-A key to profitability. *Harvard Business Review.* 53, (January-February) 21-26.

Buzzell, Robert D., and Donald F. Heany. (1974) Impact of strategic planning on profit performance. *Harvard Business Review.* 52, (March-April) 137-145.

Buzzell, Robert D., and Fred D. Wiersema. (1981) Successful share-building strategies. *Harvard Business Review.* 59, (January-February) 135-144. (*2)

Buzzell, Robert D., and Fred D. Wiersema. (1981) Modelling changes in market share: A cross sectional analysis. *Strategic Management Journal.* 2, (January-February) 27-42.

Byham, William D. (1987) *Applying a Systems Approach to Personnel Activities.* Monograph IX. Pittsburgh, PA: Development Dimensions International.

Byham, William D. (1990) *Zapp! The Lightning of Empowerment.* New York: Harmony Books.

Bylinshi, Gene. (1979) Those smart young robots on the production line. *Fortune.* (December 17) 93. (*2)

Byrd, J., and L. Moore. (1978) The application of a product mix linear programming model in corporate policy making. *Management Science.* 24, (September) 1342-1350.

Byrne, Harlan B. (1981) Deere and Co. farm-machinery leadership helps firm weather the industry's slump. *Wall Street Journal.* (February 20) 48.

Byrne, John A., Ronald Grover and Todd Vogel. (1989) Is the boss getting paid too much? *BusinessWeek.* (May) 46-52. (*3)

Byrne, Patsy Camp. (1994) Employees' perceptions of the effectiveness of total quality management training in a midsized Southeast Alabama company. Unpublished Ed.D. dissertation, College of Education, University of Alabama, Tuscaloosa, AL.

Byron, Christopher. (1981) How Japan does it. *Time.* (March) 14.

Cadotte, E. R., R. B. Woodruff and R. L. Jenkins. (1987) Expectations and norms in models of consumer satisfaction, *Journal of Marketing Research.* 24, (November) 305-314. (*2)

Cahill, Hugh E., and Richard C. Davids. (1984) Adam-a computer aid to maintainability design. *Proceedings, Annual Reliability and Maintainability Symposium.* New York: IEEE, 12-16.

Cain, J., and Michael J. Stahl. (1983) Modeling the policies of several labor arbitrators. *Academy of Management Journal.* 26, (March) 140-147.

Caine, R., T. Nolan and T. Poyer. (1982) Toward a paperless factory. *ASQC Annual Technical Quality Congress Transactions.* Milwaukee, WI: ASQC Quality Press, 584-591.

Calder, A. B. (1964) Statistical approach in analytical chemistry. *Analytical Chemistry.* 36, (August) 25A-34A.

Caldwell, B. (1994) Missteps, miscues. *Information Week.* 20, (June) 50-60.

Calvin, J. L. (1983) Microelectronics bonding real time process control. Proceedings of the 1983 ASQC Western Regional Conference, Phoenix, AZ: ASQC, 35-44.

Calvin, T. W. (1984) *How and When to Perform Bayesian Acceptance Sampling.* Milwaukee, WI: ASQC Quality Press.

Cameron, Joseph M. (1952) Tables for constructing and for computing the operating characteristics of single sampling plans. *Industrial Quality Control.* 9, (July) 37-39.

Cameron, Joseph M. (1977) *Measurement Assurance.* Washington, DC: National Bureau of Standards. (NBSIR 77-1240, April).

Cameron, K. S., and R. E. Quinn. (1988) Organizational paradox and transformation. In R. E. Quinn and K. S. Cameron (Eds.) *Paradox and Transformation: Toward a Theory of Change in Organization and Management.* Cambridge, MA: Ballinger.

Cameron, R. D. (1977) Up your quality with show and tell. *Quality.* (May) 24-25.

Camillus, J. C., and A. L. Lederer. (1985) Corporate strategy and the design of computerized information systems. *Sloan Management Review.* 26, (Spring) 35.

Camp, Robert C. (1989) *Benchmarking: The Search for Industry Best Practices that Lead to Superior Performance.* Milwaukee, WI: ASQC Quality Press. (*5)

Campanella, J. (1983) Principles of quality costs, quality progress. *Journal of the American Society for Quality Control.* (April) 16-22.

Campanella, J., and F. J. Corcoran. (1983) Principles of quality costs. *Quality Progress.* 16, (April) 21. (*2)

Campbel, D. (1985) *Take the Road to Creativity and Get off Your Dead End.* Greensboro, NC: Center for Creative Leadership. (*2)

Campbell, J. P., M. D. Dunnette, Edward E. Lawler III, and K. E. Weick., Jr. (1970) *Managerial Behavior, Performance and Effectiveness.* New York: McGraw-Hill.

Campbell, S. K. (1974) *Flaws and Fallacies in Statistical Thinking.* Englewood Cliffs, NJ: Prentice-Hall.

Can America compete? (1987) *BusinessWeek.* (April 20) 24.

Capezio, Peter and Debra Morehouse. (1993) *Taking the Mystery out of Total Quality Management.* Hawthorne, NJ: Career Press.

Caplan, Frank. (1980) *The Quality System.* Randor, PA: Chilton Book Company.

Caplan, Frank. (1984) Managing for success through the quality system. *ASQC Annual Technical Quality Congress Transactions.* Milwaukee, WI: ASQC Quality Press, 10-21.

Caplan, Frank. (1986) Letter to editors. *Quality Progress.* 19, (February) 6.

Caplan, Nathan, Marcella H. Choy, and John K. Whitmore. (1992) Indochinese refugee families and academic achievement. *Scientific American* 266, (February) 41-42.

Caplen, R. H. (1982) *Practical Approach to Quality Control.* London, UK: Business Books. (*3)

Capon, N., J. U. Farley, and S. Hoenig. (1990) Determinants of financial performance: A Meta-analysis. *Management Science.* 36, (October) 1143-1159.

Capon, N., and R. Glazer. (1987) Marketing and technology: Strategic coalignment. *Journal of Marketing.* 51, (July) 1-14.

Carlisle, Elliott. (1976) MacGregor. *Organizational Dynamics.* 36, (Summer) 74-84.

Carlisle, Elliott. (1979) The golfer. *California Management Review.* 22, (Fall) 42-52.

Carlisle, Elliott. (1983) *"Mac" Conversations About Management.* New York: McGraw-Hill.

Carlisle, John H., and Robert C. Parker. (1989) *Beyond Negotiation: Redeeming Customer-Supplier Relationships.* New York: John Wiley.

Carlisle, Rodney. (1981) Shirt-sleeve quality. *Quality.* (March) 48-49.

Carlson, H. C. (1978) The parallel organization structure at General Motors. *Personnel.* 55, (July-August) 64-69.

Carlson, R. D., J. Gerber and J. F. McHugh. (1981) *Manual of Quality Assurance Procedures and Forms*. Englewood Cliffs, NJ: Prentice-Hall.

Carlton, D. K. (1985) Plant sensory evaluation within a multi-plant international organization. *Food Technology*. 39, (November) 130.

Carlzon, Jan. (1989) *Moments of Truth*. New York: Harper and Row.

Carnegie, A. (1948) *Autobiography of Andrew Carnegie*. Boston, MA: Houghton Mifflin.

Carnevale, A. P., L. J. Gainer and A. S. Meltzer. (1988) *Workplace Basics: The Skills Employers Want*. American Society for Training and Development and U.S. Department of Labor Report 0-225-795-QL.2. Washington, DC: U.S. Government Printing Office.

Caron, J. R., S. L. Jarvenpaa, and D. B. Stoddard. (1994) Business reengineering at CIGNA Corporation: Experiences and lessons learned from the first five years. *MIS Quarterly*. (September) 233-250.

Caroselli, Marlene. (1991) Total quality transformations. *Training and Development Journal*. 45, (September) 81.

Carothers, G. Harlan, Jr. (1986) Future organizations of change. *Survey of Business*. (Spring) 16-17.

Carothers, G. Harlan, Jr., and M. Adams. (1991) Competitive advantage through customer value: The role of value-based strategies. In Michael J. Stahl and G. M. Bounds. *Competing Globally through Customer Value: The Management of Strategic Supersystems*. Westport, CT: Quorum Books.

Carothers, G. Harlan, Jr., and G. M. Bounds. (1991) Customer value determination and system improvement cycles. In Michael J. Stahl and G. M. Bounds. *Competing Globally through Customer Value: The Management of Strategic Suprasystems*. Westport, CT: Greenwood Press.

Carothers, G. Harlan, Jr., G. M. Bounds, and Michael J. Stahl. (1991) Managerial leadership. In Michael J. Stahl and G. M. Bounds. *Competing Globally Through Customer Value: The Management of Strategic Suprasystems*. Westport, CT: Quorum Books.

Carpenter, Ben H. (1982) Control of copper ore roasting exit gas quality. *ASQC Annual Technical Quality Congress Transactions*. Milwaukee, WI: ASQC Quality Press, 748-755.

Carr, B. T. (1989) An integrated system for consumer-guided product optimization. *Product Testing with Consumers for Research Guidance*. Philadelphia, PA: ASC.

Carr, Clay. (1990) Total quality training. *Training*. 27, (November) 59-60.

Carr, Clay. (1992) The three R's of training. *Training*. 29, (June) 60. (*2)

Carr, David K., and Ian D. Littman. (1990) *Excellent in Government: Total Quality Management in the 1990s*. Washington, DC: Coopers and Lybrand. (*3)

Carr, Jesse M., and E. A. McCracken. (1960) Statistical program planning for process development. *Chemical Engineering Progress*. 56, (November) 56-61.

Carrington, J. (1969) Does management owe the supervisor promotional opportunity? *Personnel Journal*. 48, (June) 23-26.

Carroll, J. M. (1969) Estimating errors in the inspection of complex products. *Transactions of Industrial Engineering*. 1, 229-235.

Carroll, S., and D. Gillen. (1987) Are the classical management functions useful in describing managerial work? *Academy of Management Review*. (January) 38-51.

Carroll, Timothy Warren. (1994) Total quality management in higher education: Implementation and barriers. Unpublished Ed.D. dissertation, University of Central Florida, Orlando, FL.

Carruth, Paul J., and Thurrell O. McClandon. (1984) How supervisors react to 'meeting the budget' pressure. *Management Accounting*. 66, (November) 50-54.

Carson, K., Robert L. Cardy, and Gregory H. Dobbins. (1992) Upgrade the employee evaluation process. *H R Magazine*. 37, (November) 88. (*2)

Carson, K., Robert L. Cardy, and Gregory H. Dobbins. (1993) Upgrade the employee evaluation process. *Survey of Business*. Knoxville, TN: College of Business, University of Tennessee. (Summer-Fall) 29-32.

Carter, Bob. (1975) Simplifying NC fixtures. *Industrial Engineering*, 7, (July) 40-41.

Carter, C. L., and G. M. Carter. (1983) A motivation program for inspectors. *ASQC Annual Technical Quality Congress Transactions*. Milwaukee, WI: ASQC Quality Press, 525-528.

Carter, L. R., and T. Huzan. (1973) *A Practical Approach to Computer Simulation in Business*. London, UK: Allen and Unwin.

Carter, L. R. (1993) Continuous improvement and the IE: Defining a new role. *Industrial Engineering*. 25, (January) 36. (*2)

Cartwright, Dorwin. (1973) Determinants of scientific progress: The case of research on the risky shift. *American Psychologist*. 28, (March) 222-231.

Cartwright, Dorwin and Alvin Zander. (1968) *Group Dynamics: Research and Theory*. Third edition. New York: Harper and Row.

Casalou, R. F. (1991) Total quality management in health care. *Hospital and Health Services Administration*. 36, 134-146.

Cascio, W. F. (1982) *Costing Human Resources: The Financial Impact of Behavior in Organizations*. New York: Van Nostrand Reinhold.

Cascio, W. F. (1988) Innovative human resource practices for the high tech firm. In L. R. Gomez-Mejia and M. W. Lawless (Eds.) *Conference Proceedings Managing the High Technology Firm.* Boulder, CO: University of Colorado Press, 9-15.

Cascio, W. F. (1988) Strategic human resource management in high technology industry. In L. R. Gomez-Mejia and M. W. Lawless (Eds.) *Conference Proceedings Managing the High Technology Firm.* Boulder, CO: University of Colorado Press, 16-24.

Case, John. (1989) Competitive advantage. *Inc.* (April) 33-34.

Case, John. (1992) Quality with tears. *Inc.* (June) 82. (*2)

Case, K., and J. B. Keats. (1982) On the selection of a prior distribution in Bayesian acceptance sampling. *Journal of Quality Technology.* 14, (January) 10-18.

Case, Tony. (1992) Total quality management. *Editor and Publisher.* 125, (May 9) 14. (*3)

Cason, Roger L. (1978) The right size: An organizational dilemma. *Management Review.* 67, (April) 27. (*2)

Castro, Janice. (1989) Making it better. *Time.* (November 13) 47.

Castro, Janice. (1989) Where did the gung-ho go. *Time.* (September) 53.

Caswell, A. R., and J. D. Zimmer. (1979) Flow chart analysis of pharmaceutical products. *ASQC Annual Technical Quality Congress Transactions.* Milwaukee, WI: ASQC Quality Press, 161-167.

Catch a falling star. (1989) *U.S. News and World Report.* (June 5) 43-44.

Caterpillar is rarely first. (1977) *BusinessWeek.* (May 4) 23-24.

Caterpillar Tractor Company (1978) *Service Quality Guide.* Peoria, IL: Caterpillar Tractor Company

Caterpillar: Sticking to basics to stay competitive. (1981) *BusinessWeek.* (May) 76. (*3)

Causal modeling: A statistical approach. (1992) *Industry Week.* (September 7) 76. (*2)

Cavallo, Gerald O., and Joel Perelmuth. (1989) Building customer satisfaction, strategically. *Bottomline.* (January) 29.

Cavallon, Michel and Scott Winslow. (1993) Strategic benchmarking make quality programs work. *American Banker.* 157, (March 29) 11-14. (*3)

Caves, R. E., Bradley T. Gale, and Michael E. Porter. (1977) Inter-firm profitability differences. *Quarterly Journal of Economics.* (November) 667-675.

Caves R. E., and Michael E. Porter. (1976) Barriers to exit. In Joe S. Bain, R. T. Mason, and P. D. Quals (Eds.) *Essays in Industrial Organization.* Cambridge, MA: Ballinger.

Caves, R. E., and Michael E. Porter. (1978) Market structure, oligopoly and the stability of market shares. *Journal of Industrial Economics.* 24, (June) 289-313.

Centamore, V. (1971) A materials management survey. *Journal of Purchasing.* (June) 79-32.

Centre for the Study of Management Learning. (1992) Team appropriateness. *University of Lancaster (UK) Studies in Management.* 23, (Part 4) 349-362.

A CEO's odyssey toward world class manufacturing. *Chief Executive.* (September) 46-49.

Chadwick, Sid. (1992) It takes more than statistics. *American Printer.* 208, (February) 78.

Chaffee, Ellen and Lawrence Sherr. (1992) *Quality: Transforming Postsecondary Education.* ASHE-ERIC Higher Education Report #3. Washington, DC: ASHE-ERIC. (*2)

Chaisson, Donald A. and William H. Sue-Ho. (1984) Reliability concepts drug ability studies. *ASQC Annual Technical Quality Congress Transactions*. Milwaukee, WI: ASQC Quality Press, 414-419.

Chalk, Mary Beth, Shirley Edwards, and Brad Eskind. (1992) Total quality management: a corporate real estate survival strategy. *Site Selection*. 37, (October) 996. (*2)

Chambers, E., IV. (1990) Sensory analysis-dynamic research for today's products. *Food Technology*. 44, (January) 92.

Chambers, J. M., W. S. Cleveland, B. Kleiner, and P. A. Tukey. (1983) *Graphical Methods for Data Analysis*. Monterey: Brooks/Cole.

Chamers, J. C., K. Mullick, and D. D. Smith. (1974) *An Executive's Guide to Forecasting*. New York: John Wiley.

Champy, James. (1990) Organizational revisionism. *CIO*. (December) 20.

Chan, W. W., and K. Rathmill. (1985) *Digital Simulation of a Proposed Flexible Manufacturing System*. Manchester, UK: Department of Mechanical Engineering.

Chancellor, J. (1990) *Peril and Promise: A Commentary on America*. New York: Harper and Row.

Chandler, Alfred D., Jr. (1962) *Strategy and Structure: Chapters in the History of Industrial Enterprise*. Cambridge, MA: MIT Press. (*5)

Chandler, Alfred D., Jr. (1977) *The Visible Hand: The Managerial Revolution in American Business*. Cambridge, MA: Harvard University Press. (*3)

Chandler, Alfred D., Jr., and Stephen Salsbury. (1971) *Pierre du Pont and the Making of the Modern Corporation*. New York: Harper and Row.

Chang, R. Y. (1993) When TQM goes nowhere. *Training and Development Journal*. 47, (January) 25-29.

Chang, R. Y. (1994) Improve processes, reengineer them, or both? *Training and Development*. 48, (March) 54-58.

Chapman, M. K. (1969) The world prosperity through quality. *Journal of Quality Assurance.* 17, (December) 28-31.

Chase, Richard B. (1974) Survey of paced assembly lines. *Industrial Engineering.* 6, (February) 20-23.

Chase, Rory L. (1988) *Total Quality Management.* New York: IFS Publications. (*2)

Chase, Richard B., and N. J. Aquila. (1981) *Production and Operations Management: A Life Cycle Approach.* Homewood, IL: Irwin.

Chase, Richard B., and David A. Tansik. (1983) The customer contact model for organization design. *Management Science*. 29, (November) 1037-1050.

Chaufournier, R., and C. St. Andre. (1993) Total quality management in an academic health center. *Quality Progress*. 26, (March) 63-66.

Chebookjian, S. L. (1980) The inspector is human. *ASQC Annual Technical Quality Congress Transactions*. Milwaukee, WI: ASQC Quality Press, 365.

Checkland, Peter. (1981) *Systems Thinking, Systems Practice*. New York: John Wiley.

Cheek, L. M. (1977) *Zero-Base Budgeting Comes of Age. What It Is and What It Takes to Make It Work.* New York: AMACOM.

Chen, G. K., and R. E. McGarrah. (1977) *Planning and Control*. San Francisco, CA: Holden-Day.

Chen, X. (1988) China's special economic zones (SEZs): Origins and initial consequences of a new development strategy. Origins and

Consequences of National Development Strategies: Latin America and East Asia Compared. Durham, NC: Duke University Press.

Cherkasky, M. (1993) Quality must put customers first. *New York Times*. (March) B 1. (*4)

Cherkasky, Stanley M. (1970) Long-term storage and system reliability. *Proceedings, Annual Reliability and Maintainability Symposium.* New York: IEEE, 120-127.

Cherry, R. (1982) The development of General Motors' team-based plants in the innovative organization. In Robert Zager and Michael P. Rosow (Eds.). (1982) *The Innovative Organization: Productivity Programs in Action*. New York: Pergamon Press, 125-148.

Cherry. D. H., J. C. Grogan, W. A. Holmes, and F. A. Perris. (1978) Availability analysis for chemical plants. *Chemical Engineering Process.* (January) 172-185.

Chestnut, H. (1965) *Systems Engineering Tools.* New York: John Wiley.

Chevrolet Motor Division. (1987) *Increasing Customer Satisfaction through Effective Corporate Complaint Handling.* Detroit, MI: Technical Assistance Research Program (TARP).

Chew, Victor (1964) *Experimental Designs in Industry.* New York: John Wiley.

Chew, W. Bounce. (1988) No-nonsense guide to measuring productivity. *Harvard Business Review.* 66, (January-February) 110-118.

Child, John. (1977) *Organization: A Guide to Problems and Practices.* New York: Harper and Row. (*3)

Chiller, Zachary. (1989) Big Blue's overhaul. *BusinessWeek.* Special issue on innovation.

Chinoy, Eli. (1955) *Automobile Workers and the American Dream.* New York: Doubleday.

Chira, Susan. (1992) Money's value questioned in school debate. *New York Times* (May 4) A 1.

Choate, P. (1990) *Agents of Influence.* New York: Alfred A. Knopf.

Choksi, Suresh. (1971) Computer can optimize manufacturing tolerances for an economical design. *ASQC Annual Technical Quality Congress Transactions.* Milwaukee, WI: ASQC Quality Press, 323-330.

Christensen, K. L. (1975) Certification program reduces costs. *Quality.* (August) 14-16.

Christofono, R. (1984) *Fundamental Statistical Process Control.* Ron Christofono Workshop Series.

Christopher, R. C. (1983) *The Japanese Mind.* New York: Linden Press. (*2)

Christopher, R. C. (1986) *Second to None: American Companies in Japan.* New York: Fawcett Columbine Books.

Chrysler on the road to recovery. (1992) *USA Today.* (March 6) B1.

Chrysler ties executive bonuses to worker profit-sharing. (1988) *Los Angeles Times.* (April) B 1.

Chrysler, Walter P. (1951) *Life of an American Workman.* New York: Dodd, Mead.

Churchill, A. V. (1956) The effect of scale interval length and pointer clearance on speed and accuracy of interpolation. *Journal of Applied Psychology.* 40, (December) 358-361.

Churchill, B. G. (1984) *People Working Together: A Seventy-Fifth Anniversary Salute to Powell.* Powell, WY: Custom Printing. (*2)

Churchill, Neil C. (1984) Budget choice: Planning vs. control. *Harvard Business Review*. 62, (July-August) 150-164.

Churchman, C. (1968) *The Systems Approach*. New York: Dell.

Churchman, C., Russell L. Ackoff, and E. Leonard Arnoff. (1957) *Introduction to Operations Research*. New York: John Wiley.

Ciampa, Dan. (1988) *Manufacturing's New Mandate*. New York: John Wiley.

Ciampa, Dan. (1992) Planning for successful steering committees. *Journal for Quality and Participation*. (December) 22-34.

Ciampa, Dan. (1992) *Total Quality: A User's Guide for Implementation*. Reading, MA: Addison-Wesley.

Civin, Robert. (1992) On the road to Utopia. *Institutional Distribution*. 28, (April) 12. (*2)

Civin, Robert. (1992) Total quality management: Competitive edge for the 90s. *Institutional Distribution*. 28, (May 1) 12. (*2)

Clark, Gordon L. (1988) Restructuring in the steel industry: Adjustment strategies and local labor relations. *America's New Market Geography*. New Brunswick, NJ: Rutgers University.

Clark, Gregory. (1982) Western reindustrialization and Japan: Why Japan works (1). *The Japan Economic Journal*. (March) 24.

Clark, Kim B. (1980) Impact of unionization on productivity: A case study. *Industrial and Labor Relations Review*. 33, (July) 451-69.

Clark, Kim B., B. W. Chew, and T. Fujimoto. (1987) Product development in the world auto industry: Strategy, organization and performance. *Brookings Paper on Economic Activity*. 3, 729-771.

Clark, Kim B., and T. Fujimoto. (1986) Overlapping problem solving in product development. Harvard Business School Working Paper. 87, 48.

Clark, Kim B., R. H. Hayes, and C. Lorenz. (1985) *The Uneasy Alliance: Managing the Productivity Technology Dilemma.* Cambridge, MA: Harvard Business School Press.

Clark, R. C. (1979) *The Japanese Company.* New Haven, CT: Yale University Press. (*2)

Clark, S. (1991) Quality isn't enough: Programs need to be market-driven. *Marketing News.* 10, (June) 15.

Clark, V. S. (1929) *History of Manufactures in the United States.* New York: McGraw-Hill.

Clarke, James and Michel Halbouty. (1952) *Spindletop.* New York: Random House.

Clatworthy, W. H. (1973) *Tables of the Two-Associate-Class Partially Balanced Designs.* Washington, DC: National Bureau of Standards Applied Mathematics Services Publication 63, U.S. Government Printing Office.

Claunch, J. (1985) Implementing JIT. Paper presented at the Spring Seminar of the Purchasing Management Association of Denver.

Clausing, Don, and Bruce H. Simpson. (1990) Quality by design. *Quality Progress.* 23, (January) 41-44.

Cleland, David I. (1981) The cultural ambience of the matrix organization. *Management Review.* 70, (November) 37-39.

Cleland, David I. (1981) Matrix management (Part II): A kaleidoscope of organizational systems. *Management Review.* 70, (December) 48-56.

Cleland, David I., and W. R. King. (Eds.). (1972) *Management: A Systems Approach.* New York: McGraw-Hill.

Cleland, David I., and W. R. King (Eds.). (1983) *Systems Analysis and Project Management.* Third edition. New York: McGraw-Hill.

Cleland, David I., and W. R. King (Eds.). (1988) *Project Management Handbook.* Second edition. New York: Van Nostrand Reinhold.

Clemen, R. (1923) *American Livestock and Meat Industry.* New York: The Ronald Press Company.

Clements, John. (1985) One-two-three-go: Part 1. *Quality Progress.* 18, (April) 92.

Clements, John. (1985) One-two-three-go: Part 2. *Quality Progress.* 18, (July) 48-50.

Clements, John. (1985) One-two-three-go: Part 3. *Quality Progress.* 18, (August) 54.

Clemmer, Jim. (1991) How total is your quality management? *The Canadian Business Review.* 18, (Spring) 38-41.

Clemons, D. S. (1993) Expanding the model of consumer satisfaction and dissatisfaction: The means-ends disconfirmation model of CS/D. Unpublished Ph.D. dissertation, Department of Marketing, Logistics and Transportation, University of Tennessee, Knoxville, TN.

Clepper, Irene. (1992) Wake-up call for service techs. *Air Conditioning, Heating and Refrigeration News.* 187, (December 21) 3. (*3)

Cleveland, H. (1985) Control: The twilight of hierarchy. *New Management.* 3, (February) 14-25. (*2)

Cleveland, W. S. (1985) *The Elements of Graphing Data.* Monterey: Wadsworth.

Cleverly, W. O. (1987) Product costing for health care firms. *Health Care Management Review.* (Winter) 39-48.

Clifford, Donald K., and Richard E. Cavanagh. (1988) *The Winning Performance: How America's High-Growth Midsize Companies Succeed.* New York: Bantam Books.

Clifford, Paul C. (1959) Control charts without calculations. *Industrial Quality Control.* 15, (May) 2-6. (*2)

Clifford, Paul C. (1971) A process capability study using control charts. *Journal of Quality Technology.* 3, (March) 107-111. (*3)

Cline, Nancy and Paula Dalla. (1982) Quality circles in the recovery room. *Nursing and Health Care.* 3, (November) 494-496.

Clover, Vernon and Howard Balsley. (1974) *Business Research Methods.* Columbus, OH: Grid.

Coate, L. Edwin. (1990) Implementing total quality management in a university setting. In Harry Ivan Costin (Ed.) (1994) *Readings in Total Quality Management.* Fort Worth, TX: Dryden Press, 447-483.

Coate, L. Edwin. *Total Quality Management at Oregon State University.* Corvallis, OR: Oregon State University. (*3)

Coch, L., and John R. P. French. Jr. (1949) Overcoming resistance to change. *Human Relations.* 1, (April) 512-533. (*4)

Cocheu, Ted. (1992) Training with quality. *Training and Development Journal.* 46, (May) 22. (*3)

Cochran, D. S., F. R. David, and C. K. Gibson. (1985) A framework for developing an effective mission statement. *Journal of Business Strategy.* 2, (Winter) 4-17.

Cochran, William G. (1977) *Sampling Techniques.* New York: John Wiley. (*3)

Cochran, William G., and Gertrude M. Cox. (1957) *Experimental Designs.* New York: John Wiley. (*3)

Cockburn, Alexander, James Ridgeway, and Andrew Cockburn. (1981) The Pentagon spends its way to omnipotence. *Village Voice.* (February) 11. (*2)

Codding, George A. (1964) *The Universal Postal Union.* New York: New York University Press.

Codman, E. A. (1914) The product of a hospital. *Surgical Gynecology and Obstetrics.* 18, 491-494.

Codman, E. A. (1917) *A Study in Hospital Efficiency: As Demonstrated by the Case Report of the First Five Years of a Private Hospital.* Boston, MA: Privately published, circa 1917.

Coeyman, Marjorie. (1993) ISO 9000 gaining ground in Asia/Pacific. *Chemical Week.* (April 28) 54.

Cohan, David, Stephen M. Haas, David L. Radloff, and Richard F. Yancik. (1984) Using fire in forest management: decision making under uncertainty. *Interfaces.* 14, (September-October) 8-19.

Cohen, A. Clifford, and Betty Jones Whitten. (1981) Estimation of a normal distributions. *American Journal of Mathematical and Management Sciences.* 1, (January) 139-153.

Cohen, H. (1980) *You Can Negotiate Anything.* Secaucus, NJ: Citadel Press.

Cohen, I. B. (1984) Florence Nightingale. *Scientific American.* 250, 128-137.

Cohen, Jack. (1991) Everyone should be a sales rep. *Marketing News.* 25, (August) 4.

Cohen, Morris A., and Hau L. Lee. (1990) Out of touch with customer need? Spare parts and after sales service. *Sloan Management Review.* 31, (Winter) 55-66.

Cohen, Stephen. S., and John Zysman. (1987) *Manufacturing Matters: The Myth of the Post-Industrial Economy.* New York: Basic Books. (*4)

Cohen-Rosenthal, Edward. (1985) Orienting labor-management cooperation toward revenue and growth. *National Productivity Review.* 4, (April) 385-396. (*2)

Cohen-Rosenthal, Edward, and Cynthia Burton. (1986) *Mutual Gains: A Practical Guide to Union Management Cooperation.* New York: Praeger.

The Cola kings are feeling a bit jumpy. (1992) *BusinessWeek.* (July 13) 112.

Cole, Raymond C., and Lee H. Hales. (1992) How Monsanto justified automation. *Management Accounting.* (January) 39-43.

Cole, Robert E. (1971) *Japanese Blue Collar: The Changing Tradition.* Los Angeles, CA: University of California Press. (*2)

Cole, Robert E. (1979) Made in Japan—Quality control circles. *Across the Board.* 16, (November) 72-78. (*2)

Cole, Robert E. (1979) *Work Mobility and Participation: A Comparative Study of American and Japanese Industry.* Berkeley, CA: University of California Press. (*6)

Cole, Robert E. (1980) Learning from the Japanese: Prospects and pitfalls. *Management Review.* 61, (September) 22-28.

Cole, Robert E. (1980) Will quality control cycles work in the U.S.? *Quality Progress.* 13, (July) 30-33. (*3)

Cole, Robert E. (1981) Common misconceptions of Japanese QC circles. *ASQC Annual Technical Quality Congress Transactions.* Milwaukee, WI: ASQC Quality Press, 188-189.

Cole, Robert E. (1981) The Japanese lesson in quality. *Technology Review.* (July) 29-34.

Cole, Robert E. (1982) Quality control practices in the auto industry: United States and Japan compared. *Ann Arbor Observer.* (February) 27-28.

Cole, Robert E. (1979) Diffusion of new work structures in Japan. IAQC 1st Annual Conference Transactions. Cincinnati, OH: International Association of Quality Circles.

Cole, Robert E. (1979) Made in Japan: A spur to U.S. productivity. *ASIA Magazine.* (June) 18-24.

Cole, Robert E. (1979) *Work, Mobility and Participation: A Comparative Study of American and Japanese Industry.* Berkeley, CA: University of California Press.

Cole, Robert E. (1981) QC warning voiced by U.S. expert on Japanese circles. *World of Work Report.* 6, (July) 49-51.

Cole, Robert E. (1981) Rationale for financial incentives for quality circle members. *Quality Circles Journal.* 8, (February) 43-46.

Cole, Robert E. (1982) Industry at the crossroads. Michigan papers in Japanese studies. Ann Arbor, MI: University of Michigan, Center for Japanese Studies.

Cole, Robert E. (1983) *Automobiles and Future: Competition, Cooperation, and Change.* Ann Arbor, MI: University of Michigan Press.

Cole, Robert E. (1983) Improving product quality through continuous feedback. *Management Review.* 72, (October) 8-12.

Cole, Robert E. (1989) *Strategies for Learning: Small-Group Activities in American, Japanese, and Swedish Industry.* Berkeley, CA: University of California Press.

Cole, Robert E. (1993) Introduction, Special Issue on Total Quality Management. *California Management Review.* 35, (Spring) 7-8.

Cole, Robert E., and D. S. Tachiki. (1984) Forging institutional links: Making quality circles work in the U.S. *National Productivity Review.* 3, (April) 417-429. (*2)

Cole, Robert E., and A. G. Walder. (1981) Structural diffusion: The politics of participative work structures in China, Japan, Sweden and the United States. *CRSO Working Paper.* (February) 28. (*2)

Cole, W. (1991) Competitive economies and the economics of competition. In Michael J. Stahl and G. M. Bounds. *Competing Globally Through Customer Value: The Management of Strategic Suprasystems*. Westport, CT: Quorum Books, 14-31.

Coleman, L. R. (1982) Detailed defect reporting: A key to productivity. *ASQC Annual Technical Quality Congress Transactions*. Milwaukee, WI: ASQC Quality Press, 574-579.

Coleman, Lynn G. (1992) Total quality management prescribed as cure for health care ailments. *Marketing News*. 26, May 11) 5. (*2)

Collard, Ron. (1981) The quality circle in context. *Personnel Management*. 13, (September) 26-30.

Collard, Ron. (1989) Total quality. *Personnel Management*. 21, (November) 77.

Colvin, G. (1990) The wee outfit that decked IBM. *Fortune*. (November 19) 165-168.

Comish, John W. (1983) Managing a multidivisional quality function. *ASQC Annual Technical Quality Congress Transactions*. Milwaukee, WI: ASQC Quality Press, 268-271.

Commin, Kevin. (1990) U.S. companies urged to adopt holistic thinking. *Journal of Commerce and Commercial*. (June 25) 4a. (*3)

Committee for Economic Development. (1981) *Social Responsibilities of Business Corporations*. New York: CED, 25-26.

Committee for Economic Development. (1983) *Productivity Policy: Key to the Nation's Economic Future*. Washington, DC: CED.

Commoner, Barry. (1971) *The Closing Circle*. New York: Alfred A. Knopf.

Communicating quality: 101 companies talk about "How to do it right the first time." (1990) *Business Marketing, the Starmark Report III*. New York: Starmark, Incorporated and Crain Communications.

Comola, Jackie P. (1988) Designing a new family of measures. *Total Quality Performance.* (Research Report Number 909). New York: The Conference Board, 59-64.

Company's courses go collegiate. (1979) *BusinessWeek.* (February) 7.

Compaq can't cope with demand for Pro Linea PCs. (1992) *Wall Street Journal.* (July 10) B1.

Competitiveness linked to quality. (1992) *CA Magazine.* (April) 15. (*2)

Computers: When will the slump end? (1986) *BusinessWeek.* (April 21) 58-66.

Comstock, Vivian C., and Gerald E. Swartz. (1980) *Predictable Developmental Stages in the Evolution of Quality Circles.* Cincinnati, OH: International Association of Quality Circle.

Condit, C. (1968) *American Building.* Chicago, IL: University of Chicago Press.

The Conference Board. (1991) *Global Perspectives on Total Quality.* New York: The Conference Board.

Conley, Dean. (1969-1970) A management team approach to hospital systems analysis. *Hospital Administration.* (Winter) 1-21.

Conlin, Joseph. (1989) The house that GE built. *Successful Meetings.* 38, (August) 50-58.

Connell, L. W. (1984) Quality at the source: The first step in just-in-time production. *Quality Progress.* 17, (November) 44-45.

Connellan, T. K. (1978) *How to Improve Human Performance: Behaviorism in Business and Industry.* New York: Harper and Row.

Conner, Roy C., Jr. (1992) A success formula. *Internal Auditor.* 49, (April) 33. (*2)

Connor, P. E. (1980) *Organizations: Theory and Design*. Chicago, IL: SRA Associates.

Connor, W. S. (1961) Group screening designs. *Industrial and Engineering Chemistry*. 53, 69-70.

Connors, Tracy Daniel. (1993) *The Non Profit Management Handbook: Operating Policies and Procedures*. New York: John Wiley.

Conot, Robert. (1974) *American Odyssey*. New York: William Morrow.

Constable, Gordon K. (1983) The role of ASQC in academic programs. *ASQC Quality Technology Program Accreditation Update*. Milwaukee, WI: ASQC Quality Press, 49-53.

Consumer complaint handling in America: An update study part II. (1986) Technical Assistance Research Program. (March 31) 21-24. Washington, DC: U.S. Government Printing Office. (*2)

Continuous Sampling Procedures and Tables for Inspection by Attributes. (1981) MIL-STD-1235b Washington, DC: U.S. Government Printing Office.

Controlling with standards. (1987) *Small Business Report*. (August) 62-65.

Conway, G. J., and G. H. Carothers. (1991) Application to government; U.S. Army, Watervliet Arsenal. In Michael J. Stahl and G. M. Bounds. *Competing Globally through Customer Values: The Management of Strategic Suprasystems*. New York: Quorum Books. (*2)

Conway, R. W., L. Maxwell, and Larry W. Miller. (1967) *Theory of Scheduling*. Reading, MA: Addison-Wesley.

Conway, W. (1981) Nashua Corporation paper. (March). Rio de Janeiro: Nashua Corporation.

Cook, J. D. (1988) Truck 54, Where are you? *U.S. News and World Report*. (March) 64.

Cook, K. (1977) Exchange and power in network of interorganizational relations. *Sociological Quarterly*. 18, 62-82.

Cook, M. H. (1982) Quality circles-they really work, but. *Training and Development Journal*. 36, (January) 4-6.

Cook, Nathan. (1975) Computer managed parts manufacture. *Scientific American*. (January) 23-29.

Cook, T. M., and R. A. Russell. (1984) *Contemporary Operations Management*. Englewood Cliffs, NJ: Prentice-Hall.

Cooke, William N. (1990) Factors influencing the effect of joint union-management programs on employee-supervisor relations. *Industrial and Labor Relations Review*. 43, (July) 33-38.

Cool, K. O., and D. Schendel. (1982) Strategic group formation and performance: The case of the U.S. pharmaceutical industry, 1963-1982. *Management Science*. 33, (September) 141-160.

Cooney, Barry D. (1989) Japan and culture. *Training and Development Journal*. 43, (August) 58-61.

Coonley, Howard and P. G. Agnew. (1941) *The Role of Standards in the System of Free Enterprise*. New York: American National Standards Institute.

Coop, Philip G. (1982) Training as a key to hazardous waste compliance. *ASQC Annual Technical Quality Congress Transactions*. Milwaukee, WI: ASQC Quality Press, 653-658.

Cooper, B. E. (1968) The extension of Yates' 2^n algorithm to any complete factorial experiment. *Technometrics*. 10, (July) 575-577.

Cooper, C. (1983) Freight consolidation and warehouse location strategies in physical distribution systems. *Journal of Business Logistics*. 453-74.

Cooper, J. E. (1977) Patrol inspection: Guide to productivity and profit. *ASQC Annual Technical Quality Congress Transactions*. Milwaukee, WI. ASQC Press, 50-52.

Cooper, J. E. (1980) Total quality design and conformance. *Quality*. (October) 24-25.

Cooper, Kenneth. (1990) New York schools will test Miami-style reforms. *Washington Post* (1 January) A 13.

Cooperative entrepreneurs at American Transtech. (1985) *World of Work Report*. (April) 15-18.

Copenhaver, L., and R. H. Guest. (1982) Quality of work life: The anatomy of two successes. *National Productivity Review*. 1, (April) 5-12. (*2)

Copulsky, W. (1991) Balancing the needs of customers and shareholders. *Journal of Business Strategy*, (November-December) 44-47.

Corbett, J. M. (1985) Perspective work design of a human-centered CNC lathe. *Behavior and Information Technology*. 4, 201-214.

Corbi, Jean-Claude, Michael J. Nay, and Philip Brown Belt. (1986) Statistical quality control in the bleach plant. *TAPPI*. 69, (February) 60-66.

Cordiner, R. J. (1956) *New Frontiers for Professional Managers*. New York: McGraw-Hill.

Cormier, Frank and William Eaton. (1970) *Reuther*. Englewood Cliffs, NJ: Prentice-Hall.

Cornell, John A. (1981) *Experiments with Mixtures*. New York: John Wiley.

Cornell, John A. (1983) How to run mixture experiments for product. *ASQC Annual Technical Quality Congress Transactions*. Milwaukee, WI: ASQC Quality Press, 1-6.

Corner, P. (1976) Quality: A common international goal. *ASQC Annual Technical Quality Congress Transactions*. Milwaukee, WI: ASQC Quality Press, 432-443.

Cornfeld, B., and O. Edwards. (1983) *Quintessence: The Quality of Having It.* New York: Crown Publishers.

Cornford, F. M. (1945) *The Republic of Plato.* New York: Oxford University Press.

Corning laboratories. (1991) *BusinessWeek.* (October 25) 158.

Cornwall, L. P. (1964) *Quality Control in International Air Freight.* Chicago, IL: Railroad Systems and Management Association.

The corporate elite. (1989) *BusinessWeek.* (October) 25-44.

The corporate culture at IBM: How it reinforces strategy. (1982) *Wall Street Journal.* (April 8) 1.

Corporate culture: The hard-to-change values that spell success or failure. (1980) *BusinessWeek.* (October 27) 148-160.

The cost of quality. (1992) *Newsweek.* (September 7) 48-49.

Costin, Harry Ivan. (1994) Exploring the concepts underlying total quality management. In Harry Ivan Costin (Ed.) *Readings in Total Quality Management.* (1994) Fort Worth, TX: Dryden Press, 7-26.

Costin, Harry Ivan (Ed.). (1994) *Readings in Total Quality Management.* Fort Worth, TX: Dryden Press.

Cound, Dana M. (1965) Quality system analysis-key to recurring cost reduction. *ASQC Annual Technical Quality Congress Transactions.* Milwaukee, WI: ASQC Quality Press, 109-115.

Cound, Dana M. (1986) Quality first. *Quality Progress.* 19, (March) 15-16.

Coulson-Thomas, C. J. (1993) Corporate transformation and business process reengineering. *Executive Development*. 6, (No. 1) 14-20.

Coulson-Thomas, C. J., and T. Coe. (1991) The flat organisation: philosophy and practice. British Institute of Management Report.

Cound, Dana. (1992) *A Leader's Journey to Quality*. Milwaukee, WI: ASQC Quality Press.

Counte, Michael A., Gerald L. Glandon, Denise M. Oleske, and James P. Hill. (1992) Total quality management in a health care organization: How are employees affected? *Hospital and Health Services Administration*. 37, (Winter) 503. (*3)

Courdy, Jean Claude. (1984) *The Japanese*. New York: Harper and Row.

Courter, Sandra Shaw. (1980) Continuing education: A growth industry. *Quality Progress*. 13, (April) 16-21.

Courtright, William. (1981) Hughes circles: An update. *Quality Circles Journal*. 4, (August) 30-34.

Covey, Stephen R. (1989) *The 7 Habits of Highly Effective People.* New York: Simon and Schuster. (*2)

Covey, Stephen R. (1992) Principles of total quality. *Modern Office Technology*. 37, (February) 10.

Covey, Stephen R., A. Roger Merrill, and Rebecca R. Merrill. (1994) *First Things First: To Live, to Love, to Learn, to Leave a Legacy*. New York: Simon and Schuster.

Cowden, D. J. (1957) *Statistical Methods in Quality Control*. Englewood Cliffs, NJ: Prentice-Hall, 489-490. (*2)

Cox, D. R. (1958) *Planning of Experiments*. New York: John Wiley.

Coyne, K. P. (1986) Sustainable competitive advantage—What it is, what it isn't. *Business Horizons*. 29, (January-February) 54-61.

Craig, Cecil C., and R. C. Harris. (1973) Total productivity measurement at the firm level. *Sloan Management Review.* 14, (Spring) 13-29.

Craig, J. A., Jr. and R. P. Bland. (1981) An empirical Bayes approach to a variables acceptance sampling plan problem. *Communication in Statistics.* 2399-2410.

Crandall, N. F., and L. M. Wooton. (1978) Developmental strategies of organizational productivity. *California Management Review.* 21, (Winter) 37-46.

Cranfill, S. M. (1991) Seven task manufacturing program. *Manufacturing Systems.* (January) 11-12.

Cravens, D., G. Hills, and R. B. Woodruff. (1987) *Marketing Management.* Homewood, IL: Irwin.

Cray, Ed. (1978) *Levi's.* Boston, MA: Houghton Mifflin. (*2)

Cray, Ed. (1980) *The Chrome Colossus.* New York: Harper and Row.

Creech, Bill. (1994) *The Five Pillars of TQM: How to Make Total Quality Management Work for You.* New York: Truman Talley Books/Plume.

Creveling, C. M., and William Fowlkes. (1995) *Engineering Methods for Robust Design: Advanced Taguchi Methods.* Reading, MA: Addison-Wesley.

Crocker, Olga L., Cyril Charney, and Johnny Sik Leung Chiu. (1986) *Quality Circles: A Guide to Participation and Productivity.* New York: New American Library.

Croisier, R. B. (1984) Mixture experiments: Geometry and pseudocomponents. *Technometrics.* 26, (August) 209-216.

Crosby, David, C. (1991) How to succeed in SPC. *Quality in Manufacturing.* (March/April) 15-19.

Crosby, Philip B. (1979) Quality is free: The art of making quality certain. In Harry Ivan Costin (Ed.) *Readings in Total Quality Management.* (1994) Fort Worth, TX: Dryden Press, 123-136.

Crosby, Philip B. (1979) *Quality is Free: The Art of Making Quality Certain.* New York: McGraw-Hill. (*13)

Crosby, Philip B. (1979) *Quality Without Tears: The Art of Hassle-Free Management.* New York: McGraw-Hill. (*10)

Crosby, Philip B. (1980) A look at the Japanese and American styles of management of quality and productivity. *Quality.* (June) 36-37.

Crosby, Philip B. (1980) Measuring maturity. *Quality.* (August) 21-24.

Crosby, Philip B. (1980) *Quality Is Free: The Art of Making Quality Certain.* New York: New American Library. (*4)

Crosby, Philip B. (1988) *Eternally Successful Organization.* New York: McGraw-Hill. (*3)

Crosby, Philip B. (1989) *Let's Talk Quality: 96 Questions You Always Wanted to Ask Phil Crosby.* New York: McGraw-Hill. (*3)

Crosby, Philip B. (1989) Working like a chef. *Quality Progress.* 22, (January) 24-25.

Crosby, Philip B. (1990) *Leading: The Art of Becoming an Executive.* New York: McGraw-Hill. (*2)

Crosby, Philip B. (1991) By George, I think I've got it. *HR Focus.* 68, (December) 23.

Crosby, Philip B. (1992) In debate: Does the Baldridge Award really work? *Harvard Business Review.* 70, (January-February) 126-147.

Crosby, Philip B. (1996) *Quality Is Still Free: Making Quality Certain in Uncertain Times.* New York: McGraw-Hill.

Cross, Kelvin F. (1984) Production modules offer flexibility: Low WIP for high tech. *Manufacturing*. 64-72.

Cross, R. (1984) PPM—parts per million—AOQL sampling plans. *Quality Progress*. 17, (November) 28-34.

Crothers, D. H. (1971) Workshop techniques for programmed audits. *Proceedings, Annual Symposium on Reliability*. New York: IEEE, 139-144.

Crow, E. L. (1966) Optimum allocation of calibration errors, industrial quality calibration errors. *Industrial Quality Control*. 22, (November) 215-219.

Crow, E. L., F. A. Davis, and M. M. Maxfield. (1960) *Statistics Manual*. New York: Dover.

Crozier, M. (1964) *The Bureaucratic Phenomenon*. Chicago, IL: University of Chicago Press.

Crystal, G. S. (1971) Motivating for the future: The long-term incentive plan. *Financial Executive*. 39, (October) 48-50.

Csikszentmihalyi, Mihalyi. (1990) *Flow: The Psychology of Optimal Experience*. New York: Harper and Row.

Cullen, J., and J. Hollingum. (1987) *Implementing Total Quality*. London, UK: IFS Limited.

Cummings, L. L. (1975) Strategies for improving human productivity. *The Personnel Administrator*. 20, (June) 40-44.

Cummings, T. G., and E. S. Molloy. (1977) *Improving Productivity and the Quality of Work Life*. New York: Praeger. (*2)

Cummings, T. G., and S. Srivastva. (1977) *Management of Work: A Sociotechnical Systems Approach*. Kent, OH: Kent State Press.

Cummins, Michael J. (1989) Total quality of telecommunications. *Business Communications Review*. 19, (December) 36.

Cunningham, Mary. (1984) *Power Play*. New York: Linden Press.

Cuppy, Will. (1950) *The Decline and the Fall of Practically Everybody*. New York: Holt, Rinehart and Winston. (*2)

Current Index to Statistics: Applications, Methods and Theory (1976) Washington, DC: American Statistical Association and Institute of Mathematical Statistics.

Currid, C. (1994) Have you taken a ride on the reengineering roller coaster? *Windows Magazine*. 1, (April) 51.

Currie, R. M. (1989) *Work Study*. London, UK: Pitman.

Curry, D. J., and D. J. Faulds. (1985) The measurement of quality competition in strategic groups. In J. Jacoby and J. C. Olson (Eds.) *Perceived Quality: How Consumers View Stores and Merchandise*. Lexington, MA: Lexington Books, 269-293.

Curtice, M. (1977) Integrity in database systems. *Datamation*. 23.

Curtis, B., M. I. Kellner, and J. Over. (1992) Process modeling. *Communications of the ACM*. 35, (No. 9) 75-90.

Curtis, Gerald. (1971) *Election Campaigning Japanese Style*. New York: Columbia University Press.

Cussler, C. (1990) *Dragon*. New York: Simon and Schuster.

Cusumano, Michael. (1985) *The Japanese Automobile Industry*. Cambridge: Harvard University Press. (*2)

Cuthbert, Daniel. (1959) Use of half-normal plots for interpreting factorial two-level experiments. *Technometrics*. 1, (September) 311-341.

Cuthbert, Daniel. (1962) Sequences of fractional replicates in the 2p-q series. *Journal of the American Statistical Association*. 57, (298) 403-429.

Cuthbert, Daniel. (1966) Parallel fractional replicates. *Technometrics.* 8, (February) 469-480.

Cuthbert, Daniel. (1976) *Applications of Statistics in Industrial Experimentation.* New York: John Wiley.

Cuthbert, Daniel and Fred S. Wood. (1971) *Fitting Equations to Data.* New York: John Wiley.

Cutts, Robert E. (1980) The productivity proposition: Notes on the Japanese approach. *Japan Airlines Travel Magazine.* (October) 4.

Cypress, H. L. (1994) Reengineering—MS/OR imperative: Make second generation of business process improvement mode work. *OR/MS Today.* (February) 18-29.

Cyert, Robert M., and James G. March. (1963) *A Behavioral View of the Firm.* Englewood Cliffs, NJ: Prentice-Hall.

Czaja, S. J., and C. G. Drury. (1981) Training programs for inspectors. *Human Factors.* 23, (April) 473-484.

Dabney, V. (1971) *Virginia: The New Dominion.* Garden City, NY: Doubleday.

Daft, Richard L. (1986) *Organization Theory.* St. Paul, MN: West Publishing.

Daft, Richard L. (1991) *Management.* Chicago, IL: Dryden Press.

Daft, Richard L., and Norman B. MacIntosh. (1981) A tentative exploration into the amount and equivocality of information processing in organizational work units. *Administrative Science Quarterly.* 26, (October) 207-224.

Daft, Richard L., and Norman B. MacIntosh. (1984) The nature and use of formal control systems for management control and strategy implementation. *Journal of Management.* 10, 43-66.

Daft, Richard L., J. Sormunen, and D. Parks. (1988) Chief executive scanning, environmental characteristics and company performance. *Strategic Management Journal*. 9, (March-April) 123-139.

Dahlinger, John C. (1975) *The Secret Life of Henry Ford.* Indianapolis, IN: Bobbs-Merrill.

Dahneman, D., B. Slovic, and Armos Tversky (Eds.). (1982) *Judgment Under Uncertainty: Heuristics and Biases*. Cambridge, UK: Cambridge University Press

Dailey, John J., Jr., and Rudolph L. Kagerer. (1982) A primer on quality circles. *Supervisory Management*. 27, (June) 40-43.

Dale, B. G., and B. Cooper. (1992) *Total Quality and Human Resources: An Executive Guide*. Oxford, UK: Basil Blackwell.

Dale, B. G., and J. J. Plunkett. (1986) The determination and use of quality related costs in manufacturing industry. *EOQC Quality*. (March) 3-6.

Daley, J. (1991) Mortality and other outcome data personnel. In D. R. Longo and D. Bohr (Eds.) *Quantitative Methods in Quality Management: A Guide to Practitioners*. Chicago, IL: American Hospital Association, 27-43.

Dalkey, N. (1969) *The Delphi Method: An Experimental Study of Group Opinion*. Santa Monica, CA: Rand Corporation.

Dalton, G., Paul R. Lawrence, and Jay W. Lorsch. (1970) *Organization Structure and Design*. Homewood, IL: Irwin Dorsey.

Dalton, M. (1959) *Men Who Manage.* New York: John Wiley.

The Dana style: Breaking with tradition. (1981) *Dana 1981 Annual Report*.

Dandekar, A. V. (1984) Group motivation and management: An Indian experience. *Proceedings, World Quality Congress*. Brighton, UK: World Quality Congress, 498-506.

Danforth, D. (1987) The quality imperative. *Quality Progress*. 20, (February) 17-19.

Dangerous precedent. (1984) *Virginia Weekly*. (April 4) 1.

Daniel, I. C. (1963) Factor screening in process development. *Industrial and Engineering Chemistry*. 55, (May) 5-7.

Daniel, Marquardt D. (1984) New technical and educational directions for managing product quality. *The American Statistician*. (February) 8-13.

Daniels, R. M., Jr., A. R. Dennis, G. S. Hayes, J. F. Nunamaker, Jr., and J. S. Valacich. (1991) Enterprise analyzer: Electronic support for group requirements elicitation. In *Proceedings of the Twenty-Fourth Annual Hawaii International Conference on System Sciences*. New York: IEEE Computer Society Press.

Darby, G. R. (1970) The metric system-practical implementation. *Quality Engineer*. 24, (July-August) 8-10.

The dark side of 1992. (1990) *Forbes*. (January) 85.

Darling, John R. (1992) Total quality management: The key role of leadership strategies. *Leadership and Organization Development Journal*. 13, (July) 3. (*2)

Darnell, D., and A. Lofflin. (1977) National airlines fuel management and allocation model. *Interfaces*. 7, (February) 1-16.

Das, S., A. Hendry, and S. Hong. (1980) The impact of imperfect repair on system reliability. *Proceedings, Annual Reliability and Maintainability Symposium*. New York: IEEE, 393-402.

Das, T. K. (1989) Organizational control: An evolutionary perspective. *Journal of Management Studies*. (September) 459-475. (*2)

Dass, Ram. (1971) *Remember, Now Be Here, Be Here Now*. San Cristobal, NM: Crown Publications.

Date, C. J. (1975) *An Introduction to Database Systems.* Reading, MA: Addison-Wesley.

Datsun's mobile training vehicle (1977) *Quality.* (September) 47.

Dauer, Sydney and Alice Dauer. (1956) A new approach to creative thinking and idea development. *IBM Engineering Seminar.* San Jose, CA.

Davenport, T. H. (1993) *Process Innovation: Reengineering Work Through Information Technology.* Cambridge, MA: Harvard Business School Press. (*3)

Davenport, T. H. (1994) Saving IT's soul: Human-centered information management. *Harvard Business Review.* 72, (March-April) 119-131.

Davenport, T. H., and J. E. Short. (1990) The new industrial engineering: Information technology and business process redesign. *Sloan Management Review.* 31, (Summer) 11-27. (*2)

Davenport, T. H., and D. B. Stoddard. (1994) Reengineering: Business change of mythic proportions? *MIS Quarterly.* (June) 121-127.

David, C. (1963) Factor screening in process development. *Industrial and Engineering Chemistry.* 55, (May) 5.

Davidow, William H. (1986) *Marketing High Technology-An Insider's View.* New York: Free Press.

Davidow, William H., and B. Utall. (1989) *Total Customer Service: The Ultimate Weapon.* New York: HarperCollins.

Davidson, D. (1982) The eye of the beholder. *Quality.* (April) 38-39.

Davidson, William H. (1982) Small group activity at Musashi semiconductor works. *Sloan Management Review.* 23, (Spring) 3-14. (*2)

Davidson, William H. (1988) A technology-based theory of management. In L. R. Gomez-Mejia and M. W. Lawless (Eds.) *Conference Proceedings Managing the High Technology Firm.* Boulder, CO: University of Colorado Press, 71-77.

Davidson, William H. (1993) Beyond reengineering: The three phases of business transformation. *IBM Journal.* 32, (No. 1) 65-79.

Davies, Owen L. (1954) *The Design and Analysis of Industrial Experiments.* New York: Hafner Publishing Company.

Davies, Owen L. (1957) *Design and Analysis of Industrial Experiments.* Third edition. Edinburgh: Oliver and Boyd. (*2)

Davies, Owen L. (1957) *Statistical Methods in Research and Production.* Edinburgh: Oliver and Boyd.

Davies, Owen L. (1958) *Statistical Methods in Research and Production.* New York: Hafner Publishing Company.

Davies, Owen L., and P. L. Goldsmith. (1972) *Statistical Methods in Research and Production.* Edinburgh: Oliver and Boyd.

Davies, Owen L., and W. A. Hay. (1950) Construction and use of fractional factorial designs in industrial research. *Biometrics.* 6, (April) 233.

Davis, David C. (1993) Where is total quality management today? Just when you think you understand TQM, along comes TQS. *Defense Electronics.* 24, (February) 30-37. (*3)

Davis, Gordon B. (1974) *Management Information Systems: Conceptual Foundations, Structure, and Development.* New York: McGraw-Hill.

Davis, L. E., and A. Chern. (1975) *The Quality of Working Life.* New York: Free Press. (*2)

Davis, L. E., and J. C. Taylor. (1979) *Design of Jobs.* Santa Monica, CA: Goodyear. (*2)

Davis, Neill M., and M. R. Cohen. (1981) *Medication Errors: Causes and Prevention.* Philadelphia, PA: George F. Stickley.

Davis, Stanley M. (1980) Establishing a new context for strategy, organization and executive pay. In David J. McLaughlin (Ed.) *Executive Compensation in the 1980's.* San Francisco, CA: Jossey-Bass.

Davis, Stanley M. (1984) *Managing Corporate Culture.* Cambridge, MA: Ballinger.

Davis, Stanley M. (1987) *Future Perfect.* Reading, MA: Addison-Wesley. (*3)

Davis, Vicky S. (1992) Self-audits: First step in TQM. *H R Magazine.* 37, (September) 39. (*2)

Day, Charles R., Jr. (1991) Total quality leadership: Without it, the total quality of everything else will be inferior. *Industry Week.* (October) 7.

Day, Charles R., Jr. (1992) Paradise lost can be found. *Industry Week.* (May 18) 7. (*2)

Day, Charles R., Jr. (1992) Quality: Make it a matter of policy. *Industry Week.* (January) 46.

Day, Charles R., Jr. (1993) What about blob? *Industry Week.* (January) 7. (*3)

Day, Charles R., Jr., and Perry Pascarella. (1980) Righting the productivity balance. *Industry Week.* (September 2) 55. (*2)

Day, Terian C. (1984) Strategies for setting up a commitment to excellence policy and making it work. *Management Review.* 73, (May) 16-24. (*2)

Day, Thomas C. (1988) Value-driven business = Long term success. *Total Quality Performance.* (Research Report Number 909). New York: The Conference Board, 27-29.

De Geus, Arie P. (1988) Planning as learning. *Harvard Business Review*. 66, (March-April) 70-74. (*2)

De Pree, Max. (1989) *Leadership Is an Art.* Garden City, NY: Doubleday. (*2)

De Simone, Mary Joan Orzolek. (1994) An ethnographic study of the formation of a continuous improvement facilitator's group in higher education. Unpublished Ph.D. dissertation, University of Maryland, College Park, MD.

De Simone, V. Daniel. (1971) A metric America: A decision whose time has come. *National Bureau of Standards Special Publication.* Washington, DC: (July) 345.

De Simone, V. Daniel. (1972) Moving to metric makes dollars and sense. *Harvard Business Review*. 60, (January-February) 100-111.

De Vos, George A. (1975) *Apprenticeship and Paternalism In Modern Japanese Organization and Decision Making*. Berkeley, CA: University of California Press.

Deal, Terrance E., and Allen A. Kennedy (1982) *Corporate Cultures: The Rites and Rituals of Corporate Life*. Reading, MA: Addison-Wesley. (*4)

Dean, James W., Jr. (1992) Integrated manufacturing and human resource management: A human capital perspective. *Academy of Management Journal*. 35, (August) 467. (*2)

Dean, R., and D. Prior. (1986) Your company could benefit from a no-layoff policy. *Training and Development Journal*. 40, (August) 38-41.

Dearden, John. (1972) How to make incentive plans work. *Harvard Business Review*. 50, (July-August) 117-124.

Dearden, John. (1983) Will the computer change the job of top management? *Sloan Management Review*. 24, (Fall) 57-60.

Debate rages over trade pact. (1992) *USA Today*. (August 10) B1.

DeBaun J., and A. M. Schneider. (1957) Some examples of multivariate analyses. *ASQC Annual Technical Quality Congress Transactions*. Milwaukee, WI: ASQC Quality Press, 19-26.

DeBusk, R. E. (1962) Evolutionary operation at the Tennessee Eastman Company. *Industrial Quality Control.* 19, (February) 15-21.

DeCario, N. M., and W. K. Sterett. (1990) History of the Malcolm Baldridge National Quality Award. *Quality Progress*. 23, (March) 17-18. (*2)

Dechant, K., and V. J. Marsick. (1991) In search of the learning organization: Toward a conceptual model of collective learning, Proceedings, Eastern Academy of Management, Annual Meeting, Hartford, CT. (May).

Deci, Edward L. (1972) The effects of contingent and non-contingent rewards and controls on intrinsic motivations. *Organizational Behavior and Human Performance*. 8, (June) 217-229.

Dedrick, Calvert L., and Morris H. Hansen. (1938) *Final Report on Total and Partial Unemployment: The Enumerative Check Census.* Washington, DC: U.S. Government Printing Office.

Defense Science Board. (1983) *Solving the Risk in Transitioning from Development of Production.* Cameron Station, Alexandria, VA: Department of Defense, Technical Information Center.

Delph, Thomas L. (1992) Total quality management. *Hardware Age*. 229, (July) 7. (*2)

Delta Consulting Group. (1990) *The Emerging Architecture of Organizations: Structures and Processes for the 1990's*. New York: Delta Consulting Group.

Deming, William Edwards. (1943) *Statistical Adjustment of Data.* New York: John Wiley.

Deming, William Edwards. (1946) Personal diary.

Deming, William Edwards. (1947) Personal diary.

Deming, William Edwards. (1950) *Elementary Principles in the Statistical Control of Quality, Union of Japanese Scientists and Engineers*. Tokyo: JUSE. (*2)

Deming, William Edwards. (1950) Personal diary.

Deming, William Edwards. (1950) *Some Theory of Sampling*. New York: John Wiley. (*3)

Deming, William Edwards. (1951) *The Elementary Principles of the Statistical Control of Quality, a Series of Lectures*. Tokyo: Nippon Kagaku Gijutsu Remmei. (*3)

Deming, William Edwards. (1952) Statistical techniques and international trade. *The Journal of Marketing*. 12, (October) 428-433.

Deming, William Edwards. (1953) On the distinction between enumerative and analytic surveys. *Journal of American Statistical Association*. 48, 244-255. (*2)

Deming, William Edwards. (1956) On some statistical aids toward economic production. In Harry Ivan Costin (Ed.) *Readings in Total Quality Management*. (1994) Fort Worth, TX: Dryden Press, 93-111.

Deming, William Edwards. (1956) On the use of theory. *Industrial Quality Control*. 8, (July) 12-14. (*3)

Deming, William Edwards. (1960) *Sample Design in Business Research*. New York: John Wiley. (*2)

Deming, William Edwards. (1965) Personal diary.

Deming, William Edwards. (1966) *Some Theory of Sampling*. New York: Dover. (*2)

Deming, William Edwards. (1972) Report to management. *Quality Progress*. 5, (July) 2.

Deming, William Edwards. (1975) On probability as a basis for action. *The American Statistician*. 29 (April) 146-152.

Deming, William Edwards. (1975) On some statistical aids towards economic production. *Interfaces*. 5, (August) 1-15. (*3)

Deming, William Edwards. (1977) Quality and productivity. *Quality Progress*. 10, (November) 21.

Deming, William Edwards. (1980) It does work. From section "Product quality USA: Quality—A management gambit." *Quality*. (August) Q26-31.

Deming, William Edwards. (1980) The statistical control of quality, Part II. *Quality*. (March) 34-36. (*2)

Deming, William Edwards. (1981-82) Improvement of quality and productivity through action by management. *National Productivity Review*. 1, (Winter) 12-22. (*5)

Deming, William Edwards. (1982) *Quality, Productivity and Competitive Position*. Cambridge: MIT Press. (*10)

Deming, William Edwards. (1985) Transformation of western style of management. *Interfaces*. 15, (March) 6-11.

Deming, William Edwards. (1986) *A Day with Dr. Deming*. Washington, DC: Office of Naval Operations, Total Quality Leadership.

Deming, William Edwards. (1986) *Out of the Crisis*. Cambridge, MA: MIT, Center for Advanced Engineering Study. (*22)

Deming, William Edwards. (1987) New principles of leadership. *Modern Materials Handling*. (October) 37. (*3)

Deming, William Edwards. (1989) Foundation for management of quality in the Western world. Paper delivered at a meeting of the Institute of Management Science in Osaka, Japan, (July 24). This paper was updated September 1, 1990.

Deming, William Edwards. (1993) *The New Economics for Industry, Government, Education*. Cambridge, MA: MIT, Center for Advanced Engineering Study. (*5)

Deming, William Edwards. (1994) *The New Economics for Industry, Government, Education*. Second edition. Cambridge, MA: MIT, Center for Advanced Engineering Study.

Deming, William Edwards and L. Geoffry. (1941) On sample inspection in the processing of census. *Journal of the American Statistical Association*. 36, (September) 17-18.

Deming's demons: The management guru thinks U.S. corporations are crushing their worker incentive. (1990) *Wall Street Journal*. (June) R39. (*2)

Demonet, Gene. (1986) Flexible manufacturing systems for super-alloy jet engine parts. SME/FMS Conference Presentation. Chicago, IL.

Demos, M. P. (1989) SQC's role in health care management. *Quality Progress*. 22, (August) 85-89.

DeMott, Joann. (1992) Integrating TQM into daily worklife. In Harry Ivan Costin (Ed.) *Readings in Total Quality Management*. (1994) Fort Worth, TX: Dryden Press, 333-340.

Denissoff, Basile A. (1980) Process control management. *Quality Process*. (June) 14-16.

Denker, S. P. (1984) Justifying your investment in automatic visual PCB testing. *Circuits Manufacturing*. (October) 56, 58, 60, 62.

Dennis, A. R., R. M. Daniels Jr., and J. F. Nunamaker Jr. (1993) Automated support for business process reengineering: A case study at IBM. In *Proceedings of the Twenty-Sixth Annual Hawaii International Conference on System Sciences*. Los Alamitos, CA: IEEE Computer Society Press.

Dennis, A. R., R. M. Daniels Jr., G. Hayes, and J. F. Nunamaker Jr. (1994) Methodology-driven use of automated support in business process reengineering. *Journal of Management Information Systems*. 10, (No. 3) 117-138.

Dennis, Pascal. (1997) *Quality, Safety, and Environment: Synergy in the 21st Century*. Milwaukee, WI: ASQC Press.

Dennison, E. F. (1972) The measurement of productivity. *The Survey of Current Business*. 52, (May) 1-111.

Dennison, E. F. (1979) *Accounting for Slower Economic Growth: The United States in the 1970's*. Washington, DC: Brookings Institution.

Denton, Keith D. (1991) Horizontal management. *SAM Advanced Management Journal*. 56, (Winter) 35-41.

Department of Defense. (1977) *Reliability Design Qualification and Production Acceptance*. Washington, DC: Defense Document Distribution Center. (August) 116.

Department of Trade and Industry. (1983) *Directory of Quality Training and Education in the U.K.* London, UK: DTI.

DePree, Max. (1987) *Leadership Is an Art*. East Lansing, MI: Michigan State University Press.

DePree, Max. (1989) *Leadership is an Art*. New York: Dell. (*2)

Derrick, Frederick, Harsha Desai, and William O'Brien. (1989) Survey shows employees at different organizational levels define quality differently. *Industrial Engineering*. 21, (April) 22-26.

Dertouzos, Michael L., Richard K. Lester, and Robert M. Solow. (1989) *Made in America: Regaining the Competitive Edge*. Cambridge, MA: MIT Press. (*7)

Dervitsiotis, K. N. (1981) *Operations Management*. New York: McGraw-Hill.

The design and introduction of the new information technologies into work organizations. *Journal of Occupational Psychology*. 59, (Fall) 287-314.

DesPias, Edward P. (1986) Reliability in the manufacturing cycle. *Proceedings Annual Reliability and Maintainability Symposium*. New York: IEEE, 139-144. (*2)

Dess, G. D., and D. W. Beard. (1984) Dimensions of organizational task environments. *Administrative Science Quarterly*. 29, (November) 52-73.

Detouzous, M., Richard K. Lester, and Robert M. Solow. (1990) *Made in America: Regaining the Productive Edge*. Cambridge, MA: MIT Press, The MIT Commission on Industrial Productivity.

Deutsch, Claudia H. (1989) The powerful push for self-service. *New York Times*. (April 9) section 3, 1, 15.

Devanna, Mary Anne, Charles J. Fombrun, and Noel M. Tichy. (1981) Human resource management: A strategic approach. *Organizational Dynamics*. 9, (Winter) 51-67.

Devanna, Mary Anne, Charles J. Fombrun, and Noel M. Tichy. (1984) A framework for strategic human resource management. In Charles J. Fombrun, Noel M. Tichy, and Mary Anne Devanna (Eds.) *Strategic Human Resource Management*. New York: John Wiley.

Developing managers not a corporate priority. (1988) *Wall Street Journal*. (April) 1.

Developments in industrial relation. (1986) *Monthly Labor Review*. (June) 21-22. (*2)

Dewar, Donald L. (1976) Measurement of results-Lockheed QC circles. *ASQC Annual Technical Quality Congress Transactions*. Milwaukee, WI: ASQC Quality Press, 40-47.

Dewar, Donald L. (1980) Implementing quality circles in your organization. IAQC Second Annual Conference Transactions. Cincinnati, OH: International Association of Quality Circles.

Dewar, Donald L. (1980) *The Quality Circle Guide to Participative Management*. Englewood Cliffs, NJ: Prentice-Hall. (*2)

Dewar, Donald L. (1980) *The Quality Circle Handbook.* Red Bluff, CA: Quality Circle Institute.

Dewar, Donald L. (1981) If Japan can—We can too. IAQC Third Annual Conference Transactions. Cincinnati, OH: International Association of Quality Circles.

Dewitt, F. (1970) A technique for measuring management productivity. *Management Review.* 59, (June) 2-11.

DeYoung, H. Garrett. (1989) Preachings of quality gurus: Do it right the first time. *Electronic Business.* 15, (October 16) 88-94. (*3)

Di Georgio, Brent S. (1981) Management and labor cooperate to increase productivity. *Supervision.* 43, (January) 5-7.

Diamond, W. (1981) *Practical Experimental Designs.* Belmont, CA: Wadsworth. (*2)

Dickie, G. (1971) *Aesthetics: An Introduction.* New York: Bobbs-Merrill.

Dickinson, Roger, Anthony Herbst, and John O'Shaughnessy. (1983) What are business schools doing for business. *Business Horizons.* 26, (November-December) 31-34.

Dickson, John. (1977) Plight of middle management. *Management Today.* (December) 16-18.

Dickson, W. (1966) An analysis of vendor selection systems and decisions. *Journal of Purchasing.* (August) 210.

Diebold Group. (1977) *Automatic Data Processing Handbook.* New York: McGraw-Hill.

Diebold, John. (1990) *The Innovators: The Discoveries, Inventions, and Breakthroughs of Our Time.* New York: Truman Talley Books/E. P. Dutton.

Dielman, Terry E., and Roger C. Pfaffenberger. (1984) Computational logarithms for calculating least absolute value and Chebyshev estimates for multiple regression. *American Journal of Mathematical and Management Sciences*. 4, (February) 169-197.

Diesch, K. H., and E. M. Malstrom. (1984) Physical modeling of flexible manufacturing systems. IIIE Fall Conference Presentation.

Diez, Roy L. (1992) Three reasons you can't afford to ignore quality revolution. *Professional Builder and Remodeler*. 57, (November) 9. (*2)

The difficult task of changing corporate culture: The case of Corning Glass. (1983) *Wall Street Journal*. (April 22) 1.

Diggins, J. P. (1988) *The Proud Decades: America in War and Peace, 1941-1960*. New York: W. W. Norton.

Diggs, E. J. (1979) Why have outgoing quality audits? *ASQC Annual Technical Quality Congress Transactions*. Milwaukee, WI: ASQC Quality Press, 506-512.

Digital believes. (1981) *Digital Equipment Corporation Annual Report 1981*. 12.

Dikov, D. (1977) Experience gained by the quality centers in Bulgaria. Proceedings, ETC Seminar. Odessa, TX: ETC. (*2)

Dillion, F. (1980) Inbound routing guides make sense. *Save Dollars Purchasing*. 89, (October) 67-70.

Dillon, Linda S. (1983) Adopting Japanese management: Some cultural stumbling blocks. *Personnel*. 60, (July) 73-77.

Dilworth, James B. (1984) *Production and Operations Management*. St. Paul, MN: West Publishing.

Dilworth, James B. (1989) *Production and Operations Management: Manufacturing and Nonmanufacturing*. New York: Random House.

Dingus, V. (1993) The strategy for achieving quality of management. Presentation at Eastman Chemicals/University of Tennessee Continuous Improvement Workshop. (August 10).

Dinosaurs: IBM, Sears, GM. (1993) *Fortune*. (May 3) 36-42.

Directory of software for quality assurance and quality control. (1984) *Quality Progress*. 17, (March) 33-53.

Directory of software for quality assurance and quality control. (1985) *Quality Progress*. 18, (March) 36-63.

Directory of software for quality assurance and quality control. (1986) *Quality Progress*. 19, (March) 37-79.

Directory of software for quality assurance and quality control. (1987) *Quality Progress*. 20, (March) 33-66.

Dirsmith, M., and S. Jablonsky. (1979) Zero-based budgeting as a management technique and political strategy. *Academy of Management Review*. (April), 555-565.

Dixon, Wilfred. J. (1983) *BMDP Statistical Software*. Berkeley, CA: University of California Press.

Dixon, Wilfred J., and Frank J. Massey Jr. (1957) *Introduction to Statistical Analysis*. New York: McGraw-Hill. (*3)

Dobbins, Gregory, Robert L. Cardy, and K. Carson. (1991) Examining fundamental assumptions: A contrast of person and system approaches to human resource management. *Research in Personnel and Human Resources Management*, 1-38.

Dobbins, Lloyd. (1990) Ed Deming wants big changes and he wants them fast. *Smithsonian*. (August) 74-83. (*4)

Dobbins, Lloyd and Clare Crawford-Mason. (1991) *Quality or Else: The Revolution in World Business*. Boston, MA: Houghton Mifflin. (*3)

Dobbins, Richard K. (1977) A dollars and cents approach to failure analysis. *ASQC Annual Technical Quality Congress Transactions.* Milwaukee, WI: ASQC Quality Press, 230-235.

Dobbins, Richard K. (1978) Quality cost and profit performance. *ASQC Annual Technical Quality Congress Transactions*. Milwaukee, WI: ASQC Quality Press, 201-206.

Dobbins, Richard K. (1980) Designing an effective procurement rating system. *ASQC Annual Technical Quality Congress Transactions.* Milwaukee, WI: ASQC Quality Press, 488-494.

Dobbins, Richard K. (1981) Your quality posture-A profit/survival challenge. *ASQC Annual Technical Quality Congress Transactions.* Milwaukee, WI: ASQC Quality Press, 485-490.

Dobler, D. W., L. Lee Jr., and D. N. Burt. (1984) *Purchasing and Materials Management: Text and Cases*. New York: McGraw-Hill.

Dodd, G. G., and L. Rossol. (1979) *Computer Vision and Sensor-Based Robots.* New York: Plenum.

Dodds, L. B. (1967) Workmanship. *ASQC Annual Technical Quality Congress Transactions*. Milwaukee, WI: ASQC Quality Press. 249-252.

Dodge, Harold F. (1928) A method of rating manufactured product. *Bell Telephone Laboratories*. (May) B-315 (*2)

Dodge, Harold F. (1932) Statistical control on sampling inspection. *American Machinist.* (October) 1085-1088.

Dodge, Harold F. (1943) A sampling plan for continuous production. *Annals of Mathematical Statistics.* 264-279.

Dodge, Harold F. (1950) Inspection for quality assurance. *Industrial Quality Control.* 6, (June) 8.

Dodge, Harold F. (1955) Chain sampling inspection plan. *Industrial Quality Control.* 12, (February) 10-13. (*2)

Dodge, Harold F. (1955) Skip-lot sampling plan. *Industrial Quality Control.* 11, (March) 3-5.

Dodge, Harold F. (1956) Skip-lot sampling plans. *Industrial Quality Control.* 12, (May) 3-5.

Dodge, Harold F. (1969) Notes on the evolution of acceptance sampling plans, Part II. *Journal of Quality Technology.* 1, (July) 155-156.

Dodge, Harold F. (1969) Notes on the evolution of acceptance sampling plans, Part I. *Journal of Quality Technology.* 1, (April) 77.

Dodge, Harold F. (1970) Notes on the evolution of acceptance sampling plans, Part V. *Journal of Quality Technology.* 2, (January) 1-8.

Dodge, Harold F., B. J. Kinsburg, and M. K. Kruger. (1953) The L3 coaxial system-quality control requirements. *Bell System Technical Journal.* 32, (January) 943-1005.

Dodge, Harold F., and R. L. Perry. (1971) A system of skip-lot plans for lot-by inspection. *ASQC Annual Technical Quality Congress Transactions.* Milwaukee, WI: ASQC Quality Press, 469-477.

Dodge, Harold F., and G. Romig. (1959) *Sampling Inspection Tables-Single Sampling and Double Sampling.* Second edition. New York: John Wiley. (*2)

Dodge, Harold F., and Kenneth S. Stephens. (1965) Some new chain sampling inspection plans. *ASQC Annual Technical Quality Congress Transactions.* Milwaukee, WI: ASQC Quality Press, 8-17.

Dodge, Harold F., and Kenneth S. Stephens. (1966) Some new chain sampling inspection plans. *Industrial Quality Control.* 12, (August) 61-67. (*2)

Dodge, Harold F., and Mary N. Torrey. (1951) Additional continuous sampling plans. *Industrial Quality Control.* 7, (March) 7-12.

Dodge, Harold F., and Mary N. Torrey. (1956) A check inspection and demerit rating plan. *Industrial Quality Control.* 13, (July) 5-12.

Dodson, Robert L. (1991) Speeding the way to total quality. *Training and Development Journal.* 45, (June) 35-42.

Doi, Takeo. (1973) *The Anatomy of Dependence.* Tokyo: Kodansha International. (*2)

Dome, Ellen R. (1993) Statistical process control: Sophisticated but simple. In Harry Ivan Costin (Ed.) *Readings in Total Quality Management.* (1994) Fort Worth, TX: Dryden Press, 277-283.

Dome, Ellen R., Robert C. Culver, and Richard H. Rawcliffe. (1994) Organizational impact of introducing concurrent engineering. In Harry Ivan Costin (Ed.) *Readings in Total Quality Management.* (1994) Fort Worth, TX: Dryden Press, 351-359.

Donabedian, A. (1980) *Explorations in Quality Assessment and Monitoring.* Volume 1: The definition of quality and approaches to its assessment. Ann Arbor, MI: Health Administration Press.

Donabedian, A. (1982) *Explorations in Quality Assessment and Monitoring.* Volume 2, The Criteria and Standards of Quality. Ann Arbor, MI: Health Administration Press.

Donahue, Thomas. (1982) Labor looks at quality of work life programs. *Journal of Contemporary Business.*

Donaldson, G., and Jay W. Lorsch. (1983) *Decision Making at the Top.* New York: Basic Books.

Donis, Peter. (1988) The genesis of annual quality improvement at Caterpillar. Speech, Juran Institute Conference, Chicago, IL.

Donnelly. James H. Jr. J. L. Gibson, and J. M. Ivancevich. (1984) *Fundamentals of Management.* Plano, TX: BPI.

Donovan, J. J. (1970) *Systems Programming.* New York: McGraw-Hill.

Donovan, J. Michael. (1979) A roadmap for solving problems in quality circles. *Quality Circles Journal.* 2, (Fourth Quarter) 16-18.

Donovan, J. Michael. (1979) Quality circles-Goldmine or fad? Skillful management of the program can make the difference. IAQC 1st Annual Conference Transactions. Cincinnati, OH: International Association of Quality Circles.

Donovan, J. Michael. (1979) Quality circles help school through financial crises. *Quality Circles Journal.* 2, (Third Quarter) 14-17.

Donovan, J. Michael. (1980) Skillful management of the program can make the difference. IAQC Second Annual Conference Transactions. Cincinnati, OH: International Association of Quality Circles.

Donovan, J. Michael. (1981) Building management support for quality circle programs. IAQC Third Annual Conference Transactions. Cincinnati, OH: International Association of Quality Circles.

Donovan, J. Michael. (1981) New tools for problem solving in quality circles. IAQC Third Annual Conference Transactions. Cincinnati, OH: International Association of Quality Circles.

Donovan, J. Michael. (1986) Self-managing work teams—Extending the quality circle concept. *Quality Circles Journal.* 9, (September) 15-20.

Donovan, J. Michael. (1988) The future of excellence and quality. *Journal for Quality and Participation.* (March) 22-24.

Donovan, J. Michael and Wingate Sikes. (1978) QC circles: An explosive formula for cutting costs. *Quality Circles Journal.* 1, (Fourth Quarter) 19-22.

Don't blame the system, blame the managers. (1980) *Dun's Review.* (September) 88.

Doody, Alton F., and Ron Bingaman. (1988) *Reinventing the Wheels: Ford's Spectacular Comeback.* Cambridge, MA: Ballinger.

Dooher, J. M. (1952) *The Development of Executive Talent: A Handbook of Management Development.* New York: American Management Association.

Doom, I. F. (1969) *Total Cost Purchasing Applied to Heavy Equipment Procurement.* Charlottesville: Virginia Highway Research Council.

Doran, P. K. (1985) A total quality improvement program. *International Journal of Quality and Reliability Management.* 18-36.

Dore, Ronald. (1958) *City Life in Japan: A Study of Tokyo Ward.* Berkeley, CA: University of California Press.

Dore, Ronald. (1973) *British Factory-Japanese Factory: The Origins of National Diversity in Industrial Relations.* London, UK: Alden and Mowbray.

Doren, P. K. (1986) A total quality improvement program. *Management Decision (UK).* 24, (June) 54-63.

Dorgan, William J., III. (1992) TQM. *Modern Machine Shop.* 65, (July) 108. (*2)

Dorin, R. (1981) *Quality of Working Life.* Ottawa, Canada: Quality of Working Life Unit, Labor Canada.

Dornheim, Michael A. (1992) NASA hopes to slash contract costs 5-10% by using TQM in procurement. *Aviation Week and Space Technology.* 137, (August) 22. (*2)

Dorsky, L. R. (1984) Management commitment to Japanese apple pie. *Quality Progress.* 17, (February) 11-12.

Doty Alan L. (1982) Far east sourcing. *ASQC Annual Technical Quality Congress Transactions.* Milwaukee, WI: ASQC Quality Press, 217-224.

Douglas, R. D. (1983) Now what do we do? *The Juran Report.* (November) 100-105.

Dove, W. F. (1947) Food acceptability-its determination and evaluation. *Food Technology*. 1, 39.

Dow Corning employees falsified data on breast implants, counsel concludes. (1992) *Wall Street Journal*. (November 3) A3.

Dowd, R. (1991) Help for would-be exporters. *Fortune*. (April 8) 13.

Dowdy, S. M., and S. Wearden (1983) *Statistics for Research*. New York: John Wiley.

Dower, John. (1979) *Empire and Aftermath: Yoshida Sigeru and the Japanese Experience, 1878-1954*. Cambridge, MA: Harvard University Press.

Dowling, P. J., and R. S. Schuler. (1990) *International Dimensions of Human Resource Management*. Boston, MA: PWS-Kent, 685-698.

Dowling, William F. (1979) At GM: System 4 builds performance and profits. *Organizational Dynamics*. 7, (Summer) 61-80.

Dowling, William F., and Edward Carlson. (1979) Conversation with Edward Carlson. *Organizational Dynamics*. 2, (Spring) 58. (*2)

Dowling, William F., and Fletcher Byrom. (1978) Conversation with Fletcher Byrom. *Organizational Dynamics*. 1, (Summer) 44. (*2)

Downer, Winston C. (1983) Management's commitment to QA includes ESD control. *ASQC Annual Technical Quality Congress Transactions*. Milwaukee. WI: ASQC Quality Press, 76-81.

Downs, Anthony. (1967) *Inside Bureaucracy*. Boston, MA: Little, Brown.

Dowst, S. (1976) Stormy economy brings payoff for management. *Systems Purchasing*. 8, (February) 59-61.

Doyle, A. C. (1976) *The Illustrated Sherlock Holmes Treasury*. New York: Crown.

Doyle, R. J. (1983) *Gainsharing and Productivity*. New York: AMACOM.

Drake, Bob. (1992) Total quality management opens doors to profit. *Pit and Quarry*. 84, (May) 18. (*2)

Draper, Norman R., and William G. Hunter. (1967) Transformations, some examples revisited. *Technometrics*. 10, (November) 23.

Draper, Norman R., and David N. Stoneman. (1964) Estimating missing values in unreplicated two-level factorial and fractional factorial designs. *Biometrics*. 20, (March) 443-458.

Dreamers, heretics, gadflies. (1980) *Newsweek*. (August) 6.

Dreager, J. (1989) *Function Point Analysis*. Englewood Cliffs, NJ: Prentice-Hall.

Dreyfus, Joel. (1988) Catching the computer wave. *Fortune*. (September 26) 78-82.

Dreyfus, Joel. (1988) Victories in the quality crusade. *Fortune*. (October 10) 80-88.

Dreyfus, Joel. (1989) Shaping up your suppliers. *Fortune*. (April 10) 116-122.

Dreyfus, Joel. (1990) Get ready for the new work force. *Fortune*. (April 23) 165-81. (*2)

Driscoll, J. W., D. J. Carroll, and T. A. Sprecher. (1978) The first-level supervisor: Still 'the man in the middle'. *Sloan Management Review*. 19, (Winter) 25-37.

Drucker, Peter F. (1950) *The New Society*. New York: Harper and Row.

Drucker, Peter F. (1954) *The Practice of Management*. New York: Harper and Row. (*3)

Drucker, Peter F. (1964) *Managing for Results*. New York: Harper and Row. (*2)

Drucker, Peter F. (1969) *The Age of Discontinuity: Guidelines to Our Changing Society*. New York: Harper and Row. (*3)

Drucker, Peter F. (1974) *Management: Tasks, Responsibilities, Practices*. New York: Harper and Row. (*8)

Drucker, Peter F. (1979) *Adventures of a Bystander*. New York: Harper and Row. (*3)

Drucker, Peter F. (1980) *Managing in Turbulent Times*. London, UK: Pan Books. (*3)

Drucker, Peter F. (1981) Behind Japan's success. *Harvard Business Review*. 59, (January-February) 83-90.

Drucker, Peter F. (1983) *Concept of the Corporation*. Second revised edition. New York: New American Library. (*3)

Drucker, Peter F. (1983) Twilight of the first-line supervisor? *Wall Street Journal*. (June 7) 1. (*2)

Drucker, Peter F. (1985) *Innovation and Entrepreneurship: Practice and Principles*. New York: Harper and Row. (*2)

Drucker, Peter F. (1986) *The Frontiers of Management*. New York: Truman Talley Books/E. P. Dutton. (*3)

Drucker, Peter F. (1986) *Managing for Results: Economic Tasks and Risk-Taking Decisions*. New York: Harper and Row.

Drucker, Peter F. (1988) The coming of the new organization. *Harvard Business Review*. 66, (January-February) 45-53. (*2)

Drucker, Peter F. (1988) Leadership: More doing than dash. *Wall Street Journal*. (January 6) 14.

Drucker, Peter F. (1988) Worker's hands bound by tradition. *Wall Street Journal*. (August) 1, 4.

Drucker, Peter F. (1989) *The New Realities: In Government and Politics/ In Economics and Business/ In Society and World View.* New York: Harper and Row. (*6)

Drucker, Peter F. (1990) The emerging theory of manufacturing. *Harvard Business Review.* 78, (May-June) 94-102. (*4)

Drucker, Peter F. (1990) *Managing the Non-Profit Organization: Practices and Principles.* New York: HarperCollins.

Drucker, Peter F. (1991) Buyer's guide to new CMMS. *Quality in Manufacturing.* (January-February) 15-18.

Drucker, Peter F. (1992) *Managing the Future: The 1990s and Beyond.* New York: HarperCollins. (*2)

Drucker, Peter F. (1992) The new society of organizations. *Harvard Business Review.* 70, (September-October) 95-104.

Drucker, Peter F. (1993) *Post-Capitalist Society.* New York: HarperCollins.

Drucker, Peter F. (1993) We need to measure, not count. *Wall Street Journal.* (Eastern Edition). (April) A18. (*2)

Drucker, Peter F. (1996) *The Executive in Action.* New York: HarperCollins.

Drummond, Helga and Elizabeth Chell. (1992) Should organizations pay for quality? *Personnel Review.* 21, (Fall) 3. (*2)

Dryfuss, Joel. (1989) Reinventing IBM. *Fortune.* (August 14) 30-39.

Dubois, Didier. (1983) Mathematical model of an FMS with limited in-process inventory. *European Journal of Operational Research.* 3, (No. 4) 61-84.

Dubois, Pierre. (1983) Quality circles: A valuable tool for effective management. *Canadian Banker and ICB Review.* 90, (April) 38-43.

Dubos, R. (1960) *Louis Pasteur: Free Lance of The Sciences*. New York: De Capo Press. (*2)

Duckworth, W. E. (1965) Statistical method in metallurgical development. *The Statistician*. 15, 7-30.

Dudewicz, Edward J. (1976) *Introduction to Statistics and Probability*. New York: Rinehart and Winston.

Duffy, D. (1994) Managing the white space (cross functional processes). *Management*. (April) 35-36.

Duhan, Stanley and John C. Catlin, Sr. (1973) Total life cost and the ileitis. *Proceedings, Annual Reliability and Maintainability Symposium*. New York: IEEE, 491-495

Dumaine, Brian. (1987) The new art of hiring smart, *Fortune*. (August 17) 78-81.

Dumaine, Brian. (1990) Who needs a boss? *Fortune*. (May 7) 52-55, 58, 60. (*3)

Dumaine, Brian. (1992) How to win quality war with Japan. *Fortune*. 126, (July 27) 162.

Dumas, Ronald A., Nancy Cushing, and Carol Laughlin. (1987) Making quality control theories workable. *Training and Development Journal*. 41, (February) 30-33.

Duncan, Acheson J. (1962) Bulk sampling problems and lines of attack. *Technometrics*. 5, (August) 319-344.

Duncan, Acheson J. (1965) *Quality Control and Industrial Statistics*. Homewood, IL: Irwin. (*5)

Duncan, Acheson J. (1965) The use of ranges in comparing variabilities. *Industrial Quality Control*. 11, (February) 31-33.

Duncan, Acheson J. (1974) *Quality Control and Industrial Statistics*. Homewood, IL: Irwin. (*2)

Duncan, D. B. (1955) Multiple range and multiple F tests. *Biometrics*. 11, (January) 1.

Duncan, J. (1986) Businessmen are good sales forecasters. *Dun's Review*. (July) 7.

Duncan, Jack W., and Joseph G. Van Matre. (1990) The gospel according to Deming: Is it really new? *Business Horizons*. 33, (July-August) 3-10. (*3)

Duncan, William L. (1988) *Just-in-Time in American Manufacturing*. Dearborn, MI: Society of Manufacturing Engineers.

Dunlap, Craig. (1992) Quality training dominates talk at International Trade Conference. *Journal of Commerce and Commercial*. 392, (May 21) 4A. (*2)

Dunlop, John T., and P. Vasilii. (1964) *Diatchenko, Labor Productivity*. New York: McGraw-Hill.

Dunn, D. S. (1966) Quality control for profit improvement in the specialty steel industry. *ASQC Annual Technical Quality Congress Transactions*. Milwaukee, WI: ASQC Quality Press, 152-155.

Dunn, Peter. (1985) FMS simulation-yet another system. *FMS Magazine*. 3, (February) 198-200.

Dunn, Peter. (1993) Sematech's quality management sparks a big response. *Electronic News*. 39, (February 8) 11. (*2)

Dunn, R., and R. Ullman. (1982) *Quality Assurance for Computer Software*. New York: McGraw-Hill.

Durand, David. (1971) *Stable Chaos*. Chicago, IL: General Learning Press.

Durant, Will. (1954) *Our Oriental Heritage*. New York: Simon and Schuster.

Durant, Will and Ariel Durant. (1968) *The Lessons of History*. New York: Simon and Schuster. (*2)

Dushman, Allan. (1970) Effect of reliability on life cycle inventory cost. *Proceedings, Annual Reliability and Maintainability Symposium.* New York: IEEE, 549-561

Dussault, Heather B. (1984) Automated FMEA-status and future. *Proceedings, Annual Reliability and Maintainability Symposium.* New York: IEEE, 1-5.

Dutton, Barbara. (1990) Switching to quality excellence. *Manufacturing Systems.* (March) 51-53.

Dwyer, P., and D. Griffiths. (1988) How the pentagon can go to war against abuse. *BusinessWeek.* (July 4) 34. (*2)

Dyer, W. G. (1987) *Team Building.* Second edition. Reading, MA: Addison-Wesley.

Dyke, R. M. (1967) *Numerical Control.* Englewood Cliffs, NJ: Prentice-Hall.

Dymtrow, Eric D. (1985) Quality improvement in information processing. *The Juran Report.* (Winter) 134-139.

Dziezak, J. D. (1987) Quality assurance through commercial laboratories and consultants. *Food Technology.* 41, (December) 110.

D'Agostino, R. B., A. Belanger, and R. B. D'Agostino Jr. (1990) A suggestion for using powerful and informative tests of normality. *The American Statistician.* 44, (April) 316.

Eagle, Alan R. (1954) A method for handling errors in testing and measuring. *Industrial Quality Control.* 10, (March) 10-15.

Ealey, Lance A. (1987) QFD-bad name for a great system. *Automotive Industries.* (July) 21.

Ealey, Lance A. (1988) *Quality by Design: Taguchi Methods and U.S. Industry.* Dearborn, MI: ASI Press. (*3)

Ealey, Lance A. (1988) Taguchi basics. *Quality Progress.* 21, (November) 30-32. (*2)

Earl, M., and B. Khan. (1994) How new is business process redesign? *European Management Journal.* 12, (No. 1) 20-30.

Early, Pete. (1988) *Family of Spies.* New York: Bantam Books.

Early, S., and R. Wilson. (1986) Do unions have a future in high technology. *Technology Review.* (October) 57-65.

Earnhart, G. L. (1983) *Statistical Control of Suspension Bushing Assembly.* Warrendale, PA: Society of Automotive Engineers. SAE Paper 830300 75-79. (*2)

Eastman Chemical to start new era. (1993) *Knoxville News-Sentinel.* (December 5) D1.

Eastman Kodak Company. (1983) *Ergonomic Designs for People at Work.* Belmont, CA: Lifetime Learning Publications.

Eastman Quality Policy. (1993) Kingsport, TN: Eastman Chemicals Company.

Ebenfelt, Hans and Stig Ogren. (1974) Some experiences from the use of an LCC. approach. *Proceedings, Annual Reliability and Maintainability Symposium.* New York: IEEE, 142-146.

Ebert, Ronald J., and Terence R. Mitchell. (1975) *Organizational Decision Processes: Concepts and Analysis.* New York: Crane, Russak and Company.

Ebrahimpour, M., and R. J. Schonberger. (1984) The Japanese just-in-time/total quality control production system: Potential for developing countries. *International Journal of Production Research.* (May-June) 21-24.

Eccles, J. (1986) Interdependence in a highly complex organization. A report submitted in partial fulfillment for the requirements for the degree of Master of Business Administration. Graduate School of Business Administration, University of California, Berkeley.

Eccles, Robert G. (1991) The performance measurement manifesto. *Harvard Business Review.* 79, (January-February) 131-137. (*2)

Echols, D., and R. Mitchell. (1990) Champion or victim? The supervisor's new role in a team-based work system. Paper presented at Seventh Annual Fall Forum, Association for Quality and Participation, Denver, CO, October.

Eden, Colin. (1975) *Management Decision and Decision Analysis.* New York: John Wiley.

Edgerton, Russ. (1993) The new public mood and what it means to higher education. *AAHE Bulletin.* 45, (June) 27-28. (*3)

Edwards, David. (1991) Total quality management in higher education. *Management Services.* 35, (Issue 12, December) 18-20.

Edwards, S. A., and M. W. McCarrey. (1973) Measuring performance of researchers. *Research Management.* 16, (January) 34-41.

Egermayer, F. (1976) Education and training program for QC. Proceedings, 20th EOQC Conference, Copenhagen: European Organization for Quality Control (EOQC) (*2)

Egermayer, F. (1978) Quality information system in integrated quality control. *Quality and Reliability.* 24, (August) 127. (*2)

Egermayer, F. (1979) Estimation of economic effect of quality control system. Proceedings, Twenty-Third EOQC Conference. 5, 133. (*2)

Egermayer, F. (1983) *Quality Control in Mechanical Engineering Works.* Prague: University Press. (*2)

Eglo, Len. (1990) Save dollars on maintenance management. *Chemical Engineering.* 97, (June) 157-162.

Ehrenfeld, S. (1972) On group sequential sampling. *Technometrics.* 14, (September) 167-174.

Eidt, Clarence M., Jr. (1992) Applying quality to RandD means 'learn-as-you-go.' *Research-Technology Management*. 35, (July-August) 24. (*2)

Eienhart C. (1968) Expression of the uncertainties of final results. *Science*. 14, (June) 1201-1204.

Eight big masters of innovation. (1984) *Fortune*. (October 15) 21-26.

Eiler, Robert G. (1990) A challenge to the financial function. *Ohio CPS Journal*. 49, (Autumn) 38.

Eiler, Robert G. (1990) Managing complexity. *Ohio CPS Journal*. 49, (Spring) 45-47.

Eilon, S., B. Gold, and J. Soesan. (1974) *Applied Productivity Analysis for Industry*. New York: Pergamon Press.

Eisenberg, Abne. (1978) *Understanding Communication in Business and the Professions*. New York: Macmillan.

Eisenhardt, K. M. (1985) Control: Organizational and economic approaches. *Management Science*. 31, (January) 12-149.

Eisenhardt, K. M. (1988) Making fast strategic decisions. *Academy of Management Journal*. 31, (July) 111-124.

Eisenhardt, K. M. (1990) Speed and strategic choice: How managers accelerate decision making. *California Management Review*. 32, (Spring) 39-54. (*2)

Eisenhardt, K. M., and L. J. Bourgeois. (1988) The politics of strategic decision making in high velocity environments: Toward a mid-range theory. *Academy of Management Journal*. 31, (September) 737-770.

Eisenhardt, K. M., and L. J. Bourgeois. (1989) Top management teams in high velocity environments. In Mary Ann Von Glinow and Susan Albers Mohrman (Eds.) *Managing Complexity in High Technology Industries: Systems and People*. New York: Oxford University Press.

Eisenhart, Churchill. (1969) Realistic evaluation of the precision and accuracy of instrument calibration systems. In Harry H. Ku. *Precision Measurement and Calibration.* (Volume 1) Washington, DC: National Bureau of Standards Special Publication 300.

Eisenhart, Tom. (1990) Total quality is the key to U.S. competitiveness. *Business Marketing.* 75, (June) 30.

Ekings J. Douglas. (1976) Profit and customer satisfaction equals the specification for commercial reliability programs. *Proceedings, Annual Reliability and Maintainability Symposium.* New York: IEEE.

Ekings, J. Douglas. (1986) A nine-step quality improvement process to improve customer satisfaction Transactions of the 30th European Organization for Quality Control, Stockholm. (June) 323-328.

Ekings, J. Douglas and Robert L. Sweetland. (1978) Burn-in forever? There must be a better way. *Proceedings, Annual Reliability and Maintainability Symposium.* New York: IEEE, 286-293.

Ekings, J. Douglas, and T. D. Hill. (1982) MTBF requirements: Nice or competitive. *Reliability Review.* 7, (April) 51-52.

Ekstein, Henry C. (1989) Better materials control with inventory cardiograms. *Small Business Reports.* 14, (August) 50-53.

El Gabry, A. A. (1972) Interrelation of quality characteristics. *ASQC Annual Technical Quality Congress Transactions.* Milwaukee, WI: ASQC Quality Press, 422-428.

Eldridge, L. A., and C. A. Aubrey, Il. Stressing quality—The path to productivity. *Magazine of Bank Administration.* 59, (June) 20-24.

Emerson, R. M. (1979) Social exchange theory. *Annual Review of Sociology.* 2, 335-362.

Emery, E. M. (1967) The role of quantitation in gas chromatography. *Journal of Gas Chromatography.* (December) 31-32.

Emery, F. E. (1969) *Systems Thinking: Selected Readings.* Baltimore, MD: Penguin Books.

Emery, F. E., and Einar Thorsrud. (1976) *Democracy at Work.* Leiden: Martinus Nijhoff Social Sciences Division.

Emery, R. E. (1980) Designing socio-technical systems for Greenfield sites. *Journal of Occupational Behavior.* 1, (January) 19-27.

Emmons, Sidney L. (1977) Auditing for profit and productivity. *ASQC Annual Technical Quality Congress Transactions.* Milwaukee, WI: ASQC Quality Press, 206-212.

Emory, C. William. (1980) *Business Research Methods.* Homewood, IL: Irwin.

Emphrain, M., Jr., and A. B. Hamilton. (1973) *Locomotive Reliability Paper 73-DGP-14, Diesel and Gas Engine Power Division.* New York: American Society of Mechanical Engineers.

Employee Development Review Guidebook. (1978) Johnson and Johnson. Skillman, NJ: Johnson and Johnson.

Enell, J. W. (1954) What sampling plan shall I choose? *Industrial Quality Control.* 10, (May) 96-100.

England, W. B. (1962) *Procurement.* Fourth edition. Homewood, IL: Irwin.

Engle, David and David Ball. (1986) Improving customer service for special orders. *Proceedings, Third Annual Conference on Quality Improvement.* Pigua, OH: Ohio Quality and Productivity Forum, 71-84.

Eppen, G. D., and E. G. Hurst. (1974) Optimal location of inspection stations in a multistage production process. *Management Science.* 20, (April) 1194-1200.

Epstein, Benjamin. (1960) Estimation from life test data. *Technometrics.* 3, (November) 447-454.

Epstein, Edward Jay. (1982) Have you ever tried to sell a diamond? *Atlantic*. (February) 23-34.

Epstein, Eugene. (1982) *People and Productivity: A Challenge to Corporate America*. New York: New York Stock Exchange.

Ercan, S. (1974) Cost minimizing single sampling plans with AIQL and AOQL constraints. *Management Sciences*. 20, 1112-1121.

Erhardt, C. C. (1980) Economic advantages of true position tolerancing. *ASQC Annual Technical Quality Congress Transactions*. Milwaukee, WI: ASQC Quality Press, 559-564.

Erickson, Tamara J. (1992) Beyond TQM: Creating the high performance business. *Management Review*. 81, (July) 58. (*2)

Erickson, Tom and Janice G. Sproul. (1979) *How Do You Know That You Have Arrived at Where You Thought You Were Going*. Cincinnati, OH: International Association of Quality Circles.

Erikson, W. J., and O. P. Hall. (1986) *Computer Models for Management Science*. Reading, MA: Addison-Wesley.

Ernst and Young Quality Improvement Consulting Group. (1990) *Total Quality: An Executive's Guide for the 1990s*. Homewood, IL: Dow Jones-Irwin.

Ernst, Raymond G. (1989) Why automating isn't enough. *Journal of Business Strategy*. (May/June) 38-42.

Erschler, J., et al. (1984) Periodic loading of flexible manufacturing systems. *Advances in Production Management Systems*. (June) 401-413.

Eshelman, Debra and Clifton Cooksey. (1992) The quality toolbox. *Training*. 29, (April) 19. (*2)

Estes, Elliott M. (1979) *World Wide Competition—Can the U.S. Meet the Challenge?* Philadelphia, PA: Wharton Entrepreneurial Center.

Ettlie, John E. (1985) *The Implementation of Programmable Manufacturing Innovations*. Ann Arbor, MI: Industrial Technology Institute.

Ettlie, John E., and Janet L. Eder. (1985) Managing the vendor-user team for successful implementation. AIM Technology 22 Conference Presentation.

Etzioni, Amitai. (1964) *Modern Organizations*. Englewood Cliffs, NJ: Prentice-Hall.

Eubanks, Paula. (1992) A new vision of hospital leadership. *Hospitals*. 66, (June 5) 34. (*2)

Eubanks, Paula. (1992) Berwik: TQM backlash prompts questions. *Hospitals*. 66, (June) 30.

Eubanks, Paula. (1992) Quality coordinator: On cutting edge of change. *Hospitals*. 66, (October 5) 78. (*2)

Eubanks, Paula. (1992) TQM/CQI. *Hospitals*. 66, (June 5) 24. (*2)

European Foundation for Quality Management. (1992) *Total Quality Management: The European Model for Self-Appraisal 1992*. Eindhoven, Netherlands: EFQM.

European Foundation for Quality Management. (1994) Total quality management: the European model for self-appraisal 1992. In Harry Ivan Costin (Ed.) *Readings in Total Quality Management*. (1994) Fort Worth, TX: Dryden Press, 598-609.

European Organization for Quality Control (1981) *Glossary of Terms Used in Quality Control*. Fifth edition. Berne, Switzerland: EOQC. (*2)

Eustis, G. E. (1977) Reduced support costs for shipboard electronic systems. *Proceedings, Annual Reliability and Maintainability Symposium*. New York: IEEE, 316-319.

Evans, David H. (1975) Background, part II. *Journal of Quality Technology*. 7, (April) 24.

Evans, David H. (1975) Methods for estimating moments, part III: Shifts and drifts. *Journal of Quality Technology*. 7, (October) 34-35.

Evans, David H. (1975) Statistical tolerancing: The state of the art, part I. *Journal of Quality Technology*. 7, (January) 27-28.

Evans, David H. (1991) The myth of customer service. *Canadian Business*. (March) 34-39.

Evans, James R., and William M. Lindsay. (1989) *The Management and Control of Quality*. St. Paul, MN: West Publishing.

Evans, M. G. (1970) Leadership and motivation: A core concept. *Academy of Management Journal*. 13, (March) 91-102.

Evans, Ralph A. (1966) Problems in probability. *Proceedings, Annual Symposium on Reliability*. New York: IEEE, 347-353.

Eveland, J. D. (1977) *The Innovation Process in Publication Organizations: Some Elements of a Preliminary Model*. Ann Arbor, MI: Department of Journalism, University of Michigan.

Eveland, J. D. (1986) Diffusion, technology transfer and implementation: Thinking and talking about change. *Knowledge*. 8, 303-322.

Evelyn, J. J., and N. DeCarlo. (1992) Customer focus helps utility see the light. *Journal of Business Strategy*. (January-February) 8-12.

Ewan, W. D. (1963) When and how to use cu-sum charts. *Technometrics*. 6, (February) 1-22.

Ewell, Peter. (1993) Total quality and academic practice. *Change*. 25, (March) 50.

Ewing, D. W. (1977) *Freedom Inside the Organization*. New York: E. P. Dutton. (*2)

Ewing, D. W. (1983) *Do it My Way or You're Fired*. New York: John Wiley. (*2)

Excellence in England. (1985) *Quality Progress*. 18, (September) 19-24.

Eysenck, H. J. (1963) The measurement of motivation. *Scientific American*. 208, (May) 130-140.

Ezer, S. (1979) Statistical models for proficiency testing. *ASQC Annual Technical Quality Congress Transactions*. Milwaukee, WI: ASQC Quality Press, 448-457.

Ezikial, M., and K. A. Fox. (1959) *Methods of Correlation and Regression Analysis*. New York: John Wiley.

Fabricant, S. (1971) *A Primer on Productivity*. New York: Random House.

Fagan, M. E. (1976) Design and code inspections to reduce errors in program development. *IBM Systems Journal*. 123-148.

Fahey, Paul P., and Stephen Ryan. (1992) Quality begins and ends with DATS. *Quality Progress*. 25 (April) 75.

Fallon, Ivan and James Srodes. (1983) *Dream Maker: The Rise and Fall of John Z. DeLorean*. New York: Putnam.

Fallows, James. (1986) Letter from Tokyo. *Atlantic Monthly*. (August) 1. (*2)

Fallows, James. (1989) *More Like Us: Making America Great Again*. Boston, MA: Houghton Mifflin. (*2)

Fallows, James. (1990) Japanese education: What can it teach American schools? *ERS Concerns in Education*. Occasional Paper.

Faltermayer, Edmund. (1977) The man who keeps those Maytag repairman lonely. *Fortune*. (November) 192. (*2)

Fargher, S. W., Jr. (1992) Managing process improvement at the Cherry Point Naval Aviation Depot. *National Productivity Review*. 11, (Autumn) 533. (*2)

Farkas, A. (1973) Some practical aspects of education and training for quality in light industry. Proceedings, Seventeenth EOQC Conference, Belgrade. (*2)

Farley, J., and N. J. Glickman. (1986) R and D as an economic development strategy: The microelectronics and computer technology corporation comes to Austin, Texas. *Journal of the American Planning Association.* 52, 407-413.

Farnham, A. (1989) The trust gap. *Fortune.* 4, (December 4) 56-76. (*2)

Farrel, Christopher, and John Hoerr. (1989) Employee ownership: Is it good for your company? *BusinessWeek.* (May 15) 116-123. (*2)

Farrel, Christopher. (1990) Why we should invest in human capital. *BusinessWeek.* 17, (December) 88-90.

Farrow, John H. (1985) A computerized approach to using stabilized p-charts. *ASQC Annual Technical Quality Congress Transactions.* Milwaukee, WI: ASQC Quality Press, 448-453.

Farrow, John H. (1987) Quality audits: An invitation to management. *Quality Progress.* 20, (January) 11-13.

Father of quality control circles doubts their long-term viability in the west. (1982) *International Management.* (August) 23-25.

Fayol, Henry. (1949) *General and Industrial Administration.* Boston, MA: Pitman. (*2)

Fear and loathing of Japan. (1992) *Fortune.* (February 26) 50.

Fed has lost much of its power to sway U.S. interest rates. (1990) *Wall Street Journal.* (March 12) 1.

Feigenbaum, Armand V. (1951) *Quality Control: Principles, Practice and Administration.* New York: McGraw-Hill. (*2)

Feigenbaum, Armand V. (1956) Total quality control. *Harvard Business Review.* 44, (November-December) 93-101 (*3)

Feigenbaum, Armand V. (1961) *Total Quality Control: Engineering and Management.* New York: McGraw-Hill. (*12)

Feigenbaum, Armand V. (1977) Quality and productivity. *Quality Progress.* 10, (November) 15-16.

Feigenbaum, Armand V. (1982) Engineering quality as a world marketing strategy. *Professional Engineer.* (June) 12-17.

Feigenbaum, Armand V. (1984) Total quality control and customer satisfaction. *Performance Management.* (Fall/Winter) 41-44. (*2)

Feigenbaum, Armand V. (1989) How to implement total quality control. *Executive Excellence.* (November) 15. (*2)

Feigenbaum, Armand V. (1989) Seven keys to constant quality. *Journal for Quality and Participation.* (March) 20-23.

Feigenbaum, Armand V. (1990) America on the threshold of quality. *Quality.* (January) 16-18. (*2)

Feigenbaum, Armand V. (1990) The criticality of quality and the need to measure it. *Financier.* (October) 33-36.

Feigenbaum, Armand V. (1992) TQM: Health care can learn from other fields. *Hospitals.* 66, (November 20) 56. (*2)

Feigenbaum, Armand V. (1994) Total quality control. In Harry Ivan Costin (Ed.) *Readings in Total Quality Management.* Fort Worth, TX: Dryden Press, 77-91.

Fein, M. (1974) Job enrichment: A reevaluation. *Sloan Management Review.* 15, (Winter) 69-88.

Fein, M. (1974) *Rational Approaches to Raising Productivity.* Norcross, GA: American Institute of Industrial Engineers.

Fein, M. (1976) Improving productivity by improved productivity sharing. *The Conference Board Record.* 13, (July) 12-29.

Fellers, Gary P. (1991) *SPC for Practitioners: Special Cases and Continuous Processes*. Milwaukee, WI: ASQC Quality Press.

Fellers, Gary P. (1994) *The Deming Vision: SPC/TQM for Administrators*. Milwaukee, WI: ASQC Quality Press.

Fennell, Thomas L., and Thomas A. Nicoli. (1984) Computer aided testability. *Proceedings, Annual Reliability and Maintainability Symposium*. New York: IEEE, 6-11.

Fenney, E. (1980) Quality circles: Using pooled effort to promote excellence. *Training and Human Resource Development*. (January) 25-28.

Fenwick, P., and Edward E. Lawler III. (1978) What you really want from your job. *Psychology Today*. (May) 43-48.

Ferguson, Gary. (1990) Printer incorporates Deming—Reduces errors, increases productivity. *Industrial Engineering*. 22, (August) 32-34.

Ferguson, M. (1980) *The Aquarian Conspiracy*. Los Angeles, CA: J. P. Tarcher.

Ferris, C. D., F. E. Grubbs, and C. L. Weaver. (1946) Operating characteristics for the common statistical tests of significance. *Annals of Mathematical Statistics*. 17, 178-192.

Ferris, T. (1988) *Coming of Age in the Milky Way*. New York: William Morrow.

Fertik, Edward. (1991) Applying TQM principles to part-time employees. *Bureaucrat*. 20, (Fall) 42-44.

Festinger, Leon. (1954) A theory of social comparison processes. *Human Relations*. 7, (June) 117-140. (*2)

Fiedler, F. A. (1967) *A Theory of Leadership Effectiveness*. New York: McGraw-Hill.

Fiedler, F. A., and L. A. Mahar. (1979) A field experiment validating contingency model leadership training. *Journal of Applied Psychology*. 64, (June) 247-254.

Fiedler, F. E. (1958) *Leader Attitudes and Group Effectiveness.* Urbana, IL: University of Illinois Press.

Fiedler, F. E. (1965) Engineer the job to fit the manager. *Harvard Business Review*. 43, (January-February) 115-122.

Fiedler, Robert M. (1978) Portal to portal product protection. *Quality*. (May) 12-14.

Field, D. L. (Ed.). (1976) *Procurement Quality Control: A Handbook of Recommended Practices*. Milwaukee, WI: ASQC Quality Press.

Fields, G. (1983) *From Bonsai to Levis.* New York: Macmillan.

Filley, A. C., and A. J. Grimes. (1967) The bases of power in decision processes. Academy of Management Decisions, Twenty-Seventh Annual Meeting, 133-160.

Finan, W. F., and A. M. LaMond. (1985) Sustaining U.S. competitiveness in microelectronics: The challenge to U.S. Policy. In B. R. Scott and G. C. Lodge, (Eds.) *U.S. Competitiveness in the World Economy*. Cambridge, MA: Harvard Business School Press.

Fine, Helene S. (1993) Just-in-time: A production system built on a code of ethics. In Harry Ivan Costin (Ed.) *Readings in Total Quality Management*. (1994) Fort Worth, TX: Dryden Press, 269-275.

Fine, Sidney. (1969) *Sit-Down: The General Motors Strike of 1936-37*. Ann Arbor, MI: University of Michigan Press.

Finison, L. J., K. S. Finison, and C. M. Bliersbach. (1993) The use of control charts to improve healthcare quality. *Journal for Healthcare Quality*. 10, (January) 21-25.

Finkel, James I. (1983) Computer models for flexible manufacturing. *CAE.* 52-60.

Finn, Chester E., Jr. (1991) *We Must Take Charge: Our Schools and Our Future.* New York: Free Press.

Finney, Edward E. (1969) Objective measurements for texture in foods. *Texture Studies.* 1, 19.

Firtz, R. (1989) *The Path of Least Resistance.* New York: Fawcett-Columbine.

Fischer, W. Robert. (1984) Design for assembly. *Proceedings, Annual Reliability and Maintainability Symposium.* New York: IEEE, 409-411.

Fisher, Anne B. (1974) *Small Group Decision Making: Communication and Group Process.* New York: McGraw-Hill. (*2)

Fisher, Anne B. (1986) GM is tougher than you think. *Fortune.* (November 10) 55. (*2)

Fisher, G. M. C. (1983) On the misuse of accounting rates of return to infer monopoly profits. *American Economic Review.* (March) 82-97.

Fisher, G. M. C. (1990) Measuring the unmeasurable. *World: The Magazine for Decision Makers.* 2, 5.

Fisher, James R. (1983) Computer assisted net weight control. *Quality Progress.* 16, (June) 22-25.

Fisher, Jim, Charlotte Heywood, and John McCutcheon. (1992) Total quality management of Canadian R and D activities. *CMA—The Management Accounting Magazine.* 66, (September) 25. (*2)

Fisher, Roger and William Ury. (1978) *Mediation: A Handbook.* New York: International Peace Academy.

Fisher, Roger and William Ury. (1981) *Getting to Yes: Negotiation Agreement Without Giving In.* New York: Penguin.

Fisher, Ronald A. (1935) *The Design of Experiments.* London, UK: Oliver and Boyd.

Fisher, Ronald A. (1936) The use of multiple measurements in taxonomic problems. *Annals of Eugenics.* 179-188.

Fisher, Ronald A. (1970) *Statistical Methods for Research Workers.* New York: Hafner Publishing Company.

Fisher, Ronald A. (1973) *Statistical Methods and Scientific Inference.* New York: Hafner Publishing Company.

Fisher, Ronald A., and F. Yates. (1964) *Statistical Tables for Biological, Agricultural and Medical Research Workers.* Sixth edition. New York: Stechert-Hafner.

Fishman, Nina and Lee Kavanaugh. (1989) Searching for your missing quality link. *Journal for Quality and Participation.* (December) 28-32.

Fitch, T. P. (1984) Putting the emphasis on quality. *United States Banker.* 95, (May) 28-32.

Fitz-Enz, Jac. (1990) *Human Value Management.* San Francisco, CA: Jossey-Bass.

Fitz-Enz, Jac and James Rodgers. (1991) Get quality performance from professional staff. *Personnel Journal.* 70, (May) 22, 24.

Fitzgerald, F. Scott. (1965) The crack-up. In Charles R. Anderson (Ed.) *American Literary Masters.* New York: Holt, Rinehart and Winston, 1007. (*2)

Fitzgerald, Laurie and Joseph Murphy. (1982) *Installing Quality Circles: A Strategic Approach.* San Diego, CA: University Associates.

Fitzgerald, Michael L. (1991) Quality: Take it to the limit. *Computerworld.* (February 11) 71-78.

Fitzgibbons, R. G., and Joseph M. Juran. (1974) Vendor relations. In Joseph M. Juran (Ed.) *Quality Control Handbook.* New York: McGraw-Hill.

Fitzsimmons, J. A., and R. S. Sullivan. (1982) *Service Operations Management.* New York: McGraw-Hill.

The five best-managed companies. (1977) *Dun's Review.* (December) 60.

Flagle, C. D., H. Huggins, and R. H. Roy. (1960) *Operations Research and Systems Engineering.* Baltimore, MD: Johns Hopkins Press. (*2)

Flaherty, Robert J. (1980) Harris corporation's remarkable metamorphosis. *Forbes.* (May 26) 46. (*2)

Flamholtz, E. G. (1974) *Human Resource Accounting.* Encino, CA: Dickenson. (*2)

Flamholtz, E. G. (1983) Accounting, budgeting and control systems in their organizational context: Theoretical and empirical perspectives. *Accounting, Organizations and Society.* 8, 153-169.

Fleenor, Patrick C., and Peter M. Scontrink. (1982) *Performance Appraisal: A Manager's Guide.* Dubuque, IA: Kendall and Hunt.

Fletcher, O. L., and E. Novy. (1972) Application of hypergeometric sampling plans in a large job shop. *ASQC Annual Technical Quality Congress Transactions.* Milwaukee, WI: ASQC Quality Press, 489-500.

Flexman, Nancy and Thomas Scanlan. (1982) *Running Your Own Business.* Boston, MA: Argus Communication.

Flink, James. (1923) *The Car Culture.* Cambridge, MA: MIT Press.

Flint, Anthony. (1992) At Dartmouth, "Educated Person" redefined. *The Boston Globe.* (April 8) 21, 25.

Flint, Perry. (1989) Total quality: The quality to total success? *Air Transport World.* 26, (November) 38-41.

Flood, R. L. (1993) *Beyond TQM.* New York: John Wiley.

Florida Power and Light Company. (1984) *Quality Improvement Program, Guidebook and Roadmap.* Miami, FL: FPL.

Flower, Joe. (1993) Benchmarking: Tales from the point. *Healthcare Forum.* 36, (Issue 1, January-February) 37-51.

Flowers, Vincent S., and Charles L. Hughes. (1973) Why employees stay. *Harvard Business Review.* 51, (July-August) 49.

Flynn, Barbara and F. Robert Jacobs. (1987) An experimental comparison of cellular (group technology) layout with process layout. *Decision Sciences.* 18, 562-581.

Flynn, M. F., and J. A. Bolcar. (1984) The road to hell. *ASQC Annual Technical Quality Congress Transactions.* Milwaukee, WI: ASQC Quality Press, 192-197. (*2)

Fody, Theodore, J. (1977) The procurement of window air conditioners using life cycle costing. *Proceedings, Annual Reliability and Maintainability Symposium.* New York: IEEE, 81-88.

Fogarty, D. W., and T. R. Hoffmann. (1983) *Production and Inventory Management.* Cincinnati, OH: South-Western.

Fogel, L. G. (1967) *Human Information Processing.* Englewood Cliffs, NJ: Prentice-Hall.

Foggin, James H. (1992) Meeting customer needs. *Survey of Business.* 28, (Issue 1, Summer) 6-9.

Foley, Patricia Fisher and Thomas J. McDonald. (1982) *The World Almanac and Book of Facts.* New York: Newspaper Enterprise Association.

Folks, W., and R. Aggarwal. (1988) *International Dimensions of Financial Management.* Boston, MA: PWS-Kent.

Follett, Mary Parker. (1941) Report. In H. C. Metcalf and L. Urwick (Eds.) *Dynamic Administration*. New York: Harper and Row.

Follini, J. R. (1971) Production certifies the quality of its work. *Industrial Engineering*. 3, (November) 10-17.

Fombrun, Charles J. (1986) Structural dynamics within and between organizations. *Administrative Science Quarterly*. 31, (December) 403-421.

Fombrun, Charles J., Noel M. Tichy, and Mary Anne Devanne. (1984) *Strategic Human Resource Management*. New York: John Wiley.

Foote, G. H. (1973) Performance shares revitalize executive stock plans. *Harvard Business Review*. 51, (November-December) 121-30.

Ford, Donald J. (1993) Benchmarking HRD. *Training and Development Journal*. 47, (June) 36-41.

Ford, Henry. (1923) *My Life and Work*. Garden City NY: Doubleday.

Ford, Henry. (1988) *Today and Tomorrow*. Cambridge, MA: Productivity Press. (*5)

Ford Motor Company. (1983) *Ford's Q-101-Quality System Standard*. Product Quality Office. Dearborn, MI: Ford Motor Company.

Ford Motor Company. (1984) *Continuing Process Control and Process Capability Improvement*. Plymouth MI: Statistical Methods Publications.

Ford, R. N. (1968) The art of reshaping jobs. *Bell Telephone Magazine, AT and T*. 47, (September-October) 5.

Ford, R. N. (1969) *Motivation Through the Work Itself*. New York: American Management Association. (*2)

Ford, R. N. (1973) Job enrichment lessons from AT and T. *Harvard Business Review*. 51, (January-February) 96-106.

Ford's Q1 program drives suppliers. (1985) *Quality*. (September) 36-38.

Forrester, J. W. (1961) *Industrial Dynamics*. Cambridge, MA: MIT Press.

Fortuna, Ronald M. (1988) Beyond quality: Taking SPC upstream. *Quality Progress*. 21, (June) 15-18.

Fortuna, Ronald M. (1990) The quality imperative. *Executive Excellence*. (March) 1.

Fortune Editors. (1956) *The Executive Life*. Garden City, NY: Doubleday.

Forward Quality. (1992) *Training*. 29, (August) 14. (*2)

Forward, Robert L. (1980) Spinning new realities. *Science 80*. (December) 40. (*2)

Fosse, Chris J. (1987) Quality assurance through strategic product development. *Proceedings, Fifth Annual Conference on Quality Improvement*. Piqua, OH: Ohio Quality and Productivity Forum, 81-92.

Foster, D. (1968) Limitations of subjective measurement of odors. *Correlation of Subjective-Objective Methods in the Study of Odors and Taste*. Philadelphia, PA: American Society for Testing and Materials.

Foster, Geoffery. (1976) Dana's strange disciplines. *Management Today*. (September) 61. (*2)

Foster, R. (1986) *Innovation: The Attacker's Advantage*. New York: Summit. (*2)

Foster, Thomas A., and Joseph V. Barks. (1990) The right chemistry for single sourcing. *Distribution*. 89, (September) 44-52.

Fowler, Elizabeth M. (1988) New regard for the ideas of workers. *New York Times*. (July 5) D10. (*3)

Foxman, Loretta D., and Walter L. Polsky. (1989) Cross-cultural understanding. *Personnel Journal*. 68, (November) 12-14. (*2)

Foy, Nancy. (1977) Action learning comes to industry. *Harvard Business Review*. 55, (September-October) 158-168.

Fraker, Susan. (1984) High speed management for the high-tech age. *Fortune*. (March 5) 62-68. (*2)

Fram, Eugene H., and Martin L. Presburg. (1992) TQM is a catalyst for new marketing applications. *Marketing News*. 26, (November 9) 17. (*3)

Francis, Ivor (1981) *Statistical Software: A Comparative Review*. New York: Elsevier Science Publishing.

Francis, Philip H. (1992) Putting quality into the RandD process. *Research-Technology Management*. 35, (July-August) 16. (*2)

Frank, G. R. (1977) Tolerance challenge. *ASQC Annual Technical Quality Congress Transactions*. Milwaukee, WI: ASQC Quality Press, 72-78.

Frank, Norman C. (1982) Ten commandments for laboratory notebooks. *Quality Progress*. 15, (November) 40-41.

Frank, Victor E. (1959) *Man's Search for Meaning*. New York: Simon and Schuster. (*2)

Fraser, Jill Andresky. (1990) Straight talk. *Inc*. (March 19) 97-98.

Fraser, R. A., and J. E. Talbert. (1974) Preparation for change in management of the future industrial complex. *Proceedings of the 1974 SAVE Conference*, Chicago, IL: Society of American Value Engineers, 108-115.

Frederickson, J. (1984) The comprehensiveness of strategic decision processes: Extensions, observations, future directions. *Academy of Management Journal*. 27, (March) 445-466.

Freedman, J. (1985) The case for a free labor market. *Across the Board*. (January) 42-48.

Freedman, Jonathan L. (1978) *Social Psychology*. Englewood Cliffs, NJ: Prentice-Hall.

Freedman, Jonathan L., and Scott C. Fraser. (1966) Compliance without pressure: The foot-in-the-door technique. *Journal of Personality and Social Psychology*. 4, (May) 195-202.

Freedman, Jonathon L., David O. Sears, and J. Merrill Carlsmith. (1978) *Social Psychology*. Englewood Cliffs, NJ: Prentice-Hall.

Freedman, Marion. (1992) Quest for quality: The payoff for a quality program can be significant for insurers with patience and the willingness to expend considerable effort. *Property-Casualty Insurance Edition*. 93, (September) 28. (*2)

Freeman, H. A., M. Friedman, Frederick Mosteller, and W. A. Wallis. (1948) *Sampling Inspection*. New York: McGraw-Hill.

Freeman, Richard. (1984) *Strategic Management: A Stakeholder Approach*. Boston, MA: Pitman.

Freeman, Richard. (1992) *Quality Assurance in Training and Education*. London, UK: Kogan Page Limited. (*8)

Freeston, Kenneth R. (1992) Getting started with TQM. *Educational Leadership*. (November) 10-13.

French, John R. P., Jr. and B. Raven. (1960) The bases of social power. In Dorwin Cartwright, and Alvin Zander. (Eds.) *Group Dynamics*. Evanston, IL: Row, Peterson, 607-623.

Freund, F. A. (1985) Definitions and basic quality concepts. *Journal of Quality Technology*. 17, (January) 50-56.

Freund, J. E., and F. J. Williams. (1959) *Modern Business Statistics.* Englewood Cliffs, NJ: Prentice-Hall.

Freund, J. E., and F. J. Williams. (1982) *Elementary Business Statistics.* Englewood Cliffs, New Jersey: Prentice-Hall.

Freund, Richard A. (1957) Acceptance control charts. *Industrial Quality Control.* 13, (October) 13-23. (*2)

Freund, Richard A. (1981) The role of quality technology. In H. J. Bajaria, (Ed.) *Quality Assurance: Methods, Management and Motivation.* Dearborn, MI: Society of Manufacturing Engineers. (*2)

Freund, Richard A. (1985) Definitions and basic quality concepts. *Journal of Quality Technology.* 17, (January) 52-54.

Freund, Richard A., and H. B. Trulli (1982) Quality assurance review technique. *Quality Assurance.* 8, (March) 17-22.

Frey, William C. (1962) A plan for outgoing quality. *Modern Packaging.* (October) 9.

Friar, J., and M. Horwitch. (1986) The emergence of technology strategy: A new dimension of strategic management. *Technology in Society.* 7, 143-178.

Friedman, H. H., J. E. Whitney, and A. S. Szczesnial. (1963) The texturometer-a new instrument for objective measurements. *Food Science.* 28, 390.

Friedman. Milton. (1962) *Capitalism and Freedom.* Chicago, IL: University of Chicago Press.

Friedman. Milton. (1970) The social responsibility of business is to increase its profits. *New York Times Magazine.* (September 13) 21-24.

Friedman, Thomas L. (1981) Talking business. *New York Times.* (June) D2. (*2)

Friedmann, G. (1955) *The Emergence of the Human Problems of Automation.* New York: Free Press.

Frito-Lay shortens its business cycle. *Fortune.* (January 19) 11.

Frost, C. F., J. H. Wakely, and R. A. Ruh. (1974) *The Scanlon Plan for Organization Development: Identity, Participation, and Equity.* East Lansing, MI: Michigan State University Press.

Fry, D. (1993) A quest for total quality. *Mortgage Banking.* 53, (May) 83.

Fry, P. (1976) Evolution of database management systems. *Computing Surveys.* 8.

Fry, W. Darryl. (1993) A quest for total quality. *Mortgage Banking.* 53, (February) 83. (*2)

Fuchs, V. R. (1969) *Production and Productivity in the Service Industries.* New York: Columbia University Press.

Fuchsberg, G. (1990) Gurus of quality are gaining clout. *Wall Street Journal.* 27, (November) B1.

Fuchsberg, G. (1991) Non-profits may get own Baldrige prize. *Wall Street Journal.* (March 5) 1.

Fuchsberg, G. (1993) Baldridge Awards may be losing some luster. *Wall Street Journal.* (April 19) 1, 7. (*3)

Fuchsburg, G. (1992) Quality programs showing shoddy results. *Wall Street Journal.* (May 14) B1.

Fuchsburg, G. (1992) Total quality' is termed only partial success. *Wall Street Journal.* (October 1) B1.

Fuji Xerox. (1983) *Fuji Xerox: The First Twenty Tears: 1962-1982.* Tokyo: Fuji Xerox.

Fujita, Yoshitaka. (1981) The workers autonomous small group activities and productivity in Japan. *Management Japan.* 14, (Summer) 16-18.

Fujita, Yoshitaka. (1982) Participative work practices in the Japanese auto industry: Some neglected considerations. *Industry at the Crossroads.* 7, 75-86.

Fujita, Yoshitaka. (1983) Development of Japanese quality control. *Standardization.* 13, (November) 13-16.

Fukada, R. (1982) Japanese management not magic, but science. *The Japan Times Weekly.* (March 13) 5.

Fukuda, R. (1981) Introduction to the CEDAC. *Quality Progress.* 14, (November) 14-19.

Fukuda, R. (1981) Quality control factor in methods engineering. *ASQC Annual Technical Quality Congress Transactions.* Milwaukee, WI: ASQC Quality Press, 268-273.

Fukuda, R. (1983) *Managerial Engineering: Techniques for Improving Quality and Productivity in the Workplace.* Cambridge, MA: Productivity Inc. (*4)

Fuld, Leonard M. (1992) Achieving total quality through intelligence. *Long Range Planning.* 25, (February) 109-115.

Fullan, Michael G. (1992) *The New Meaning of Educational Change.* New York: Teachers College Press, 1991. (*2)

Fullan, Michael G., and Matthew Miles. (1992) Getting reform right: What works and what doesn't. *Phi Delta Kappan.* 73, (June) 750.

Fuller, F. Timothy. (1985) Eliminating complexity from work: Improving productivity by enhancing quality. *National Productivity Review.* 4, (Autumn) 327-344.

Furey, T. R. (1993) A six-step guide to process reengineering. *Planning Review.* (March/April) 20-23. (*2)

Furr, Diana S., and Joseph A. Petrick. (1995) *Total Quality in Managing Human Resources*. Delray Beach, FL: St. Lucie Press.

Furukawa, O., M. Kogure, and S. Ishizu. (1981) Systems approach to production. *ASQC Annual Technical Quality Congress Transactions.* Milwaukee, WI: ASQC Quality Press, 225-262.

Gabor, Andrea. (1987) GM's bootstrap battle: The factory-floor view. *U.S. News and World Report*. (September 21) 52-53. (*2)

Gabor, Andrea. (1988) The leading light of quality: An innovative Florida utility borrows a page from Japan, Inc. *U.S. News and World Report*. (November 28) 53-56.

Gabor, Andrea. (1988) The man who changed the world of quality. *International Management.* (March) 42-46. (*6)

Gabor, Andrea. (1989) The front lines of quality. *U.S. News and World Report.* 27, (November) 57-59.

Gabor, Andrea. (1990) *The Man Who Discovered Quality: How W. Edwards Deming Brought the Quality Revolution to America-The Stories of Ford, Xerox and G.M.* New York: Time Books. (*5)

Gabor, Andrea, Mary Lord, Peter Dworkin, Steve L. Hawkins, and Jack A. Seamonds. (1987) What they don't teach you at business school. *U.S. News and World Report*. (July 13) 44-46.

Gabor, Carol. (1986) Special project task teams: An extension of a successful Quality Circle Program. *Quality Circles Journal.* 9, (September) 40-43.

Gacula, M. C. (1978) Analysis of incomplete block designs with reference samples in every block. *Food Science*. 43, 14-61.

Gadd, Ken W., and John S. Oakland. (1995) Discontinuous change in total quality environment. D2D Ltd: A case study. *Business Process Reengineering and Management Journal*. 7, (No. 2) 18-40.

Gadd, Ken W., and John S. Oakland. (1996) Chimera or culture? Business process reengineering for total quality management. *Quality Management Journal.* 3, (No. 3) 20-38.

Gadon, H. (1984) Making sense of quality of work life programs. *Business Horizons.* 27, (January-February) 42-44.

Gaines, B. R., and M. Shaw. (1986) Knowledge engineering for an FMS advisory system. Simulation in Manufacturing Conference. San Francisco, CA, 144-163.

Gainsburgh, M. R. (1971) Productivity, inflation and economic growth. *Michigan Business Review.* 23, (January) 15-21.

Gaither, Norman. (1981) The effect of inflation and fuel scarcity upon inventory policies. *Production and Inventory Management.* 22, 37-48.

Gaither, Norman. (1990) *Production and Operations Management: A Problem-Solving and Decision-Making Approach.* Fifth edition. Chicago, IL: Dryden Press.

Gaither, Norman. (1992) *Production and Operations Management.* Sixth edition. Orlando, FL: Jovanovich Publishers.

Galagan, Patricia A. (1992) How to get your TQM training back on track. *Nation's Business.* 80, (October) 24. (*2)

Galaskiewicz, J. (1979) *Exchange Networks and Community Politics.* Beverly Hills, CA: Sage.

Galaskiewicz, J., and K. R. Krohn. (1984) Positions, roles and dependencies in a community interorganizational system. *Sociological Quarterly.* 25, 527-550.

Galatowitsch, Sheila. (1993) ISO 9000 perceived as TQM enigma. *Defense Electronics.* (February) 17-18. (*3)

Galbraith, Jay R. (1973) *Designing Complex Organizations.* Reading, MA: Addison-Wesley.

Galbraith, Jay R. (1977) *Organization Design*. Reading, MA: Addison-Wesley. (*2)

Galbraith, Jay R. (1982) Designing the innovating organization. *Organizational Dynamics*. 10, (Winter) 3-24.

Galbraith, Jay R. (1989) Technology and global strategies and structures. In Mary Ann Von Glinow and Susan Albers Mohrman (Eds.) *Managing Complexity in High Technology Industries: Systems and People*. New York: Oxford University Press.

Galbraith, Jay R., and D. A. Nathanson. (1978) *Strategy Implementation*. St. Paul, MN: West Publishing.

Galbraith, Jay R., D. A. Nathanson, and Greg R. Oldham. (1978) *Strategy Implementation: The Role of Structure and Process*. St. Paul, MN: West Publishing. (*3)

Galbraith, Jay R., and D. E. Schendel. (1983) An empirical study of strategy types. *Strategic Management Journal*. 4, (May-June) 153-173.

Galbraith, John Kenneth. (1952) *American Capitalism: The Concept of Countervailing Power*. Boston, MA: Houghton Mifflin.

Galbraith, John Kenneth. (1961) *The Great Crash, 1929*. Boston, MA: Houghton Mifflin.

Galbraith, John Kenneth. (1978) *The New Industrial State*. Boston, MA: Houghton Mifflin.

Gale, Bradley T. (1980) Can more capital buy higher productivity? *Harvard Business Review*. 61, (July-August) 78-86.

Gale, Bradley T. (1985) *Quality as a Strategic Weapon*. Cambridge, MA: The Strategic Planning Institute.

Gale, Bradley T. (1987) How quality drives market share. *The Quality Review*. (Summer) 18-23.

Gale, Bradley T. (1989) Beyond customer satisfaction: Four key mistakes companies make. *The Quality Executive.* (October) 8.

Gale, Bradley T. (1994) *Managing Customer Value: Creating Quality and Service That Customers Can See.* New York: Free Press.

Gale, Bradley T., and B. Branch. (1982) Concentration versus market share: Which determines performance and why does it matter? *Antitrust Bulletin.* 27, (Spring) 83-106.

Gale, Bradley T., and Robert D. Buzzell. (1989) Market perceived quality: Key strategic concept. *Planning Review.* (March/April) 6-15.

Gall, Norman. (1981) It's later than we think. *Forbes.* (February) 65. (*2)

Gall, Norman. (1983) The rise and decline of industrial Japan. *Commentary.* (October) 29. (*2)

Gallagher, B. M., and W. H. Knobloch. (1971) Helicopter auxiliary power unit cost of ownership. *Proceedings, Annual Reliability and Maintainability Symposium.* New York: IEEE, 285-291.

Gallagher, W. E., Jr., and H. J. Einhorn (1976) Motivation theory and job design. *Journal of Business.* 49, (July) 358-373.

Galloway, Robert A. (1992) Quality improvement and heightened self-esteem: The Brighton police story. *National Productivity Review.* 11, (Autumn) 453. (*2)

Galluccio, Nick. (1980) The housecleaning is over. *Forbes.* (November) 74.

Gallup Survey. (1987) *Executives Perceptions Concerning the Quality of American Products of Services Gallup Organization.* Princeton, NJ.

Gallup Survey. (1990) *A Survey of Employees' Attitudes Toward Their Jobs and Quality*; Survey conducted by the Gallup Organization for the American Society for Quality Control. Milwaukee, WI: ASQC Quality Press.

Gallwey, Timothy W. (1979) *The Inner Game of Tennis*. New York: Bantam Books.

Galvin, Robert W. (1991) *The Idea of Ideas*. Schaumburg, IL: Motorola University Press.

Gannes, Stuart. (1987) Sun's sizzling race to the top. *Fortune*. (August) 27.

Gansler, J. S. (1974) Application of life cycle costing to the DOD. System acquisition decision process. *Proceedings, Annual Reliability and Maintainability Symposium*. New York: IEEE, 147-148.

Gantt J. S. (1959) Let's take the guesswork out of inspection. *American Machinist.* (March) 1959, 1-6.

Ganushkin, V. V. (1980) Information supply of quality management system in the ministry of electronics and electrical engineering in Bulgaria. Proceedings, Twenty-Fourth EOQC Conference, Warsaw. 3, 409. (*2)

Gardner, Edward P. (1985) A systems approach to bank credential management and supervision: The utilization of feed forward control. *Journal of Management Studies*. 22, 1-24.

Gardner, John W. (1965) *Self Renewal: The Individual and the Innovative Society*. New York: Harper Colophon Books. (*2)

Gardner, John W. (1978) *Morale*. New York: W. W. Norton. (*2)

Gardner, John W. (1986) The nature of leadership: Introductory considerations. Leadership Papers /1. The first in a series of papers prepared for the Leadership Studies Program sponsored by Independent Sector (January). Washington, DC.

Gardner, John W. (1986) The tasks of leadership. Leadership Papers /2. The second in a series of papers prepared for the Leadership Studies Program sponsored by Independent Sector (March), Washington, DC.

Gardner, John W. (1986) The heart of the matter: Leader-constituent interaction. Leadership Papers /3. The third in a series of papers prepared for the Leadership Studies Program sponsored by Independent Sector (June). Washington, DC.

Gardner, John W. (1986) Leadership and power. Leadership Papers /4. The fourth in a series of papers prepared for the Leadership Studies Program sponsored by Independent Sector (October). Washington, DC.

Gardner, John W. (1987) The moral aspect of leadership. Leadership Papers /5. The fifth in a series of papers prepared for the Leadership Studies Program sponsored by Independent Sector (January). Washington, DC.

Gardner, Ralph., Jr. (1984) *Young, Gifted, and Rich.* New York: Simon and Schuster.

Gardner, Scott A. (1992) Completing the triangle. *Telephone Engineer and Management.* 96, (June 1) 86. (*2)

Garrick, B. John and Robert J. Mulvihill. (1974) Reliability and maintainability of mechanized bulk mail systems. *Proceedings, Annual Reliability and Maintainability Symposium.* New York: IEEE, 32-33

Garvin, David A. (1982) Japanese quality management. *Columbia Journal of World Business.* 19, (Fall) 4.

Garvin, David A. (1983) Quality on the line. *Harvard Business Review.* 61, (September-October) 65-75. (*8)

Garvin, David A. (1984) What does product quality really mean. *Sloan Management Review.* 25, (Fall) 31-40.

Garvin, David A. (1986) Quality problems, policies and attitudes in the United States and Japan: An exploratory study. *Academy of Management Journal.* 29, (December) 653-673. (*2)

Garvin, David A. (1987) Competing on the eight dimensions of quality. *Harvard Business Review*. 65, (November-December) 101-109. (*2)

Garvin, David A. (1988) History and evolution of the quality movement. In Harry Ivan Costin (Ed.) *Readings in Total Quality Management*. (1994) Fort Worth, TX: Dryden Press, 27-44.

Garvin, David A. (1988) *Managing Quality: The Strategic and Competitive Edge*. New York: Free Press. (*9)

Garvin, David A. (1991) How the Baldrige award really works. *Harvard Business Review*. 69, (November-December) 80-90.

Garwood, D. R. (1984) Explaining JIT, MRP II, *Kanban. P and IM Review and APICS News*. (October) 14-17.

Garwood, R. D. (1971) Delivery as promised: Production and inventory management. *APICS Journal*. (Third Quarter) 21-28. (*2)

Gatfinkel, D., and S. Clodfelter. (1984) Contract inspection comes into its own. *American Machinist*. (October) 90-92.

Geber, Beverly. (1992) Can TQM cure health care? *Training*. 29, (August) 25. (*2)

Geber, Beverly. (1992) From manager into coach. *Training*. 29, (February) 21-24.

Gebhardt, C. (1982) Color me calibrated. *Quality*. (March) 62-63.

Geipel, Gary. (1986) At today's supermarket, the computer is doing it all. *BusinessWeek*. (August 11) 64-65.

Geldman, S. B. (1990) Supplier recognition award. *Quality*. (August) 15-16.

Gelinas, Mary V. (1982) A systems approach to quality circles. IAQC Fourth Annual Conference Transactions. Cincinnati, OH: International Association of Quality Circles.

Gellagher, B. M., and L. X. Ball. (1976) Productivity jumps with computer-controlled engine test. *Quality*. (October) 12.

Gellerman, S. W., and W. G. Hodgson. (1988) Cyanamid's new take on performance appraisal. *Harvard Business Review*. 66, (May-June) 36-41. (*2)

Gelsanliter, David. *Jump Start: Japan Comes to the Heartland.* New York: Farrar, Straus and Girou. 1990. (*2)

Gendron, G., and B. Burlingham. (1989) The entrepreneur of the decade. *Inc*. (April) 114.

Geneen, Harold and Alvin Moscow. (1985) *Managing*. New York: Avon Books. (*3)

George, A. (1980) *Presidential Decision Making in Foreign Policy.* Boulder, CO: Westview Press.

George, Claude S., Jr. (1972) *The History of Management Thought.* Englewood Cliffs, NJ: Prentice-Hall. (*2)

George, Stephen. (1992) *The Baldrige Quality System: The Do-It-Yourself Way to Transform Your Business.* New York: John Wiley.

George, Stephen. (1994) *Total Quality Management: Strategies and Techniques Proven at Today's Most Successful Companies*. New York: John Wiley.

George, William W. (1977) Task teams for rapid growth. *Harvard Business Review*. 55, (March-April) 71-80.

Gepner, L. (1977) User ratings of software packages. *Datamation.* 23.

Gerber, Beverly. (1987) Teaming up with unions. *Training*. 34, (August) 12-13.

Gerhard, Larry and Walter T. Sparrow. (1988) Pride teams: A quality circle that works. *Journal for Quality and Participation.* (June) 32-36.

Gerhart, Clifford. (1992) Quality in Alaska. *Alaska Business Monthly.* 8, (October) 99. (*2)

Gerigk, K., H. Stephen Hildebrandt, and J. Wegener. (1986) Lebensmittelrechtliche Beurteilung von Leberwurst. *Fleischwirtsch.* 66, (March) 310.

Gerpott, T. J., and M. Domsch. (1985) The concept of professionalism and the management of salaried technical professionals: A cross national perspective. *Human Resource Management.* 24, (Spring/Summer) 207-226.

Gershwin, Stanley B. (1982) *Material and Information Flow in an Advanced Automated Manufacturing System.* Cambridge, MA: MIT Press.

Gerston, Jill. (1981) Tiffany's unbashed guardian of good taste relinquishes helm. *San Francisco Examiner.* (January) C2.

Gerwin, Donald. (1984) *A Theory of Innovation Processes for Computerized Manufacturing Technology.* Milwaukee, WI: University of Wisconsin.

Getting high tech back on track. (1990) *Fortune.* (January 1) 74.

Getting personal: At Fidelity Investments, computers are designed to make the company seem more human. (1992) *Wall Street Journal.* (April 6) R19.

Gevirtz, D. (1984) *Business Plan for America.* New York: Putnam.

Gharajedaghi, Jamshid. (1984) *On the Nature of Development.* Los Angeles, CA: Human Systems Management.

Gharajedaghi, Jamshid. (1985) *Toward a System Theory of Organization.* Seaside, CA: Intersystems Publications.

Ghemawat, P. (1986) Sustainable advantage. *Harvard Business Review.* 64, (September-October) 53-58.

Ghosh, B. K. (1970) *Sequential Tests of Statistical Hypotheses.* Reading, MA: Addison-Wesley.

Giamatti, A. Bartlett. (1988) *The Free and Ordered Space.* New York: W. W. Norton.

Gibb, C. (1990) TQM and the quality professional. The Quality Management Forum. *ASCQ Management Division Newsletter.* (Winter) 1.

Gibbon, E. (1900) *The Decline and Fall of the Roman Empire.* New York: Modern Library. First published 1776-1788. London, UK: W. Strahan and T. Cadell.

Gibbons, Jean D. (1982) Methods for selecting the best process. *Journal of Quality Technology.* 14, (February) 80-88.

Gibbons, Jean D. (1983) How do you recognize a qualified inspector? *Quality Assurance for the Offshore Industry.* (April) 55-56.

Gibbons, Jean D. (1985) *Nonparametric Methods for Quantitative Analysis.* Second edition. Columbus, OH: American Sciences Press.

Gibney, Frank. (1953) *Five Gentlemen of Japan.* New York: Farrar, Straus and Young.

Gibney, Frank. (1979) *The Fragile Superpower.* New York: W. W. Norton. (*3)

Gibney, Frank. (1982) *Miracle by Design.* New York: Time Books. (*3)

Gibney, G. (1985) *Japan: The Fragile Superpower.* New York: Meridian.

Gibra, I. N. (1975) Recent developments in control chart techniques. *Journal of Quality Technology.* 7, (April) 183-192.

Gibra, I. N. (1978) Economically optimal determination of parameters of np control charts. *Journal of Quality Technology.* 10, (January) 12-19.

Gibson, C. H. (1973) Volvo increases productivity thru job enrichment. *California Management Review.* 15, (Summer) 64-66.

Gibson, Cyrus G., and Richard L. Nolan. (1974) Managing the four stages of EDP growth. *Harvard Business Review.* 52, (January-February) 76-88.

Gibson, D. V., and E. M. Rogers. (1988) The MCC comes to Texas. In F. Williams (Ed.) *Measuring the Information Society: The Texas Studies.* Newbury Park, CA: Sage.

Gibson, Price. (1981) Full-time facilitation. *Quality Circles Journal.* 4, (August) 9.

Gibson, Price. (1981) Short term fad or long term fundamental. *Quality Circles Journal.* 4, (May) 25-26.

Gibson, Price. (1982) Assess readiness, measure change and survive. *Quality Circles Journal.* 4, (May) 19-31.

Gibson, Price. (1982) Challenges for quality circles and quality of work life. IAQC Fourth Annual Conference Transactions. Cincinnati, OH: International Association of Quality Circles.

Gibson, R. (1987) Managing the techies: Closing the lab coat-pinstripe gap. *Wall Street Journal.* Special report. (June 12) 23. (*2)

Gibson, Thomas C. (1987) The total quality management resource. *Quality Progress.* 20, (November) 62-66.

Gibson, Thomas C. (1990) Helping leaders accept leadership of Total Quality Management. *Quality Progress.* 23, (November) 45-47.

Giddens, Paul Henry. (1938) *The Birth of the Oil Industry.* New York: Macmillan.

Giegold, W. (1978) *Management By Objectives, A Self-Instructional Approach: Objective Setting and the MBO Process.* Volume 1. New York: McGraw-Hill.

Giegold, W. (1978) *Management By Objectives, A Self-Instructional Approach: Strategic Planning and the MBO Process*. Volume 2. New York: McGraw-Hill.

Gift, Bob and Doug Mosel. (1993) Benchmarking: Tales from the front. *Healthcare Forum*. (January/February) 37-51.

Gilbert, James D. (1992) TQM flops—A chance to learn from the mistakes of others. *National Productivity Review*. 11, (Autumn) 491. (*2)

Gilbert, John P., Richard J. Light, and Frederick Mosteller. (1975) Assessing social innovations: An empirical base for policy. In Carl A. Bennett and Arthur A. Lumsdaine (Eds.) *Evaluation and Experiment: Some Critical Issues in Assessing Social Programs*. New York: Academic Press, 39-193.

Gilbert, K. (1991) The production and inventory control system. In Michael J. Stahl and G. M. Bounds. *Competing Globally Through Customer Value*. Westport, CT: Quorum Books, 533-552.

Gilbert, N. (1988) Foreign companies use democracy to prosper in the US. *Management Review*. 77, (Summer) 25-29.

Gilbreth, Frank B. (1985) *Primer of Scientific Management*. Easton, PA: Hive Publishing. Reprint of original 1912 publication. New York: Van Nostrand Reinhold.

Gilder, George. (1981) *Wealth and Poverty*. New York: Basic Books. (*2)

Gilks, John F. (1990) Total quality: wave of the future. *The Canadian Business Review*. 17, (Spring) 17-20.

Gill, Mark Stuart. (1990) Stalking six stigma. *Business Month*. (January) 42-46. (*2)

Gillem, T. (1988) Deming's 14 points and hospital quality: Responding to the consumer's demand for the best value in health care. *Journal of Nursing Quality Assurance*. 2, (January) 70-78.

Gilman, J. R. (1963) Quality reports to management. *Industrial Quality Control.* 19, (May) 15-17.

Gilmore, Harold L. (1983) Consumer product quality control costs revisited. *Quality Progress.* 16, (April) 28-32. (*2)

Gilmore, Harold L. (1990) Continuous incremental improvement: An operations strategy for higher quality, lower costs and global competitiveness. In Harry Ivan Costin (Ed.) *Readings in Total Quality Management.* (1994) Fort Worth, TX: Dryden Press, 45-53.

Gilmore, Harold L., and Herbert C. Schwartz. (1986) *Integrated Products Testing and Evaluation: A Systems Approach to Improved Reliability and Quality.* Milwaukee, WI: ASQC Quality Press.

Ginsburg, Alan. (1992) Integrating evaluation into decision making. *The Public Manager: The New Bureaucrat.* 21, (Winter) 24. (*3)

Ginsburg, E. (1955) *What Makes an Executive?* New York: Columbia University Press.

Girshick, M. A., and H. Rubin. (1952) A Bayes approach to a quality control model. *Annals of Mathematical Statistics.* 23, 114-125.

Gitlow, Howard C. (1983) Product defects and productivity. *Harvard Business Review.* 61, (September-October) 131-41.

Gitlow, Howard C. (1986) Union-management relations: An important piece of the quality puzzle. *International Review of Economics and Business.* (August) 43-50.

Gitlow, Howard C., and Shelly J. Gitlow. (1987) *The Deming Guide to Achieving Quality and Competitive Position.* Englewood Cliffs, NJ: Prentice-Hall. (*5)

Gitlow, Howard C., Shelly J. Gitlow, A. Oppenheim, and R. Oppenheim. (1989) *Tools and Methods for the Improvement of Quality.* Homewood, IL: Irwin. (*7)

Gitlow, Howard C., and P. T. Herts. (1983) Product defects and productivity. *Harvard Business Review.* 61, (September-October) 131-41. (*3)

Gittler, H. (1973) Why not put inspectors on incentive? *Quality Management and Engineering.* (December) 22-24.

Gladstein, D. L. (1984) Groups in context: A model of task group effectiveness. *Administrative Science Quarterly.* 29, (January) 499-517.

Glaser, E. M. (1976) *Productivity Gains Through Worklife Improvement.* New York: Harcourt Brace Jovanovich.

Glaser, E. M. (1980) Productivity gain through worklife improvement. *Personnel.* 57, (January) 71-77.

Glaser, Rollin. (1990) *Moving Your Team Toward Self-Management.* King of Prussia, PA: Organization Design and Development.

Glaser, Rollin and C. Glaser. (1981) *Managing by Design.* Reading, MA: Addison-Wesley. (*2)

Glasser, William. (1965) *Reality Therapy.* New York: Harper and Row.

Glasser, William. (1980) *Control Theory.* New York: Harper and Row.

Glasser, William. (1990) *The Quality School: Managing Students Without Coercion.* New York: HarperCollins.

Glasser, William. (1994) *The Control Theory Manager.* New York: Harper Business. (*2)

Glauser, Michelle J. (1982) Factors which facilitate or impede upward communication in organizations. Paper presented at the Academy of Management meeting, New York.

Glaushenner A. (1984) *How to Buy Software.* New York: St. Martin's Press.

Gleason, Daniel. (1981) The cost of test system requirements. *Proceedings, Annual Reliability and Maintainability Symposium.* New York: IEEE, 108-113.

Gleick, J. (1987) *Chaos: Making a New Science.* New York: Viking.

Glen, Thomas G. (1990) *It's Not My Department! How to Get the Service You Want, Exactly the Way You Want It!* New York: William Morrow.

Glen, Thomas G. (1991) The formula for success in TQM. *Bureaucrat.* 20, (Spring) 17-20.

Glen, Thomas G. (1992) Getting people to do what they want to do. *The Public Manager: The New Bureaucrat.* 21, (Fall) 14. (*2)

Glichev, A. V. (1971) Objectives of qualimetry estimation of quality with quantitative methods. Proceedings of the Fifteenth EOQC Conference, Moscow, 117-124.

Glichev, A. V. (1977) Quality control and personnel training. Proceedings, ETC Seminar, Odessa, TX: ETC. (*2)

Glichev, A. V. (1978) Quality improvement and efficiency of social production. Proceedings of the International Conference on Quality Control. (*2)

Glichev, A. V. (1981) The Soviet QC experience. *Quality Progress.* 14, (October) 16. (*2)

Glickman, C. (1990) Klear Knit brings back the sewing circle. *The Charlotte Observer.* (March 19) 1D, 14D.

Glickman, C. (1991) Pretending not to know what we know. *Educational Leadership* 48 (May) 7.

Glover, J. (1992) Achieving the organisational change necessary for successful TQM. *International Journal of Quality and Reliability.* 10, (No. 6) 47-64.

Glover, J. G. (1951) *The Development of American Industries.* Englewood Cliffs, NJ: Prentice-Hall.

Glover, J. G., and L. Maze. (1937) *Managerial Control.* New York: Ronald Press.

Glubb, J. (1976) *The Fate of Empires and Search for Survival.* Edinburgh, UK: William Blackwood.

Gluck, F., S. Kaufman, and A. S. Wallach (1982) The four phases of management. *Journal of Business Strategy.* 2, (Winter) 9-21.

GM posts record loss of $4.45 billion, sends tough message to UAW on closings. (1992) *Wall Street Journal.* (February 25) A3.

GM settles strike at Louisiana plant sparked by effort to boost productivity. (1994) *Wall Street Journal.* (January 17) A2.

GM tightens the screws. (1992) *BusinessWeek.* (June 22) 30.

GM's Smith wants leaner firm, more rivalry among its divisions. (1981) *Wall Street Journal.* (May) 43.

Goal/QPC. (1985) Interrelationship digraph. *Goal Newsletter.* (November) 3-4.

Goal/QPC. (1986) Matrix diagram. *Goal Newsletter.* (March-April) 7-10.

Goal/QPC. (1986) Program decision process chart (PDPC) *Goal Newsletter.* (July-August) 3-4.

Goal QPC Research Report. (1988) *The Memory Jogger: A Pocket Guide of Tools For Continuous Improvement.* Methuen, MA: Goal/QPC.

Goal QPC Research Report. (1994) Hoshin planning: A planning system for implementing total quality management. In Harry Ivan Costin (Ed.) *Readings in Total Quality Management.* (1994) Fort Worth, TX: Dryden Press, 285-300.

Goal QPC Research Report. (1994) Quality function deployment: A process for translating customers' needs into a better product and profit. In Harry Ivan Costin (Ed.) *Readings in Total Quality Management.* (1994) Fort Worth, TX: Dryden Press, 321-329.

Goddard, Robert W. (1989) Work force 2000. *Personnel Journal.* 68, (February) 64-71. (*2)

Godfrey, A. Blanton. (1986) The history and evolution of quality at AT&T. *AT&T Technical Journal.* 65, (March-April) 9-19. (*2)

Godfrey, A. Blanton. (1990) Strategic quality management. *Quality.* (March) 17-22.

Godfrey, A. Blanton. (1993) Ten areas for future research in total quality management. *Quality Management Journal.* (October) 57.

Godfrey, A. Blanton and August B. Mundel. (1984) Guide for selection of an acceptance sampling plan. *Journal of Quality Technology.* 16, (January) 50-55.

Godfrey, A. Blanton, M. S. Phadke, and A. C. Shoemaker. (1986) The development and application of robust design. Taguchi's impact in the United States. *Journal of the Japanese Society for Quality Control.* (April) 145-153.

Godfrey, James T., and William R. Pasewark. (1988) Controlling quality costs. *Management Accounting.* (March) 48-51.

Goel, A. L., and S. M. Wu. (1971) Determination of ARL and a contour nomogram for CUSUM charts to control a normal mean. *Technometrics.* 13, (December) 229-230.

Goepp, Daniel J. (1994) Leaning, inquiry, and problem solving in/and resulting from interdisciplinary management teams. Unpublished Ed.D. dissertation, University of Illinois at Urbana-Champaign, Urbana, IL.

Goff, Barry A., Barry G. Shbeckley, and Sandra L. Hastings. (1992) Lessons for a learning organization. In Harry Ivan Costin

(Ed.) *Readings in Total Quality Management.* (1994) Fort Worth, TX: Dryden Press, 393-402.

Gold, B. (1982) CAM sets new rules for production. *Harvard Business Review.* 60, (November-December) 88-94.

Goldbeck, J. M. (1981) Measuring inspector's productivity. *ASQC Annual Technical Quality Congress Transactions.* Milwaukee, WI: ASQC Quality Press, 343-347.

Goldberg, Philip. (1983) *The Intuitive Edge: Understanding and Developing Intuition.* Los Angeles, CA: Tarcher.

Goldhar, Joel D., and Mariann Jelinek. (1983) Plan for economies of scope. *Harvard Business Review.* 61, (November-December) 141-148.

Goldman, Alfred E., and Susan Schwartz McDonald. (1987) *The Group Depth Interview.* Englewood Cliffs, NJ: Prentice-Hall.

Goldratt, Eliyahu M. (1987) Hierarchical management—The inherent conflict. *The Theory of Constraints Journal.* 1, (October/November) 1-17.

Goldratt, Eliyahu M. (1987) A visit . . . Modine, the McHenry plant. *The Theory of Constraints Journal.* 1, (October/November) 19-40.

Goldratt, Eliyahu M. (1988) Apologia or in the move toward the third stage. *The Theory of Constraints Journal.* 1, (April/May) 23-38.

Goldratt, Eliyahu M. (1988) The fundamental measurements. *The Theory of Constraints Journal.* 1, (August/September) 1-21.

Goldratt, Eliyahu M. (1988) Laying the foundation. *The Theory of Constraints Journal.* 1, (April/May) 1-20.

Goldratt, Eliyahu M. (1988) A visit . . . When quoted lead times are a problem. *The Theory of Constraints Journal.* 1, (August/September) 23-46.

Goldratt, Eliyahu M. (1989) How complex are our systems? *The Theory of Constraints Journal.* 1, (July/August) 1-14.

Goldratt, Eliyahu M. (1989) The importance of a system's constraints. *The Theory of Constraints Journal.* 1, (February/March) 1-12.

Goldratt, Eliyahu M. (1989) A visit . . . Looking beyond the first stage; Just in time. *The Theory of Constraints Journal.* 1, (February/March) 13-46.

Goldratt, Eliyahu M. (1989) A visit . . . Looking beyond the first stage; Just in time, Part two. *The Theory of Constraints Journal.* 1, (July/August) 15-48.

Goldratt, Eliyahu M. (1990) The paradigm shift. *The Theory of Constraints Journal.* 1, (April/May) 1-23.

Goldratt, Eliyahu M. (1990) *Theory of Constraints and How It Should Be Implemented.* Croton-on-Hudson, NY: North River Press. (*2)

Goldratt, Eliyahu M. (1990) A visit . . . Looking beyond the first stage; Just in time, Part three. *The Theory of Constraints Journal.* 1, (April/May) 25-43.

Goldratt, Eliyahu M. (1991) *The Haystack Syndrome: Sifting Information Out of the Data Ocean.* Croton-on-Hudson, NY: North River Press. (*5)

Goldratt, Eliyahu M. (1991) Late-night discussion: Time for total quality management to confront the real issues. *Industry Week.* (December) 51-52.

Goldratt, Eliyhau M. (1992) Late-night discussions. *Industry Week.* (June 3) 38.

Goldratt, Eliyahu M. (1994) *It's Not Luck.* Great Barrington, MA: North River Press.

Goldratt, Eliyahu M. (1997) *Critical Chain: A Business Novel.* Great Barrington, MA: North River Press.

Goldratt, Eliyahu M., and Jeff Cox. (1984) *The Goal: Excellence in Manufacturing*. Croton-on-Hudson, NY: North River Press. (*2)

Goldratt, Eliyahu M., and Jeff Cox. (1986) *The Goal: Excellence in Manufacturing*. Second edition. Croton-on-Hudson, NY: North River Press. (*2)

Goldratt, Eliyahu M., and Jeff Cox. (1992) *The Goal: Excellence In Manufacturing*. Second revised edition. Croton-on-Hudson, NY: North River Press. (*2)

Goldratt, Eliyahu M., and Robert E. Fox. (1986) *The Race*. Croton-on-Hudson, NY: North River Press.

Goldsmith, C. H., and D. W. Gaylor. (1970) Three stage nested designs for estimating variance components. *Technometrics*. 12, (August) 487-498.

Goldstein, D. K. (1986) Hallmark Cards. Harvard Business School Case No. 9-186-044. (July) Cambridge, MA: Harvard Business School.

Goldstein, Nora. (1988) Production strategies when business booms. *In Business*. 10, (March-April) 32-34.

Goldstein, Raymond. (1983) The two-tier audit system. *ASQC Annual Technical Quality Congress Transactions*. Milwaukee, WI: ASQC Quality Press, 14-16.

Goldzimer, Linda Silverman. (1989) *"I'm First." Your Customer's Message to You*. New York: Macmillan.

Goleman, Daniel. (1985) *Vital Lies, Simple Truths*. New York: Simon and Schuster. (*2)

Gomersall, A. (1984) *Machine Intelligence: An International Bibliography with Abstracts on Sensors Automated Manufacturing*. New York: Springer-Verlag.

Gomez-Mejia, L. R., and D. B. Balkin. (1985) Managing a high-tech venture. *Personnel.* 62, (December) 31-36.

Gomez-Mejia, L. R., and D. B. Balkin. (1985) Managing a high tech venture. *Organizational Dynamics.* 8, (Winter) 42-51.

Gomez-Mejia, L. R., and D. B. Balkin. (1988) The perceived effectiveness of individual and aggregate compensation strategies in an R and D setting. *Industrial Relations.* 28, (Winter) 20-25.

Gomez-Mejia, L. R., D. B. Balkin, and T. Welbourne. (1988) The influence of venture capitalists on human resource management practices in the high technology industry. In L. R. Gomez-Mejia and M. W. Lawless (Eds.) *Conference Proceedings Managing the High Technology Firm.* Boulder, CO: University of Colorado Press, 23-28.

Gomez-Mejia, L. R., J. E. McCann, and R. C. Page. (1985) The structure of managerial behaviors. *Industrial Relations.* 24, (Spring) 147-154.

Gooch, J., M. George, and D. Montgomery. (1987) *America Can Compete!* Dallas, TX: Institute of Business Technology.

Goodfellow, Mathew. (1981) Quality control circle programs-what works and what doesn't. *Quality Progress.* 14, (August) 32-33.

Goodman, Alan L. (1982) Cumulative sum control and continuous processes. *ASQC Annual Technical Quality Congress Transactions.* Milwaukee, WI: ASQC Quality Press, 270-274.

Goodman, John and Cynthia J. Grimm. (1990) A quantified case for improving quality now. *Journal for Quality and Participation.* (March) 50-55.

Goodman, John, Arlene Malech, and Theodore Marra. (1987) I can't get no satisfaction. *The Quality Review.* (Winter) 11-14.

Goodman, P. (1979) *Assessing Organizational Change: The Rushton Quality of Work Experiment.* New York: John Wiley. (*2)

Goodman, R. K., J. H. Waheley, and R. H. Rich. (1972) What employees think of the Scanlon Plan. *Personnel*. 49, (September-October) 30-36.

Goodspeed, Shannon and Michael Goodspeed. (1992) The customers inside your business - 6 steps to make you more competitive. *Saskatchewan Business*. 13, (September-October) 12. (*4)

Goodyear squares off to protect its turf from foreign rivals. (1989) *Wall Street Journal.* (December 29) A1.

Gopal, Krishan, Suresh Rai, K. K. Aggarwarl, and J. S. Gupta. (1981) Reliability education in India, present and future. *Institute of Electrical and Electronic Engineers Transactions on Reliability.* 1 (April) 4-7.

Gordon, Maynard M. (1985) *The Iacocca Management Technique.* New York: Dodd, Mead. (*2)

Gordon, T. (1955) *Group Centered Leadership.* Boston, MA: Houghton Mifflin. (*2)

Gordon, T. (1970) *P.E.T.: Parent Effectiveness Training.* New York: Wyden Books.

Gordon, T. (1978) *Effective Leader Training-E.L.T.* New York: Bantam Books.

Gordon, William J. (1956) Operational approach to creativity. *Harvard Business Review*. 34, (November-December) 41-51.

Goree, Paul F., and Thomas A. Musson. (1984) DOD/industry-RandM case study analysis. *Proceedings, Annual Reliability and Maintainability Symposium*. New York: IEEE, 91-98.

Gorlin, H., and L. Schein. (1984) *Innovations in Managing Human Resources.* New York: Conference Board. (*2)

Gorman, J. W., and J. E. Hinman. (1962) Simplex lattice designs for multicomponent systems. *Technometrics*. 4, (April) 463-487.

Gort, Michael. (1979) Structure as a reorganizing device: shifting attention and altering the flow of biases. Unpublished Manuscript.

Goskel, A. K., W. T. Sekino, and W. W. Troutman. (1986) Tools and techniques for VLSI quality. *AT&T Technical Journal*. 65, (March-April) 77-84.

Goss, G., and J. Hartmanis. (1984) *Digital Image Processing Systems*. New York: Springer-Verlag.

Goss, T., Richard Tanner Pascale, and Anthony G. Athos. (1993) The reinvention roller coaster: Risking the present for a powerful future. *Harvard Business Review*. 71, (November-December) 97-108.

Gotlieb, Leo. (1992) Quality comes to the information systems function. *CMA-The Management Accounting Magazine*. 66, (September) 15. (*2)

Gould, Stephen Jay. (1980) *The Panda's Thumb: More Reflections in Natural History*. New York: W. W. Norton. (*2)

Gouldner, A. W. (1954) *Patterns of Industrial Bureaucracy*. New York: Free Press. (*2)

Gouldner, A. W. (1957) Cosmopolitans and locals—Toward an analysis of latent social roles. *Administrative Science Quarterly*. 2, (December) 281-306.

Gouldner, A. W. (1957) Theoretical requirements of the applied social sciences. *American Sociological Review*. 22, 91-102.

Govindarajulu, Z. (1981) *The Sequential Statistical Analysis of Hypothesis Testing, Point and Interval Estimation, and Decision Theory*. Columbus, OH: American Sciences Press.

Gow, Ernest. (1980) Would our use of the Japanese 'quality circle' bring cost savings. *Management Accounting*. 58, (February) 18.

Grabowski, H. (1968) The determinants of industrial research and development. *Journal of Political Economy*. 292-305.

Grady, R. B. (1992) *Practical Software Metrics for Project Management and Process Improvement.* Englewood Cliffs, NJ: Prentice-Hall.

Graham-Moore, Brian and Timothy L. Ross. (1990) *Gainsharing: Plans for Improving Performance.* Washington, DC: Bureau of National Affairs.

Grant, Eugene L. (1952) *Statistical Quality Control.* New York: McGraw-Hill.

Grant, Eugene L. (1953) Industrialists and professors in quality control: A look back and a look ahead. *Industrial Quality Control.* 9, (July) 31. (*2)

Grant, Eugene L., and Richard S. Leavenworth. (1972) *Statistical Quality Control.* Fourth edition. New York: McGraw-Hill. (*3)

Grant, Eugene L., and Richard S. Leavenworth. (1980) *Statistical Quality Control.* Fifth edition. New York: McGraw-Hill. (*3)

Grant, R. M., R. Shani, and R. Krishnan. (1994) TQM's challenge to management theory and practice. *Sloan Management Review.* 35, (Winter) 25-35.

Graves, S. (1971) Better records: The first step to better quality. *Modern Hospital.* 116, (April) 46-48.

Gray, H. L., and Truman Lewis. (1967) A confidence interval for the availability ratio. *Technometrics.* 16, (January) 465-471.

Gray, I., A. L. Bases, C. H. Martin, and A. Sternberg. (1975) *Product Liability, a Management Response.* New York: John Wiley.

Grayson, C. J., Jr. (1967) *Financial Research and Management Decisions.* New York: John Wiley.

Grayson, C. J., Jr. (1972) Eight ways to raise productivity-and profits. *Nations Business.* 60, (November) 30-36.

Grayson, C. J., Jr. (1975) Productivity's impact on our economic future. *The Personnel Administrator.* 20, (June) 20-24.

Grayson, C. J., Jr. (1993) Experience talks: Shun price controls. *Wall Street Journal.* (December 15) A17-18.

Grayson, C. J., Jr., and Carla O'Dell. (1988) *American Business: A Two-Minute Warning.* New York: Free Press. (*2)

Grayson, Mary A. (1992) Benchmark TQM survey tracks a new management era in administration. *Hospitals.* 66, (June) 26-27.

Greb, D. J. (1976) Does bad test equipment accept bad product? A quantitative analysis. *ASQC Annual Technical Quality Congress Transactions.* Milwaukee, WI: ASQC Quality Press, 389-391.

Green, C. M. (1956) *Eli Whitney and the Birth of American Technology.* Boston, MA: Little, Brown.

Green, D. (1991) Quality improvement versus quality assurance? *Topics in Health Records Management.* 11, 58-70.

Green, R. (1995) *Competent Reengineering: Advice, Warnings, and Recipes from Eye Witnesses.* Reading, MA: Addison-Wesley.

Green, R. R. (1981) Productivity improvements for J. C. Penney catalog. *AIIE Proceedings.* (Spring) 489-493.

Green, Stephen G., and M. Ann Welsh. (1988) Cybernetics and dependence: Reframing the control concept. *Academy of Management Review.* (January) 287-301.

Greenberg, Eric Rolf. (1990) Customer service: The key to competitiveness. *Management Review.* 79, (December) 29-31.

Greenberg, L. (1973) *A Practical Guide to Productivity Measurement.* Rockville, MD: BNA Book.

Greenridge, R. M. C. (1953) The case of reliability vs. defective components et al. *Electronic Applications Reliability Review.* 1-12.

Greenwood, Frank and Mary M. Greenwood. (1990) How to raise productivity while cutting costs. *Records Management Quarterly.* (July) 8-15. (*3)

Greer, L. (1961) Leader indulgence and group performance. *Psychological Monographs.* 75, 1-33.

Gregory, Carl, E. (1967) *Management of Intelligence: Scientific Problem Solving and Creativity.* New York: McGraw-Hill.

Gregory, G., and G. J. Resnikoff. (1955) *Some Notes on Mixed Variables and Attributes of Sampling Plans.* Stanford, CA: Stanford University Press.

Griffin, John M. (1990) Demographic opportunities for the '90's and beyond. *Vital Speeches.* 56, (May) 437-440. (*2)

Griffin, R. J. (1980) Aerospace and defense metric system impact. *ASQC Annual Technical Quality Congress Transactions.* Milwaukee, WI: ASQC Quality Press, 606-609.

Griffin, R. W. (1980) Relationship among individual, task design and leader behavior variables. *Academy of Management Journal.* 23, (June) 665-683.

Griffiths, D. (1990) *Implementing Quality With a Customer Focus.* Milwaukee, WI: ASQC Quality Press.

Griggs, W. H., and S. Manring. (1986) Increasing the effectiveness of technical professionals. *Management Review.* 75, (Summer) 21-28.

Griliches, Z. (1979) Issues in assessing the contribution of research and development to economic growth. *The Bell Journal of Economics.* 10, (Spring) 92-116.

Grimlin, D. R., and A. M. Breipohl. (1972) Bayesian acceptance sampling. *IEEE Transactions on Reliability.* (August) 176-180.

Grimm, A. F. (1974) Quality costs: Where are they in the accounting process? *ASQC Annual Technical Quality Congress Transactions.* Milwaukee, WI: ASQC Quality Press, 190-200.

Grinding wheel quality improvement hints. (1977) *Quality*. (April) 44.

Grindley, K. (1973) *The Effective Computer: A Management by Objectives Approach.* New York: McGraw-Hill.

Grissom, G. R., and K. J. Lombardo. (1985) The role of the high-tech human resources professional. *Personnel.* 62, (June) 15-17.

Groff, G. K. (1971) Worker productivity: An integrated view. *Business Horizons.* 14, (April) 78-86.

Gronroos, Christian. (1990) *Management and Marketing: Managing the Moments of Truth in Service Competition.* Lexington, MA: Lexington Books.

Groocock, John. M. (1974) *The Cost of Quality.* London, UK: Pitman.

Groocock, John M. (1976) ITT Europe's 1975 quality cost improvement program quality assurance. *Journal of the Institute of Quality Assurance.* (March) 235-239.

Groocock, John M. (1977) Quality costs and no-failure costs. *EOQC Quality.* (January) 18-19. (*2)

Groocock, John M. (1978) The recall of the nova fritex quality assurance. *Journal of the Institute of Quality Assurance.* 4, (June) 29-11.

Groocock, John M. (1981) Conformance or fitness for use? II: Quality. *EOQC Quality.* (March) 43-46. (*3)

Groocock, John M. (1986) *The Chain of Quality.* New York: John Wiley. (*2)

Groover, M. P., and E. W. Zimmers. (1980) Energy constraints and computer power will greatly impact automated factories in the year 2000. *Industrial Engineering.* 12, (November) 34-43.

Gross, Gilbert. (1963) The gentle bulldozers of Peoria. *Fortune*. (July 1) 167.

Gross, Irwin. (1978) *Insights from Pricing Research, in Pricing Practices and Strategies*. New York: E. L. Bailey. 34-39.

Grossi, Giovanni. (1992) Quality certifications. *Internal Auditor*. 49, (October) 33. (*2)

Grossman, Sanford J., and Oliver D. Hart. (1986) The costs and befefits of wonership: A theory of vertical and lateral integration. *Journal of Political Economy*. (August) 691-719.

Grove, A. S. (1983) *High Output Management*. New York: Random House. (*2)

Grove, A. S. (1984) Why training is the boss's job. *Fortune*. (January 15) 47-54. (*2)

Grubbs, Frank E. (1969) Procedures for detecting outlying observations in samples. *Technometrics*. 12, (February) 1-21. (*2)

Grubbs, Frank E. (1983) An optimum procedure for setting machines. *Journal of Quality Technology*. 15, (October) 155-208. (*3)

Grubbs, Frank E., and H. Coon. (1954) On setting test limits relative to specification limits. *Industrial Quality Control*. 10, (March) 15-20. (*2)

Grubman, S. Martin and William R. Pabst Jr. (1969) MIL-STD-69OB. Failure rate sampling plans and procedures. *Journal of Quality Technology*. 1, (July) 205-216.

Gryna, Frank M., Jr. (1970) *User costs of poor product quality*. Iowa City, IA: University of Iowa Press.

Gryna, Frank M., Jr. (1972) User quality costs. *Quality Progress*. 5, (November) 18-21.

Gryna, Frank M., Jr. (1977) Quality costs: User vs. manufacturer. *Quality Progress*. 10, (June) 10-13. (*2)

Gryna, Frank M., Jr. (1978) Quality costs: What does management expect? *ASQC Technological Conference Transactions*. Milwaukee, WI: ASQC Quality Press, 210-217.

Gryna, Frank M., Jr. (1981) *Quality Circles: A Team Approach to Problem Solving*. New York: American Management Association. (*2)

Gryna, Frank M., Jr., N. J. McAfee, C. M. Ryerson, and S. Zwerling. (1960) *Reliability Training Text*. New York: Institute of Radio Engineers.

Guaspari, J. (1985) *I Know It When I See It*. New York: AMACOM. (*2)

Gudden, G. K., and R. H. Reck. (1991) Combining quality and reengineering for operational superiority. *Perspectives on the Management of Information Technology*. 8, (No. 1) 1-12.

Guest, R. H. (1979) Quality of worklife—Learning from Tarrytown. *Harvard Business Review*. 57, (July-August) 76-87. (*3)

Guest, R. H. (1981) Gauging: The next five years. *Quality Assurance*. 7, (December) 113-115.

Guha, S., W. J. Kettinger, and J. T. C. Teng. (1994) Business process reengineering: Building a comprehensive methodology. *Information Systems Management*. (Spring) 13-22.

Guide for Sampling Inspection. (1965) MIL-HDBK-53 Washington, DC: U.S. Government Printing Office. (*2)

Gulliver, Frank R. (1987) Post-project appraisals pay. *Harvard Business Review*. 65, (March-April) 128-131. (*2)

Gumpert, David E. (1986) The joys of keeping the company small. *Harvard Business Review*. 64, (July-August) 6-14.

Gunn, Thomas G. (1987) *Manufacturing for Competitive Advantage: Becoming a World Class Manufacturer*. Cambridge, MA: Ballinger.

Gunter, B. (1983) The fallacy of 100% inspection. *ASQC Statistical Division Newsletter*. 5, (September) 1-2.

Gunter, Berton. (1987) A perspective on the Taguchi methods. *Quality Progress*. 20, (June) 44-52.

Gupta, Ashok K., and Vijay Govindarajan. (1984) Build, hold, harvest: Converting strategic intentions into reality. *Journal of Business Strategy*. 4, (Winter) 34-47.

Gupta, Ashok K., and Vijay Govindarajan. (1984) Business unit strategy, managerial characteristics and business unit effectiveness at strategy implementation. *Academy of Management Journal*. 27, (January) 11.

Gupta, Ashok K., and D. Wilemon. (1986) Rand and marketing managers in high-tech companies: Are they different? *IEEE Transactions on Engineering Management*. 1, (February) 21-25.

Gupta, Sushil K. (1993) Quality improvement in teaching. *Explorations in Teaching and Learning*. 3, (January) 4-5.

Gushue, John M., and N. S. Shashidhara. (1986) Quality assurance for hazardous waste management. *ASQC Annual Technical Quality Congress Transactions*. Milwaukee, WI: ASQC Quality Press, 492-498.

Gust, Lawrence J. (1985) Non-manufacturing quality improvement. *The Juran Report*. (Winter) 112-120. (*2)

Gutman, N. (1984) *The Matrix Management*. New York: Marcel Dekker.

Gutt, J. D., and G. F. Gruska. (1977) Variation simulation. *ASQC Annual Technical Quality Congress Transactions*. Milwaukee, WI: ASQC Quality Press, 557-563.

Guyon, Janet. (1980) Family feeling at Delta creates loyal workers, enemy of unions. *Wall Street Journal*. (July 7) 13. (*2)

Gwiazdecki, M. (1978) Good work competition: Essential element of quality policy in Poland. Proceedings, Twentieth Conference, Dresden. 1, 150. (*2)

Gwynne, S. C. (1990) The right stuff. *Time*. (October 29) 74-84. (*2)

Gyllenhammar, P. G. (1977) *People at Work*. Reading, MA: Addison-Wesley. (*2)

Haas, E. (1987) Breakthrough manufacturing. *Harvard Business Review*. 65, (March-April) 75-81.

Haavind, Robert. (1989) Hewlett-Packard unravels the mysteries of quality. *Electronic Business*. 15, (October 16) 101-105.

Haberler, Gottfried. (1964) *Prosperity and Depression*. New York: W. W. Norton.

Haberman, Martin. (1991) The pedagogy of poverty versus good teaching. *Phi Delta Kappan*. 73, (December) 292-200.

Hackman, J. Richard. (1975) Is job enrichment just a fad? *Harvard Business Review*. 53, (October-November) 129-138.

Hackman, J. Richard. (1984) *Designing Research That Works*. Reading, MA: Addison-Wesley.

Hackman, J. Richard. (1987) The design of work teams. In Jay W. Lorsch (Ed.) *Handbook of Organizational Behavior*. Englewood Cliffs, NJ: Prentice-Hall.

Hackman, J. Richard. (1989) *Groups That Work (And Those That Don't): Creating Conditions for Effective Teamwork*. San Francisco, CA: Jossey-Bass.

Hackman, J. Richard and Edward E. Lawler III. (1971) Employee reactions to job characteristics. *Journal of Applied Psychology*. 55, (June) 259-286. (*2)

Hackman, J. Richard and Greg R. Oldham. (1975) Development of the job diagnostic survey. *Journal of Applied Psychology*. 59, (April) 111-128.

Hackman, J. Richard and Greg R. Oldham. (1980) *Work Redesign.* Reading, MA: Addison-Wesley. (*2)

Hackman, J. Richard, Greg R. Oldham, R. Janson, and K. Purdy. (1975) A new strategy for job enrichment. *California Management Review.* 17, (Summer) 57-71.

Hackman, J. Richard and Lloyd Suttle. (1977) *Improving Life at Work: Behavioral Science Approaches to Organizational Change.* Santa Monica, CA: Goodyear. (*3)

Hadesky, John L. (1988) *Productivity and Quality Improvement.* New York: McGraw-Hill.

Hadley, G. (1967) *Introduction to Probability and Statistical Decision Theory.* San Francisco, CA: Holden-Day.

Haefele, John W. (1962) *Creativity and Innovation.* New York: Van Nostrand Reinhold.

Hagan, J. T. (1968) *A Management Role for Quality Control.* New York: American Management Association.

Hagan, J. T. (1984) The management of quality: Preparing for a competitive future. *Quality Progress.* 17, (December) 21.

Hagan, J. T. (1985) Quality cost II: The economics of quality improvement. *Quality Progress.* 18, (October) 48-51.

Hahn, G. J. (1970) Additional factors for calculating prediction intervals for samples from a normal distribution. *Journal of the American Statistical Association.* 75, (311) 1668-1676.

Hahn, G. J. (1970) Statistical intervals for a normal population, formulas, assumptions, some derivations. *Journal of Quality Technology.* 2, (January) 115-125, 195-206.

Hahn, G. J. (1971) How abnormal is normality? *Journal of Quality Technology*. 3, (January) 18-22.

Hahn, G. J. (1984) Discussion. *Technometrics*. 26, (February) 110-115.

Hahn, G. J. (1985) More intelligent statistical software and statistical expert systems, future directions. *The American Statistician*. 39, (January) 1-8.

Hahn, G. J., and A. F. Dershowitz. (1974) Evolutionary operations today—some survey results and observations. *Applied Statistics*. 23, 214-218.

Hahn, G. J., and S. S. Shapiro (1967) *Statistical Models in Engineering*. New York: John Wiley. (*2)

Haidinger, T. P., and P. Richardson. (1975) *A Managers Guide to Computer Timesharing*. New York: John Wiley.

Hains R. W. (1969) Economics of quality. *ASQC Annual Technical Quality Congress Transactions*. Milwaukee, WI: ASQC Quality Press, 439-443.

Hains, R. W. (1978) Measurement of subjective variables. *ASQC Annual Technical Quality Congress Transactions*. Milwaukee, WI: ASQC Quality Press. 237-244.

Haire, M. (1959) *Modern Organizational Theory*. New York: John Wiley.

Halberstam, David. (1960) *The War Effort during WWII: Lectures, Articles and Interview Notes*. New York: Dover.

Halberstam, David. (1983) Can we rise to the Japanese challenge? *Parade Magazine*. (October) 7. (*2)

Halberstam, David. (1984) Quality—what we can learn from the American who taught Japan. *Parade Magazine*. (July 8) 6.

Halberstam, David. (1984) Yes we can. *Parade Magazine*. (July) 4.

Halberstam, David. (1987) *The Reckoning*. New York: Avon Books. (*7)

Hald, A. (1952) *Statistical Theory with Engineering Applications*. New York: John Wiley.

Hald, A. (1960) The compound hypergeometric distribution and a system of single sampling inspection plans based on prior distributions and costs. *Technometrics.* 2, (August) 275-340. (*2)

Hald, A. (1972) Asymptotic properties of Bayesian decision rules for two terminal decisions and multiple sampling. *Journal of the Royal Statistical Society.* 34, (April) 55-74.

Hald, A. (1981) *Statistical Theory of Sampling Inspection by Attributes*. New York: Academic Press. (*2)

Hale, Guy A. (1982) *Process Management Skills*. Walnut Creek, CA: Alamo Learning Systems.

Hales, H. L. (1984) How small firms can approach and benefit from computer-integrated manufacturing systems. *Industrial Engineering.* 16, (June) 43-51.

Hall, D., and K. Nougaim. (1968) An examination of Maslow's need hierarchy in an organizational setting. *Organizational Behavior and Human Performance.* 3, (January) 12-35.

Hall, D. J., and M. A. Saias. (1980) Strategy follows structure. *Strategic Management Journal.* 1, (May-June) 156.

Hall, Frank. (1971) Participation improves quality . . . because it changes attitudes. *Machinery.* (July) 46-50.

Hall, Frank. (1980) Made in Japan. *Plastics Engineering.* (November) 38-48.

Hall, G., J. Rosenthal, and J. Wade. (1993) How to make reengineering really work. *Harvard Business Review.* 71, (November-December) 119-131.

Hall, James L., and Joe K. Leidecker. (1981) Is Japanese-Style Management anything new? *Human Resource Management*. 20, (Winter) 14-21.

Hall, Phil. (1992) Living with TQM. *Risk Management*. 39, (March) 20.

Hall, R. J. (1985) Professional management relations: Imagery vs. action. *Human Resource Management*. 24, (Spring/Summer) 227-236.

Hall, R. J., and J. Nakane. (1990) *Flexibility: Manufacturing Battlefield of the 90s*. Wheeling, IL: Association for Manufacturing Excellence.

Hall, Robert W. (1983) *Zero Inventories*. Homewood, IL: Dow Jones-Irwin. (*3)

Hall, Robert W. (1987) *Attaining Manufacturing Excellence*. Homewood, IL: Dow Jones-Irwin. (*3)

Hall, Robert W. (1987) Measuring progress: Manufacturing essential. *Target*. (Summer) 7.

Hall, William D. (1980) Survival strategies in a hostile environment. *Harvard Business Review*. 58, (January-February) 75-85.

Halliday, David and Robert Resnick. (1974) *Fundamentals of Physics*. New York: John Wiley.

Halligan, Beate. (1992) ISO 9000 standards prepare you to compete. *Industrial Distribution*. 81, (May) 100. (*2)

Halloran, Richard. (1969) *Japan: Images and Realities*. New York: Random House.

Halperin, S. (1985) ESD—what, where and why. *Quality*. (September) 18-24.

Halpin, J. F. (1966) *Zero Defects: A New Dimension in Quality Assurance*. New York: McGraw-Hill. (*2)

Hamaker, H. C. (1951) Some basic principles of sampling inspection by attributes. Proceedings of the International Statistical Conference.

Hamaker, H. C. (1958) Some basic principles of sampling inspection by attributes. *Applied Statistics*. 7, 149-159.

Hamaker. H. C. (1979) Acceptance sampling for percent defective by variables and by attributes. *Journal of Quality Technology*. 11, (July) 139-148.

Hambrick, D. C. (1982) Environmental scanning and organizational strategy. *Strategic Management Journal*. 3, (July-August) 159-174.

Hambrick, D. C., and D. Lei. (1985) Toward an empirical prioritization of contingency variables for business strategy. *Academy of Management Journal*. 28, (April) 763-788.

Hamel, G., and C. K. Prahalad. (1989) Strategic intent. *Harvard Business Review*. 67, (May-June) 63-76.

Hamel, G., and C. K. Prahalad. (1990) The core competence of the corporation. *Harvard Business Review*. 68, (May-June) 70-91.

Hamel, G., and C. K. Prahalad. (1991) Corporate imagination and expeditionary marketing. *Harvard Business Review*. 69, (July-August) 81-92.

Hamel, G., Y. L. Diz, and C. K. Prahalad. (1989) Collaborate with your competitors and win. *Harvard Business Review*. 67, (January-February) 133-139.

Hamilton, E. (1948) *The Greek Way*. New York: New American Library. (*2)

Hamilton, Sharon Gale. (1994) An examination of total quality management at the United Way of Dade County, Incorporated (Florida). Unpublished Ph.D. dissertation, University of Miami, Coral Gables, FL.

Hamilton, W. F. (1986) Corporate strategies for managing emerging technologies. *Technology in Society*. 7, 197-212.

Hamlin, J. (1978) Productivity improvement: An organized effort. American Institute of Industrial Engineers. 1978 Spring Annual Conference Proceedings. Norcross, GA: AIIE, 223-228.

Hammel, Lisa. (1980) *Solutions in Statistics and Probability.* Columbus, OH: American Sciences Press.

Hammel, Lisa. (1983) Heteroscedasticity. *Encyclopedia of Statistical Sciences*. New York: John Wiley.

Hammel, Lisa and Zaven A. Karian. (1985) *Modern Design and Analysis of Discrete-Event Computer Simulations.* Los Angeles, CA: Los Angles Press.

Hammel, Lisa, Zaven A. Karian, and Rudolph James Marshal III. (1985) Random number generation on microcomputers. Proceedings of the Conference on Simulation on Microcomputers. La Jolla, CA.

Hammel, Lisa and S. N. Mishra. (1988) *Modern Mathematical Statistics*. New York: John Wiley.

Hammel, Lisa and Thomas G. Ralley. (1981) *The Handbook of Random Number Generation and Testing with Testrand Computer Code.* Columbus, OH: American Sciences Press.

Hammer, Michael. (1990) Reengineering work: Don't automate, obliterate. *Harvard Business Review*. 68, (July-August) 104-112. (*4)

Hammer, Michael. (1991) Why we need both continuous and discontinuous improvement. *Perspectives on the Management of Information Technology*. 8, (No. 1) 6-7.

Hammer, Michael and James Champy. (1993) *Reengineering the Corporation: A Manifesto for Business Revolution*. New York: Harper Business. (*24)

Hammer, Michael and Steven A. Stanton. (1995) *The Reengineering Revolution: A Handbook*. New York: Harper Business. (*2)

Hammer, Willie. (1980) *Product Safety Management and Engineering*. Englewood Cliffs, NJ: Prentice-Hall.

Hammons, Charles. (1990) Total quality management in the public sector. *Management Decision (UK)*. 28, (June) 15-19.

Hammons, Charles and Gary A. Maddux. (1987) An obligation to improve. *Management Decision.* 27, (November 6) 5-8. (*3)

Hampton, David R. (1986) *Management.* New York: McGraw-Hill.

Hampton, David R., C. E. Summer, and R. A. Webber. (1968) *Organizational Behavior and the Practice of Management.* Glenview, IL: Scott Foresman.

Hampton, David R., C. E. Summer, and R. A. Webber. (1975) *Manufacturing Organization and Management.* Third edition. Englewood Cliffs, NJ: Prentice-Hall.

Hampton, William J. (1988) GM bets an arm and a leg on a people-free plant. *BusinessWeek.* (September 12) 72-73.

Hamscher, W. (1994) AI in business-process reengineering: A report of the 1994 workshop. *AI Magazine.* 15, (No. 4) 71-72.

Hamson, Ned. (1990) TQM can save nearly $300 billion for nation. *Journal for Quality and Participation.* (December) 54-56.

Hanami, Tadashi. (1982) *Labor Relations in Japan Today.* Tokyo: Kodansha International.

Hancock, G. (1984) Quality brings sales dividends at Jaguar. *Quality Progress.* 17, (May) 32.

Handfield, R. (1989) Quality management in Japan versus the United States. *Production and Inventory Management.* (Second Quarter) 79-84.

Handy, C. B. (1981) *Understanding Organizations.* New York: Penguin.

Handy, C. B. (1989) *The Age of Unreason*. London: Century Business.

Hanley, J. (1980) Our experience with quality circles. *Quality Progress*. 13, (February) 22-24. (*2)

Hanlon, M. D., David A. Nadler, and D. Gladstein. (1985) *Attempting Work Reform*. New York: John Wiley. (*2)

Hansel, John L. (1985) The cult of technical rationality. *AAACJC Journal*. (March) 39-41.

Hansen, G. (1994) A complex process: The case for automated assistance in business process reengineering. *OR/MS Today*. (August) 34-41.

Hanson, Bertrand L. (1960) *Work Sampling for Modern Management*. Englewood Cliffs, New Jersey: Prentice-Hall.

Hanson, Bertrand L. (1963) *Quality Control Theory and Applications*. Englewood Cliffs, NJ: Prentice-Hall.

Harari, Oren. (1992) Quality is a good bit-box. *Management Review*. 81, (December) 8. (*3)

Harari, Oren. (1993) Ten reasons why TQM doesn't work. *Management Review*. 82, January) 33. (*3)

Harari, Oren. (1993) Three very difficult steps to total quality. *Management Review*. 82, (April) 39. (*3)

Harbison, F., and A. Myers. (1959) *Management in the Industrial World*. New York: McGraw-Hill.

Hard, Rob. (1992) Hospitals look to hospitality service firms to meet TQM goals. *Hospitals*. 66, (May 20) 56. (*2)

The Hare and the Tortoise. (1989) Milwaukee, WI: ASQC Quality Press.(*2)

Hare, Paul. (1952) A study of interaction and consensus in different sized groups. *American Sociological Review.* 17, (June) 261-268.

Hare, Paul A., F. Borgatta, and R. F. Bales. (1955) *Small Groups.* New York: Alfred A. Knopf.

Harmon, Kenneth L., Jr. (1988) Total quality and management of performance improvement. *SAM Advanced Management Journal.* 53, (Autumn) 4-12.

Harper, Sam T. (1982) I was operations manager. *Personal Communication.* (January) 14-18.

Harrigan, K. R. (1983) *Strategies for Vertical Integration.* Lexington, MA: Lexington Books.

Harrigan, K. R. (1985) *Strategies for Joint Ventures.* Lexington, MA: Lexington Books.

Harrington, E. C., Jr. (1965) The desirability function. *Industrial Quality Control.* 21, (April) 10.

Harrington, H. James. (1981) Process qualification-manufacturing's insurance policy. *IBM Technical Report.* San Jose, CA.

Harrington, H. James. (1984) *Understanding the Manufacturing Process.* New York: Marcel Dekker.

Harrington, H. James. (1986) *Poor-Quality Cost.* Milwaukee, WI: ASQC Quality Press.

Harrington, H. James. (1987) *The Improvement Process: How America's Leading Companies Improve Quality.* New York: McGraw-Hill. (*2)

Harrington, H. James. (1988) *Excellence the IBM Way.* Milwaukee, WI: ASQC Quality Press. (*2)

Harrington, H. James. (1990) Worklife in the year 2000. *Journal for Quality and Participation.* (March) 56-57.

Harrington, H. James. (1991) *Business Process Improvement: The Breakthrough Strategy for Total Quality, Productivity, and Competitiveness.* New York: McGraw-Hill. (*3)

Harrington, H. James and Wayne S. Rieker. (1988) The end of slavery: Quality control circles. *Journal for Quality and Participation.* (March) 16-20. (*3)

Harrington, Joseph, Jr. (1979) *Computer Integrated Manufacturing.* Huntington, NY: Robert E. Krieger.

Harris, C. (1981) What ails IBM. *Financial World.* (May) 17.

Harris, C. (1985) Information power. *BusinessWeek.* (October 14) 53-55.

Harris, D. H., and F. B. Chaney. (1969) *Human Factors in Quality Assurance.* New York: John Wiley.

Harris, F. W. (1915) *Operations and Cost.* Chicago, Il: A. W. Shaw. (*2)

Harris, R. D., and R. F. Gonzalez. (1981) *The Operations Manager: Role, Problems, and Techniques.* St. Paul, MN: West Publishing.

Harrison, Dan. (1992) You can play an important role in your company's focus on quality. *Institutional Distribution.* 28, (July) 18. (*2)

Harrison, H. L., and J. G. Bollinger. (1966) *Introduction To Automatic Controls.* Third edition. Scranton, PA: International Textbook. (*2)

Harrison, J. F. (1978) *Improving Performance and Productivity: Why Won't They Do What I Want Them to Do?* Reading, MA: Addison-Wesley.

Hart, Christoper W. L. (1990) The profitable art of service recovery. *Harvard Business Review.* 68, (July-August) 148-156. (*3)

Hart, Christopher W. L. (1993) *Extraordinary Guarantees: A New Way to Build Quality Throughout Your Company and Ensure Satisfaction for Your Customers*. New York: AMACOM.

Hart, Christopher W. L., E. Bogan, and D. O'Brien. (1990) Winning isn't everything. *Harvard Business Review*. 68, (January-February) 208.

Hart, Marilyn K., and R. F. Hart. (1989) *Quantitative Methods for Quality and Productivity Improvement*. Milwaukee, WI: ASQC Quality Press. (*4)

Hart, Roger D. (1994) *Quality Handbook for the Architectural, Engineering, and Construction Community*. Milwaukee, WI: ASQC Quality Press.

Hart, W. (1992) MD-directed critical pathways: It's time. *Hospitals*. 66, (December) 56. (*3)

Hart, W. (1992) Using the Baldrige criteria for assessment and continuous improvement. *Human Resources Policies and Practices*. 8, (April) 40.

Harter, H. Leon. (1983) *The Chronological Annotated Bibliography of Order Statistics*. Columbus: American Sciences Press.

Harter, H. Leon and Satya D. Dubey. (1967) *Theory and Tables for Tests of Hypotheses concerning the Mean and the Variance of a Weibull Population*. Washington, DC: U.S. Department of Commerce.

Harty, J. D., G. W. Plossl, and O. W. Wight. (1963) Management of lot-size inventories. *APICS Special Report*. 1, 33-40. (*2)

Hartz, Ove. (1982) Quality management and cooperation in small firms. *Quality Progress*. 15, (April) 18-21.

Harvey, Jeff B. (1988) *The Abilene Paradox and Other Meditations on Management*. Lexington, MA: Lexington Books. (*2)

Harwood, C. C. (1984) The view from the top. *Quality Progress.* 17, (October) 26-30.

Hassan, Z. (1979) An optimal quality control design for a single-product serial manufacturing system. *Journal of Quality Technology.* 11, (January) 1.

Hassan, Z. (1982) Quality control design for a single product manufacturing system subject to inspection error. *Engineering Costs and Production Economics*, 699-117.

Hatch, M. J. (1987) Physical barriers, task characteristics and interaction activity in research and development firms. *Administrative Science Quarterly.* 32, (September) 387-399.

Hattrup, Colleen. (1982) The changing roles of participants in a self-facilitation mode. IAQC Fourth Annual Conference Transactions. Cincinnati, OH: International Association of Quality Circles.

Hatvany, Nina and Vladimir Pucik. (1981) Japanese management practices and productivity. *Organization Dynamics.* 9, (July) 44-64.

Hauenstein, P., and William C. Byham. (1989) *Understanding Job Analysis.* Monograph XI. Pittsburgh, PA: Development Dimensions International.

Haugen, Robert and Terrence Langetieg. (1975) An empirical test for synergism in merger. *Journal of Finance.* (September)

Hauser, John R., and Don Clausing. (1988) The house of quality. *Harvard Business Review.* 66, (May-June) 63-73. (*3)

Hawken, Paul. (1987) Mastering the numbers. *Inc.* (October) 19-20.

Hawken, Peter. (1983) *The Next Economy.* New York: Random House.

Hawley, K. (1989) *Executive Quality Management—What You Get Is What You Lead.* Minneapolis, MN: Undersea Systems Division, Honeywell Corporation.

Hax, A. C., and N. C. Majluf. (1984) *Strategic Management*. Englewood Cliffs, NJ: Prentice-Hall, 383-399.

Hay, Edward J. (1988) *The Just-in-Time Breakthrough: Implementing the New Manufacturing Basics*. New York: John Wiley. (*2)

Hayakawa, S. I. (1974) *Language in Thought and Action*. London, UK: Allen and Unwin. (*2)

Hayashi, Alden M. (1988) GE says solid state is here to stay. *Electronic Business*. 14, (April 1) 52-56.

Hayashi, Ryozo. (1990) National policy on the information service industry. *Business Japan*. (March) 49-61.

Hayes, Glenn E. (1982) Quality and productivity—The education gap. *Quality*. (October) 50-51.

Hayes, Glenn E. (1985) The box plot. *Quality Progress*. 18, (December) 12-17.

Hayes, Glenn E. (1985) Random sampling and the assembly line. *Quality*. (March) 3.

Hayes, Glenn E. (1985) Quality and productivity: Challenges for management. *Quality vs Progress*. (October) 42-46.

Hayes, Glenn E. (1985) *Quality and Productivity: The New Challenge*. Wheaton, IL: Hitchcock Publishing.

Hayes, Glenn E. (1990) Three views of TQM. *Quality Magazine*. (April) 14-19.

Hayes, Glenn E., and H. G. Roming. (1982) *Modern Quality Control*. Revised edition. Encino, CA: Free. (*3)

Hayes, J. J. (1962) *Creative Management*. New York: John Wiley.

Hayes, J. J. (1963) *Problem Solving Discussions and Conferences*. New York: McGraw-Hill.

Hayes, R. H. (1981) Reflections on Japanese factory management. Harvard Business School Working Paper. (January) 47-56.

Hayes, R. H. (1981) Why Japanese factories work. *Harvard Business Review.* 59, (July-August) 57-66. (*2)

Hayes, R. H. (1985) Strategic planning: Forward in reverse? *Harvard Business Review.* 63, (November-December) 111-119. (*2)

Hayes, R. H., and W. J. Abernathy. (1980) Managing our way to economic decline. *Harvard Business Review.* 68, (July-August) 67-77. (*4)

Hayes, R. H., and Kim B. Clark. (1986) Why some factories are more productive than others. *Harvard Business Review.* 64, (September-October) 66-73.

Hayes, R. H., and R. W. Schmenner. (1978) How should you organize for manufacturing? *Harvard Business Review.* 56, (January-February) 105-118.

Hayes, R. H., and Steven C. Wheelwright. (1979) Link manufacturing process and product life cycles. *Harvard Business Review.* 57, (January-February) 133-140. (*2)

Hayes, R. H., Steven C. Wheelwright, and Kim B. Clark. (1988) *Dynamic Manufacturing: Creating the Learning Organization.* New York: Free Press. (*5)

Hayes, R. H., and Steven C. Wheelwright. (1984) *Restoring Our Competitive Edge: Competing Through Manufacturing.* New York: John Wiley. (*10)

Hayes, Thomas C. (1991) Behind Wal-Mart's surge, a web of suppliers. *New York Times.* (July 1) C1, C2.

Haylet, K., J. Plewa, and M. Watts. (1993) Reengineering tops CIO menu. *Datamation.* (April 15) 73-74.

Hayre, L. S. (1985) Group sequential sampling with variable group sizes. *Journal of the Royal Statistical Society.* 47, (May) 90-97.

Hayter, W. T. (1961) Process and quality control for management. *ASQC Annual Technical Quality Congress Transactions*. Milwaukee WI: ASQC Quality Press, 61-66.

Hazama, Hiroshi. (1979) Characteristics of Japanese corporate management. *Toyota Quarterly Review*. 8, (Winter) 1-8.

Healy, John. (1986) Modeling IC failure rates. *Proceedings, Annual Reliability and Maintainability Symposium*. New York: IEEE, 307-311.

Heaton, H. (1977) *Productivity in Service Organizations*. New York: McGraw-Hill.

Heckel, Jim. (1984) Purchasing considerations under the JIT concept. *Quality*. (February) 36.

Heckscher, C. (1988) *The New Unionism*. New York: Basic Books.

Hegland, Ronald E. (1981) Quality circles: Key to productivity with quality. *Production Engineering*. (June) 26-31.

Heiko, L. (1988) The role of manufacturability in managing new product development. In L. R. Gomez-Mejia and M. W. Lawless (Eds.) *Conference Proceedings Managing the High Technology Firm*. Boulder, CO: University of Colorado Press, 149-153.

Heiner, J., and E. Jacobson. (1976) A model of task group development in complex organizations and a strategy of implementation. (1976) *Academy of Management Review*. (April) 98-111.

Heizer, Jay H. (1993) *Production Operations Management: Strategies and Tactics*. Boston, MA: Allyn and Bacon.

Heldt, John and Robert J. Pinschmidt. (1977) Learning by doing. *Quality Progress*. 10, (August) 30-32.

Heldt, John. (1975) *Quality and Reliability Cases, Projects and Exercises*. Los Altos Hills, CA: Deanza College Book Store.

Hellend, Kris L., Jr. (1978) Motivating management on maintainability. *Proceedings, Annual Reliability and Maintainability Symposium*. New York: IEEE, 32-37.

Heller, Joseph. (1975) *Something Happened.* New York: Ballantine Books.

Heller, Joseph. (1984) *God Knows.* New York: Alfred A. Knopf.

Heller, Robert. (1984) *The Supermanagers.* New York: E. P. Dutton.

Heller, Robert. (1991) Driving necessity. *Management Today.* (January) 32.

Heller, Robert. (1992) How BA engineered its turnaround. *Management Today*. (September) 50. (*2)

Heller, Robert. (1993) TQM: Not a panacea but a pilgrimage. *Management Today*. (January) 36. (*3)

Helm, E and B. Trolle. (1946) Selection of a test panel. *Wallerstein Laboratories Communications*. 9, 181-194.

Henderson, B. D. (1979) *Henderson on Corporate Strategy.* Cambridge, MA: Abt Books.

Henderson, J. C., and N. Venkatraman. (1993) Strategic alignment: Leveraging information technology for transforming organizations. *IBM Systems Journal*. 32, (No. 1) 4-16.

Henderson, J. T. (1979) A computerized LCC/ORLA methodology. *Proceedings, Annual Reliability and Maintainability Symposium*. New York: IEEE, 51-55.

Henderson, Richard. (1980) *Performance Appraisal: Theory to Practice*. Reston, VA: Reston Publishing Company. (*2)

Hendricks, Charles F., and Arlene Triplett. (1989) TQM: Strategy for '90s management. *Personnel Administrator*. 34, 42.

Henkoff, A. (1989) What Motorola learns from Japan. *Fortune.* (April 15) 157.+

Henley, Ernest J. (1979) Analytical methods in risk and safety assessment. *ASQC Annual Technical Quality Congress Transactions.* Milwaukee, WI: ASQC Quality Press, 717-725.

Henry William A., III. (1990) Beyond the melting pot. *Time.* (April 9) 28-31. (*2)

Here come the baby boomers. (1984) *U.S. News and World Report.* (November 5) 27.

Herip, Walter M. (1982) Forging ahead. *Quality Circles Journal.* 5, (November) 9-11.

Herndon, Booton. (1969) *Ford: An Unconventional Biography of the Men and Their Times.* New York: Weybright and Talley.

Herrold, George R. (1976) GIDEP data aids technical problem solving. *Proceedings, Annual Reliability and Maintainability Symposium.* New York: IEEE, 46-51.

Herschdoerfer, S. M. (1986) *Quality Control in the Food Industry.* New York: Academic Press. (*2)

Hersey, P., and Kenneth Blanchard. (1982) *Management of Organizational Behavior.* Fourth edition. Englewood Cliffs, NJ: Prentice-Hall.

Hershauer, J. C., and W. A. Ruch. (1978) A worker productivity model and its use at Lincoln Electric. *Interfaces.* 8, (May) 80-89.

Hershfield, D. C. (1976) Barriers to increased labor productivity. *The Conference Board Record.* 13, (July) 38-41.

Hershkowitz, Brian. (1992) TQM in mortgage banking. *Mortgage Banking.* 53, (December) 89. (*3)

Hertzberg, Agnes M., and D. R. Cox. (1969) Recent work on the design of experiments: A bibliography and a review. *Journal of the Royal Statistical Society.* 132, (January) 29-67.

Herzberg, Fredrick. (1966) *Work and the Nature of Man.* New York: World Publishing Company. (*3)

Herzberg, Fredrick. (1968) One more time: How do you motivate employees? *Harvard Business Review.* 44, (January-February) 53-62. (*2)

Herzberg, Fredrick. (1979) *The Motivation of Work.* New York: John Wiley.

Herzberg, Fredrick. (1987) One more time: How do you motivate employees? *Harvard Business Review.* (January-February) 109-120. (*4)

Herzberg, Fredrick, Bernard Mauser, and Barbara Bloch Snyderman. (1959) *The Motivation to Work.* New York: John Wiley. (*2)

Heskett, James L. (1986) *Managing in the Service Economy.* Boston, MA: Harvard Business School Press.

Heskett, James L. (1987) Lessons in the service sector. *Harvard Business Review.* 65, (March-April) 118-126. (*2)

Heskett, James L., W. Earl Sasser Jr., and Christopher W. L. Hart. (1990) *Service Breakthroughs: Changing the Rules of the Game.* New York: Free Press.

Heslop, S. (1981) Practical experience in implementing quality assurance in a small business. *Quality Assurance.* 7, (March) 10-14.

Hess, Mary Abbot. (1991) Minding your TQM's. *Journal of the American Dietetic Association.* 91, (September) 1126.

Hewins, Ralph. (1967) *The Japanese Miracle Men.* London, UK: Secker and Warburg.

Hewlett, William R., and David Packard. (1980) *The HP Way*. Palo Alto, CA: Hewlett-Packard. (*4)

Heymann, Kenneth. (1992) Quality management: A ten-point model. *Cornell H.R.A. Quarterly*. (October) 51-60.

Hickerson, Mel. (1968) *Ernie Breech: The Story of His Remarkable Career at General Motors, Ford, and TWA*. Des Moines, IA: Meredith Corporation.

Hickey, J. J. (1974) *Employee Productivity: How to Improve and Measure Your Company's Performance.* Stratford, CT: Institute for the Advancement of Scientific Management and Control.

Hickman, C. R. (1984) *Creating Excellence*. New York: New American Library.

Hicks, C. R. (1955) Some applications of Hotelling's T. *Industrial Quality Control*. 11, (June) 23-26.

Hicks, C. R. (1964) *Fundamental Concepts in the Design of Experiments*. New York: Holt, Rinehart and Winston.

Hicks, C. R. (1982) *Fundamental Concepts in the Design of Experiments.* New York: Holt, Rinehart and Winston.

Higgins, J. C. (1964) Subtracting the blank value. *Analyst*. 89, 211-215.

Higgins, J. C. (1976) *Information Systems for Planning and Control: Concepts and Cases*. New York: Edward Arnold.

High tech to the rescue. (1986) *BusinessWeek*. (June 16) 17-18.

Higman, B. A. (1967) *A Comparative Study of Programming Languages*. New York: Elsevier Science Publishing.

Hill, C., and W. Cartwright. (1978) Quality circles work. *Quality Circles Journal*. 1, (Third Quarter) 27-36.

Hill, C. W. (1988) Differentiation versus low cost or differentiation and low cost: A contingency framework. *Academy of Management Review*. (March) 401.

Hill, D. A. (1952) Control of complicated product. *Industrial Quality Control*. 8, (June) 18-22.

Hill, David J. (1960) The economic incentive provided by sampling inspection. *Applied Statistics*. 9, 69-81.

Hill, F. J., and R. Peterson. (1973) *Digital Systems: Hardware Organization and Design*. New York: John Wiley.

Hill, Hubert M., and R. H. Brown. (1966) Statistical methods in chemistry. *Analytical Chemistry*. 38, (April) 440R-442R.

Hill, Hubert M., and R. H. Brown. (1968) Statistical methods in chemistry. *Analytical Chemistry*. 40, (April) 376R-380R.

Hill, Hubert M., and David J. McClaskey. (1980) Developing awareness of quality responsibilities. *ASQC Annual Technical Quality Congress Transactions*. Milwaukee, WI: ASQC Quality Press, 160-167.

Hill, Hubert M., and Lynn D. Sorrell. (1985) The key to quality. *ASQC Annual Technical Quality Congress Transactions*. Milwaukee, WI: ASQC Quality Press, 406-421.

Hill, I. D. (1962) Sampling inspection and defense specification DEF-131. *Journal of Royal Statistical Society*. 125, (January) 31-73.

Hill, John S., and Richard R. Still. (1984) Adapting products to LDC tastes. *Harvard Business Review*. 62, (March-April) 92-101.

Hill, P. (1976) *Towards a New Philosophy of Management*. Essex, UK: Gower Press. (*2)

Hill, S. and A. Wilkinson. (1995) In search of TQM. *Employee Relations*. 17, (No. 3) 8-20.

Hill, T. (1985) *Manufacturing Strategy: The Strategic Management of the Manufacturing Function.* London, UK: Macmillan.

Hill, W. J., and William G. Hunter. (1966) A review of response surface methodology: A literature survey. *Technometrics.* 8, (March) 571-590.

Hill, W. J., and R. A. Wiles. (1975) Plant experimentation (PLEX). *Journal of Quality Technology.* 7, (March) 115-122.

Hillier. F. S. (1969) X and R—Chart control limits based on a small number of subgroups. *Journal of Quality Technology.* 1, (January) 17-26.

Hillkirk, J. (1989) Bush hands out Baldrige Awards. *USA Today.* (November 3) 1.

Hillkirk, J. (1991) This month will focus on quality. *USA Today.* (October) 1.

Himmelblau, D. M. (1970) *Process Analysis by Statistical Methods.* New York: John Wiley.

Hinchen, J. D. (1968) Multiple regression in process development. *Technometrics.* 10, (May) 257-269.

Hinchen, J. D. (1968) Multiple regression in process development. *Journal of Quality Technology.* 10, (May) 257-269.

Hinchen, J. D. (1970) Multiple regression with unbalanced data. *Journal of Quality Technology.* 12, (January) 22-29.

Hinreiner, E. H. (1956) Organoleptic evaluation by industry panels-the cutting bee. *Food Technology.* 31, (November) 62.

Hinrichs, J. R. (1978) *Practical Management for Productivity.* New York: Van Nostrand Reinhold.

Hinrichs, J. R. (1982) What's wrong with traditional productivity improvement programs? *Training.* 19, (March) 90.

Hinrichs, J. R. (1983) Avoid the 'quick fix' approach to productivity problems. *Personnel Administrator.* 29, (July) 39-43.

Hirose, Katsusada. (1989) Corporate thinking in Japan and the U.S. *The Japanese Economic Foundation Journal of Japanese Trade and Industry.* (July) 21-28.

Hiroyuki, Yoshikawa. (1977) *Computer Graphics Theory.* Tokyo: JUSE Press.

Hirschhorn, Larry and Thomas Gilmore. (1992) The new boundaries of the boundaryless company. *Harvard Business Review.* 70, (May-June) 104-115.

Hirschman, A. (1958) *The Strategy of Economic Development.* New Haven, CT: Yale University Press.

History shows: The five best-managed companies. (1977) *Dun's Review.* (December) 50.

Hitchcock, T. S., and G. L. Parker. (1976) Productivity: Man and machine. *Management International Review.* 4, (Fourth Quarter) 9-11.

Hoadley, B. (1981) The universal sampling plan. *ASQC Annual Technical Quality Congress Transactions.* Milwaukee, WI: ASQC Quality Press, 80-87.

Hoaglin, D. C., Frederick Mosteller, and John W. Tukey. (1983) *Understanding Robust Exploratory Data Analysis.* New York: John Wiley.

Hoare, C. A., and H. Perrott. (1972) *Operating System Techniques.* London, UK: Academic Press.

Hobsbawm, E. J. (1969) *Industry and Empire.* Baltimore, MD: Penguin Books. (*2)

Hocking, R. R., and R. N. Leslie. (1967) Selection of the best subset in regression analysis. *Technometrics.* 9, (April) 531-540.

Hodgeson, Alan. (1987) Deming's never-ending road to quality. *Personal Management*. (July) 40-45. (*3)

Hoerl, Arthur E., and Robert W. Kennard. (1970) Ridge regression biased estimation for nonorthogonal problems. *Technometrics*. 12, (February) 55-68. (*2)

Hoerl, Arthur E., and Robert W. Kennard. (1970) Ridge regression application to nonorthogonal problems. *Analyst*. 12, (February) 69-82.

Hoerl, Arthur E., and Robert W. Kennard. (1981) Ridge regression, advanced algorithms and applications. *American Journal of Mathematical and Management Sciences*. 1, (January) 5-83.

Hoerr, J. (1986) Power-sharing between management and labor: It's slow going. *BusinessWeek*. (February) 11-12.

Hoerr, J. (1987) Getting man and machine to live happily ever after. *BusinessWeek*. (April 20) 61-62.

Hoerr, J., (1988) Work teams can rev up paper pushers, too. *BusinessWeek*. (November 28) 68-69. (*2)

Hoerr, J. (1989) Is teamwork a management plot? Mostly not. *BusinessWeek*. (February) 20-21.

Hoerr, J. (1989) The cultural revolution at A. O. Smith. *BusinessWeek*. (May 29) 41-45. (*2)

Hoerr, J. (1989) The payoff from teamwork. *BusinessWeek*. (July) 21-25. (*4)

Hoerr, J. (1990) Sharpening minds for a competitive edge. *BusinessWeek*. (December) 72-78. (*2)

Hoerr, J. (1990) The strange bedfellows backing workplace reform. *BusinessWeek*. (April 30) 17-19.

Hoerr, J., and M. A. Pollock. (1986) Management discovers the human side of automation. *BusinessWeek*. (September 29) 74-77.

Hofer, C. W., and D. Schendel. (1978) *Strategy Formulation: Analytical Concepts.* St. Paul, MN: West Publishing.

Hoff, B. (1982) *The Tao of Pooh.* New York: E. P. Dutton.

Hoffer, P. (1985) Moving to prevention: An industry in transition. *Quality Progress.* 18, (April) 22-26.

Hoffherr, G. D., J. D. Moran, and G. Nadler. (1994) *Breakthrough Thinking in Total Quality Management.* Englewood Cliffs, NJ: Prentice-Hall.

Hoffman, Frank O. (1983) A quality atmosphere: Quality circles demand a supportive business philosophy. *Management World.* 12, (January) 44.

Hoffman, R. J. (1933) *Great Britain and the German Trade Rivalry.* Philadelphia, PA: University of Pennsylvania Press.

Hofheinz, Roy, Jr., and Kent E. Calder. (1982) *The East Asia Edge.* New York: Basic Books. (*4)

Hofstadter, Richard. (1959) *Social Darwinism in America Thought.* New York: George Braziller.

Hofstede, Geert. (1980) Motivation, leadership and organization: Do American theories apply abroad? *Organizational Dynamics.* 3, (Summer) 42-62.

Hohner, Gregory. (1993) Quality leadership at Baxter Healthcare Corporation. *Industrial Engineering.* 25, (January) 31. (*3)

Hohnson, Richard Tanner and William G. Ouchi. (1974) Made in America (under Japanese management). *Harvard Business Review.* 52, (September-October) 61-69.

Holden, Constance. (1980) Innovation: Japan races ahead as U.S. falters. *Science.* 26, (November) 41-51.

Holland, M. (1987) *When the Machine Stopped: A Cautionary Tale from Industrial America*. Cambridge, MA: Harvard Business School Press.

Hollander, Myles and Douglas Wolfe. (1973) *Nonparametric Statistical Methods*. New York: John Wiley.

The hollow corporation: The decline of manufacturing threatens the entire U.S. Economy. *BusinessWeek*. (March 3) 57.

Holm, Robert A. (1985) Quality improvement in the oil patch. *The Juran Report*. (Winter) 47-51.

Holmes, Arthur W., and Wayne S. Overmeyer. (1976) *Basic Auditing*. Homewood, IL: Irwin.

Holmes, D. S., and A. E. Mergen. (1987) A good tool for process control: The cumulative sum chart. *Quality*. (February) 71-72.

Holmes, H. (1974) Computer assisted inspection. *The Quality Engineer*. 38, (September) 211-213.

Holmes, Richard K., and Joseph M. Michalek. (1982) Optimizing quality through variation simulation. *ASQC Annual Technical Quality Congress Transactions*. Milwaukee, WI: ASQC Quality Press, 382-390.

Holpp, Lawrence. (1989) 10 reasons why total quality is less than total. *Training*. 26, (October) 93-103.

Holpp, Lawrence. (1990) Ten steps to total service quality. *Journal for Quality and Participation*. (March) 92-96.

Holpp, Lawrence. (1992) Making choices: Self-directed teams or total quality management? *Training*. 29, (May) 69. (*4)

Holsapple, C. W., K. Tam, and A. B. Whinston. (1988) Adapting expert system technology to financial management. *Financial Management*. (Autumn) 1-19.

Holt, Donald D. (1980) How Amoco finds all that oil. *Fortune.* (September 8) 51. (*3)

Holt, J. (1976) Elaboration and implementation of a quality control system in Nordisk Ventilator Co. Proceedings, Twentieth Conference. (June) Berne: EOQC, 65-75.

Holt, Maurice. (1993) The educational consequences of W. Edwards Deming. *Phi Delta Kappan.* 74, (January) 382. (*3)

Holub, Aleta. (1990) The added value of the customer-provider partnership. *Making Total Quality Happen.* (Research Report Number 937). New York: The Conference Board, 60-63.

Holusha, John. (1985) Detroit experimenting with the plastic look. *New York Times.* (November 29) D1. (*2)

Holusha, John. (1987) G.M. chief sees profit gain soon. *New York Times.* (February 12) D1. (*2)

Holusha, John. (1989) Beating Japan at its own game. *New York Times.* (July 16) section 3, 1, 7.

Holusha, John. (1989) No utopia, but to workers it's a job. *New York Times.* Business section. (January 29) 1, 10.

Holusha, John. (1989) Raising quality: Consumers star. *New York Times.* (January 5) D1. (*2)

Holy Bible: King James Text (1981) Wheaton, IL: Tyndale House.

Holzer, M. (1976) *Productivity in Public Organizations.* New York: Kennikat Press

Holzinger, Albert G. (1992) How to succeed by really trying. *Nation's Business.* 80, (August) 50. (*2)

Hombruch, F. W., Jr. (1977) *Raising Productivity.* New York: McGraw-Hill.

Homans, George. (1950) *The Human Group*. New York: Harcourt Brace Jovanovich.

The Honda's star gets another sequel. (1993) *New York Times*. (August 27) C.

Honeywell quality circles: Part of a growing American trend. (1981) *Journal of Organizational and Behavior Management*. 3, 97-101.

Hooke, R. (1983) *How to Tell the Liars from the Statisticians*. New York: Marcel Dekker.

Hopeman, R. J. (1980) *Production and Operations Management*. Columbus, OH: Charles E. Merrill.

Hopkins, David S., and Earl Bailey. (1971) New product pressures. *The Conference Record*. (June) 16-24.

Hopper, Kenneth. (1982) Creating Japan's new industrial management: The Americans as teachers. *Human Resource Management*. 21, (Spring/Summer) 13-34. (*2)

Hoppmann, W. H., II, C. Liu, C. James, and Roberto J. Rivello. (1980) Models of professions: Law, medicine and engineering. *Mechanical Engineering*. (May) 44-49.

The horizontal corporation. (1993) *BusinessWeek*. (December 20) 76.

Horn, Roy L., and Fred M. Hall. (1983) Maintenance-centered reliability. *Proceedings, Annual Reliability and Maintainability Symposium*. New York: IEEE, 197-204.

Horonec, S. M., and H. L. Chassang. *Cost Management Steps into the Future*. Chicago, IL: Arthur Anderson and Company.

Horovitz, J. H. (1980) *Top Management Control in Europe*. London, UK: Macmillan.

Horton, Thomas R. (1986) *What Works for Me: 16 CEOs Talk About Their Careers and Commitments*. New York: Random House.

Horton, Thomas R. (1990) The people side of quality. *Supply House Times.* (October) 150.

Horton, Thomas R. (1990) Wallace goes for the Baldrige. *Supply House Times.* (October) 143.

Hosmer, L. T. (1991) *The Ethics of Management.* Fourth edition. Homewood, IL: Irwin.

Hosotani, K. (1992) *Japanese Quality Concepts: An Overview.* English translation. White Plains, NY: Quality Resources.

Hospitals expand focus to include TQM. (1992) *Industrial Engineering.* 24, (July) 6. (*2)

Hosseini, J. R., and N. S. Fard. (1991) A system for analyzing information to manage the quality-control process. *Interfaces.* 21, (March-April) 48.

Hostage, G. M. (1975) Quality control in a service business. *Harvard Business Review.* 53, (September-October) 98-118.

Hought, T. M. (1987) Working better and faster with fewer people. *Wall Street Journal.* 15, (May) 3.

Houghton, James R. (1993) It's time for a new management system. *USA Today.* 121, (March) 62. (*2)

Houle, C. O. (1984) *Patterns of Learning.* San Francisco, CA: Jossey-Bass.

Hounshell, D. A. (1984) *From the American System to Mass Production, 1800-1932.* Baltimore, MD: Johns Hopkins University Press.

House, R. J. (1971) A path-goal theory of leader effectiveness. *Administrative Science Quarterly.* 16, (September) 321-328.

House, R. J. (1976) A 1976 theory of transformational leadership. In J. G. Hunt and L. L. Larson. (Eds.) *Leadership: The Cutting Edge.* Carbondale, IL: Southern Illinois University Press, 189-207.

House, R. J., and Terence. R. Mitchell. (1979) Path-goal theory of leadership. *Journal of Contemporary Business.* 3 (Autumn) 81-97.

Housel, T. J., C. J. Morris, and C. Westland. (1993) Business process reengineering at Pacific Bell. *Planning Review.* (May/June) 28-33.

Houston, P. (1989) Timberrr! *Business Month.* (December) 50-56.

Houston, P. (1990) Baldie, we hardly knew ye. *Business Month.* (July) 41-44.

Houston, P. (1992) What's right with school. *American School Board Journal* (April): 24-29.

Hout, Thomas M., and George Stalk Jr. (1990) *Competing Against Time.* New York: Free Press.

How American industry stacks up. (1992) *Fortune.* (March 9) 30.

How Ford hit the bull's eye with Taurus. (1986) *BusinessWeek.* (June 30) 69-70. (*2)

How power will be balanced on Saturn's shop floor. (1985) *BusinessWeek.* (August 5) 17-18.

How to build quality. (1989) *The Economist.* (September 23) 91-92.

How to get a bright idea. (1980) *The Economist.* (December 17) 61.

How to spread the gospel of quality. (1992) *BusinessWeek.* (November 30) 122. (*2)

Howard, Nigel and Yoshiya Teramoto. (1981) The really important difference between Japanese and western management. *Management International Review.* (February) 19-30.

Howard, R. (1990) Values make the company. *Harvard Business Review.* 78, (September-October) 132-145.

Howe, C. L. (1986) Big labor and big blue. *Datamation.* (January) 30-32.

Howe, Irving and B. J. Widick. (1949) *The UAW and Walter Reuther.* New York: Random House.

Howe, J. (1976) The determinants of R and D expenditures. *Canadian Journal of Economics.* (February) 57-71.

Howe, Roger J., Dee Baikkert, and Maynard A. Howe. (1992) *Quality on Trial.* St Paul, MN: West Publishing.

Howell, Vincent W. (1981) Quality control factor in methods engineering. *ASQC Annual Technical Quality Congress Transactions.* Milwaukee, WI: ASQC Quality Press, 268-273.

Hradesky, J. (1988) *Productivity and Quality Improvement.* New York: McGraw-Hill.

Hromi, John D. (1980) Training quality control technicians. *Quality Progress.* 13, (October) 35-37.

Hsi, B. P. (1966) Optimization of quality control in the chemical laboratory. *Technometrics.* 8, (August) 519-534.

Huang, P. Y., L. P. Rees, and B. W. Taylor III. (1983) A simulation analysis of the Japanese just-in-time technique (with *Kanbans*) for a multiline, multistage production system. *Decision Sciences.* (July) 31-38.

Hubbard, M. R. (1990) *Statistical Quality Control for the Food Industry.* New York: Van Nostrand Reinhold.

Hubele, N. F., and J. B. Keats. (1987) Automation: The challenge for SPC. *Quality.* (March) 14-18, 20, 22.

Huber, G. (1980) *Managerial Decision Making.* Glenview, IL: Scott Foresman.

Huddleston, Kenneth and Dorothy Fenwick. (1983) The productivity challenge: Business/education partnership. *Quality*. (April) 21-24.

Huettner, D. (1974) *Plant Size, Technological Change and Investment Requirements*. New York: Praeger.

Huff, D. (1954) *How to Lie with Statistics*. New York: W. W. Norton.

Huff, Lenard, Claes Fornell, and Eugene Anderson. (1996) Quality and productivity: Contradictory and complementary. *Quality Management Journal*. 4 (Issue 1) 22-39.

Huff, S. L. (1992) Reengineering the business. *National Productivity Review*. 11, (Winter) 38-42.

Huge, E. C., and A. D. Anderson. (1988) *The Spirit of Manufacturing Excellence: An Executive's Guide to the New Mind Set*. Homewood, IL: Dow Jones-Irwin.

Huge, Ernest C. (1987) *The Spirit of Manufacturing Excellence*. Homewood, IL: Irwin.

Hugh, Sidney. (1980) Majesty, poetry and power. *Time*. (October) 39.

Hughes, B. (1991) 24 stepping stones for self-directed teams. *Training*. 28, (December) 22-44. (*2)

Hughes, E. (1967) Professions. In Lynn Davenport (Ed.) *The Professions in America*. Boston, MA: Beacon Press.

Hughes, John. (1987) It's methodology, not technology, that counts. *FMS Magazine*. 5, (April) 81-85.

The human side of quality. (1990) *Fortune*. (September 24) 138.

Humble, J. (1989) Five ways to win the service war. *The International Management Development Review*. 61.

Humphrey, W. S. (1987) *Managing for Innovation.* Englewood Cliffs, NJ: Prentice-Hall.

Hunt, Bonnie. (1981) Measuring results in a quality circle pilot test. *Quality Circles Journal.* 4, (August) 26-29.

Hunt, V. D. (1986) *Artificial Intelligence and Expert Systems Sourcebook.* New York: Chapman and Hall.

Hunter, J. Stuart. (1959) Determination of optimum operating conditions by experimental methods Parts I, II and III. *Industrial Quality Control.* 15, (January-February) 28-37.

Hunter, J. Stuart. (1966) The inverse Yates algorithm. *Technometrics.* 8, (January) 177-183.

Hunter, J. Stuart. (1980) The national system of scientific measurement. *Science.* 26, (November) 869-874.

Hunter, J. Stuart. (1984) The status of U.S. quality. *Quality.* (January) 52.

Hunter, J. Stuart. (1985) Statistical design applied to product design. *Journal of Quality Technology.* 7, (March) 210-221.

Hunter, J. Stuart. (1985) The technology of quality. *RCA Engineer.* 30, (March) 8-15.

Hunter, R. S. (1987) Objective methods for food appearance assessment. In J. G. Kapsalis (Ed.) *Objective Methods in Food Quality Assessment.* Boca Raton, FL: CRC Press.

Hunter, William G. (1977) Some ideas about teaching design of experiments with 2^5 examples of experiments conducted by students. *The American Statistician.* 31, (January) 2-5.

Hunter, William G., and J. R. Kitrell, (1966) Evolutionary operation: A review. *Technometrics,* 8, (April) 389-397.

Hunting for creative minds. (1985) *New York Times.* (February 10) 7.

Huntoon, R. B., and L. G. Scharpf Jr. (1987) Quality control of flavoring materials. In J. G. Kapsalis (Ed.) *Objective Methods in Food Quality Assessment*. Boca Raton, FL: CRC Press.

Huseman, Richard C., and Edward W. Miles. (1988) Organizational communication in the information age: Implications of computer-based systems. *Journal of Management*. 14, 181-204.

Hutchins, David. (1981) How quality goes round in circles. *Management Today*. (January) 26-29.

Hutchins, David. (1985) *The Quality Circle Handbook*. London, UK: Pitman.

Hutchins, David and Naoto Sasaki. (1984) *The Japanese Approach to Product Quality: Its Applicability to the West*. Oxford, UK; Pergamon Press.

Hutchins, Dexter. (1986) And now, the home-brewed forecast. *Fortune*. (January 20) 53-54.

Hutchins, Dexter. (1986) Having a hard time with just in time. *Fortune*. (June 9) 64-66.

Hutchins, G. (1992) *Purchasing Strategies for Total Quality*. Homewood, IL: Irwin. (*2)

Hutchinson, R. (1984) Flexibility is the key to economic feasibility of automated small batch manufacturing. *Industrial Engineering*. 16, (June) 16-19.

Hutter, R. G. (1966) Inspection manpower planning. *Industrial Quality Control*. 22, (April) 521-523.

Hwang, C. L., and K. Yoon. (1981) *Multiple Attribute Decision Making-A State of the Art Survey*. New York: Springer Verlag.

Hwang, F. K. (1984) Robust group testing. *Journal of Quality Technology*. 16, (March) 189-195.

Hyde, Albert C. (1990) Rescuing quality measurement from TQM. *Bureaucrat.* 19, (Winter) 16-20.

Hyde, Albert C. (1992) A brief glossary of quality jargon. *The Public Manager: The New Bureaucrat.* 21, (Winter) 48. (*3)

Hyer, C. W. (1979) *Principal Aspects of U.S Laboratory Accreditation Program.* Ridgefield, CT: The Marley Organization. (January) 24.

Hymowitz, Carol. (1981) Employers take over where schools fail to teach the basics. *Wall Street Journal.* (January) 1.

Iacocca, Lee A., and William Novak. (1984) *Iacocca: An Autobiography.* New York: Bantam Books. (*31)

Iacocca, Lee A., with Sonny Kleinfield. (1988) *Talking Straight.* New York: Bantam.

IBM and Motorola: Michael Brody. (1987) Helping workers to work smarter. *Fortune.* (June 15) 86-88.

IBM Corporation. (1984) *IBM FSD Owego Excellence Plus Manual.* Owego, NY: IBM, 9-15.

IBM to introduce in February a series of more powerful AS/400 computers. *Wall Street Journal.* (January 31) B3.

IBM: A special company. (1989) *Think.* (September) 51.

Ibuka, Masaru. (1980) Management opinion. *Administrative Management.* (May) 86.

Ikezawa, et al. (1987) Features of companywide quality control in Japan. Report of Forty-fourth Quality Control Symposium, International Conference on Quality Control, Tokyo.

Imai, Masaaki. (1975) *Never Take Yes for an Answer: An Inside Look at Japanese Business.* Tokyo: Simul Press.

Imai, Masaaki. (1982) From Taylor to Ford to Toyota: *Kanban* system another challenge from Japan. *The Japan Economic Journal.* (March) 12.

Imai, Masaaki. (1982) Plant-wide campaigns: Voluntary activities extended beyond small group. *The Japan Economic Journal.* (July) 12.

Imai, Masaaki. (1982) Productivity in disarray: its hard and soft aspects. *The Japan Economic Journal.* (January) 12.

Imai, Masaaki. (1982) Quality control and small group activities: The key to improve productivity. *The Japan Economic Journal.* (April) 12.

Imai, Masaaki. (1982) Small group activities-five times ROI? The case of Nissan chemical industries. *The Japan Economic Journal.* (May) 14-17. (*2)

Imai, Masaaki. (1982) Total quality control as corporate strategy. *The Japan Economic Journal.* (December) 12.

Imai, Masaaki. (1983) Policy development: Japanese management's new strategic tool. *The Japan Economic Journal.* (February) 12.

Imai, Masaaki. (1986) *Kaizen: The Key to Japan's Competitive Success.* New York: McGraw-Hill. (*10)

Iman, Ronald L. (1982) Graphs for use with the Lillefors test for normal and exponential distributions. *The American Statistician.* 36, (February) 109-112.

Imberman, Woodruff. (1982) Why quality control circles don't work. *Canadian Business.* (May) 103-106.

In search of the retentive incentive. (1984) *Inc.* (May) 12-13.

The incredible explosion of startups. (1982) *BusinessWeek.* (August 2) 53-54.

Ingle, Sud. (1986) Job shop sampling. *Quality Assurance*. 12, (September) 28-30.

Ingle, Sud. (1982) How to avoid quality circle failure in your company. *Training and Development Journal*. 36, (June) 54-59.

Ingle, Sud. (1982) *Quality Circles Master Guide: Increasing Productivity with People Power.* Englewood Cliffs, NJ: Prentice-Hall. (*2)

Ingman, Lars C. (1992) We are only halfway there. *Pulp and Paper International*. 66, (July) 113. (*3)

Ingrassia, Lawrence. (1980) Staid Maytag puts its money on stoves but may need to invest expertise, too. *Wall Street Journal.* (July) 25. (*2)

Ingrassia, Paul. (1987) G.M. quality can be hazardous to your health. *Wall Street Journal.* (December 2) 28. (*2)

Inguanzo, Joe M. (1991) Communicating mission: Research is vital. *Hospital*. 65, (August) 45-46.

Inguanzo, Joe M. (1992) Taking a serious look at patient expectations. *Hospitals*. (September 5) 68.

Innovation: The global race. (1990) *BusinessWeek.* (June) 32-33.

Innovative thinking cited in recognition of three companies. (1992) *American Paint and Coatings Journal*. (December 14) 40. (*2)

Inside the Entrepreneur. (1984) *Venture*. (May) 28-37.

Inspection can make an impression with a saving. (1975) *Quality*. (September) 37.

Institute of Industrial Engineers. (1990) Productivity and quality in the USA today. *Management Services (UK)*. (January) 27-31.

Institute of Quality Assurance. (1975) *A Guide to Process Capability Studies*. London, UK: IQA.

Instrumentation in the chemical and petrol industries. (1986) Proceedings of the 1985 Spring Symposium. Research Triangle Park, NC: ISA.

International Conference on Quality Control. (1978) Proceedings. Union of Japanese Scientists and Engineers, Tokyo. (*2)

Inventory management: Controlling costs to maximize profits. *Small Business Report*. (August) 50-53.

Ireland, R. D., et al. (1987) Strategy formulation process. *Strategic Management Journal*. 8, (July-August) 469-486.

Ireson, W. Grant. (1982) *Reliability Handbook*. New York: McGraw-Hill.

Irving, Robert R. (1978) QC circles spur productivity, improve product quality. *Iron Age*. 221, (June) 61-63.

Irving, Robert R. (1979) QC payoff attracts top management. *Iron Age*. 222, (August) 64-65.

Irwin, Ross. (1986) Corporations take aim at illiteracy. *Fortune*. (September 29) 47-54.

Is TQM a part of your company's management strategy? (1992) *Oregon Business*. (May) 69. (*2)

Ishibashi, Kanichiro. (1983) TQC as a tool: It works at Bridgestone. *Automotive News*. (June) D8.

Ishihara, S. (1990) Warning from Japan: Trust yourselves not your leaders. *Washington Post*. 7, (October) 6.

Ishihara, Z. (1979) Where should management and computer applications go from here? *Management Japan*. 12, (Spring) 14-21.

Ishikawa, Kaoru. (1962) *Kanrizu-ho*. Tokyo: JUSE Press. (*2)

Ishikawa, Kaoru. (1965) Recent trend of quality control. *Reports of Statistical Applications and Research.* JUSE Press. 12, (January) 1-17. (*2)

Ishikawa, Kaoru. (1968) QC circles activities. *QC in Japan.* Tokyo: JUSE Press.

Ishikawa, Kaoru. (1969) Education for quality control in Japanese industry. *Reports of Statistical Applications and Research.* 16, (March) Tokyo: JUSE Press, 21-40.

Ishikawa, Kaoru. (1969) Ten principles of vendee-vendor relations from the standpoint of quality control. *Proceedings, International Conference on Quality Control.* Tokyo: JUSE Press, 333-336.

Ishikawa, Kaoru. (1972) Quality control starts and ends with education. *Quality Progress.* 5, (August) 18. (*2)

Ishikawa, Kaoru. (1975) Process flow chart for management. *Hinshitsu Kanri.* 26, (January) 332-333.

Ishikawa, Kaoru. (1976) Cause and effect diagram—CE diagram—Tokusei Yo-In Zu-Ishikawa diagram. In Davida M. Amsden, and Robert T. Amsden (Eds.) *QC Circles: Applications, Tools and Theory.* Milwaukee, WI: ASQC Quality Press, 91-94.

Ishikawa, Kaoru. (1976) *Guide to Quality Control.* Milwaukee, WI: ASQC Quality Press.

Ishikawa, Kaoru. (1976) *Guide To Quality Control.* Tokyo: Asian Productivity Organization. (*4)

Ishikawa, Kaoru. (1978) QC specialists and standardization. *Proceedings, International Conference on Quality Control.* Tokyo: JUSE Press, A6-5 through A6-10. (*2)

Ishikawa, Kaoru. (1980) *QC Circle Koryo: General Principles of the QC Circle.* Tokyo: JUSE Press (Union of Japanese Scientists and Engineers). (*3)

Ishikawa, Kaoru. (1980) Quality in Japan: QC circles activities. *Quality*. (May) 97.

Ishikawa, Kaoru. (1983) *Guide to Quality Control*. Tokyo: Asian Productivity Organization. (*5)

Ishikawa, Kaoru. (1984) Quality and standardization: Program for economic success. *Quality Progress*. 17, (January) 18.

Ishikawa, Kaoru. (1985) *What is Total Quality Control? The Japanese Way*. Translated by David J. Lu. Englewood Cliffs, NJ: Prentice-Hall. (*20)

Ishikawa, Kaoru. (1986) *Guide to Quality Control*. Second revised edition. Tokyo: Asian Productivity Organization.

Ishikawa, Kaoru. (1987) The quality control audit. *Quality Progress*. 20, (January) 39-41. (*2)

Ishikawa, Kaoru. (1990) *Introduction to Quality Control*. Tokyo: 3A Corporation. (*3)

Ishikawa, Kaoru and K. Kondo. (1969) Education and training for quality control in Japanese industry. *Quality*. (March) 90-96.

It seemed like a good idea at the time. (1982) *Science*. (January-February) 86.

Itoh, S. (1974) Executive reports on quality: Audit reports and quality reports. *Reports of Statistical Applications and Research*. 21, (March) Toyko: JUSE Press, 65-77.

It's so beautiful: How to get a bright idea. (1980) *The Economist*. (December 17) 61.

Ivancevich, John, J. Timothy McMahon, J. William Streidl, and Andrew D. Szilagyi. (1978) Goal setting: The Tenneco approach to personnel development and management effectiveness. *Organizational Dynamics*. 3, (Winter) 48-80.

Ives, B., S. L. Jarvenpaa, and R. O. Mason. (1993) Global business drivers: Aligning information technology to global business strategy. *IBM Systems Journal.* 32, (No. 1) 143-161.

Iwahashi, Masaru. (1986) Research program on the new Product X through seven management tools for QC. *Reports of Statistical Applications and Research.* 33, (June) Toyko: JUSE Press 43-52.

Iwasaki, Iwao (1974) Mechanical Components. *Quality Control Handbook.* Third edition. New York: McGraw-Hill.

J. Alexander's opens in Dayton. (1993) *Nation's Restaurant News.* (March 8) 11. (*2)

Jablonski, Joseph R. (1990) Implementing total quality management. *Training and Development Journal.* 44, (December) 71-72. (*2)

Jablonski, Joseph R. (1990) *Implementing Total Quality Management-Competing in the 1990s.* New Mexico: Technical Management Consortium.

Jackson, J. E. (1956) Quality control methods for two related variables. *Industrial Quality Control.* 12, (January) 4-8.

Jackson, Susan. (1992) What you should know about ISO 9000. *Training.* 29, (May) 48-52. (*2)

Jacobs, H. S., and K. Jillson. (1974) *Executive Productivity.* New York: American Management Association.

Jacobs, Richard M. (1967) Implementing formal design reviews. *Industrial Quality Control.* 23, (February) 398-404.

Jacobsen, T., and R. W. Gunderson. (1986) Applied cluster analysis. In J. R. Piggott (Ed.) *Statistical Procedures in Food Research.* New York: Elsevier Science Publishing.

Jacobson, C., and J. Hillkirk. (1986) *Xerox: American Samurai.* New York: Macmillan. (*4)

Jacobson, G. (1951) The use of the role concept in the study of complex organizations. *Journal of Social Issues.* 7, (March) 21-26.

Jaech, J. L. (1980) Determination of acceptance numbers and sample sizes for attribute sampling plans. *Journal of Quality Technology.* 10, (April) 159-163.

Jaehm, A. H. (1982) Maintaining the credibility of your quality control department. *TAPPI.* 65, (May) 187.

Jaffe, Thomas. (1980) When opportunity knocks. *Forbes* (October 13) 96-100. (*2)

Jaffe, Thomas. (1981) Is this it. *Forbes.* (February) 48.

Jaikumar, R. (1986) Postindustrial manufacturing. *Harvard Business Review.* 64, (November-December) 75. (*6)

Jamieson, A. (1982) *Introduction to Quality Control.* Englewood Cliffs, NJ: Prentice-Hall.

Janesky, A. J. (1969) Computerized control in a small company. Proceedings, APICS Conference. (*2)

Janis, I. L. (1971) Groupthink. *Psychology Today.* (November) 43-46.

Janis, I. L. (1982) *Groupthink.* Boston, MA: Houghton Mifflin.

Japan's high-tech challenge. (1982) *Newsweek.* (August) 48-54.

Japan's industrial competitiveness: The human factor. (1982) *Japan Labor Bulletin.* (May) 5-8.

Jardim, Anne. (1970) *The First Henry Ford: A Study in Personality and Business Leadership.* Cambridge, MA: MIT Press. (*2)

Jarrett, Joyce R. (1990) Long term strategy . . . A commitment to excellence. *Journal for Quality and Participation.* (July/August) 28-33.

Jay, Antony. (1967) *Management and Machiavelli: An Inquiry into the Politics of Corporate Life.* New York: Holt, Rinehart and Winston. (*2)

Jayachandran, Toke and Louis R. Moore. (1976) A comparison of reliability growth models. *IEEE Transactions on Reliability.* (April) 49-51.

Jehring, J. J. (1970) Profit sharing, motivation and productivity. *Personnel Administration.* 33, (March-April) 17-21.

Jelinek, M. (1979) *Institutionalizing Innovation: A Study of Organizational Learning Systems.* New York: Praeger. (*4)

Jelinek, M., and C. B. Schoonhoven. (1988) Lessons for the future in high technology management: The strategy of innovation where it counts. In L. R. Gomez-Mejia and M. W. Lawless (Eds.) *Conference Proceedings Managing the High Technology Firm.* Boulder, CO: University of Colorado Press, 318-323.

Jenkins, G. M., and V. Yule. (1971) *Systems Engineering.* New York: Watts Publication.

Jenkins, K. M., and J. Shimada. (1981) Quality circles in the service sector. *Supervisory Management.* 26, (August) 2-7.

Jennings, D. F., and D. H. Sexton. (1985) Managing innovation in established firms: Issues, problems and the impact on economic growth and employment. Proceedings, Conference on Industrial Science and Technological Innovation. Sponsored by National Science Foundation. The Center for Research and Development, State University of New York at Albany, New York.

Jennings, E. (1961) The anatomy of leadership. *Management of Personnel Quarterly.* (Autumn) 35-44.

Jensen, Michael C., and William H. Meckling. (1976) Theory of the firm. *Journal of Financial Economics.* 3, (October) 305-360.

Jerahov, G. E. (1984) *Training requirements for an interactive CAD/CAM system.* Autofact 6.

Jerome, John. (1972) *The Death of the Automobile.* New York: W. W. Norton.

Jessup, H. R. (1992) New roles in team leadership. *Training and Development Journal.* 46, (November) 79-83. (*2)

Jessup, Peter T. (1985) The value of continuing improvements. Proceedings of the International Communications Conference, June. (*2)

Jewell, R., and H. L. Ariey (1984) *British Social Attitudes: The 1984 Report.* Aldershot, UK: Gower Press. (*2)

Jiro, Kondo. (1973) *Operations Research.* Tokyo: JUSE Press, 128-136.

Joch, Alan. (1982) Quality circles: The key to better management? *Metal Center News.* (June) 64-69.

Jocobs, R. M., and August B. Mundel. (1975) Quality tasks in product recall. *Quality Progress.* 8, (June) 16-19.

Johansson, Hank J., and Dan McArther. (1988) Rediscovering the fundamentals of quality. *Management Review.* 77, (January) 34-37.

Johansson, Hank J., P. McHugh, J. Pendlebury, and W. A. Wheeler III. (1993) *Business Process Reengineering: Breakpoint Strategies for Market Dominance.* New York: John Wiley. (*2)

John F. Ackers: Turning the corner at IBM. (1989) *The Quality Executive.* (August) 6-7.

John, Peter W. M. (1966) Augmenting 2^n-1 designs. *Technometrics.* 8, (March) 469-480.

Johnson, Bryan. (1983) Brave new world of Nissan—U.S.A. *The Globe and Mail.* (June) 21-24.

Johnson, C. (1972) *Conspiracy at Matsukawa.* Berkeley, CA: University of California Press.

Johnson, C. (1982) *MIT and the Japanese Miracle.* Stanford, CA: Stanford University Press. (*2)

Johnson, C. (1984) *The Industrial Policy Debate.* San Francisco, CA: ICS Press.

Johnson, D. A. (1975) Product problem control through warranty analysis: Ford's approach. *ASQC Automotive Division Second Annual Agricultural, Industrial, and Construction Equipment Conference.* Milwaukee, WI: ASQC Quality Press, 61-78.

Johnson, D. W., and F. P. Johnson. (1982) *Joining Together: Group Theories and Group Skills.* Englewood Cliffs, NJ: Prentice-Hall. (*2)

Johnson, H. Thomas. (1987) The decline of cost management: A reinterpretation of 20th-century cost accounting history. *Journal of Cost Management.* (Spring) 5-12.

Johnson, H. Thomas. (1990) Beyond product costing: A challenge to cost management's conventional wisdom. *Journal of Cost Management.* (Fall) 17-19.

Johnson, H. Thomas and Robert S. Kaplan. (1987) *Relevance Lost: The Rise and Fall of Management Accounting.* Cambridge, MA: Harvard Business School Press. (*5)

Johnson, I. (1968) Interactive graphics in data processing: Principle of interactive systems. *IBM Systems Journal.* 7, (No. 1) 123-141.

Johnson, J. A., W. J. Jones, and L. M. Schilling. (1992) Quality service management: A challenge for the 1990s. *Journal of the American Dietetic Association.* 92, (August) 985. (*2)

Johnson, J. Lynn and Ralph Kuehn. (1987) The small business owner/manager's search for external information. *Journal of Small Business Management.* (July) 53-60.

Johnson, L. M. (1982) *Quality Assurance Program Evaluation.* Santa Fe Springs, CA: Stockton Trade Press.

Johnson, Michael. (1986) Letter to editors. *Quality Progress*. 19, (February) 6.

Johnson, Norman L., and F. C. Leone. (1964) *Statistics and Experimental Design*. New York: John Wiley, 347-348.

Johnson, Norman L., and Samuel Kotz. (1969) *Discrete Distributions*. Boston, MA: Houghton Mifflin

Johnson, R. (1989) Volvo's new assembly plant has no assembly line. *Automotive News*. (July 10) 22, 24.

Johnson, R. W. (1984) Vendor self-inspection sets the stage for just-in-time deliveries. *Quality Progress*. 17, (November) 46-47.

Johnson, Richard A., Fremont E. Kast, and James Rosenweig. (1967) *Management of Systems*. New York: McGraw-Hill.

Johnson, Ross and Richard Webber. (1985) *Buying Quality*. New York: Watts Publication.

Johnson, Ross and William O. Winchell. (1989) *Management and Quality*. Milwaukee, WI: ASQC Quality Press. (*2)

Johnson, S. (1984) Comparing R and D strategies of Japanese and U.S. firms. *Sloan Management Review*. 25, (Spring) 25-34. (*2)

Johnson, S. L., and D. J. Funke. (1980) An analysis of human reliability measure in visual inspection. *Journal of Quality Technology*. 12, (April) 71-74.

Johnson, T. (1974) Made in America (under Japanese management). *Harvard Business Review*. 52, (September-October) 61-69.

Johnsson, Julie. (1992) TQM: Best antidote for MD practice problems. *Hospitals*. 66, (March) 64.

Johnston, Catharine G., and Mark J. Daniel. (1991) Customer satisfaction through quality. *The Canadian Business Review*. 18, (Winter) 12-15.

Johnston, Catharine G., and Mark J. Daniel. (1992) Total quality management: customer satisfaction guaranteed? *CMA—The Management Accounting Magazine*. 66, (April) 15. (*2)

Johnston, Joseph and Associates. (1986) *Educating Managers*. San Francisco, CA: Jossey-Bass.

Johnstone, Bob. (1990) Prophet with honor. *Far Eastern Economic Review [Hong Kong]*. (December 27) 50.

Joiner Associates. (1990) *The Joiner 7 Step Method*. Madison, WI: Joiner Associates.

Joiner Associates. (1993) *A Practical Guide to Quality: Selected Readings in Quality Improvement*. Madison, WI: Joiner Associates.

Joiner, Brian L., and Marie Gaudard. (1990) Variation, management, and W. Edwards Deming. *Quality Progress*. (December) 29-37.

Joiner, Brian L., in collaboration with Sue Reynard. (1994) *Fourth Generation Management: The New Business Consciousness*. New York: McGraw-Hill. (*2)

Joiner, Charles W. (1983) One manager's story of how he made the theory Z concept work. *Management Review*. 72, (May) 48-53.

Joiner, Charles W. (1985) The key role of statisticians in the transformation of North American industry. *The American Statistician*. 3, (August) 224-234.

Jones, E. (1963) Tactics of integration among leaders and subordinates in a status hierarchy. *Psychological Monographs*. 77, 1-20.

Jones, Ken. (1988) High performance manufacturing: A break with tradition. *Industrial Management* (Canada). (June) 30-32.

Jones, Russell A. (1985) *Total Quality Objective*. Cleveland, OH: TRW's Automotive Worldwide Sector.

Jones, Russell A. (1977) *Self-Fulfilling Prophecies: Social, Psychological and Physiological Effects of Expectancies*. Hillsdale, NJ: Lawrence Erlbaum Associates.

Jordan, Jennifer. (1992) Everything you wanted to know about TQM. *The Public Manager: The New Bureaucrat*. 21, (Winter) 45. (*3)

Jorgensen, Barbara. (1992) Industry to B schools: Smarten up on TQM or else. *Electronics Business*. (October) 85-90.

Jorgenson, W. (1967) The explanation of productivity change. *Review of Economic Studies*. 34, (July) 249-83.

Joyce, Bruce. (1991) The doors to school improvement. *Educational Leadership*. 48 (May) 17-20.

Judge, Joanne M. (1992) Bill Arnold: TQM champion. *Healthcare Financial Management*. 46, (September) 20. (*2)

Judge, W., R. Scott, and R. Millender. (1991) Long-term quality improvement and cost reduction at Capsugel/Warner-Lambert. In Michael J. Stahl and G. M. Bounds. *Competing Globally Through Customer Value: The Management of Strategic Suprasystems*. Westport, CT: Quorum Books, 703-709.

Judson, A. S. (1976) New strategies to improve productivity. *Technology Review*. (July-August) 61-67.

Judson, A. S. (1982) The awkward truth about productivity. *Harvard Business Review*. 54, (September-October) 93-97.

Judson, Horace F. (1980) *Search for Solutions*. New York: Holt, Rinehart and Winston. 3. (*3)

Juechter, W. Matthew and Tom Utne. (1982) Wellness: Addressing the whole person. *Training and Development Journal*. 36, (May) 112-116.

Julien R. Phillips and Allan A. Kennedy. (1980) Shaping and managing shared values. *McLinsey Staff Paper*. (December) 1.

Juran Institute. (1987) *Juran on Quality Planning (video cassette series)*. Wilton, CT: Juran Institute.

Juran Institute. (1989) Check sheets. In Harry Ivan Costin (Ed.) *Readings in Total Quality Management*. (1994) Fort Worth, TX: Dryden Press, 205-216.

Juran Institute. (1989) Histograms. In Harry Ivan Costin (Ed.) *Readings in Total Quality Management*. (1994) Fort Worth, TX: Dryden Press, 195-203.

Juran, Joseph M. (1935) Inspector's errors in quality control. *Mechanical Engineering*. 59, (October) 643-644.

Juran, Joseph M. (1945) *Management of Inspection and Quality Control*. New York: Harper and Row.

Juran, Joseph M. (1951) *Quality Control Handbook*. New York: McGraw-Hill. (*4)

Juran, Joseph M. (1952) Is your product too fussy? *Factory Management and Maintenance*. 110, (August) 125-128.

Juran, Joseph M. (1956) *Lectures on Quality Control*. (In Japanese). Tokyo: JUSE Press.

Juran, Joseph M. (1959) A note on economics of quality. *Industrial Quality Control*. 15, (February) 20-23.

Juran, Joseph M. (1962) *Quality Control Handbook*. Second edition. New York: McGraw-Hill.

Juran, Joseph M. (1964) *Managerial Breakthrough: A New Concept of the Manager's Job*. New York: McGraw-Hill. (*10)

Juran, Joseph M. (1966) Quality problems remedies, and nostrums. *Industrial Quality Control*. 22, (June) 647-653.

Juran, Joseph M. (1967) The QC circle phenomenon. *Industrial Quality Control*. 23, (January) 336. (*2)

Juran, Joseph M. (1968) Vendor relations—An overview. *Quality Progress.* 1, (July) 10-16. (*2)

Juran, Joseph M. (1969) Mobilizing for the 1970's. *Quality Progress.* 2, (August) 8-17.

Juran, Joseph M. (1969) Mobilizing for the 1970's. *Quality Progress.* 2, (December) 21.

Juran, Joseph M. (1970) Consumerism and product quality. *Quality Progress.* 3, (July) 18-27. (*3)

Juran, Joseph M. (1970) *Quality Planning and Analysis: From Product Development Through Usage.* New York: McGraw-Hill.

Juran, Joseph M. (1972) Product safety. *Quality Progress.* 5, (July) 3-32.

Juran, Joseph M. (1973) The Taylor system and quality control. *Quality Progress.* 6, (May) 11-12. (*2)

Juran, Joseph M. (1975) Quality control service—The 1974 Japanese symposium. *Quality Progress.* 8, (April) 10-13.

Juran, Joseph M. (1975) Standardization and quality. *Quality Progress.* 8, (February) 4-5.

Juran, Joseph M. (1975) The non-Pareto principle: Mea culpa. *Quality Progress.* 8, (May) 8-9.

Juran, Joseph M. (1976) Emerging professionalism in quality assurance. *Quality Assurance.* 2, (September) 71-77.

Juran, Joseph M. (1977) Auto safety a decade later. *Quality.* (October) 26-32. (*2)

Juran, Joseph M. (1977) Quality and its assurance-an overview. *Second NATO Symposium on Quality and Its Assurance.* London, UK: North Atlantic Treaty Organization, 1-24.

Juran, Joseph M. (1978) Japanese and Western quality: A contrast in methods and results. *Management Review.* 67, (November) 20-28, 39-45.

Juran, Joseph M. (1978) Japanese and Western quality: A contrast. *Quality Progress.* 11, (December) 10-18. (*3)

Juran, Joseph M. (1979) Japanese and Western quality: A contrast. *Quality.* (January and February) A3-25. (*2)

Juran, Joseph M. (1979) *Managerial Breakthrough.* New York: McGraw-Hill.

Juran, Joseph M. (1980) International significance of the QC circle movement. *Quality Progress.* 13, (November) 18-22.

Juran, Joseph M. (1981) *Juran on Quality Improvement.* Danbury CT: Juran Institute.

Juran, Joseph M. (1981) Product quality—A prescription for the west. Proceedings, Twenty-Fifth Conference EOQC, Paris. 3, (June) 221-242. (*6)

Juran, Joseph M. (1982) Product quality—A prescription for the West: Part I: Training and improvement programs. *Control and Applied Statistics.* 27, (June) 719-720.

Juran, Joseph M. (1982) *Upper Management and Quality.* Danbury, CT: Juran Institute.

Juran, Joseph M. (1984) *Upper Management and Quality.* Wilton, CT: Juran Institute.

Juran, Joseph M. (1985) A prescription for the West: Four years later. Proceedings of the Twenty-ninth Annual Conference of the European Organization for Quality Control.

Juran, Joseph M. (1985) Catching up: How is the west doing. *Quality Progress.* 18, (November) 18-22.

Juran, Joseph M. (1985) Charting the quality course. *The Juran Report.* (Summer) 10-15.

Juran, Joseph M. (1986) Letter to editors. *Quality Progress.* 19, (April) 10. (*2)

Juran, Joseph M. (1986) The product trilogy: A universal approach to managing for quality. *Quality Progress.* 19, (August) 19-24. (*3)

Juran, Joseph M. (1986) The quality trilogy: A universal approach to managing for quality. In Harry Ivan Costin (Ed.) *Readings in Total Quality Management.* (1994) Fort Worth, TX: Dryden Press, 113-122.

Juran, Joseph M. (1987) QC Circles in the West. *Quality Progress.* 20, (September) 60-61.

Juran, Joseph M. (1988) *Juran on Planning for Quality.* New York: Free Press. (*11)

Juran, Joseph M. (1988) *Juran's Quality Control Handbook.* Fourth edition. New York: McGraw-Hill. (*5)

Juran, Joseph M. (1988) *Planning for Quality.* New York: Free Press. (*4)

Juran, Joseph M. (1989) A tale of the twentieth century. *The Juran Report.* (Autumn) 4-13.

Juran, Joseph M. (1989) *Juran on Leadership for Quality: An Executive Handbook.* New York: Free Press. (*6)

Juran, Joseph M. (1989) Universal approach to managing for quality. *Executive Excellence.* (May) 15-17.

Juran, Joseph M. (1991) Made in USA—A quality resurgence. *Journal for Quality and Participation.* (March) 6-8. (*2)

Juran, Joseph M. (1991) Strategies for world-class quality. *Quality Progress.* 24, (March) 81-85. (*3)

Juran, Joseph M. (1992) Acing the quality quiz. *Across the Board.* (July-August) 58. (*2)

Juran, Joseph M. (1992) *Juran on Quality by Design: New Steps for Planning Quality into Goods and Services.* New York: Free Press.

Juran, Joseph M. (1993) Made in the U.S.A.: A renaissance in quality. *Harvard Business Review.* 71, (July-August) 47.

Juran, Joseph M. (Ed.). (1995) *A History of Managing for Quality: The Evolution, Trends, and Future Directions of Managing for Quality.* Milwaukee, WI: ASQC Quality Press.

Juran, Joseph M. (1995) *Managerial Breakthrough: The Classic Book on Improving Management Performance.* New York: McGraw-Hill.

Juran, Joseph M., and Frank M. Gryna Jr. (1993) *Quality Planning and Analysis from Product Development Through Use.* Third edition. New York: McGraw-Hill. (*8)

Juran, Joseph M., Frank M. Gryna Jr., and Richard S. Bingham. (1976) *Quality Control Handbook.* Third edition. New York: McGraw-Hill. (*8)

Kackar, Raghu N. (1985) Off-line quality control, parameter design and the Taguchi method. *Journal of Quality Technology.* 17, (April) 176-188. (*4)

Kackar, Raghu N. (1986) Taguchi's quality philosophy: Analysis and commentary. *Quality Progress.* 19, (April) 18-23.

Kackar, Raghu N. (1986) Taguchi's quality philosophy: Analysis and commentary. *Quality Progress.* 19, (December) 21-29.

Kackar, Raghu N., and A. C. Shoemaker. (1986) Robust design: A cost-effective method for improving manufacturing processes. *AT&T Technical Journal.* 65, (March-April) 39-50.

Kador, J. (1992) Reengineering to boost software productivity. *Datamation.* (December 15) 57-58.

Kahn, Herman and Thomas Pepper. (1979) *The Japanese Challenge.* New York: Thomas Y. Crowell. (*3)

Kahn, L. (1956) Human relations research in large organizations. *Journal of Social Issues.* 12, (January) 23-30.

Kahn, R., and Michael Katz. (1953) *Leadership Practices in Relation to Productivity and Morale.* Evanston, IL: Row, Peterson and Company.

Kahnerman, Daniel J., Paul Slovic, and Armos Tversky (Eds.). (1982) *Judgment Under Uncertainty: Heuristics and Biases.* New York: Cambridge University Press.

Kaihatsu, Hidy. (1989) The new Xerox movement: TQC in Japan. Speech at the Second Annual Quality Conference, May 16-17, New York City.

Kaluzny, Arnold D., Curtis P. McLaughlin, and Kit Simpson. (1992) Applying total quality management concepts to public health organizations. *Public Health Reports.* 107, (May-June) 257-264. (*3)

Kamata, Satoshi. (1982) *Japan in the Passing Lane: An Insider's Account of Life in a Japanese Auto Factory.* New York: Pantheon Books.

Kamber, Igor. (1989) Thank labor for our high quality of life. *Los Angeles Times.* (September) 1.

Kaminski, B. (1991) Training-key to success in TQM. *Quality in Manufacturing.* 2, (January-February) 12-13.

Kamizawa, N., N. Ishizuka, and Yoji Akao. (1978) Quality evolution system and FMEA. *Proceedings, International Conference on Quality Control.* Tokyo: JUSE Press, B4-19 through B4-28.

Kanarick, A. F., and D. L. Dotlich. (1984) Honeywell's agenda for organizational change. *New Management.* 2, (January) 14-19. (*2)

Kanban: The just-in-time Japanese inventory system. *Small Business Report.* (February) 69-71.

Kane, Edward J. (1986) IBM's quality focus on the business process. *Quality Progress.* 19, (April) 24-32. (*2)

Kane, Edward J. (1992) Implementing TQM at Dun and Bradstreet Software. *National Productivity Review.* 11, (Summer) 405. (*2)

Kane, Roger W. (1984) Fitness reviews: Key to a total quality program. *ASQC Annual Technical Quality Congress Transactions.* Milwaukee, WI: ASQC Quality Press, 263-267.

Kane, Victor E. (1986) Process capability indexes. *Journal of Quality Technology.* 18, (January) 41-52. (*2)

Kanevsky, V., and T. J. Housel (1994) Value-based business process reengineering: An objective approach to value added. Pacific Bell working paper number 96.

Kano, Noriaki. (1978) Comparison of the background of quality between Japan and the west. *Proceedings, International Conference on Quality Control.* Tokyo: JUSE Press, C3-1 to C3-8.

Kano, Noriaki. (1984) Problem solving in new product development-application of T-Typed Matrix. *Quality.* (April) 45-55. (*2)

Kano, Noriaki. (1993) A perspective on quality activities in American firms. *California Management Review.* 36, (Spring) 12-31.

Kano, Noriaki, N. Seraku, F. Takahashi, and S. Tsuji. (1984) Attractive quality and just-be-quality. *Journal of Japanese Society for Quality Control.* 14, (February) 39-48.

Kanter, Rosabeth Moss. (1983) *The Change Masters: Innovations for Productivity in the American Corporation.* New York: Simon and Schuster. (*5)

Kanter, Rosabeth Moss. (1983) Frontiers for strategic human resource planning and management. *Human Resource Management.* 22, (Spring-Summer) 9-21.

Kanter, Rosabeth Moss. (1984) Variations in management career structure in high technology firms: The impact of organizational characteristics on internal labor market patterns. In P. Osterman (Ed.) *Internal Labor Markets.* Cambridge, MA: MIT Press.

Kanter, Rosabeth Moss. (1986) Pay and hierarchy. *Management Review.* 75, (June) 11-12.

Kanter, Rosabeth Moss. (1987) The attack on pay. *Harvard Business Review.* 65, (March-April) 6-67.

Kanter, Rosabeth Moss, Barry A. Stein, and Todd D. Jick. (1992) *The Challenge of Organizational Change: How Companies Experience It and Leaders Guide It.* New York: Simon and Schuster. (*3)

Kaplan, Robert S. (1986) Must CIM be justified by faith alone? *Harvard Business Review.* 64, (March-April) 87-91. (*2)

Kaplan, Robert S. (1991) The topic of quality in business school education and research. *Selections (SEL).* (Autumn) 13-21.

Kaplan, Robert S., and L. Murdoch. (1991) Core process design. *The McKinsey Quarterly.* (February) 27-43.

Kapur, K. C., and L. R. Lamberson. (1977) *Reliability in Engineering Design.* New York: John Wiley.

Karabatsos, Nancy. (1983) Quality is instrumental at Steinway. *Quality.* (October) 19-22.

Karabatsos, Nancy. (1983) Serving quality. *Quality.* (September) 65-68.

Karabatsos, Nancy. (1983) Update on coordinate measuring machines. *Quality.* (December) 23-28, 30, 32, 34.

Karabatsos, Nancy. (1989) Quality in transition: Part one. *Quality Progress.* 22, (December) 22-26.

Karabatsos, Nancy. (1990) Absolutely, positively quality. *Quality Progress.* 23, (May) 24-28.

Karakaya, Fahri W., and Michael J. Stahl. (1991) *Entry Barriers and Market Entry Decisions*. New York: Quorum Books.

Karasek, F. W. (1975) Analytical service laboratories. *Research/Development*. 26, (April) 32, 34, 36.

Karasek, R. A. (1979) Job demands, job decision latitude and mental strain: Implications for jobs redesign. *Administrative Science Quarterly*. 24, (June) 285-308.

Karatsu, Hajime. (1966) *Quality Control to Extend a Company: From Top Management to the Factory Floor*. Tokyo: JUSE Press.

Karatsu, Hajime. (1982) What makes Japanese products better. *SAM Advanced Management Journal*. 47, (Spring) 4-7.

Karatsu, Hajime. (1988) *Tough Words for American Industry*. Cambridge, MA: Productivity Press. (*2)

Karatsu, Hajime. (1988) *TQC Wisdom of Japan: Managing for Total Quality Control*. Cambridge, MA: Productivity Press. (*2)

Karlgaard, R. (1994) ASAP interview: Susan Cramm and John Martin. *Forbes ASAP*. 29, (August) 67-70.

Kassalow, E. M. (1987) The unions' stake in high tech development. In A. Kleingartner and C. S. Anderson (Eds.) *Human Resource Management in High Technology Firms*. Lexington, MA: D. C. Heath, 157-182.

Kast, Fremont E., and James E. Rosenweig. (1974) *Organization and Management: A Systems Approach*. Second edition. New York: McGraw-Hill. (*2)

Kastenbaum, M. A., D. G. Hoel, and K. O. Bowman. (1970) Sample size requirements: Randomized block designs. *Biometrika*. 57, (1) 573-578. (*2)

Kato, Osamu, Yosho Sakai and Katsuo Sasaki. (1981) Improvement of the rust preventive method for the body panel of a motor vehicle. *Reports of Statistical Applications and Research*. 28, (March) 40-55.

Katz, Daniel and Robert L. Kahn. (1978) *The Social Psychology of Organizations*. Revised edition. New York: Wiley, (*2)

Katz, Donald R. (1988) Coming home. *Business Month*. (October) 57-62. (*2)

Katz, Robert L. (1987) The skills of an effective administrator. *Harvard Business Review*. 65, (September-October) 90-102. (*2)

Katzan H. (1984) *Management Support Systems: A Pragmatic Approach*. New York: Van Nostrand Reinhold. (*2)

Katzean, Harry, Jr. (1989) *Quality Circle Management*. New York: Tab Books.

Katzell, M. E. (1975) *Productivity: The Measure and the Myth*. New York: AMACOM.

Katzell, M. E., and D. Yankelovich. (1965) *Work Productivity and Job Satisfaction*. New York: Harcourt Brace Jovanovich.

Katzenbach, J. R., and D. K. Smith (1993) The discipline of teams. *Harvard Business Review*. 71, (September-October) 134-142.

Katzenbach, J. R., and D. K. Smith (1993) *The Wisdom of Teams: Creating the High-Performance Organization*. Cambridge, MA: Harvard School Press.

Kaufman, J. J. (1981) *Value Engineering: An Executive Overview*. Houston, TX: Cooper.

Kaufman, R. J. (1969) Life cycle costing decision-making tool for capital equipment acquisitions. *Journal of Purchasing*. (August) 16-31.

Kaufman, Roger and Atsusi Hirumi. (1992) Ten steps to TQM plus. *Educational Leadership*. (November) 33-34.

Kaufman, Steve. (1989) Quest for quality. *Business Month*. (May) 60-65.

Kawamata, Katsuji. (1964) *My Career*. Tokyo: Keizai Shimbunsha.

Kay, T. G. (1972) Timeless work sampling. *Journal of Industrial Engineering*. 4, (June) 30-33.

Kazemek, Edwards A., and Kristine E. Peterson. (1989) Hospitals must demonstrate commitment to total quality. *Healthcare Financial Management*. 43, (March) 114.

Keane, John (1981) Computers and quality. *ASQC Annual Technical Quality Congress Transactions*. Milwaukee, WI: ASQC Quality Press, 625-631.

Kearney, Francis J. (1984) Management of product quality without a quality department. *ASQC Annual Technical Quality Congress Transactions*. Milwaukee, WI: ASQC Quality Press, 249-252.

Kearns, David T. (1990) Leadership through quality. *Academy of Management Executive*. 4, (May) 86-89. (*3)

Kearns, David T., and David A. Nadler. (1992) *Prophets in the Dark: How Xerox Reinvented Itself and Beat Back the Japanese*, New York: HarperCollins.

Kececioglu, D., and D. Cormier. (1964) *Designing a Specified Reliability into a Component*. Washington, DC: Society of Automotive Engineers.

Keefe, John P. (1981) Part-time facilitation. *Quality Circles Journal*. 4, (August) 8.

Keehley, Pat (1992) Total quality management: Getting started. *Public Management*. 74, (October) 10. (*2)

Keehley, Pat. (1992) TQM for local governments. *Public Management*. 74, (August) 10. (*2)

Keen, Peter G. W. (1986) *Competing in Time: Using Telecommunications for Competitive Advantage*. Cambridge, MA: Ballinger.

Keene, Margaret Rahn. (1991) *The Training Investment: Banking on People for Superior Results*. Homewood, IL: Business One Irwin.

Kegarise, Ronald J., and George D. Miller. (1985) An Alcoa-Kodak joint team. Proceedings of the Third Annual Conference on Quality Improvement. (*2)

Kegg, Richard L. (1984) Quality and productivity in manufacturing systems. Second Bi-Annual Machine Tool Technical Conference. Gaithersburg, MD: MTTC, 9-71 to 9-86.

Kegg, Richard L. (1985) Quality and productivity in manufacturing systems annals of the CIRP. *Rivis*. 34, (February) 531-534.

Keidel, R. (1985) *Game Plans*. New York: E. P. Dutton.

Keil, P. J., B. G. Burns, and A. D. Woyewoda. (1984) Recommended procedures and guidelines for quality evaluation of Atlantic short-fin squid. *Lebersmittelwissenschaft U. Technology*. 17, 276.

Keirsey, D. B., and M. Bates. (1978) *Please Understand Me-Character and Temperament Types*. Delmar, CA: Prometheus Nemesis.

Keller, E. F. (1983) *A Feeling for the Organism: The Life and Work of Barbara McClintock*. New York: W. H. Freeman.

Keller, E. F. (1987) Demarketing public from private values in evolutionary discourses. The project on interdependence at Radcliffe College, Working paper series, No. 3.

Keller, Maryann. (1989) *Rude Awakening: The Rise, Fall, and Struggle for Recovery of General Motors*. New York: William Morrow.

Keller, Maryann. (1993) *Collision: GM, Toyota, Volkswagen and the Race to Own the 21st Century*. New York: Doubleday.

Keller, R., and R. Chinta. (1990) International technology transfer: Strategies for success. *Academy of Management Executive*. 4, (May) 33-43.

Keller, T. A. (1975) Inspection by exception through automated video techniques. *ASQC Annual Technical Quality Congress Transactions*. Milwaukee, WI: ASQC Quality Press, 1-7.

Kelley, H., and J. Thibaut (1969) Group problem solving. In G. Lindzey and G. Aronson (Eds.) *The Handbook of Social Psychology*. Reading, MA: Addison-Wesley.

Kelley, R. E. (1985) *The Gold Collar Worker: Harnessing the Brainpower of The New Workforce*. Reading, MA: Addison-Wesley.

Kelly, C. M., and J. M. Norman. (1983) The fusion process for productivity improvement. *National Productivity Review*. 2, (Spring) 164-72.

Kelly, Kevin. (1992) How the states are playing midwife to "baby Baldriges." *BusinessWeek*. (November 30) 69. (*3)

Kelly, Lane and Reginald Worthley. (1981) The role of culture in comparative management. *Academy of Management Journal*. 24, (February) 164-173.

Kelman, H., and C. A. Kraus. (1958) Compliance, identification and internalization: three processes of attitude change. *Journal of Conflict Resolution*. 2, (March) 51-60.

Kemeny, J. G., J. L. Snell, and G. L. Thomson. (1957) *Introduction to Finite Mathematics*. Englewood Cliffs, NJ: Prentice-Hall.

Kemp, K. W. (1962) The use of cumulative sums for sampling inspection schemes. *Applied Statistics*. 11, 16-31.

Kemper, Robert E. (1992) Global quality at Federal Express. In Samuel C. Certo. *Modern Management*. Boston, MA: Allyn and Bacon, 684-685.

Kemper, Robert E. (1992) If it isn't broken at Florida Power and Light, they fix it anyway. In Samuel C. Certo. *Modern Management*. Boston, MA: Allyn and Bacon, 680-681.

Kemper, Robert E., and Deborah A. Codding. (1994) *The Conflict: The People Who Nobody Knows* . New York: McGraw-Hill.

Kemper, Robert E., and Deborah A. Codding. (1994) *The Resolution: Handbook for Win-Win-WIN Organizations.* New York: McGraw-Hill.

Kemper, Robert E., and Joseph Yehudai. (1991) *Experiencing Operations Management: A Walk Through.* Boston, MA: PWS-Kent.

Kempthorne, O. (1950) *Design and Analysis of Experiment.* New York: John Wiley.

Kempthorne, O. (1957) *An Introduction to Generic Statistics.* New York: John Wiley.

Ken, J. (1984) The (Artificial) eyes have it. *Electronic Business.* 10, (September 16) 154-162.

Kendrick, J. W. (1978) *Understanding Productivity: An Introduction to the Dynamics of Productivity Change.* Baltimore: Johns Hopkins University Press.

Kendrick, J. W. (1984) *Improving Company Productivity.* Baltimore, MD: Johns Hopkins University Press. (*2)

Kendrick, J. W. (1984) *International Comparisons of Productivity and Causes of The Slowdown.* Cambridge, MA: Ballinger.

Kendrick, J. W., and D. Creamer. (1965) *Measuring Company Productivity: Handbook with Case Studies.* New York: Conference Board. (*2)

Kendrick, J. W., and E. S. Grossman. (1980) *Productivity in the United States: Trends and Cycles.* Baltimore: Johns Hopkins University Press.

Kendrick, J. W., and N. Vaccara. (1975) *New Developments in Productivity Measurement and Analysis.* Chicago, IL: University of Chicago Press.

Kennedy, Larry W. (1991) *Quality Management in the Nonprofit World.* San Francisco, CA: Jossey-Bass.

Kennedy, P. (1989) *The Rise and Fall of the Great Powers.* New York: Vintage Books.

Kennedy, Ray. (1980) Howard Head says, 'I'm giving up the thing world.' *Sports Illustrated.* (September) 72.

Kenworthy, Harry W., and Angela George. (1989) Quality and cost efficiency go hand in hand. *Quality Progress.* 22, (October) 40-41.

Kenyon, Richard L., and Richard J. Newell. (1982) FMEA technique for microcomputer assemblies. *Proceedings, Annual Reliability and Maintainability Symposium.* New York: IEEE, 117-120.

Kepner, C., and B. Tregoe. (1965) *The Rational Manager.* New York: McGraw-Hill.

Kepner, C., and B. Tregoe. (1981) *The New Rational Manager.* Princeton, NJ: Princeton Research Press.

Kepper, R. E. (1985) Quality motivation. *Food Technology.* 39, (September) 51.

Kerr, C., and J. M. Rosow. (1979) *Work in America: The Decade Ahead.* New York: Van Nostrand Reinhold. (*2)

Kerr, C., John T. Dunlop, Frederick Harbison, and Charles A. Myers. (1964) *Industrialism and Industrial Man.* New York: Oxford University Press.

Kerr, J. L. (1985) Diversification strategies and managerial rewards: An empirical study. *Academy of Management Journal.* 28, (January) 115-179.

Keryner, Harold (1979) *Project Management: A Systems Approach to Planning, Scheduling, and Controlling.* New York: Van Nostrand Reinhold.

Ketchum, L. D. (1984) How redesigned plants really work. *National Productivity Review.* 3, (February) 246-254. (*2)

Keuls, M. (1952) The use of the studentized range in connection with an analysis of variance. *Euphytica.* 112.

Keynes, John Maynard. (1963) *Essays in Persuasion.* New York: W. W. Norton. (*2)

Keynes, John Maynard. (1965) *The General Theory of Employment, Interest and Money.* New York: Harcourt Brace Jovanovich. (*2)

Khojecki, H. (1974) *Quality Optimization: Psychological Methods.* Warsaw: WEC. (*2)

Khwialkowski, H. (1980) New form of education and training of the managerial staff in the field of QC in Poland. Proceedings, Twenty-Fourth Conference, Warsaw. 1, 93. (*2)

Kida, Hiroshi. (1981) Life-long learning: Education for all people at all ages. *Look Japan.* (December) 1-3.

Kidder, Tracy. (1981) *The Soul of a New Machine.* Boston, MA: Little, Brown.

Kidder, Tracy. (1989) *Among School Children.* Boston, MA: Houghton Mifflin.

Kierkegaard, Sören. (1937) In *Bartlett's Familiar Quotations.* Boston, MA: Little, Brown.

Kiesche, Elizabeth S. (1992) Going beyond expectations: The competitive edge. *Chemical Week.* 151, (September 30) 52. (*2)

Kikuchi, Senchi. (1982) Japanese quality control method increasingly finds its way abroad. *The Japan Economic Journal.* (June) 11.

Kilbridge, M. D. (1960) Reduced costs through job enrichment: A case. *Journal of Business*. 33, (April) 357-362.

Kilduff, Francis B. (1985) For small shops: Low cost Q.C. *Quality Assurance*. 11, (March) 20.

Killian, Ceil S. (1988) *The World of W. Edwards Deming*. Rockville, MD: Cee Press Books/Mercury Press. (*2)

Killian, Ceil S. (1992) *The World of W. Edwards Deming*. Second edition. Knoxville, TN: SPC Press. (*2)

Kilingel, Sally and Ann Martin (Ed.). (1988) *A Fighting Chance*. New York: ILR Press.

Kilmann, R. H. (1984) *Beyond the Quick Fix: Managing Five Tracks to Organizational Success*. San Francisco, CA: Jossey-Bass. (*5)

Kimberly, J. R., and H. Miles. (1980) *Organization Life Cycles*. San Francisco, CA: Jossey-Bass.

Kimble, Roger G. (1982) Serviceability analysis. *Proceedings of the Quality in Electronics Conference*. Milwaukee, WI: ASQC Quality Press, 79-81.

Kimemia, Joseph and Stanley B. Gershwin. (1983) Algorithm for the computer control flexible manufacturing system. *IIE Transactions*. 15, 353-362.

Kimmerling, George F. (1989) The future of HRD. *Training and Development Journal*. 43, (June) 50. (*2)

Kindelberger, C. (1974) An American economic climacteric. *Challenge*. (January-February) 35.

Kindelberger, C. (1980) The economic aging of America. *Challenge*. (January-February) 48.

Kindlarski, E. (1984) Ishikawa diagrams for problem solving. *Quality Progress*. 17, (December) 26-30.

King, Bob. (1987) *Better Designs in Half the Time: Implementing QFD in America.* Methuen, MA: Goal/QPC. (*5)

King, Bob. (1989) *Hoshin Planning: The Developmental Approach.* Methuen, MA: Goal/QPC.

King customer. (1990) *BusinessWeek* (March 12) 88-94. (*2)

King, J. L., and B. Konsynski. (1990) Singapore Tradenet: A tale of one city. Harvard Business School Case No. 9-191-009. Cambridge, MA: Harvard Business School.

King, James R. (1971) *Probability Charts for Decision Making.* New York: The Industrial Press. (*2)

King, W. R. (1988) Strategic planning for information resources. *Information Resource Management Journal.* (Fall) 2-3.

Kinlaw, Dennis C. (1989) *Coaching for Commitment: Managerial Strategies for Obtaining Superior Work Teams.* San Diego: Pfeiffer and Company. (*2)

Kinlaw, Dennis C. (1990) *Inter-Group Feedback Questionnaire.* Norfolk, VA: Kinlaw Associates. (*2)

Kinlaw, Dennis C. (1991) *Developing Superior Work Teams: Building Quality and the Competitive.* Lexington, MA: Pfeiffer and Company. (*2)

Kinlaw, Dennis C. (1991) *Superior Team Development Inventory.* Norfolk, VA: Kinlaw Associates. (*2)

Kinnucan, Paul. (1983) Flexible systems invade the factory. *High Technology.* (July) 32-42.

Kinsella, Bridget. (1993) Commitment begets quality. *Graphic Arts Monthly.* 25, (February) 44. (*3)

Kirby, Bill. (1992) Improving productivity in sponsored research administration. *SRA Journal.* (Fall) 41-54.

Kirby, Kenneth E., and Charles F. Moore. (1989) Process control and quality in the continuous process industries. *Survey of Business.* (Summer) 62-66.

Kirk, R. E. (1968) *Experimental Design: Procedures for the Behavioral Sciences*. Belmont, CA: Wadsworth.

Kirk, R. E. (1992) Exploding myths over quality. *Marketing*. (August 27) 20. (*2)

Kirkpatrick, D. L. (1985) *How to Manage Change Effectively*. San Francisco, CA: Jossey-Bass. (*2)

Kirkpatrick, R. L. (1970) Confidence limits on a percent defective characterized by two specification limits. *Journal of Quality Technology*. 2, (March) 150-155.

Kirschner, Elisabeth. (1992) Incorporating the green angle. *Chemical Week*. 151, (September 30) 60. (*2)

Kirwan, M. S. (1972) Guaranteed accurate numerical tapes. *Mechanical Engineering*. (August) 13-17.

Kivenko, K. (1979) Surviving the operational audit. *Production Engineering*. (June) 21-24.

Kivenko, K. (1984) *Quality Control for Management.* Englewood Cliffs, NJ: Prentice-Hall. (*2)

Klauss, Hans. (1990) Total quality at Siemens' Wurzburg electric motor factory. *International Journal of Technology Management*. 5, 114-121.

Klein, B. (1977) *Dynamic Economics.* Cambridge, MA: Harvard University Press. (*2)

Klein, Gerald D. (1981) Implementing quality circles: A hard look at some of the realities. *Personnel*. 58, (November-December) 11-21.

Klein, J. A. (1983) First-line supervisory reactions and accommodations to worker involvement programs. Unpublished Ph.D. dissertation, MIT, Sloan School of Management, Cambridge, MA.

Klein, J. A. (1984) Why supervisors resist employee involvement. *Harvard Business Review.* 62, (September-October) 87-95.

Klein, J. A. (1989) The human costs of manufacturing reform. *Harvard Business Review.* 67, (March-April) 60-66.

Klein, J. A., and P. Posey. (1986) Traditional versus New Work systems supervision: Is there a difference? Harvard Business School Working Paper 1-786-036, (April).

Klein, M. M. (1994) Reengineering methodologies and tools: A prescription for enhancing success. *Information Systems Management.* (Spring) 30-35.

Klein, Walter F., and Thom Schamberger. (1982) Part-time facilitators and quality control circles in the hospital environment. IAQC Fourth Annual Conference Transactions. Cincinnati, OH: International Association of Quality Circles, 528-540.

Kleinfeld, N. D. (1989) Wanted: C.F.O. with "flair for funk." *New York Times.* (March 26) D4. (*2)

Kleingartner, A., and C. S. Anderson. (1987) *Human Resource Management in High Technology Firms.* Lexington, MA: Lexington Books. (*2)

Kline, James J. (1992) Total quality management in local government. *Government Finance Review.* 8, (August) 7. (*2)

Klompmaker Jay E., David G. Hughes, and Russell I. Haley. (1976) Test marketing in new product development. *Harvard Business Review.* 54, (May-June) 128-138.

Kmetz, J. L. (1984) An information-processing study of a complex work flow in aircraft electronic repair. *Administrative Science Quarterly.* 29, (July) 255-280.

Knakal, Jan C. (1992) Historical sources of Japanese management practices. In Harry Ivan Costin (Ed.) *Readings in Total Quality Management.* (1994) Fort Worth, TX: Dryden Press, 341-350.

Knickerbocker, I. (1948) Leadership: A conception and some implications. *Journal of Social Issues.* 423-40.

Knight, L. J. (1983) Quality circles in action: A Canadian experience. *The Human Element.* (February) 20-21.

Knotts, Rose. (1991) Rambo doesn't work here anymore. *Business Horizons.* 34, (January-February) 44-46.

Knowles, M. (1970) *The Modern Practice of Adult Education.* New York: Association Press.

Knuth, D. E. (1973) *The Art of Computer Programming. Volume 3: Sorting and Searching.* Reading, MA: Addison-Wesley.

Kobayashi, Iwao. (1990) *20 Keys to Workplace Improvement.* Cambridge, MA: Productivity Press.

Kobayashi, Koji. (1986) *Computers and Communications.* Cambridge, MA: MIT Press. (*2)

Kobayashi, Koji. (1986) Quality management at NEC corporation. *Quality Progress.* 20, (April) 18-23. (*2)

Koch, Richard A. (1974) Consumer product reliability: The role of the retailer. *Proceedings, Annual Reliability and Maintainability Symposium.* New York: IEEE, 27-29.

Kochen, T. A. (1983) Strategic choice and industrial relations theory and practice. Sloan School of Management working paper.

Kochen, T. A., and B. McKensie. (1985) *Handbook of Organizational Behavior.* Englewood Cliffs, NJ: Prentice-Hall.

Kochhar, A. K. (1979) *Development of Computer Based Production System.* New York: John Wiley.

Kodak. Managing. (1987) *Fortune.* (April 27) 26.

Koehler, T. L. (1959) Evolutionary operation. *Chemical Engineering Progress.* 55, 76-79.

Koestler, Arthur. (1967) *The Ghost in the Machine.* New York: Macmillan. (*2)

Kofoed, Carl A. (1982) The integration phase. *ASQC Annual Technical Quality Congress Transactions.* Milwaukee, WI: ASQC Quality Press, 433-440.

Koger, Dan and Greg Brower. (1992) If total quality seems like a revolution, that's because it is. *Communication World.* 9, (October) 18. (*2)

Kogure, Masao. (1975) *Theory of Process Capability and Its Applications.* Tokyo: JUSE Press.

Kogure, Masao and Yoji Akao. (1983) Quality function deployment and CWQC in Japan. *Quality Progress.* 16, (October) 25-29. (*2)

Kohil, Ajay K., and Bernard J. Jaworski. (1990) Market orientation: The construct, research propositions and managerial implications. *Journal of Marketing.* 50, (April) 1-18.

Kohl, R. (1982) Can America meet foreign competition? A treatise on productivity. *Journal of Small Business Management.* 20, (January) 56-58.

Kohn, Alfie. (1986) *No Contest: The Case Against Competition.* Boston, MA: Houghton Mifflin. (*5)

Kohn, Alfie. (1990) *The Brighter Side of Human Nature.* New York: Basic Books.

Kohnka, Edward. (1984) Zero inspectors. Is it attainable? *ASQC Annual Technical Quality Congress Transactions.* Milwaukee, WI: ASQC Quality Press, 152-156.

Kohnke, Luane. (1990) Designing a customer satisfaction measurement program. *Bank Marketing.* (July) 29.

Kohoutek, Henery J. (1983) Commitment to quality through a strategic plan. *ASQC Annual Technical Quality Congress Transactions.* Milwaukee, WI: ASQC Quality Press, 82-86.

Kolb, John and Steven S. Ross. (1980) *Product Safety and Liability: A Desk Reference.* New York: McGraw-Hill.

Kolmin, F. W. (1973) Measuring productivity and efficiency. *Management Accounting.* 55, (November) 32-34

Kolthoff, I. M., and P. J. Elving. *Treatise on Analytical Chemistry.* New York: John Wiley.

Konarick, Ronald B., and Wayne Reed. (1981) A military approach: Work environment improvement teams. *Quality Circles Journal.* 4, (August) 35-40.

Kondo, Y. (1969) Internal QC audit in Japanese companies. *Quality.* (April) 97-103.

Kondo, Y. (1976) The role of managers in QC circle movement. In Davida M. Amsden and Robert T. Amsden (Eds.) *QC Circles: Applications, Tools and Theory.* Milwaukee, WI: ASQC Quality Press.

Kondo, Y. (1976) The roles of manager in QC circle movement. *Reports of Statistical Applications and Research.* 23, 71-81.

Kondo, Y. (1977) Creativity in daily work. *ASQC Annual Technical Quality Congress Transactions.* Milwaukee, WI: ASQC Quality Press, 430-439.

Kondo, Y. (1978) JUSE—A center of quality control in Japan. *Quality Progress.* 16, (August) 14-15.

Kondrasuk, Jack N. (1981) Studies in MBO effectiveness. *Academy of Management Review.* (June) 419-430.

Konz, Stephen A. (1979) Quality circles: An annotated bibliography. *Quality Progress*. 14, (April) 30-35.

Konz, Stephen A. (1979) Quality circles: Japanese success story. *Industrial Engineering*. 11, (October) 24-37.

Konz, Stephen A. (1983) *Work Design and Industrial Ergonomics*. Columbus, OH: Grid.

Konz, Stephen A., G. Peterson, and A. Joshi. (1981) Reducing inspector errors. *Quality Progress*. 14, (July) 24-26.

Koons, Paul F. (1991) Getting comfortable with TQM. *Bureaucrat*. 20, (Summer) 35-38.

Koontz, Harold and C. O'Donnell. (1972) *Principles of Management: An Analysis of Managerial Functions*. Fifth edition. New York: McGraw-Hill.

Koopmans, L. H. (1981) *Introduction to Contemporary Statistics*. Boston, MA: Duxbury Press.

Kopelman, R. E. (1985) Job redesign and productivity: A review of the evidence. *National Productivity Review*. 4, (March) 237-255. (*2)

Kopelman, R. E. (1986) *Managing Productivity in Organizations*. New York: McGraw-Hill. (*2)

Kosaky, Yoshida. (1989) Deming management philosophy: Does it work in the U.S. as well as in Japan? *Columbia Journal of World Business*. (Fall) 10-18. (*2)

Koshiro, Kazuyoshi. (1981) The quality of working life. *Toyota Quarterly Review*. 10, (June) 1-8.

Koska, Mary T. (1990) Adopting Deming's quality improvement ideas: A case study. *Hospitals*. (July) 58-63. (*4)

Koska, Mary T. (1992) CEOs say hospitals must learn from each other for TQM success. *Hospitals*. 66, (June 20) 42. (*2)

Kosnik, T. J. (1985) Ambiguity of preference and brand flexibility: How we know our options open when we don't know what we want. Unpublished Ph.D. dissertation, Stanford University, Palo Alto, CA.

Kosnik, T. J. (1988) Five stumbling blocks to global strategic alliances. *Items Integration Age.* (October) 21-24.

Kosnik, T. J., and R. T. Moriarty. (1988) High-tech vs. low-tech market, what's the difference? AMA Research Workshop. Research at the Market Entrepreneurship Interface Proceedings.

Kosnik. T. J. (1986) Flexibility seeking and delay: The effects of ambiguity preference and experience on selecting a short list. Unpublished work paper, Harvard Business School.

Kotkin, Joel. (1988) The great American revival. *Inc.* (February) 52-63.

Kotter, John P. (1982) *The General Managers.* New York: Macmillan.

Kotter, John P. (1985) *Power and Influence.* New York: Free Press.

Kotter, John P. (1988) *The Leadership Factor.* New York: Free Press.

Kotter, John P., L. Fahey, and S. Jatusripitak. (1985) *The New Competition.* Englewood Cliffs, NJ: Prentice-Hall. (*2)

Kotter, John P., L. A. Schlesinger, and V. Sathe. (1986) *Organization: Text, Cases, and Readings on the Management of Organizational Design and Change.* Second edition. Homewood, IL: Irwin. (*2)

Kouzes, J., and P. Posner. (1987) *The Leadership Challenge.* San Francisco, CA: Jossey-Bass.

Koyanagi, Kenichi. (1952) Statistical quality control in Japanese industry. *ASQC Annual Technical Quality Congress Transactions.* Milwaukee, WI: ASQC Quality Press.

Kozol, J. (1985) *Illiterate America.* New York: New American Library.

Kozol, J. (1992) From a speech presented at the annual convention of American Association of School Administrators, San Diego, February.

Kraakman, Reinier. (1984) Corporate liability strategies and the costs of legal controls. *Yale Law Journal.* 93, (April) 857-898.

Kraar, Louis. (1975) The Japanese are coming—With their own style of management. *Fortune.* (March 15) 116-21.

Kraar, Louis. (1980) Japan's automakers shift strategies. *Fortune.* (August 1) 109. (*2)

Kraar, Louis. (1991) Twenty-five who help the U.S. win. *Fortune.* (August 15) 34.

Kraemer, H. C., and S. Thiemann. (1987) *How Many Subjects.* Newbury Park, CA: Sage.

Kramer, A., and B. A. Twigg. (1970) *Quality Control for the Food Industry.* Westport Connecticut: The Avi Publishing Company.

Kramer, C. Y., and D. R. Jensen, (1969) Fundamentals of multivariate analysis. *Journal of Quality Technology.* 1, (February) 120-133.

Krause, T. R., J. Hidley, and S. J. Hodson. (1990) *The Behavior-Based Safety Process: Managing Involvement for an Injury-Free Culture.* New York: Van Nostrand Reinhold.

Krautkramer, J., and H. Krautkramer. (1961) *Ultrasonic Testing of Materials.* New York: Springer-Verlag.

Kreitner, Robert. (1976) Identifying and managing the basics of individual productivity. *Arizona Business.* 23, (May) 3-8.

Krishnamoorthi, K. S. (1985) *Why the Control Chart Ticks?* Metals Park, OH: American Society for Testing and Materials.

Krishnamoorthi, K. S. (1986) Predicting quality cost changes using regression. *ASQC Annual Technical Quality Congress Transactions*. Milwaukee, WI: ASQC Quality Press, 406-410.

Kroc, Ray. (1977) *Grinding it Out: The Making of McDonald's*. New York: Berkeley. (*2)

Krone, Bob. (1990) Total quality management: An American odyssey. *Bureaucrat*. (Fall) 35-38. (*2)

Krone, C. (1974) *New Technologies in Organization Development*. La Jolla, CA: University Associates. (*2)

Krouse, John. (1982) *What Every Engineer Should Know about Computer-Aided Design and Computer-Aided Manufacturing*. New York: Marcel Dekker.

Krulee, K. (1955) The Scanlon Plan: Cooperation through participation. *Journal of Business*. 28, (February) 33-42.

Krutchkoff, R. G. (1972) Empirical Bayes estimation. *The American Statistician*. (December) 14-16.

Ku, Harry H. (Ed.). (1969) *Precision Measurement and Calibration-Statistical Concepts and Procedures*. Washington, DC: U.S. Government Printing Office.

Ku, Harry H. et al. (1969) *The Measurement Process*. Special Publication Number 300. Washington, DC: National Bureau of Standards.

Kubota, Hitoshi. (1983) Japan: Social structure and work ethic. *Asia Pacific Community*. 20, (Spring) 42-47.

Kudrna, D. A. (1975) *Purchasing Managers Decision*. Boston, MA: Cahners Publishing.

Kuhlmann, C. (1929) *The Development of the Flour Milling Industry in the U.S.*. Boston, MA: Houghton Mifflin.

Kuhn, T. S. (1970) *The Structure of Scientific Revolutions.* Chicago, IL: University of Chicago Press. (*2)

Kume, Hitoshi. (1980) Quality control in Japan's industries. *Toyota Quarterly Review.* 9, (Spring) 7-12.

Kume, Hitoshi. (1985) Business management and quality cost: The Japanese view. *Quality Progress.* 18, (May) 13-18. (*2)

Kume, Hitoshi. (1985) *Statistical Methods for Quality Improvement.* Tokyo: The Association for Overseas Technical Scholarship. (*4)

Kume, Hitoshi. (1986) Reply to letters to editors. *Quality Progress.* 19, (February) 8.

Kume, Hitoshi. (1990) The quality cultural exchange. *Quality Progress.* 23, (October) 33-35.

Kuretz, G. (1989) The acquisition boom has lost a lot of its thunder. *BusinessWeek.* (June 12) 234.

Kurland, Leonard T., and Craig A. Molgaard. (1981) The patient record in epidemiology. *Scientific American.* (October) 54-63.

Kurnow, Ernest J., Gerald J. Glasser, and Fred R. Ottman. (1959) *Statistics for Business Decisions.* Homewood, IL: Irwin.

Kurtz, T. E, B. F. Link, J. W. Turkey, and D. L. Wallace. (1965) Short-cut multiple comparisons for balanced single and double classifications. *Technometrics.* 7, (February) 95-165.

Kurtzman, J. (1990) Japan's mythical trade surplus. *New York Times.* (December 9) 13.

Kurzman, Dan. (1960) *Kishi and Japan.* New York: Odolensky.

Kusaba, I. (1981) *The QC Circle Activities in Japan.* Tokyo: JUSE Press.

Kuzela, Lad. (1980) Putting Japanese-style management to work. *Industry Week*. (September 16) 61. (*2)

Kuznets, S. (1966) *Modern Economic Growth*. New Haven, CT: Yale University Press.

Kyd, Charles. (1987) Quality nightmares. *Inc*. 9, (October) 155-158.

LaBarre, Kenneth C. (1978) Building a field resident quality program. *Quality Progress*. 11, (October) 24-27.

Labich, Kenneth. (1989) Hot company, warm culture. *Fortune*. (February 27) 74-78.

Labich, Kenneth. (1990) American takes on the world. *Fortune*. (September 24) 38-44.

Lacey, Robert. (1981) *The Kingdom*. New York: Harcourt Brace Jovanovich.

Lacey, Robert. (1986) *Ford: The Men and the Machine*. Boston, MA: Little Brown. (*2)

Lacking a gut feeling: Revitalizing the U.S. economy. (1980) *BusinessWeek*. (June) 78.

Lader, James I. (1988) Getting emotional about quality. *The Quality Review*. (Summer) 32-37.

Laetrile. (1977) The political success of a scientific failure. *Consumer Reports*. (August) 444-447.

Laffel, G., and D. Blumenthal. (1992) The case for using industrial quality management science in health care organizations. *Journal of the American Medical Association*. 262, 2869-2872.

Laffel, G., and Donald M. Berwick. (1992) Quality in health care. *The Journal of the American Medical Association*. 268, (July 15) 407. (*2)

LaFord, Richard J., and Robert R. Steers. (1979) Receiving inspection or ship to stock parts 1 and 2. *ASQC Annual Technical Quality Congress Transactions.* Milwaukee, WI: ASQC Quality Press, 69-78.

LaForge, R. Lawrence. (1981) Education. *Quality Progress.* 14, (June) 13-15.

Lalonde, J. (1975) Management of purchasing in an uncertain economy. *Journal of Purchasing and Materials Management.* 11, (Winter) 3-8.

Lamb, Robert Boyden. (1987) *Running American Business: Top CEOs Rethink Their Major Decisions.* New York: Basic Books.

Lamberson, L. R. (1985) Reliability tutorial. *ASQC Annual Technical Quality Congress Transactions.* Milwaukee, WI: ASQC Quality Press, 88-99.

Lambert, Hope. (1983) *Till Death Do Us Part.* San Diego: Harcourt Brace Jovanovich.

Lammers, C. J. (1967) Power and participation in decision making in formal organizations. *American Journal of Sociology.* 73, 201-16.

LaMotte, L. R., and R. R. Hocking. (1970) Computational efficiency in the selection of regression variables. *Technometrics.* 12, (January) 92-93.

Lampe, David (1983) CIT scanners: Industry's new see through anything eyes. *Popular Science,* 223, (September) 52-56.

Lancaster, K. (1980) Competition and product variety. *Journal of Business.* 53, (Spring) 79-89.

Lancianese, F. W. (1981) Small plant's safety success formula. *Occupational Hazards.* 13, (July) 15-18.

Land, William E., and John J. Heldt. (1981) New dimensions in quality education. *Quality Progress.* 14, (July) 20-22.

Landau, M. (1969) Redundancy, rationality and the problem of duplication and overlap. *Public Administration Review*. 29, 348-358.

Landes, D. (1969) *The Unbound Prometheus*. Cambridge, MA: Harvard University Press. (*2)

Lang, H., and B. Lefebvre. (1991) Total quality concept. *International Journal of Technology Management*. 6, 149-154.

Langer, Ellen. (1989) *Mindfulness*. New York: Addison-Wesley.

Langevin, R. G. (1977) *Quality Control in the Service Industries*. New York: AMACOM.

Langevin, R. G. (1979) What's ahead for quality control in the 1980's. *Quality Progress*. 12, (October) 11-16.

Lansing, Rick L. (1989) The power of teams. *Supervisory Management*. (February) 39-43. (*2)

Lapham, Lewis H. (1981) Gifts of the Magi. *Harper's*. (February) 11. (*2)

Lareau, William. (1991) *American Samurai: Warrior for the Coming Dark Ages of American Business*. Clinton, NJ: New Win Publishing.

Larkin, Howard. (1992) Redefining quality. *American Medical News*. 35, (October 26) 15. (*2)

Larmond, E. (1976) Sensory methods-choices and limitations. *Correlating Sensory Objective Measurements-New Methods for Answering Old Problems*. Philadelphia, PA: American Society for Testing and Materials.

Larson, C., and M. LaFasto. (1989) *Teamwork*. Newbury Park, CA: Sage.

Larson, Harry T. (1974) A 20-year ripoff. *Info Systems*. (November) 75-89.

LaSala, Kenneth P., and Arthur I. Siegel. (1983) Improved R and M in productivity by designs for people. *Proceedings Annual Reliability and Maintainability Symposium.* New York: IEEE, 490-500.

Lascelles, D. M., and B. G. Dale. (1989) The buyer-supplier relationship in the total quality management. *Journal of Purchasing and Material Management.* 25, (Summer) 10-19.

Lashof, T. W. (1964) Ranking laboratories and evaluating methods of measurement in round robin tests. *Materials Research and Standards.* 4, (August) 397-407.

Laskin, R., and W. L. Smithhisler. (1979) The economics of standard electronic packaging. *Proceedings, Annual Reliability and Maintainability Symposium.* New York: IEEE, 67-72.

Lasky, Victor. (1981) *Never Explain, Never Complain.* New York: Richard Marek.

Latzko, William J. (1982) Reduction of mistakes in a bank. In William Edwards Deming (Ed.) *Quality, Productivity, and Competitive Position.* Cambridge, MA: MIT, Center for Advanced Engineering.

Latzko, William J. (1985) Process capability in administrative applications. *ASQC Annual Technical Quality Congress Transactions.* Milwaukee, WI: ASQC Quality Press, 168-173.

Latzko, William J. (1986) *Quality and Productivity for Bankers and Financial Managers.* Milwaukee, WI: ASQC Quality Press.

Latzko, William J. (1987) *Quality and Productivity for Bankers and Financial Managers.* New York: Marcel Dekker.

Latzko, William J. (1989) Control charts in the board room. *ASQC Annual Technical Quality Congress Transactions.* Milwaukee, WI: ASQC Quality Press.

Latzko, William J., and David M. Saunders. (1995) *Four Days with Dr. Deming: A Strategy for Modern Methods of Management.* Reading, MA: Addison-Wesley.

Latzko, William J., and J. D. Dowhin. (1991) Achieving service quality by charting. *ASQC Annual Technical Quality Congress Transactions*. Milwaukee, WI: ASQC Quality Press.

Lauenstein, M. C., and W. Skinner. (1980) Formulating a strategy of superior resources. *The Journal of Business Strategy*. 1, (January-February) 410.

Laufer, A. C. (1984) *Production and Operations Management*. Cincinnati, OH: South-Western.

Law, Joe M. (1981) Quality circles at a naval shipyard: Employee involvement ups productivity. *World of Work Report*. 6, (January) 3-4.

Lawler, Edward E., III. (1969) Job design and employee motivation. *Personnel Psychology*. 22, (April) 426-435. (*2)

Lawler, Edward E., III. (1971) *Pay and Organizational Effectiveness: A Psychological View*. New York: McGraw-Hill. (*2)

Lawler, Edward E., III. (1973) *Motivation in Work Organizations*. Monterey, CA: Brooks/Cole. (*3)

Lawler, Edward E., III. (1978) The new plant revolution. *Organizational Dynamics*. 6, (March) 2-12. (*2)

Lawler, Edward E., III. (1981) *Pay and Organization Development*. Reading, MA: Addison-Wesley. (*2)

Lawler, Edward E., III. (1983) Human resource productivity in the 80's. *New Management*. (Spring) 46-49.

Lawler, Edward E., III. (1985) Education, management style and organizational effectiveness. *Personnel Psychology*. 38, (January) 1-26. (*2)

Lawler, Edward E., III. (1986) *High-Involvement Management: Participative Strategies for Improving Organizational Performance*. San Francisco, CA: Jossey-Bass. (*6)

Lawler, Edward E., III. (1986) The new pay. In Sara L. Rynes and G. T. Milkovich (Eds.) *Current Issues in Human Resources Management: Commentary and Readings.* Plano, TX: BPI, 404-412.

Lawler, Edward E., III. (1987) Pay for performance: A strategic analysis. Unpublished manuscript. University of Southern California.

Lawler, Edward E., III. (1992) Building relationships: Siemens adds the personal touch to the technical sell. *Business Marketing.* 77, (August) 34. (*2)

Lawler, Edward E., III., and J. Richard Hackman. (1971) Corporate profits and employee satisfaction: Must they be in conflict? *California Management Review.* 14, (Fall) 34-46.

Lawler, Edward E., III., and Gerald E. Ledford Jr. (1982) Productivity and the quality of worklife. *National Productivity Review.* 1, (January) 23-36. (*2)

Lawler, Edward E., III., and Gerald E. Ledford Jr. (1985) Skill based pay. *Personnel.* 62, (September) 30-37. (*2)

Lawler, Edward E., III., and Susan Albers Mohrman. (1985) Quality circles after the fad. *Harvard Business Review.* 85, (January-February) 64-71. (*2)

Lawler, Edward E., III., and Susan Albers Mohrman. (1987) Quality circles: After the honeymoon. *Organizational Dynamics.* 15, (Spring) 42-54.

Lawler, Edward E., III., David A. Nadler, and Cortland Cammann. (1980) *Organizational Assessment.* New York: John Wiley. (*2)

Lawler, Edward E., III., and L. Ozley. (1979) Winning union-management cooperation on quality of work life projects. *Management Review.* 68, (March). 20-27. (*2)

Lawler, Edward E., III., P. A. Renwick, and R. J. Bullock. (1981) Employee influence on decisions: An analysis. *Journal of Occupational Behavior.* 2, (February) 115-123. (*2)

Lawler, Edward E., III., and J. G. Rhode. (1976) *Information and Control in Organizations*. Pacific Palisades, CA: Goodyear. (*2)

Lawless, J. F. (1982) *Statistical Models and Methods for Lifetime Data.* New York: John Wiley.

Lawlor, A. J. (1978) Quality assurance in design and development. *Quality Assurance.* 4, (September) 87-91.

Lawrence, J., and J. R. Dawson. (1982) The interrelationship between components in a FMS. *Engineer's Digest.* 43.

Lawrence, Paul R. (1969) How to deal with resistance to change. *Harvard Business Review.* 47, (January-February) 4-12.

Lawrence, Paul R. (1989) A reassessment of why organizations change. In Allan M. Mohrman, Jr., Susan Albers Mohrman, Gerald E. Ledford, Jr., T. Cummings and Edward E. Lawler III (Eds.) *Large Scale Organizational Change.* San Francisco, CA: Jossey-Bass.

Lawrence, Paul R., and D. Dyer. (1983) *Renewing American Industry: Organizing for Efficiency and Innovation.* New York: Free Press.

Lawrence, Paul R., and Davis Dyer. (1983) *Renewing American Industry.* New York: Free Press. (*2)

Lawrence, Paul R., and Jay W. Lorsch. (1967) *Organization and Environment.* Boston, MA: Harvard University Press. (*2)

Lawrence, Paul R., and Jay W. Lorsch. (1969) *Organization and Environment.* Cambridge, MA: Division of Research, Harvard Business School.

Lawrence, R. Z. (1984) *Can America Compete?* Washington, DC: Brookings Institute.

Lawton, William H. (1993) Design, marketing and quality management. In Joiner Associates. *A Practical Guide to Quality: Selected Readings in Quality Improvement.* Madison, WI: Joiner Associates.

Lawton, William H., and E. A. Sylvestre. (1971) *Self Modeling Curve Resolution.* 13, (August) 617-634.

Layden, J. E. (1993) Reengineering the human/machine partnership. *Industrial Engineering.* 25, (April) 14.

Laza, Robert W., and Perry L. Wheaton. (1990) Recognizing the pitfalls of total quality management. *Public Utility Fortnightly.* 125, (April) 17-21.

Lazes, W. T. (1986) Employee involvement activities: Saving jobs and money too. *New Management.* 3, (Winter) 7-14.

Leach, Llewelyn S. (1992) U.S. managers focus on boosting quality. *Christian Science Monitor.* 85, (October 1) 9.

Leader, Charles. (1989) Making total quality management work: Lessons from industry. *Aviation Week and Space Technology.* 131, (October) 65.

Leaders of the most admired. (1990) *Fortune.* (January 29) 40-54.

Leaky water law, Editorial. (1987) *Los Angeles Times.* (April 15) 4. (*2)

Leaman, David C. (1975) *Education and Training Column of Quality Progress.* 8, (November) 34.

Leaman, David C. (1979) *Education and Training Column of Quality Progress.* 12, (December) 5.

Leaman, David C. (1981) Quality technology program accreditation update. *Quality Progress.* 14, (May) 4.

Leap, Terry L. (1991) *Collective Bargaining and Labor Relations.* New York: Macmillan.

Leavenworth, Richard S., and Eugene L. Grant. (1996) *Statistical Quality Control.* Seventh edition. Milwaukee, WI: ASQC Quality Press.

Leavitt, Harold J. (1955) Small groups in large organizations. *Journal of Business*. 28, (January) 21-32.

Leavitt, Harold J. (1958) *Managerial Psychology*. Chicago, IL: University of Chicago Press. (*2)

Leavitt, Harold J. (1965) Applying organizational change in industry: Structural, technological and humanistic approaches. In James G. March (Ed.) *Handbook of Organizations*. Chicago, IL: Rand McNally.

LeBoeuf, Michael. (1982) *The Productivity Challenge: How to Make It Work for America and You*. New York: McGraw-Hill.

Ledford, Gerald E., Jr. (1989) *The Design of Skill-Based Pay Plans*. COE Pub. 689-15. Los Angeles, CA: University of Southern California, Center for Effective Organization.

Ledvinka, J. (1982) *Federal Regulation of Personnel and Human Resource Management*. Boston, MA: PWS-Kent.

Lee, A. (1988) *Call Me Roger*. Chicago, IL: Contemporary Books. (*2)

Lee, Bruce. (1988) Worker harmony makes NUMMI work. *New York Times*. Business section. (December 25) 2.

Lee, C. (1990) Beyond teamwork. *Training*. 27, (June) 25-32. (*2)

Lee, L., and W. Dobler. (1971) *Purchasing and Materials Management*. Second edition. New York: McGraw-Hill.

Lee, M. M. and U. S. Karmarkar. (1983) Good product support is smart marketing. *Harvard Business Review*. 61, (November-December) 127.

Lee, Sang M., Fred Luthans, and Richard M. Hodgetts. (1992) Total quality management: Implications for central and Eastern Europe. *Organizational Dynamics*. 20, (Spring) 42-55.

Lee, Sang M., L. Moore, and B. Taylor. (1981) *Management Science.* Dubuque, IA: W. C. Brown.

Lee, Yong Y., and Larry W. Fegley. (1979) How QC circles were started in AMP, Inc. IAQC 1st Annual Conference Transactions. Cincinnati, OH: International Association of Quality Circles.

Leebov, W., and C. J. Ersoz. (1991) *The Healthcare Manager's Guide to Continuous Quality Improvement.* Chicago, IL: American Hospital Publishing. (*2)

Leerhsen, Charles. (1989) How Disney does it. *Newsweek.* (April 3) 17-24.

Lefcourt, Herbert M. (1976) *Locus of Control: Current Trends in Theory and Research.* Hillsdale, New Jersey: Lawrence Erlbaum Associates.

Lefevre, H. (1989) *Quality Service Pays: Six Keys to Success.* Milwaukee, WI: ASQC Quality Press.

Leffler, K. B. (1982) Ambiguous changes in product quality. *American Economic Review.* (December) 956-967.

Lefton, R. E., and V. Buzzotta. (1987) Teams and teamwork: A study of executive-level teams. *National Productivity Review.* 6, (Winter) 21-28.

Lefton, R. E., V. Bussotta, and M. Sherberg. (1981) *Improving Productivity Through People Skills.* Cambridge, MA: Ballinger.

Lehr, Lewis W. (1980) How 3M develops entrepreneurial spirit through the organization. *Management Review.* 69, (October) 31. (*2)

Leidecker, Joel K., and Albert V. Bruno. (1984) Identifying and using critical success factors. *Long Range Planning.* 17, (January) 23-32.

Lele, M. M., and N. Jagdish. (1987) *The Customer Is Key: Gaining an Unbeatable Advantage Through Customer Satisfaction.* New York: John Wiley.

Lele, M. M., and U. S. Karmarkar. (1983) Good product support is smart marketing. *Harvard Business Review.* 61, (November-December) 124-32. (*2)

Lemann, Nicholas. (1991) *The Promised Land.* New York: Alfred A. Knopf.

Lennard, Andrew. (1993) The death knell for historical cost? *Accountancy (UK).* (May) 91.

Lenter, M. M. (1965) Listing expected mean square components. *Biometrics.* 21, (February) 459-466.

Lentzen, Donald E. (1982) Methods and QA for asbestos measurements. *ASQC Annual Technical Quality Congress Transactions.* Milwaukee, WI: ASQC Quality Press, 760-766.

Lenz, John. (1983) MAST: A simulation tool for designing computerized factories. *Simulation Magazine.* 40, (July) 51-58.

Lenz, John. (1986) Benefits of FMS: Reducing work-in-process levels. *FMS Magazine.* 4, (May) 83-86.

Lenz, John. (1986) *General Theories of Flexible Integration.* Pasadena, CA: Jacobs Engineering Group.

Lenz, John. (1989) *Flexible Manufacturing-Benefits for the Low-Inventory Factory.* New York: Marcel Dekker.

Leonard-Barton, D. (1987) The case for integrative innovation: An expert system at Digital. *Sloan Management Review.* 29, (January) 7-19.

Leonard-Barton, D. (1988) Implementation as mutual adaptation of technology and organization. *Research Policy.* 17, (October) 1-17.

Leonard-Barton, D. (1988) Implementation characteristics in organizational innovations. *Communication Research.* 15, (October) 31-36.

Leonard, F. S., and W. Earl Sasser, Jr. (1982) The incline of quality. *Harvard Business Review.* 60, (September-October) 163-71. (*2)

Leonard, James F. (1986) Quality improvement in recruiting and employment. *The Juran Report.* 6, (Summer) 111-118.

Leonard, James F. (1991) Applying Deming's principles to our schools. *South Carolina Business Journal.* 11, (January) 11-16.

Leonard, James F. (1996) *The New Philosophy for K-12 Education: A Deming Framework for Transforming America's Schools.* Milwaukee, WI: ASQC Quality Press.

Leonard, Richard. (1992) Quality becomes a new priority for railroads. *Journal of Commerce and Commercial.* 392, (April 28) 11C. (*3)

Lerz, William H. (1992) Deming revolution changing the way builders deal with subcontractors. *Professional Builder and Remodeler.* 57, (September) 56. (*2)

Lesieur, F. G. (1958) *The Scanlon Plan.* Cambridge, MA: MIT Press. (*3)

Lesieur, F. G., and E. S. Puckett. (1969) The Scanlon Plan has proved itself. *Harvard Business Review.* 47, (September-October) 109-18. (*2)

Lesikar, Raymond V. (1979) *Basic Business Communication.* Homewood, IL: Irwin.

Lessard, D. (1986) Finance and global competition: Exploiting financial scope and coping with volatile exchange rates. In Michael E. Porter. *Competition in Global Industries.* Cambridge, MA: Harvard Business School Press, 147-148.

Lessons from Japan, Inc. (1980) *Newsweek.* (September) 61-62.

Lessons of a government lawsuit. (1984) *New York Times.* (March 15) 1.

Letza, S. L., and Ken W. Gadd. (1994) Should activity-based costing be considered as the costing method of choice for total quality organizations? *The TQM Magazine.* 6, (No. 5) 57-63.

Levering, R. (1988) *A Great Place to Work.* New York: Random House.

Levering, R., M. Moskowitz, and Michael Katz. (1984) *The 100 Best Companies to Work For in America.* Reading, MA: Addison-Wesley. (*2)

Leveson, Nancy G. (1984) Software safety in computer controlled systems. *Computer.* (February) 53.

Levin, Doron P. (1986) GM falls below rivals in auto profit margins. *Wall Street Journal.* (June 22) 1. (*2)

Levin, Doran P. (1989) The campaign to be 'American'. *New York Times.* (February 14) 2.

Levin, Doran P. (1990) GM Saturn plant makes friends. *New York Times.* (January 23) D1, D7.

Levine, H. (1986) The squeeze on middle management. *Personnel.* 63, (January) 21-26.

Levine, Jonathan B. (1988) How HP built a better terminal. *BusinessWeek.* (March 7) 114.

Levine, Solomon B. (1958) *Industrial Relations in Postwar Japan.* Urbana, IL: University of Illinois Press.

Levine, Solomon B., and P. E. White. (1961) Exchange as a conceptual framework for the study of intraorganizational relationships. *Administrative Science Quarterly.* 5, (August) 538-601.

Levinson, Harry. (1968) *The Exceptional Executive.* Cambridge, MA: Harvard University Press.

Levinson, Harry. (1982) The fifty largest private industrial companies. *Fortune.* (May 31) 7.

Levinson, Harry and Robert Rosenthal. (1984) *CEO: Corporate Leadership in Action.* New York: Basic Books.

Levinson, Mark. (1987) Asking for protection is asking for trouble. *Harvard Business Review.* 65, (July-August) 42-47.

Levitt, D. J. (1974) The use of sensory and instrumental assessment of organoleptic characteristics in multivariate statistical methods. *Texture Studies.* 5, (February) 183.

Levitt, Theodore. (1960) Marketing myopia. *Harvard Business Review.* 38, (July-August) 45-56. (*4)

Levitt, Theodore. (1965) Exploit the product life cycle. *Harvard Business Review.* 43, (November-December) 81-94.

Levitt, Theodore. (1975) Marketing myopia. *Harvard Business Review.* 33, (September-October) 26.

Levitt, Theodore. (1978) A heretical view of management science. *Fortune.* (December 1) 50. (*2)

Levitt, Theodore. (1981) Ideas are useless unless used. *Inc.* (February) 96. (*2)

Levitt, Theodore. (1983) After the sale is over. *Harvard Business Review.* 61, (September-October) 87-93. (*2)

Levitt, Theodore. (1983) *The Marketing Imagination.* New York: Free Press. (*5)

Levy, Frank S., and Richard C. Michel. (1985) The economic future of the baby boom. *The Urban Institute.* (December 5) 14. (*2)

Levy, George C., and Charles L. Dumoulin. (1984) *The Lab One NMRL Spectroscope Data Analysis Software System.* Revision 2.00 User's Manual. Syracuse NY: Department of Chemistry, Syracuse University.

Levy, I. (1983) Quality assurance in retailing: A new professionalism. *Quality Assurance.* 9, (January) 3.

Levy, Robert. (1980) Legends of business. *Dun's Review*. (June) 92.

Lewis, Aleen and Frederick Lewis. (1931) *Only Yesterday*. New York: Harper and Row.

Lewis, Clarence Irving. (1929) *Mind and the World-Order*. New York: Scribners. (*3)

Lewis, David. (1976) *The Public Image of Henry Ford*. Detroit, MI: Wayne State University Press.

Lewis, F. (1984) The Tiffany model. *New York Times*. (June 7) 1.

Lewis, J. (1976) Service levels: A concept for the user and the computer center. *IBM Systems Journal*. 15, (No. 1) 81-89.

Lewis, Ralph G., and Douglas H. Smith. (1994) *Total Quality in Higher Education*. Delray Beach, FL: St. Lucie Press.

Lieberman, G. J., and D. B. Owen. (1961) *Tables of the Hypergeometric Probability Distribution*. Stanford, CA: Stanford University Press.

Lieberman, G. J., and H. Solomon. (1955) Multi-level continuous sampling plans. *Annals of Mathematical Statistics*. 686-704. (*2)

Lieberman, Marvin B. (1987) Strategies for capacity expansion. *Sloan Management Review*. 28, (Summer) 19-27.

Liebesman, S. (1979) The use of military-standard-105d to control average outgoing quality. *Journal of Quality Tech*. 11, (May) 36-43.

Liebesman, S. (1982) The continuing evolution of the military standard 105d sampling system Bell System. *Technical Journal*. 1, 137-157.

Liebman, Michael S. (1992) Getting results from TQM. *H R Magazine*. 37, (September) 34. (*2)

Light, Richard J. (1992) *The Harvard Assessment Seminars, Second Report*. Cambridge: Harvard University.

Likert, Rensis. (1961) *New Patterns of Management*. New York: McGraw-Hill. (*2)

Likert, Rensis. (1977) *Past and Future Perspectives on System 4*. Ann Arbor, MI: Renis Likert Association.

Lili, H. (Ed.). (1979) *Quality Control and Standardization Handbook*. Berlin, GR: Die Wirtschaft. (*2)

Lillis, C., J. Cook, R. Best, and D. Hawkins. (1985) Marketing strategy to achieve market share goals. In H. Thomas and D. Gardner (Eds.) *Strategic Marketing and Management*. New York: John Wiley, 181-192.

Lillrank, Paul and Noriaki Kano. (1989) *Continuous Improvement: Quality Control Circles in Japanese Industries*. Michigan Papers in Japanese Studies No. 19. Ann Arbor, MI: Center for Japanese Studies, University of Michigan. (*3)

Lima Declaration and Plan of Action on Industrial Development and Co-Operation. (1975) Vienna: United Nations Industrial Development Organization.

Lincoln, J. R. (1982) Intra (and inter) organizational networks. In S. B. Bacharach (Ed.) *Research in the Sociology of Organizations*. Greenwich, CT: JAI Press, 1-38.

Linczenyi, A. (1978) International collaboration in the domain of QC in the C.M.E.A. countries. Proceedings, International Conference QC, Tokyo. A1, 5. (*2)

Lindbergh, Charles A. (1970) *The Wartime Journals of Charles A. Lindbergh*. New York: Harcourt Brace Jovanovich.

Lindblom, C. B. (1990) *Inquiry and Change*. New Haven, CT: Yale University Press. (*2)

Linden, Russell. (1992) Meeting which customer's needs? *The Public Manager: The New Bureaucrat*. 21, (Winter) 49. (*3)

Lindgren, L. H. (1969) Auditing management information systems. *Journal of Systems Management*. (June) 34-40.

Lindsay, William M. (1982) Can quality circles bridge the Japanese/American culture gap. IAQC Fourth Annual Conference Transactions. Cincinnati, OH: International Association of Quality Circles.

Linsenmeyer, Adrienne. (1991) Fad or fundamental? *Financial World*. (September 17) 34.

Lippitt, G. L., P. Langseth, and J. Mossop. (1985) *Implementing Organizational Change*. San Francisco, CA: Jossey-Bass. (*2)

Lippitt, R., J. Watson, and B. Westley. (1958) *Dynamics of Planned Change: A Comparative Study of Principles and Techniques*. New York: Harcourt Brace Jovanovich.

Lishka, K. (1977) Training and upgrading of top management of chemical and light industries in QC. Proceedings, ETC Seminar, Odessa, TX. 99. (*2)

List, G. R. (1984) The role of the Northern Regional Research Center in the development of quality control procedures for fats and oils. *JAOCS*. 61, (June) 1017.

Liswood, L. A. (1989) New system for rating service quality. *Journal of Business Strategy*. (July-August) 27-34. (*2)

The little engine that could. (1988) *Fortune*. (February 15) 39. (*2)

Little, A. C. (1976) Physical measurements as predictors of visual appearance. *Food Technology*. 30, (October) 74.

Little, A. C., and G. MacKinney. (1969) The sample as a problem. *Food Technology*. 23, (January) 25.

Livesay, H. (1975) *Andrew Carnegie*. Boston, MA: Little, Brown.

Livingston, Jon, Joe Moore, and Felicia Oldfather (Eds.). (1973) *Postwar Japan: 1945 to the Present*. New York: Pantheon Books.

Livonia example. (1983) *BusinessWeek.* (May 16) 17.

Lloyd, D. K., and M. Lipow. (1962) *Reliability: Management, Methods, and Mathematics.* Englewood Cliffs, NJ: Prentice-Hall. (*2)

Locher, A. H., and K. S. Teal. (1977) Performance appraisal—A survey of current practices. *Personnel Journal.* 56, (January) 245-247, 254.

Locke, E. A., and D. M. Schweiger (1979) Participation in decision making: One more look. In Barry M. Staw (Ed.) *Research in Organizational Behavior.* Greenwich, CT: JAI Press.

Locke, E. A., and G. P. Latham. (1984) *Goal Setting: A Motivational Technique That Works.* Englewood Cliffs, NJ: Prentice-Hall. (*2)

Locke, E. A., et. al. (1980) The relative effectiveness of four methods of motivating employee performance. In K. D. Duncan, M. M. Greeneberg, and D. Wallis (Eds.) *Changes in Working Life.* Chichester, UK: John Wiley. (*2)

Locks, Mitchell O. (1973) *Reliability, Maintainability, and Availability Assessment.* Rochelle Park, NJ: Hayden.

Lodge, G. C. (1975) *The New American Ideology.* New York: Alfred A. Knopf.

Lodge, G. C., and F. Vogel. (1987) *Ideology and National Competitiveness.* Cambridge, MA: Harvard Business School Press.

Loeb, Marshall. (1980) A guide to taking charge. *Time.* (February 25) 82. (*2)

Logsdon, Gene. (1987) Partners in pasta. *In Business.* 9, (May-June) 28-31.

Loguri, Tadao. (1982) *Providing Incentives to the QC Circle Through an Evaluation System.* Tokyo: Asian

Lohr, Steve. (1981) Overhauling America's business management. *New York Times Magazine.* (January 4) 15. (*2)

Lokiec, M. (1977) *Productivity and Incentives.* Columbia, SC: Bobbins Publications.

Long, Larry E. (1982) *Design and Strategy for Corporate Information Services*. Englewood Cliffs, NJ: Prentice-Hall.

Longenecker, Justin G., and Carlos W. Moore. (1991) *Small Business Management: An Entrepreneurial Emphasis*. Cincinnati, OH: South-Western.

Longley, J. W. (1967) An appraisal of least squares programs for the electronic computers from the point of view of the user. *Journal of the American Statistical Association.* 62, (319) 819-841.

Longo, D. R., and D. Bohr. (1991) *Quantitative Methods in Quality Management: A Guide for Practitioners.* Chicago, IL: American Hospital Organization.

Looking for a good compact? (1984) *Consumer Reports.* (January) 7-15.

Lorange, Peter and Declan Murphy. (1984) Considerations in implementing strategic control. *Journal of Business Strategy*. 4, (Spring) 27-35.

Lorange, Peter, Michael F. Scott Morton, and Sumantra Ghoshal. (1986) *Strategic Control Systems*. St. Paul, MN: West Publishing. (*3)

Lorenz, Christopher. (1981) Pioneers: The anti-merger specialists. *Financial Times*. (October) 79.

Lorin, H. (1975) *Sorting and Sort Systems.* Reading, MA: Addison-Wesley.

Lorsch, Jay W. (1986) Managing culture: The invisible barrier to strategic change. *California Management Review*. 29, (Fall) 95-109.

Lorsch, Jay W., and Paul R. Lawrence. (1965) Organizing for product innovations. *Harvard Business Review*. 43, (January-February) 109.

Lorsch, Jay W., and John J. Morse. (1974) *Organizations and Their Members: A Contingency Approach*. New York: Harper and Row.

Loss of middle management jobs. (1986) *Wall Street Journal*. (December 23) 1.

Lossin, Richard D. (1983) Quality improvement at Westinghouse Furniture Systems. *The Juran Report*. (Winter) 31-34.

Lounds, Andrew C., and Larry G. Pearson. (1985) A team project for improving office productivity and communication. *The Juran Report*. (Winter) 40-45.

Love, Kenneth S. (1982) Quality auditing of new products. *ASQC Annual Technical Quality Congress Transactions*. Milwaukee, WI: ASQC Quality Press, 534-537.

Lowenstein, Louis and Ira M. Millstein. (1988) The American corporation and the institutional investor: are there lessons from abroad? *Columbia Business Law Review*. 3, 739-749. (*2)

Lowenthal, J. N. (1994) *Reengineering the Organization: A Step-by-Step Approach to Corporate Revitalization*. Milwaukee, WI: ASQC Quality Press.

Lowry, Daniel W. (1970) Maintainability demonstration test performed on a computer system. *Proceedings, Annual Reliability and Maintainability Symposium*. New York: IEEE, 27-36.

Lozano, Robert. (1982) Quality circles-blue collar, white collar and other hues. *ASQC Annual Technical Quality Congress Transactions*. Milwaukee, WI: ASQC Quality Press, 422-428.

Lozano, Robert and Philip C. Thompson. (1980) QC circle implementation in the space shuttle external tank program at the Marietta Corp. *ASQC Annual Technical Quality Congress Transactions*. Milwaukee, WI: ASQC Quality Press, 320-334.

LTV knocks rust off its labor relations. (1985) *BusinessWeek.* (June 30) 37. (*2)

Lu, D. J. (1987) *Inside Corporate Japan-The Art of Fumble-Free Management.* Cambridge, MA: Productivity Press.

Lubar, R. (1981) Rediscovering the factory. *Fortune.* (July 15) 52-64. (*2)

Lucas, J. M. (1976) The design and use of V-Mask control schemes. *Journal of Quality Technology.* 14, (February) 51-59.

Lucas, J. M. (1985) Cumulative sum (cusum) control schemes. *ASQC Annual Technical Quality Congress Transactions.* Milwaukee, WI: ASQC Quality Press, 367-372.

Lucas, J. M. (1985) Cumulative sum (CUSUM) control schemes. *Common Statistics—Theory and Methods.* 14, (November) 2689-2704.

Lucas, J. M., and R. B. Crosier. (1982) Fast initial response (FIR) for cumulative sum quality control schemes. *Technometrics.* 24, (April) 199-204.

Lucas, J. M., and R. B. Crosier. (1982) Robust CUSUM. *Common Statistics—Theory and Methods.* 11, (February) 2669-2687.

Luce, D., and Howard Raiffa. (1957) *Games and Decisions.* New York: John Wiley.

Lucier, Christopher, Michael Boucher, Jesse White, Joseph Cangemi, and Casimir Kowalski. (1992) Exploring values of Japanese and American management systems. *Education.* 112, (Summer) 487. (*2)

Ludeman, Kate. (1992) Using employee surveys to revitalize TQM. *Training.* 29, (December) 51-57.

Ludlum, Robert. (1980) *The Matarese Circle.* New York: Bantam Books.

Luft, J. (1969) *Of Human Interaction.* Palo Alto, CA: National Press Books. (*2)

Luke, H. D. (1972) *Automation for Productivity.* Huntington, NY: Krieger.

Lumsdon, Kevin. (1992) TQM shifts hospital-vendor focus to total value. *Hospitals.* 66, (July 5) 114.

Lumsdon, Kevin. (1993) Hospitals, suppliers put TQM to the test. *Hospitals.* 67, (March 20) 58.

Lund, Robert T. (1977) Making products live longer. *Technology Review.* (January) 50-51.

Lund, Robert T. (1978) Life cycle costing: A business and societal instrument. *Management Review.* 67, (April) 17-23.

Lundstedt, S. B., and E. W. Colglazier Jr. (1982) *Managing Innovation.* New York: Pergamon Press.

Lupton, Tom. (1985) Efficiency and the quality of life. *Organizational Dynamics.* 15, (Autumn) 68. (*2)

Lurz, William H. (1992) Road to total quality management: Long, arduous—but worth it. *Professional Builder and Remodeler.* 57, (December) 58. (*3)

Luscher, Max. (1969) *The Luscher Color Test.* Translated and edited by Ivan Scott. New York: Simon and Schuster.

Lusk, Harold F., Charles M. Hewitt, John D. Donnell, and James A. Barnes. (1982) *Business Law and the Regulatory Environment: Concepts and Cases.* Homewood, IL: Irwin.

Lusser, R. (1958) *Reliability through Safety Margins.* Redstone Arsenal, AL: United States Army Ordnance Missile Command.

Luthans, F., and K. Thompson. (1987) Theory D and organization behavior modification: Synergistic or opposite approaches to performance improvement. In Thomas C. Mawhenny (Ed.)

Organizational Behavior Management and Statistical Process. New York: Hawthorne Press, 109-119.

Luthans, F., W. S. Maciag, and S. A. Posencrantz. (1983) O.B. mod: Meeting the productivity challenge with human resources management. *Personnel*. 60, (March-April) 28-36.

Luther, David. (1992/1993) Advanced TQM: Measurements, missteps and progress through key result indicators at Corning. *National Productivity Review*. 11, (Winter) 23-36.

Lynch, John J. (1992) Eliminate the auditors? *Internal Auditor*. 49, (April) 26. (*2)

Lynch, R. L., and K. F. Cross. (1991) *Measuring UP! Yardsticks for Continuous Improvement*. Cambridge, MA: Blackwell.

Lynn, George F. (1992) 'TQM' delivers as promised. *Modern Healthcare*. 22, (March 23) 23. (*2)

Lynton, R., and U. Pareek. (1967) *Training for Development*. Homewood, IL: Irwin.

Maass, R. A. (1988) *A World Class Quality: An Innovative Prescription for Survival*. Milwaukee, WI: ASQC Quality Press.

Maccoby, Michael. (1976) *The Gamesman*. New York: Simon and Schuster.

Maccoby, Michael. (1981) *The Leader*. New York: Ballantine Books.

Maccoby, Michael. (1984) *Management Information Systems*. Chicago, IL: Spectrum. (*2)

Maccoby, Michael. (1988) *Why Work*. New York: Simon and Schuster.

Maccoby, Michael. (1990) Deming critiques American management. *Research-Technology Management*. 33, (May-June) 43.

Maccoby, Michael. (1992) Creating an empowered organization. *Research-Technology Management.* 35, (May-June) 50. (*2)

MacDonald, Joyce and Carol Robinson. (1981) Concept for management. *The Quality Circles.* 4, (November) 13-15.

Mace, Arthur E. (1952) The use of limit gages in process control. *Industrial Quality Control.* 8, (January) 24, 28-31.

Mace, M. L. (1950) *The Growth and Development of Executives.* Cambridge, MA: Harvard University Press.

MacGowan, T. G. (1957) Competitive pricing. In *National Industrial Conference Board Studies in Business Policies.* Washington, DC: National Industrial Conference Board, 84-112.

Machines in automated systems. *Journal of Applied Psychology.* 47, (July) 161-165.

Mackey, Terry and Kitty Mackey. (1992) Think quality! The Deming approach does work in libraries. *Library Journal.* 117, (May 15) 57. (*2)

MacKinney, G., A. C. Little, and L. Brinner. (1966) Visual appearance of foods. *Food Technology.* 20, (October) 1300.

MacNiece, E. H. (1958) Integrating consumer requirements in engineering specifications. *Quality Control in Action.* New York: American Management Association.

MacRae, Norman. (1976) The coming entrepreneurial revolution: A survey. *The Economist.* (December 25) 41-43. (*2)

Macy, B. A. (1979) Progress report on the Bolivar quality of work experiment. *Personnel Journal.* 20, (August) 527-559. (*2)

Macy, B. A., et. al. (1990) The bottom line impact of new design and the design: North America from 1961-1990. Paper presented at International Conference on Self-Managed Work Teams. (September) Denton, TX.

Maddison, Angus. (1982) *Phases of Capitalist Development*. Oxford: Oxford University. (*3)

Made in America: An eight-industry study by MIT, Sets five imperatives for a more productive America. (1989) *The Quality Executive*. (June) 1-3.

Made in the U.S.A. (1990) Manufacturers start to do it right. *Fortune*. (May 21) 54-64.

Madigan, M. J. (1981) Introduction to statistical quality control. *Xerox Training Manual*. 2, 42.

Madique, M. A., and R. H. Hayes. (1984) The art of high-technology management. *Sloan Management Review*. 25, (Winter) 17-31. (*2)

Madlin, Nancy. (1986) Streamlining the PERT chart. *Management Review*. 75, (September) 67-68.

Magaziner, Ira C., and Mark Patinkin. (1989) Cold competition: GE wages the refrigerator war. *Harvard Business Review*. 67, (March-April) 114-124.

Magaziner, Ira C., and Robert B. Reich. (1982) *Minding America's Business: The Decline and Rise of the American Economy*. New York: Harcourt Brace Jovanovich. (*2)

Magee, John F., and D. M. Boodman. (1967) *Production and Inventory Control Handbook*. New York: McGraw-Hill. (*2)

Magenau, J., J. Martin, and M. Peterson. (1988) Dual and unilateral commitment among stewards and rank-and-file union members. *Academy of Management Journal*. 31, (June) 359-376

Mager, Robert F., and Peter Pipe. (1970) *Analyzing Performance Problems: "You Really Oughta Wanna."* Belmont, CA: Fearon Publishers.

Magjuka, Richard. (1992) Should membership in employee involvement (E.I.) programs be voluntary? *National Productivity Review*. 11, (Spring) 40-47.

Magnet, Myron. (1982) Corning glass shapes up. *Fortune.* (December 13) 90-109.

Magnet, Myron. (1982) Managing by mystique at Tandem Computers. *Fortune.* (June 28) 84-91.

Magrath, Allan J. (1992) Marching to a different drummer? *Across the Board.* (June) 53. (*4)

Maguire, Mary A., and Richard Tanner Pascale. (1978) Communication, decision making and implementation among managers in Japanese and American managed companies in the United States. *Sociology and Social Research.* 63, 1-23.

Mahler, R. (1955) Appraisal of executive performance: The Achilles' heel of management development. *Personnel.* 31, (May) 5-14.

Mahler, W. (1974) *Diagnostic Studies.* Reading, MA: Addison-Wesley.

Mahoney, T. A., and J. R. Deckop. (1986) Evolution of concept and practice in personnel administration/human resources management (PA/HRM). In J. G. Hunt and J. D. Blair (Eds.) *1986 Yearly Review of Management of the Journal of Management.* 12, 223-241.

Maidique, Modesto A. (1980) Entrepreneurs, champions and technological innovation. *Sloan Management Review.* 21, (Winter) 60. (*2)

Maier, M. (1988) The final hours of flight 51-L: Using the space shuttle tragedy to teach about ethics and organizational (Mis) communication. A bibliography of references compiled for Second Annual Regional Organizational Behavior Teaching Conference. Philadelphia, PA, (March 12).

Maier, Norman R. (1952) *Principles of Human Behavior.* New York: John Wiley.

Maier, Norman R. (1955) *Psychology in Industry.* Boston, MA: Houghton Mifflin.

Maier, Norman R. (1958) *The Appraisal Interview.* New York: John Wiley.

Maier, Norman R., R. Solem, and A. A. Maier. (1957) *Supervisory and Executive Development: A Manual for Role Playing.* New York: John Wiley.

Main, Jeremy. (1980) The battle for quality begins. *Fortune.* (December 29) 28-33. (*2)

Main, Jeremy. (1981) Toward service without a snarl. *Fortune.* (March 15) 66. (*2)

Main, Jeremy. (1983) Ford's drive for quality. *Fortune.* (April 18) 62-70. (*3)

Main, Jeremy. (1984) The curmudgeon who talks tough on quality. *Fortune.* (June 25) 122.

Main, Jeremy. (1987) Detroit's cars really are getting better. *Fortune.* (February 2) 90-98.

Main, Jeremy. (1989) At last, software CEOs can use. *Fortune.* (March 13) 77-81.

Main, Jeremy. (1990) How to win the Baldrige award. *Fortune.* (April 15) 108.

Main, Jeremy. (1991) Is the Baldrige overblown? *Fortune.* (July 1) 63.

Maital, S. (1992) Zen and the art of total quality. *Across the Board.* (March) 50-51.

Maital, S., and N. M. Meltz. (1980) *Lagging Productivity Growth.* Cambridge, MA: Ballinger.

Majchrzak, A., T. Chang, W. Barfield, R. Eberts, and G. Salvendy. (1987) *Human Aspects of Computer-Aided Design.* Philadelphia, PA: Taylor and Francis.

Majumdar, Amit, Megan Smolenyak, and Nancy Yencho. (1991) Planting the seeds of TQM. *National Productivity Review.* 10, (Autumn) 491-497.

Makay, G., and E. Tarnoy. (1977) A complex method for teaching QC in the engineering industry in Hungary. Proceedings, Twenty First EOQC Conference, Varna. 1, 14-29. (*2)

The making of the all new Thunderbird. (1988) *Washington Post Magazine.* (November 6) 43.

Malabre Alfred L., Jr. (1987) *Beyond Our Means.* New York: Random House. (*2)

Malcolm Baldrige National Quality Award Criteria—1993. (1993) Washington, DC: U.S. Department of Commerce, National Institute of Standards and Technology.

Malcolm Baldrige National Quality Award: 1991 Application Guidelines. (1991) Washington, DC: U.S. Department of Commerce, National Institute of Standards and Technology.

Malec, William F. (1992) A funny thing happened on the way to quality. *Public Utilities Fortnightly.* 129, (April 1) 16. (*2)

Mali, P. (1978) *Improving Total Productivity.* New York: John Wiley.

Mallinger, M. (1993) Ambush along the TQM trail. *Journal of Organizational Change Management.* 6, (No. 4) 30-42.

Malott, R. H. (1983) Let's restore balance to product liability law. *Harvard Business Review.* 61, (May-June) 67.

Mamis, Robert A. (1987) Taking control. *Inc.* (February) 87-88.

Mammone, J. L. (1980) Productivity measurement: A conceptual overview. *Management Accounting.* 61, (May) 36-42.

A management standard for economical inspection. (1976) *Quality.* (January) 28-30.

Management by walking away. (1983) *Inc.* (October) 11-12.

Management Development: A Ten-Year Case Study. (1953) Washington, DC: National Industrial Conference Board.

Management leadership critical to CQI success. (1992) *Hospitals.* (July 20) 64. (*2)

Management: Quality programs show shoddy results. (1992) *Wall Street Journal.* (May 14) B1.

Managing, a study in neglect. (1988) *Los Angeles Times.* (May) 17.

Manchester, William. (1974) *The Glory and The Dream.* Boston, MA: Little, Brown. (*2)

Manchester, William. (1978) *American Caesar: Douglas MacArthur, 1880-1964.* New York: Dell. (*2)

Manchester, William. (1980) *Good-bye, Darkness: A Memoir of the Pacific War.* Boston, MA: Little, Brown. (*2)

Mandel, John and F. L. McRackin. (1963) Analysis of families of curves. *Journal of Research of the National Bureau of Standards.* 67A, (March) 259.

Mandel, John. (1954) Chain block designs with two-way elimination of heterogeneity. *Biometrics.* 10, (February) 251-272.

Mandel, John. (1964) *Statistical Analysis of Experimental Data.* New York: McGraw-Hill.

Mandell, Steven L. (1985) *Computers and Data Processing.* St. Paul, MN: West Publishing.

Mandl, Vladimir. (1990) Team up for performance. *Manufacturing Systems.* (June) 34-41.

Mangan, Katherine S. (1992) TQM: Colleges embrace the total concept of 'total quality management.' *The Chronicle of Higher Education.* 38, (August 12) A25. (*2)

Mangelsdorf, Martha E. (1989) Beyond just-in-time. *Inc.* (February) 21.

Manley, Robert and John Manley. (1996) Sharing the wealth: TQM spreads from business to education. *Quality Progress.* 29, (June) 51-56.

Mann, M. (1960) *How Things Work.* New York: Thomas Y. Crowell.

Mann, Nancy R. (1984) Profile: Dr. W. Edwards Deming. *Road and Track.* (February) 14-16.

Mann, Nancy R. (1985) *The Keys to Excellence: The Story of the Deming Philosophy.* Los Angeles: Prestwick Books. (*5)

Mann, Nancy R., Raymond Schafer, and Nozer E. Singpurwall. (1974) *Methods for Statistical Analysis of Reliability and Life Data.* New York: John Wiley.

Mann, Robert W. (1990) A building-blocks approach to strategic change. *Training and Development Journal.* 44, (August) 23-25.

Manners, G. (1975) Another look at group size: Group problem solving and member consensus. *Academy of Management Journal.* 18, (August) 715-724.

Mansfield, E. (1977) *The Production and Application of New Industrial Technology.* New York: W. W. Norton.

Mansfield, Harold. (1966) *Vision: The Story of Boeing.* New York: Duell, Sloan and Pearce. (*2)

Mant, Alistair. (1979) *The Rise and Fall of the British Manager.* London, UK: Pan Books Limited. (*4)

Mantel, Nathan. (1951) On a rapid estimation of standard errors for the means of small samples. *American Statistician.* 5, (October) 26-27.

Manufacturing Studies Board. (1984) *Computer Integration of Engineering Design and Production: A National Opportunity.* Washington, DC: National Academic Press. (*2)

Manufacturing the right way. (1990) *Fortune.* (May 21) 54-72. (*2)

Manz, Charles C., and Henry P. Sims Jr. (1989) *Superleadership: Leading Others to Lead Themselves.* Englewood Cliffs, NJ: Prentice-Hall.

Marash, Stanley A. (1966) Performing quality audits. *Industrial Quality Control.* 22, (January) 11-12.

Marash. Stanley A. (1982) Conducting an audit. *Medical Device and Diagnostic Industry.* (December) 31-35.

March, Artemis. (1986) A note on quality: The views of Deming, Juran, and Crosby. Note 9.687-011. Cambridge, MA: Harvard Business School Press. (*2)

March, James G. (1978) Bounded rationality, ambiguity and the engineering choice. *Bell Journal of Economics.* (March) 58-88.

March, James G. (1980) The technology of foolishness. In Harold J. Leavitt, Louis R. Pondy, and David M. Boje (Eds.) *Readings in Managerial Psychology.* Chicago, IL: University of Chicago Press, 576. (*2)

March, James G., and John P. Olsen. (1976) *Ambiguity and Choice in Organizations.* Bergen, Norway: Universitetsforlaget. (*3)

March, James G., and Herbert A. Simon. (1985) *Organizations.* New York: John Wiley. (*2)

Marchese, Ted. (1991) TQM reaches the academy. In Harry Ivan Costin (Ed.) *Readings in Total Quality Management.* (1994) Fort Worth, TX: Dryden Press, 433-446.

Marchese, Ted. (1991) TQM reaches the academy. *American Association of Higher Education Bulletin.* 6, (November) 21-34.

Marchington, M. (1992) ***Managing the Team: A Guide to Successful Employee Involvement.*** **Oxford, UK: Basil Blackwell, 115-123.**

Marchisio, O., and G. Guiducci. (1983) Effect of the introduction of the CAD system upon organizational systems and professional roles. In U. Briefs, D. Ciborra, and L. Schneider (Eds.) *Systems Design For, With, and By the Users*. Amsterdam: North Holland.

Marcus, Stanley. (1975) *Minding the Store*. New York: New American Library. (*2)

Marcuse, S. (1949) Optimum allocation and variance components in nested sampling with an application to chemical analysis. *Biometrics*. 5, (September) 189-216.

Margolin, B. H. (1969) Results on factorial designs of resolution IV. *Technometrics*. 11, (March) 431-444

Marguglio, B. W. (1971) Quality factors to be considered in implementing changes. *ASQC Annual Technical Quality Congress Transactions*. Milwaukee, WI: ASQC Quality Press, 189-191.

Marguglio, B. W. (1981) Environmental compliance and universal quality assurance. *Quality Progress*. 14, (September) 14-18.

Marketing in the public sector. (1992) *European Journal of Marketing*. 52, (June) 55.

Markland, B. E. (1979) *Topics in Management Science*. New York: John Wiley.

Markoff, John. (1989) Xerox vs. Apple: Standard dashboard is an issue. *New York Times*. (December 20) D7.

Markowitz, Oscar (1975) Failure free warranty/reliability improvement warranty, buyer viewpoints. *ASQC Annual Technical Quality Congress Transactions*. Milwaukee, WI: ASQC Quality Press, 18-97.

Marks, Mitchell Lee. (1982) Conducting and employee attitude survey. *Personnel Journal*. 61, (September) 684-91.

Marks, P. (1985) *Sink or CIM?* Campbell, CA: Automation Technology Products.

Maroney, B. P., and M. R. Buckley. (1992) Does research in performance appraisal influence the practice of performance appraisal? Regretfully not! *Public Personnel Management.* 21, (No. 2) 185-196.

Marquardt, Donald W. (1970) Generalized inverses, ridge regression, biased linear estimation and nonlinear estimation. *Analytical Chemistry.* 12, (August) 591-612.

Marquardt, Donald W. (1992) ISO 9000: A universal standard of quality. *Management Review.* 81, (January) 11-24. (*4)

Marquez, Manuel.(1985) Quality improvement at Challenger Caribbean Corporation. *The Juran Report.* (Winter) 52-56.

Marquis, Samuel. (1923) *Henry Ford: An Interpretation.* Boston, MA: Little, Brown.

Marrow, A. (1964) *Behind the Executive Mask.* New York: American Management Association.

Marrow, A. (1974) *Making Waves in Foggy Bottom.* Washington, DC: NTL Institute.

Marrow, A., G. Bowers, and Stanley E. Seashore. (1968) *Management by Participation.* New York: Harper and Row.

Marsh, Robert M., and Hiroshi Mannari. (1976) *Modernization and the Japanese Factory.* Princeton, NJ: Princeton University Press.

Martin, Charles C. (1976) *Project Management: How to Make It Work.* New York: AMACOM.

Martin, H. (1956) Patterns of mobility within industrial organizational. *Journal of Business.* 29, (February) 21-26.

Martin, J. (1967) *Design and Realtime Computer System.* Englewood Cliffs, NJ: Prentice-Hall.

Martin, J. (1969) *Telecommunication and the Computer.* Englewood Cliffs, NJ: Prentice-Hall.

Martin, J. (1975) *Computer and Database Organization.* Englewood Cliffs, NJ: Prentice-Hall.

Martin, J. (1980) Stories and scripts in organizational sellings. *Stanford University.* (July) 3.

Martin, J., and C. McClure. (1983) Buying software off the rack. *Harvard Business Review.* 61, (November-December) 40.

Martin, M. J. C. (1984) *Managing Technological Innovation and Entrepreneurship.* Reston, VA: Reston Publishing Company.

Martin Marietta Corporation. (1966) *Reliability for the Engineer, Book 5: Testing for Reliability.* Orlando FL: Martin Marietta.

Martin, Paula K. (1992) The missing piece of the total quality puzzle. *Training.* 29, (September) 90. (*2)

Martin, Wallace. (1981) What management can expect from an employee attitude survey. *Personnel Administrator.* (July) 75-79.

Martz, H. F. (1975) Empirical Bayes single sampling plans for specified posterior consumer and producer risks. *Naval Research Logistic Quarterly.* (December) 651-665.

Marx, K. (1959) *Capital.* Moscow: Foreign Languages Publishing House.

Marx, R., C. Stubbart, V. Traub, and M. Cavanaugh. (1986) The NASA space shuttle disaster: A case study. *Journal of Management Case Studies.* 3, 300-318.

Mascari, Patricia A. (1992) Think quality. *Association Management.* 44, (Junc) 57. (*2)

Maser, Marjorie. (1982) Mount Sinai invests in quality circles. *Health Services Manager.* 14, (February) 44-48.

Mash, Barbara. (1985) *A Corporate Tragedy: The Agony of International Harvester*. Garden City, NY: Doubleday.

Maskery, Mary Ann. (1991) Quality time: Forty years later, Japanese still revere Deming and his teachings. *Automotive News*. (November 18) 3.

Maslow, Abraham H. (1943) A theory of human motivation. *Psychological Review*. 50, 370-396. (*2)

Maslow, Abraham H. (1954) *Motivation and Personality*. New York: Harper and Row. (*5)

Mass-producing gas turbines for megawatts. (1973) *Mechanical Engineering*. (November) 34-43.

Masternak, Robert L. (1991) Gainsharing at B. F. Goodrich: Succeeding together achieves rewards. *Tapping the Network Journal*. (Fall/Winter) 13-16.

Masters, F., and June A. Schmele. (1991) Total quality management: An idea whose time has come. *Journal of Nursing Quality Assurance*. 5, (November) 7-16.

Masters, M. (1980) The effect of consolidation on customer service. *Journal of Business Logistics*. (July) 255-274.

Mastrian, L. K. (1985) The sensory evaluation program within a small processing operation. *Food Technology*. 39, (November) 127.

Matar, Joseph E., and Robert H. Lochner. (1990) *Designing for Quality: An Introduction to the Best of Taguchi and Western Methods of Statistical Experimental Design*. Milwaukee, WI: ASQC Quality Press.

Matejka, Ken. (1991) *Why This Horse Won't Drink: How to Win—and Keep—Employee Commitment*. New York: AMACOM.

Mathews, Jay and Peter Katel. (1992) The cost of quality; faced with hard times, business sours on 'Total Quality Management.' *Newsweek*. 120, (September 7) 48. (*2)

Matsumoto, Michihiro. (1988) *The Unspoken Way—Haragei: Silence in Japanese Business and Society.* Tokyo: Kodansha International.

Matthews, William E. (1993) The missing element in higher education. *Journal for Quality Participation.* 16, (Issue 1, January-February) 102-108.

Matulis, Scott. (1988) The customer is king. *Entrepreneur.* 16, (September) 69.

Maul, Gary P., and John Scott Gillard. (1993) Training today's managers to effectively use TQM. *Industrial Engineering.* 25, (January) 49. (*3)

May, R. M. (1974) *Stability and Complexity in Model Ecosystems.* Princeton, NJ: Princeton University Press.

Mayer, Allan J., and Michael Ruby. (1977) One firm's family. *Newsweek.* (November) 84.

Mayer, R. R. (1982) *Production and Operations Management.* New York: McGraw-Hill.

Maynard, J. (1972) *Modular Programming.* Princeton, NJ: Auerbach Publishers.

Maynes, E. S. (1976) The concept and measurement of product quality. In N. E. Terlecky (Ed.) *Household Production and Consumption.* New York: National Bureau of Economic Research.

Mayo, Elton. (1933) *The Human Problems of Industrial Civilization.* New York: Macmillan.

Mayo, Elton. (1946) *The Social Problems of an Industrial Civilization.* Cambridge, MA: Harvard University Press.

Mayo, Elton. (1947) *The Political Problems of an Industrial Civilization.* Cambridge, MA: Harvard University Press.

Mayo, Elton. (1977) *The Human Problems of Industrial Civilization.* New York: Arno Press.

Mayo, J. (1984) Process design as important as product design. *Wall Street Journal.* (November 17) A25.

Mazique, Mignon. (1981) The quality circle transplant. *Issues and Observation.* 1, (May) 1-3.

McArthur, C. D. (1984) Automation, JIT inventory systems and quality. *Quality Progress.* 17, (April) 64-67.

McBeath, G. (1974) *Productivity Through People.* New York: John Wiley.

McBrayer, Eugene H. (1992) Other views. *Chemical Week.* 151, (October 21) 4. (*2)

McCabe, T. J., and E. S. Williamson. (1992) Tips on reengineering redundant software. *Datamation.* (April 15) 71-74.

McCabe, William J. (1985) A service organization improved quality and cut costs at the same time. *Quality Progress.* 18, (June) 85-89.

McCabe, William J. (1986) Quality methods applied to the business process. *ASQC Annual Technical Quality Congress Transactions.* Milwaukee, WI: ASQC Quality Press, 201-204.

McCall, J., P. Richards, and G. Walters. (1977) Factors in software quality concepts are: Definitions of software quality. *Joint General Electric-U.S. Air Force Report.* Radio TR-77-369, (November) 3-5.

McCarthy, Rita. (1975) Configuration management and software reliability. *ASQC Annual Technical Quality Congress Transactions.* Milwaukee, WI: ASQC Quality Press, 49-55.

McCartney, Laton. (1985) Companies get a competitive edge using strategic computer systems. *Dun's Business Month.* (December) 13-14.

McCasland, C. (1985) JIT + SQC = Quality. *Manufacturing Systems*. 3, (July) 47-48.

McClain, J. O., and L. J. Thomas. (1980) *Operations Management*. Englewood Cliffs, NJ: Prentice-Hall.

McClelland, David C. (1961) *The Achieving Society*. New York: Van Nostrand Reinhold. (*2)

McClelland, David C. (1975) *Power: The Inner Experience*. New York: Irvington Publishers. (*2)

McClelland, David C., and R. E. Boyatzis. (1982) Leadership motive pattern and long term success in management. *Journal of Applied Psychology*. 67, (September) 737-743.

McClenahan, John S. (1981) Bringing home Japan's lessons. *Industry Week*. (February 2) 69-73.

McClenahan, John S. (1981) Moving GTE off hold. *Industry Week*. (January 1) 67. (*2)

McClure, J. Y. (1979) Procurement quality control within the multinational environment. *ASQC Annual Technical Congress Transactions*. Milwaukee, WI: ASQC Quality Press, 643-654.

McCollough, Mark. (1993) Total quality management: What gets in industry's way? *Air Conditioning, Heating, and Refrigeration News*. 188, (March 8) 1. (*3)

McConnell, C. (1979) Why is U.S. productivity slowing down? *Harvard Business Review*. 57, (March-April) 36-44, 48-60.

McConnell, J. (1986) *The Seven Tools of TQC*. Sydney, Australia: Enterprise Australia Publications.

McCormick, E. (1976) Job and task analysis. In M. Dunnette (Ed.) *Handbook of Industrial and Organizational Psychology*. Chicago, IL: Rand McNally, 651-696.

McCubbin, Robert E. (1971) Machine tool information system. *ASQC Annual Technical Quality Congress Transactions.* Milwaukee, WI: ASQC Quality Press, 235-243.

McDonald, E. (1987) The sweet smell of success. *Powerline.* (Winter) 9-25. (*2)

McDonald, Marshall (1987) Why FPL pursued quality improvement. *The Juran Report.* (Winter) 17-19. (*2)

McDonald, Martha. (1990) Valuing experience: How to keep older workers healthy. *Business and Health.* 8, (January) 35-38. (*2)

McEachern, J. E. (1992) *Understanding of Quality Management Processes. Pioneers in Health Care Quality.* Chicago, IL: American Hospital Association.

McEachern, J. E., and D. Neuhauser. (1988) The continuous improvement of quality at the Hospital Corporation of America. *Health Matrix.* 7, (January) 5-11.

McEachern, J. E., L. Schiff, and O. Cogan. (1992) How to start a direct patient care team. *Quality Review Bulletin.* 18, (June) 191-200.

McEachron, N. B., and H. S. Javitz. (1981) Managing quality: A strategic perspective. Business Intelligence Program Report Number 658. New York: SRI International.

McElroy, James L. (1982) Making just-in-time production pay off. *Automotive Industries.* 162, (February) 77-80.

McFarland, F. Warren. (1971) Problems in planning in information systems. *Harvard Business Review.* 49, (March-April) 75-89.

McFarland, L., L. Senn, and J. Childress. (1993) *21st Century Leadership.* New York: The Leadership Press.

McFarren, Al. (1970) *Criteria for Judging Acceptability of Analytical Methods Analytical Chemistry.* (March) 358.

McGarry, Charles. (1972) *Citizen Nader*. New York: Saturday Review Press.

McGrath, James H. (1985) Preparation of improvement team leaders and facilitators. *The Juran Report.* (Winter) 95-101.

McGrath, James H. (1986) Successful institutionalized improvement in manufacturing areas. Proceedings of the Third Annual Conference on Quality Improvement. (*2)

McGraw, T. K. (1986) *America Versus Japan.* Cambridge, MA: Harvard Business School Press.

McGregor, Douglas. (1948) The staff function in human relations. *Journal of Social Issues.* 4, (March) 32-36.

McGregor, Douglas. (1960) *The Human Side of Enterprise.* New York: McGraw-Hill. (*7)

McGregor, Douglas. (1967) *The Professional Manager.* New York: McGraw-Hill.

McGregor, Douglas. (1972) An uneasy look at performance appraisal. *Harvard Business Review.* 50, (September-October) 133-134.

McGregor, Douglas. (1985) *The Human Side of Enterprise.* Twenty-fifth anniversary printing. New York: McGraw-Hill.

McKee, Keith E. (1983) Quality in the 21st century. *Quality Progress.* 16, (June) 16-20.

McKenna, Joseph F. (1992) Laying siege to Washington. *Industry Week.* (June 15) 20. (*2)

McKenna, Joseph F. (1993) Empowerment thins a forest of bureaucracy. *Industry Week.* (April 5) 64. (*3)

McKenna, R. (1985) *The Regis Touch Million-Dollar Advice from America's Marketing Consultant.* Reading, MA: Addison-Wesley.

McKenzie, F. A. (1901) *The American Invaders.* London, UK: Howard Wilford Bell. (*2)

McLean, Gary N., and Susan H. DeVogel. *Role of Organization Development in Quality Management and Productivity Improvement.* Minneapolis, MN: University of Minnesota and ASTD.

McLean, M., G. Preton, and K. Jillson. (1975) *The Manger and Self-Respect.* AMA Survey Report. New York: AMACOM.

McLuhan, Marshall. (1964) *Understanding Media.* New York: McGraw-Hill.

McManus, Kevin. (1983) The cookie wars. *Forbes.* (November 7) 150-152.

McMillan, Charles J. (1980) Is Japanese management really so different? *Business Quarterly.* 45, (Autumn) 26-31.

McMillan, Charles J. (1982) From quality control to quality management: Lesson from Japan. *Business Quarterly.* 47, (Spring) 31-40.

McMillan, Charles J. (1989) *The Japanese Industrial System.* Berlin: W. de Gruyter.

McNeil, D. R. (1977) *Interactive Data Analysis.* New York: John Wiley.

McNeil, Ronald D. (1992) Benchmarking: Staying at the head of the pack! In Harry Ivan Costin (Ed.) *Readings in Total Quality Management.* (1994) Fort Worth, TX: Dryden Press, 361-367.

McNeil, Ronald D. (1992) Managing for high productivity and quality. In Harry Ivan Costin (Ed.) *Readings in Total Quality Management.* (1994) Fort Worth, TX: Dryden Press, 55-57.

McNeill, W. H. (1986) *Mythistory and Other Essays.* Chicago, IL: University of Chicago Press.

McNiece, Eugene H. (1953) *Industrial Specifications*. New York: John Wiley.

McNutt, K. (1988) Consumer attitudes and the quality control function. *Food Technology*. 42, 97.

McPartin, J. P. (1993) Just chasing rainbows? Critics brand much of the reengineering clamor as sheer marketing hype. *InformationWeek*. 11, (December) 55.

McPherson, J. M. (1988) *Battle Cry of Freedom: The Civil War Era*. Oxford: Oxford University Press.

McPherson, Rene C. (1980) GSB deanship is his way to reinvest in the system. *Stanford GSB*. (Fall) 15. (*2)

McQuade, Walter. (1980) Making a drama out of shopping. *Fortune*. (March 15) 107. (*2)

McQuade, Walter. (1984) Easing tensions between man and machine. *Fortune*. (March 15) 58-66.

McQuarrie, Edward F. (1991) The customer visit: Qualitative research for business-to-business marketers. *Marketing Research*. (March) 15-28.

McRobb, R. M. (1982) Customer-perceived quality levels. *ASQC Annual Technical Quality Congress Transactions*. Milwaukee, WI: ASQC Quality Press, 428-432.

Mead, Margaret. (1955) *Cultural Patterns and Technical Change*. New York: Mentor Books.

Mead, R., and D. J. Pike. (1975) A review of response surface methodology from a biometric point of view. *Biometrics*. 31, (October) 803.

Meadows, Edward. (1978) Close-up look at the productivity lag. *Fortune*. (December 4) 82-90.

Meadows, Edward. (1980) How three companies increased their productivity. *Fortune.* (March 10) 97. (*3)

Meal, Harlan C. (1984) Putting production decisions where they belong. *Harvard Business Review.* 62, (March-April) 102-111. (*2)

Mears, Peter and Frank Voehl. (1994) *Team Building: A Structured Learning Approach.* Delray Beach, FL: St Lucie Press.

Measurement and Interpretation of Productivity. (1979) Washington, DC: National Academy of Sciences.

Meier, K. J., and L. Brundney. (1981) *Applied Statistics for Public Administration.* Boston, MA: Duxbury Press.

Meilgaard, M., G. V. Civille, and B. T. Carr. (1987) *Sensory Evaluation Techniques.* Boca Raton, FL: CRC Press.

Meisenheimer, C. (1991) The consumer: Silent or intimate player in the quality revolution. *Holistic Nursing Practice.* 5, 39-50.

Meister, David. (1978) Subjective data in human reliability estimated. *Proceedings, Annual Reliability and Maintainability Symposium.* New York: IEEE, 380-384.

Meister, Jeanne C. (1990) Companies weave the Disney 'magic' into their own business. *Marketing News.* 24, (February 5) 12-13.

Melan, E. H. (1985) Process management in service and administrative operations. *Quality Progress.* 18, (June) 52-59.

Melan. E. H. (1987) Quality improvement in an engineering laboratory. *Quality Progress.* 20, (June) 18-25.

Melan, E. H., R. T. Curtis, and G. A. Snyder. (1984) Quality data systems in semiconductor manufacturing. *Quality Progress.* 17, (June) 32-36.

Melko, M. (1969) *The Nature of Civilization.* Reading, MA: Porter Sargent.

Melman, Seymour. (1983) *Profits Without Production.* New York: Alfred A. Knopf.

Melum, Mara Minerva. (1990) Total quality management: Steps to success. *Hospital.* 64, (December) 42.

Mendelowitz, Allen I. (1991) *Management Practices: U.S. Companies Improve Performance Through Quality Efforts.* U.S. General Accounting Office, Washington, DC.

Mendenhall, W., and J. E. Reinmuth. (1974) *Statistics for Management and Economics.* Boston, MA: Duxbury Press.

Menipaz, E. (1984) *Essentials of Production and Operations Management.* Englewood Cliffs, NJ: Prentice-Hall.

Menning, J. H., C. W. Wilkinson, and Peter B. Clarke. (1976) *Communicating Through Letters and Reports.* Homewood, IL: Irwin.

Menon, H. G. (1992) *TQM in New Product Manufacturing.* New York: McGraw-Hill.

Mensch, Gerhard. (1979) *Stalemate in Technology.* Cambridge, MA: Ballinger.

Mentch, C. C. (1980) Manufacturing process quality optimization studies. *Journal of Quality Technology.* 12, (March) 119-129.

Mercer, David. (1991) Key quality issues. *Global Perspectives on Total Quality.* New York: The Conference Board.

Merchant, Kenneth A. (1985) *Control in Business Organizations.* Boston, MA: Pitman.

Meredith, Jack R., and Marianne M. Hill. (1987) Justifying new manufacturing systems: A managerial approach. *Sloan Management Review.* 28, (Summer) 49-61.

Meredith, Jack R., and T. E. Gibbs. (1984) *The Management of Operations.* New York: John Wiley.

Merolli, A. (1980) Sensory evaluation in operations. *Food Technology*. 34, (November) 63.

Merritt, Richard H. (1963) Vegetative and floral development of plants resulting from differential precooling. *Proceedings of the American Society of Horticulture*. 82, 517-525.

Merry, M. (1990) Total quality management for physicians: Translating the new paradigm. *Quality Review Bulletin*. 16, (May) 101-105.

Merton, Robert K. (1968) *Social Theory and Social Structure*. New York: Free Press. (*2)

Merwin, J. (1986) A tale of two worlds. *Forbes*. (June 16) 17-18.

Mesdag, L. M. (1983) The appliance boom begins. *Fortune*. (July 25) 55.

Messina, William S. (1983) A tool for measuring manufacturing quality. *ASQC Annual Technical Quality Congress Transactions*. Milwaukee, WI: ASQC Quality Press, 11-20.

Messina, William S. (1984) Applications of statistical methods to manufacturing production. *Proceedings, Fortieth Rochester Quality Control Conference*. Rochester, NY: Rochester Institute of Technology. 40, 199-214.

Messina, William S. (1985) Use of trimmed means in manufacturing production. *Proceedings, Fourteenth Measurement Science Conference*. Cincinnati, OH: Measurement Science Association, 101-105.

Messina, William S. (1985) Use of variation analysis to monitor chemical batch processes. *Proceedings, Forty-first Rochester Quality Control Conference*. Rochester, NY: Rochester Institute of Technology. 41, 81-97.

Messina, William S. (1987) How do you sell SQC to the plant site? *Proceedings, Forty-third Rochester Quality Control Conference*. Rochester, NY: Rochester Institute of Technology. 43, 211-216.

Messina, William S. (1987) *Statistical Quality Control for Manufacturing Managers*. New York: John Wiley. (*2)

Messina, William S., and V. A. Pershing. (1987) *Vendor Certification Using Process Performance Statistics*. Unpublished technical report, IBM-Tucson.

Metcalf, H. C., and L. Urwick. (1942) *Dynamic Administration*. New York: Harper and Row. (*2)

Metz, Edmund J. (1981) Diagnosing readiness. *Quality Circles Journal*. 4, (November) 16-20.

Metz, Edmund J. (1981) The Verteam circle. *Training and Development Journal*. 35, (December) 78-85.

Metzger, B. (1975) *Profit Sharing in 38 Large Companies*. Evanston, IL: Profit Sharing Research Foundation. (*2)

Metzger, B. (1980) Increasing productivity through profit sharing. Evanston, IL: Profit Sharing Research Foundation.

Metzger, B., and Mary Ann Von Glinow. (1988) Off-site workers at home and abroad. *California Management Review*. 30, (Spring) 101-111.

Meyer, C. (1994) How the right measures help teams excel. *Harvard Business Review*. 72, (May-June) 95-103.

Meyer, Gordon and Randall Stott. (1986) Quality circles: Panacea or Pandora's box? *Organizational Dynamics*. 9, (Spring) 34-60.

Meyer, H. H., E. Kay, and John R. P. French Jr. (1965) Split roles in performance appraisal. *Harvard Business Review*. 43, (January-February) 123-129.

Meyer, Herbert. (1980) How Fingerhut beat the recession. *Fortune*. (November 15) 103. (*2)

Meyer, Robert P. (1982) Marriage of your P's and Q's through quality circle. *ASQC Annual Technical Quality Congress Transactions*. Milwaukee, WI: ASQC Quality Press, 21-26.

Meyers, M. (1970) *Every Employee a Manager—More Meaningful Work Through Job Enrichment*. New York: McGraw-Hill.

Michael, S. R. (1981) *Techniques of Organizational Change.* New York: McGraw-Hill. (*2)

Michalak, D. F., and G. Yager. (1979) *Making the Training Process Work.* New York: Harper and Row.

Michalek, Joseph M., and Richard K. Holmes. (1981) *Quality Engineering Techniques in Product Design/Process*. SAE Paper 810392. Warrendale, PA: Society of Automotive Engineers.

Midas, Michael, Jr. (1982) A measure. *Quality*. (August) 9-10.

Middlebrook, W. D. (1994) Reengineering the procurement process: Reducing cycle time through EDI and various automation techniques. *EDI World*. (May) 46-48.

Middlemist, R. Dennis and Michael A. Hitt. (1981) *Organizational Behavior: Applied Concepts*. Palo Alto, CA: Science Research Associates.

Mihalasky, John. (1980) The human factor in product safety. *ASQC Annual Technical Quality Congress Transactions*. Milwaukee, WI: ASQC Quality Press, 33-40.

Mikayama, M. (1978) Development of quality control in the whole of Kubota Ltd. *Reports of Statistical Applications and Research.* 25, (February) 54-77.

Milakovich, Michael E. (1991) Total quality management in the public sector. *National Productivity Review*. 10, (Spring) 195-213.

Milbank, Dana. (1992) Academe gets lessons from big business. *Wall Street Journal*. (December 15) B1.

Miles, Gregory L. (1989) Heinz ain't broke, but it's doing a lot of fixing. *BusinessWeek.* (December 11) 84-88. (*2)

Miles, L. D. (1972) *Techniques of Value Analysis and Engineering.* New York: McGraw-Hill.

Miles, Raymond E., and Charles C. Snow. (1978) *Organizational Strategy, Structure, and Process.* New York: McGraw-Hill.

Miles, Raymond E., and Charles C. Snow. (1984) Designing strategic human resource systems. *Organizational Dynamics.* 13, (Summer) 36-52.

Miles, Raymond E., and Charles C. Snow. (1986) New concepts for new forms. *California Management Review.* 28, (Spring) 31-36.

Miles, Robert H. (1982) *Coffin Nails and Corporate Strategy.* Englewood Cliffs, NJ: Prentice-Hall.

Milgram, Stanley. (1974) *Obedience to Authority.* New York: Harper and Row.

Milgrom, Paul and John Roberts. (1982) Predation, reputation, and entry deterrence. *Journal of Economic Theory.* 27, (August) 280-312.

Milgrom, Paul and John Roberts. (1990) *The economics of modern manufacturing: Technology, strategy and organization.* American Economic Review. 80, (June) 511-528.

Miljus, R. C., and R. L. Smith. (1987) Key human resource issues for management in high tech firms. In A. Kleingartner and C. S. Anderson (Eds.) *Human Resource Management in High Technology Firms.* Lexington, MA: D. C. Heath, 115-131. (*2)

Milkovich, G. T. (1987) Compensation systems in high technology companies. In A. Kleingartner and C. S. Anderson (Eds.) *Human Resource Management in High Technology Firms.* Lexington, MA: D. C. Heath, 103-114.

Miller, Cyndee. (1992) TQM's value criticized in new report. *Marketing News.* 26, (November 9) 1. (*2)

Miller, D. B. (1977) How to improve the performance and productivity of the knowledge workers. *Organizational Dynamics.* 5, (Winter) 62-80.

Miller, D. B. (1986) *Managing Professionals in Research and Development.* San Francisco, CA: Jossey-Bass. (*2)

Miller, D. W., and M. K. Starr. (1960) *Executive Decisions and Operations Research.* Englewood Cliffs, NJ: Prentice-Hall.

Miller, E. W. (1971) *Maintenance Index, A Design Tool.* SAE Paper 710680. Warrendale, PA: Society of Automotive Engineers.

Miller, Ervin F. (1982) Corporate quality audit/survey. *ASQC Annual Technical Quality Congress Transactions.* Milwaukee, WI: ASQC Quality Press, 538-545.

Miller, G. (1956) The magical number seven, plus or minus two: Some limits on our capacity for processing information. *Psychological Review*, 81-97.

Miller, G. D. (1979) Materials managers: Who needs them? *Harvard Business Review.* 57, (July-August) 143-153.

Miller, G. D., and Ronald J. Kegaris. (1986) An Alcoa-Kodak joint team. *The Juran Report.* (Summer) 29-34.

Miller, J. (1992) Selecting areas for improvement. *CMA—The Management Accounting Magazine.* 66, (September) 33. (*2)

Miller, J. G., and T. E. Vollmann. (1985) The hidden factory. *Harvard Business Review.* 43, (September-October) 142-151. (*2)

Miller, Lawrence M. (1975) How many should you check? *Quality Progress.* 8, (March) 14-15.

Miller, Lawrence M. (1978) *Behavior Management: The New Science of Managing People at Work.* New York: John Wiley.

Miller, Lawrence M. (1985) *American Spirit: Visions of a New Corporate Culture.* New York: Warner Books.

Miller, Lawrence M. (1989) *Barbarians to Bureaucrats: Corporate Life Cycle Strategies: Lessons from the Rise and Fall of Civilizations*. New York: Clarkson N. Potter.

Miller, M. (1984) Profitability = Productivity + Price recovery. *Harvard Business Review*. 42, (March-April) 145-153.

Miller, R., and M. Cote. (1985) Growing the next Silicon Valley. *Harvard Business Review*. 43, (July-August) 114-123.

Miller, R. L., and J. P. Cangemi. (1993) Why total quality management fails: Perspective of top management. *Journal of Management Development*. 12, (No. 7) 40-50.

Miller, Thomas O. (1992) A customer's definition of quality. *Journal of Business Strategy*. 13, (January-February) 4-7.

Miller, William C. (1989) *The Creative Edge, Fostering Innovation Where You Work*. Garden City, NY: Doubleday.

Miller, William H. (1992) Textbook turnaround. *Industry Week*. (April 20) 11. (*2)

Milliken, R. (1992) Perspectives on TQ in industry. Presentation at Total Quality Forum IV. Cincinnati, OH, November 11.

Mills, D. Q. (1985) *The New Competitors*. New York: John Wiley.

Mills, Richard. (1987) Getting it right every time. *Accountancy*. 99, (April) 134.

Mills, Ted. (1975) Human resources: Why the new concern. *Harvard Business Review*. 53, (March-April) 120-134.

Mintzberg, Henry. (1973) *The Nature of Managerial Work*. New York: Harper and Row. (*3)

Mintzberg, Henry. (1973) A new look at the chief executive's job. *Administrative Dynamics*. (Winter) 20-40.

Mintzberg, Henry. (1975) The manager's job: Folklore and fact. *Harvard Business Review.* 53, (July-August) 49.

Mintzberg, Henry. (1976) Planning on the left side and managing on the right. *Harvard Business Review.* 54, (July-August) 53. (*2)

Mintzberg, Henry. (1978) Patterns in strategy formation. *Management Science.* 24, (August) 934-948.

Mintzberg, Henry. (1979) *The Structuring of Organizations: A Synthesis of the Research.* Englewood Cliffs, NJ: Prentice-Hall. (*4)

Mintzberg, Henry. (1990) The design school: Reconsidering the basic premises of strategic management. *Strategic Management Journal.* 11, (March-April) 171-196.

Mintzberg, Henry, and A. McHugh. (1985) Strategy formation in an adhocracy. *Administrative Science Quarterly.* 30, (June) 160-197. (*2)

Mintzberg, Henry, and J. A. Waters. (1982) Tracking strategy in an entrepreneurial firm. *Academy of Management Journal.* 25, (May) 465-499.

Mintzberg Henry, and J. A. Waters. (1985) Of strategies, deliberate and emergent. *Strategic Management Journal.* 6, (July-August) 257-271.

Mintzberg, Henry, D. Raisinghani, and A. Theoret. (1976) The structure of 'unstructured' decision processes. *Administrative Science Quarterly.* 21, (September) 241-275.

Mirvis, Phillip H., and Edward E. Lawler III. (1987) Accounting for the quality of work life. *Journal of Occupation Behavior.* 5, 197-212. (*2)

Missed opportunities. (1988) *Wall Street Journal.* (November 14) R21.

MIT Commission on Industrial Productivity. (1989) *Working Papers of the MIT Commission on Industrial Productivity. Volume 1.* Cambridge, MA: MIT Press.

MIT Commission on Industrial Productivity. (1989) *Working Papers of the MIT Commission on Industrial Productivity. Volume 2.* Cambridge, MA: MIT Press.

Mitchell, A. (1994) Marketing's new model army. *Management Today.* (March) 42-49.

Mitchell, G. R. (1986) New approaches for the strategic management of technology. *Technology in Society.* 7.

Mitchell, J. A. (1947) Control of the accuracy and precision of industrial tests analysis. *Analytical Chemistry.* 19, (December) 961-967.

Mitchell, Terence R. (1978) *People in Organizations: Understanding Their Behavior.* New York: McGraw-Hill.

Mito, Tadashi. (1981) The internationalization of Japanese management. *Toyota Quarterly Review.* 9, (Summer) 2-9.

Mitroff, I., and Susan Albers Mohrman. (1987) The slack is gone: How the United States lost its competitive edge in the world economy. *Academy of Management Executive.* 1, (February) 66.

Mitsuya, Chikao. (1977) *Automatic Designing and Drafting System of Elevators.* JUSE Press, 24, (June) 18-27.

Mittelstaedt, Robert E., Jr. (1992) Benchmarking: How to learn from the best-in-class practices. *National Productivity Review.* 11, (Summer) 301. (*2)

Miyai, I. (1990) Human resources: Japan's sole natural wealth. *International Productivity Journal.* (Spring) 45-52.

Mizell, Michael and Lawrence Strattner. (1981) Diagnostic measuring in manufacturing. *Quality.* (September) 29-32.

Mizruchi. M., and D. Bunting. (1981) Influence in corporate networks: An examination of four measures. *Administrative Science Quarterly.* 26, (October) 475-489.

Mizuno, S. (1967) Execution of internal QC audit. *Hinshitsu Kanri.* 18, (February) 835-839.

Mizuno, S. (1979) Seven new QC tools. In Harry Ivan Costin (Ed.) *Readings in Total Quality Management.* (1994) Fort Worth, TX: Dryden Press, 229-253.

Mizuno, S. (1988) *Company-Wide Total Quality Control.* Tokyo: Asian Productivity Organization.

Mizuno, S. (1988) *Management for Quality Improvement: The Seven New QC Tools.* Cambridge, MA: Productivity Press. (*2)

Mizuno, S., and Hitoshi Kume. (1978) Development of education and training in quality control. Reports of statistical applications and research, JUSE Press, 25, (June) 36-59. (*2)

Mladjov, L. A. (1977) Bulgarian variants of the integrated QC system on the basis of standardization. Proceedings, Twenty First EOQC Conference, Varna. 1, 214. (*2)

Mlambo, S. (1983) Application of second level product tracking to 62PC disk enclosures. Unpublished technical report, IBM-Tucson.

Moacoby, Michael. (1990) How to be a quality leader. *Research-Technology Management.* (September/October) 51-52.

Mobil's successful exploration. (1980) *BusinessWeek* (October 13) 114.

Mobley, M. (1988) Marketing research and the manufacturing process. In *News and Views.* Augusta, GA: Augusta College School of Business Administration. (Fall) 1.

Mockler, R. J. (Ed.). (1970) *Readings in Management Control.* New York: Appleton-Century-Crofts.

Moder, J. J. (1956) A teaching aid of regression, correlation, analysis of variance and other statistical techniques. *Industrial Quality Control.* 13, (July) 16-21.

Modic, Stanley J. (1991) Simultaneous engineering, tooling and production. *Heubcore.* (February) 6.

Moehlenbrock, Maxine. (1985) Control teams contrasted with breakthrough teams. *The Juran Report.* (Winter) 175-179.

Moen, Ronald D. (1989) The performance appraisal system: Deming's deadly disease. *Quality Progress.* 22, (November) 62-66.

Moen, Ronald D., Thomas W. Nolan, and Lloyd P. Provost. (1991) *Improving Quality through Planned Experimentation.* New York: McGraw-Hill. (*2)

Moffat, George T. (1983) New initiatives in quality assurance. *AT&T Bell Laboratories Record.* (December) 17-20.

Moffat, S. (1990) Japan's new personalized production. *Fortune.* (October 22) 132-135.

Mohr, W., and H. Mohr. (1983) *Quality Circles: Changing Images of People at Work.* Reading, MA: Addison-Wesley.

Mohri, N. (1982) In-process monitoring of tool breakage based on auto-regressive model. *Manufacturing Technology.* 41-45.

Mohrman, Allan M., Jr., and Edward E. Lawler III. (1985) The diffusion of QWL as a paradigm shift. In Warren G. Bennis, K. D. Benne, and R. Chin (eds) *The Planning of Change.* New York: Holt, Rinehart and Winston. (*2)

Mohrman, Allan M., Jr., Susan Albers Mohrman, and C. G. Worley. (1987) Technical report on performance management in an aerospace corporation. *The Center for Effective Organizations.* Los Angles, CA: University of Southern California.

Mohrman, Allan M., Jr., and Susan Albers Mohrman. (1988) Technical report on performance management in an oil company. *The Center for Effective Organizations.* Los Angles, CA: University of Southern California.

Mohrman, Allan M., Jr., Susan Albers Mohrman, and C. G. Worley. (1988) Performance management in the highly interdependent world of high technology. In L. R. Gomez-Mejia and M. W. Lawless (Eds.) *Proceedings, Managing the High Technology Firm*. Boulder, CO: University of Colorado Press, 43-49.

Mohrman. Allan M., Jr., Susan Albers Mohrman, and C. G. Worley. (1989) Performance management in high technology settings. In Mary Ann Von Glinow and Susan Albers Mohrman (Eds.) *Managing Complexity in High Technology Industries: Systems and People.* New York: Oxford University Press, 110-128.

Mohrman, Allan M., Jr., Susan M. Resnick-West, and Edward E. Lawler III. (1989) *Designing Performance Appraisal Systems: Aligning Appraisals and Organizational Realities*. San Francisco, CA: Jossey-Bass.

Mohrman, Susan Albers and T. G. Cummings (1994). *Self Designing Organizations: Learning How to Create High Performance*. Reading, MA: Addison-Wesley.

Mokyr, J. (1990) *The Lever of Riches*. London, UK: Oxford University Press.

Mollo, Marco, et al. (1983) Modular software for FMS applications. *FMS Magazine*. 1, (June) 217-221.

Moment, D., and Abraham Zaleznik. (1963) *Role Development and Interpersonal Competence.* Cambridge, MA: Harvard University Press.

Monahan, E. (1982) A survey of partially observable Markov decision processes: Theory, models and algorithms. *Management Science.* 28, (April) 1-16.

Monczka, R. M., P. L. Carter, J. H. Hoagland, and L. W. Foster. (1978) Purchasing performance: Measurement and control. *APR 75-20557*. Washington, DC: National Science Foundation, (August).

Monden, Yasuhiro. (1981) Adaptable *Kanban* system helps Toyota maintain production. *Industrial Engineering*. 13, (May) 29-46. (*2)

Monden, Yasuhiro. (1981) What makes the Toyota production system really tick? *Industrial Engineering.* 13, (January) 36-40.

Monden, Yasuhiro. (1983) *Toyota Production System.* Atlanta, GA: Industrial Engineering and Management Press. (*3)

Monden, Yasuhiro. (1984) A simulation analysis of the Japanese just-in-time technique (with *Kanbans*) for a multiline multistage production system: A comment. *Decision Sciences.* (Summer) 33-42.

Monden, Yasuhiro. (1985) *Innovations in Management: The Japanese Corporation.* Norcross, GA: Industrial Engineering and Management Press.

Monden, Yasuhiro. (1986) *Applying Just-in-Time.* Norcross, GA: Industrial Engineering and Management Press.

Monks, J. G., and T. E. Hendrick. (1982) *Operations Management: Theory and Problems.* New York: McGraw-Hill.

Monoky, John F. (1992) Unleash the power of TQM. *Industrial Distribution.* 81, (June 15) 77. (*3)

Monroe, Linda K. (1993) A quality guarantee. *Buildings.* 87, (February) 8. (*3)

Montag, Alfred C. (1984) Flexible automation for high-volume production. *Manufacturing Engineering.* (July) 79-80.

Montana, Anthony J. (1992) If it isn't perfect, make it better. *Research-Technology Management.* 35, (July-August) 38. (*2)

Montgomery, D. C. (1976) *Design and Analysis of Experiments.* New York: John Wiley.

Montgomery, D. C. (1980) The economic design of control charts: A review and literature survey. *Journal of Quality Technology.* 12, (February) 75-87.

Montgomery, D. C. (1984) *Design and Analysis of Experiments.* New York: John Wiley. (*2)

Montgomery, D. C. (1985) *Introduction to Statistical Quality Control.* New York: John Wiley. (*5)

Montgomery, D. C., and E. A. Peck. (1982) *Introduction to Linear Regression Analysis*. New York: John Wiley.

Montgomery, D. C., and Harrison M. Wadsworth Jr. (1972) Some techniques for multivariate quality control applications. *ASQC Annual Technical Quality Congress Transactions*. Milwaukee, WI: ASQC Quality Press, 427-435.

Montgomery M. R. (1982) Making it right. *Boston Globe Magazine.* 3, (October) 29-30.

Montgomery, Robert L. (1979) *A Master Guide to Public Speaking.* New York: Harper and Row.

Mood, Alexander. (1950) *Introduction to the Theory of Statistics.* New York: McGraw-Hill.

Moody, P. (1990) *Strategic Manufacturing.* Homewood, IL: Dow Jones-Irwin.

Mooney, M. (1982) Productivity Management, Research Bulletin Number 127, New York: Conference Board.

Moore, B. E., and Timothy L. Ross. (1978) *The Scanlon Way to Improved Productivity.* New York: John Wiley. (*2)

Moore, D. (1992) TQM—not LBOs. *International Business Magazine.* (September) 1.

Moore, F. G., and T. E. Hendrick. (1984) *Production/Operations Management.* Homewood, IL: Irwin.

Moore, T. (1988) Would you buy a car from this man? *Fortune.* (April 11) 72.

Moran, J., R. Talbot, and R. Benson. (1990) *A Guide to Graphical Problem-Solving Processes.* Milwaukee, WI: ASQC Quality Press.

Moran, Jack, et al. (1990) *Daily Management*. Methuen, MA: Goal/QPC.

Moran, John W., Jr. (1991) Leading the organization to perfection through daily management. In Harry Ivan Costin (Ed.) *Readings in Total Quality Management.* (1994) Fort Worth, TX: Dryden Press, 257-267.

Morgan, Gareth. (1986) *Images of Organization*. Newbury Park, CA: Sage.

Morgan, T. K. (1984) Planning for the introduction of FMS. *FMS Magazine*. 86, (July) 13-15.

Moriarty, M. (1985) Design features of forecasting systems involving management judgments. *Journal of Marketing Research*. 22, (November) 353-364.

Moriarty, R. T., and T. J. Kosnik. (1987) High-tech vs. low-tech market where's the beef? Harvard Business School Case Series. #9-588-012. Cambridge, MA: Harvard Business School.

Morita, Akio, with Edwin M. Reingold, and Mitsuko Shimomura. (1986) *Made in Japan: Akio Morita and Sony.* New York: E. P. Dutton. (*3)

Moritani, M. (1982) *Japanese Technology: Getting the Best for the Least.* Japan: Simul Press.

Moritz, Michael and Barrett Seaman. (1981) *Going for Broke: The Chrysler Story*. Garden City, NY: Doubleday.

Morland, Julia. (1981) *Quality Circles*. London, UK: Industrial Society.

Moroney, M. J. (1951) *Facts from Figures*. Baltimore: Penguin Books.

Moroney, M. J. (1978) *Facts from Figures*. Harmondsworth, UK: Penguin.

Morris, C. N. (1983) Parametric empirical Bayes inference: Theory and applications. *Journal of the American Statistical Association.* 88, (March) 47-55.

Morris, Charles R. (1990) *The Coming Global Boom: How to Benefit Now from Tomorrow's Dynamic World Economy.* New York: Bantam Books.

Morris, Rosemary. (1981) *Quality Circles Consulting: Marketing Survey and Industrial Analysis.* San Jose, CA: FMC Corporation, Ordnance Division Engineering.

Morris, Ruby Turner and Claire Sekulski Bronson. (1969) The chaos of competition indicated by consumer reports. *Journal of Marketing.* 29, (July) 26-34.

Morrisey, George S. (1983) *Performance Appraisals in the Public Sector: Key to Effective Supervising.* Reading, MA: Addison-Wesley. (*2)

Morrisey, George S. (1992) Young personal mission statement: A foundation for your future. *Journal of Traveling and Development.* 46 (November) 71. (*2)

Morrison, D. F. (1976) *Multivariate Statistical Methods.* New York: McGraw-Hill.

Morrison, David C. (1987) Up in Arms. *National Journal.* (July 11) 1782-1786.

Morrison, David C. (1988) Right at the start. *National Journal.* (April 8) 978.

Morrocco, John D. (1987) GAO warns of potential risks in major new weapons programs. *Aviation Week and Space Technology.* (April 13) 98-102.

Morrow, Mark. (1993) International agreements increase clout of ISO 9000. *Chemical Week.* (April 7) 32.

Morrow, R. L. (1946) *Time and Motion Economy*. New York: Ronald Press.

Morse, Jay. (1983) Measuring quality costs. *Cost and Management.* (July-August) 16-20.

Mortimer, John. (1984) Building framework for FMS in high volume industries. *FMS Magazine.* 4, (August) 28-30.

Morton, M., and John F. Rockart. (1984) Implications of changes in information technology for corporate strategy. *Interfaces* (January-February) 84-95.

Mosbacher, Robert A. (1989) U.S. must produce quality products. *American Metal Market.* 97, (August 30) 14.

Moses, L. E. (1956) Some theoretical aspects of the lot plot sampling inspection plan. *Journal of the American Statistical Association.* 61, (273) 84-107.

Mosier, Charles T., and Brian Hoyler. (1986) Machine cell formulation for FMS design. *FMS Conference Presentation.*

Moskal, B. S. (1990) The wizards of Buick city. *Industry Week.* (May 7) 22-28.

Moskal, B. S. (1991) Is industry ready for adult relationships? *Industry Week.* (January 21) 18-27.

Moskowitz, Milton, Robert Levering, and Michael Katz. (1990) *Everybody's Business: A Field Guide to the 400 Leading Companies in America.* Garden City, NY: Doubleday.

Mosley, Donald C. (1975) *Management: The Art of Working with and Through People.* Encino, CA: Dickenson.

Mosteller, Frederick and John W. Tukey. (1977) *Data Analysis and Regression.* Reading, MA: Addison-Wesley.

Mottle, N. J., and P. M. Shiah. (1974) Prepared consumer standards. *ASQC Annual Technical Quality Congress Transactions*. Milwaukee, WI: ASQC Quality Press, 218-222.

Moult, John F. (1963) Critical agents in bearing fatigue testing. *Lubrication Engineering.* (December) 503-511.

Mount-Campbell, C. A., and J. B. Neuhardt. (1980) Selecting cost-optimal main effects fractions of 3 factorials. *ASQC Annual Technical Quality Congress Transactions*. Milwaukee, WI: ASQC Quality Press, 80-86

Mouradian, G. (1966) Tolerance limits for assemblies and engineering relationships. *ASCQ Annual Technical Quality Congress Transactions.* Milwaukee, WI: ASQC Quality Press, 598-606.

Muczyk, Jan P. (1979) Dynamics and hazards of MBO applications. *Personnel Administrator*. 24, (May) 52.

Muczyk, Jan P., and Bernard C. Reimann. (1989) MBO as a complement to effective leadership. *The Academy of Management Executive.* 3, (June) 131-138.

Mudel, M. E. (Ed.). (1977) *Productivity: A Series for Industrial Engineers.* Norcross, GA: American Institute of Industrial Engineers.

Mudge, A. E. (1971) *Value Engineering*. New York: McGraw-Hill.

Mullen, H. (1990) Owners need not apply. *Incorporated.* (August) 76-78.

Mullin, Rick. (1992) CEOs on the long march to quality. *Chemical Week.* 151, (September 30) 58. (*2)

Mullin, Rick. (1992) Keeping total quality on track: Perspectives on the consultant's fee. *Chemical Week.* 151, (September 30) 48. (*2)

Mundel, August B. (1972) Vendor-vendee accreditation. *ASQC Annual Technical Quality Congress Transactions.* Milwaukee, WI: ASQC Quality Press, 408-416.

Mundel, August B. (1984) Group testing. *Journal of Quality Technology*. 16, (June) 181-188.

Mundel, Marvin E. (1970) *Motion and Time Studies*. Revised edition. Englewood Cliffs, NJ: Prentice-Hall.

Mundy, Ray A., Russell Passarella, and Jay Morse. (1986) Applying SPC in service industries. *Survey of Business*. (Spring) 24-29.

Munoz, A. M. (1986) Development and application of texture reference scales. *Sensory Studies*. 1, 55.

Munro, Bruce (1982) The quality information system. *ASQC Annual Technical Quality Congress Transactions*. Milwaukee, WI: ASQC Quality Press, 327-334. (*2)

Murakami, Kishii and Inamura Murakami. (1984) PPM control for electronic parts. *Quality Progress*. 17, (November) 24-27.

Murata, Kiyoaki. (1982) What makes Japan tick. *The Japan Times Weekly*. (February) 3.

Murata, T. (1968) Internal QC audit by the top management. *Hinshitsu Kanri*. 19, (March) 300-305.

Murdoch, J. (1979) *Control Charts*. London, UK: Macmillan.

Murdoch, J., and James A. Barnes. (1975) *Statistical Tables for Science, Engineering, Management and Business Studies*. London, UK: Macmillan.

Muroi, Akira. (1987) Customer's needs: How to identify and how to use resultant information. Proceedings of the International Conference on Quality Control.

Murphy, R. B. (1959) Stopping rules with CSP-I sampling inspection plans in continuous production. *Industrial Quality Control*. 15, (November) 10-16.

Murray, T. J. (1987) Meeting the new quality challenge. *Research Management*. (November-December) 25-30.

Musashi, Miyamoto. (1982) *The Book of Five Rings: The Real Art of Japanese Management.* Translation and commentary by Nihon Services Corporation: Bradford J. Brown, Yuko Kashiwagi, William H. Barrett, and Eisuke Sasagawa. New York: Bantam Books.

Musselman, Kenneth J. (1984) Computer simulation: A design tool for FMS. *Manufacturing Engineering.* (August) 117-120.

Mutual benefits. (1984) *Inc.* (April) 7.

Myer, R. (1989) Suppliers-manage your customers. *Harvard Business Review.* 67, (November-December) 160-168.

Myers, David G. (1980) How do I love me? Let me count the ways. *Psychology Today.* (May) 16.

Myers, David G. (1980) The inflated self. *Psychology Today.* (May) 16.

Myers, I. B. (1980) *Gifts Differing.* Palo Alto, CA: Consulting Psychology Press.

Myers, I. B. (1985) Making organizations adaptive to change: Eliminating bureaucracy at Shenandoah Life. *National Productivity Week.* 4, (February) 131-38. (*2)

Myers, Ken and Ron Ashkens. (1993) Results-driven quality . . . Now! *Management Review.* 82, (March) 40. (*3)

Myers, R. H. (1971) *Response Surface Methodology.* Boston, MA: Allyn and Bacon.

Myers, S. (1964) Who are your motivated workers? *Harvard Business Review.* 42, (January-February) 64-88.

Nachi-Fujikoshi Corporation and Japan Institute of Plant Maintenance (Eds.). (1990) *Training for TPM: A Manufacturing Success Story.* Cambridge, MA: Productivity Press.

Nader, Ralph. (1965) *Unsafe at Any Speed.* New York: Grossman.

Nadler, David A. (1977) *Feedback and Organization Development: Using Data-Based Methods.* Reading, MA: Addison-Wesley. (*4)

Nadler, David A. (1982) *Concepts for the Design of Organizations.* New York: OR and C. (*2)

Nadler, David A., J. Richard Hackman, and Edward E. Lawler III. (1979) *Managing Organization Behavior.* Boston, MA: Little Brown.

Nadler, David A., M. Hanlon, and Edward E. Lawler III. (1982) Factors influencing the success of labor-management quality of work life projects. *Journal of Occupational Behavior.* 1, (March) 53-67. (*2)

Nadler, Gerald M., and Shozo Hibino. (1990) *Breakthrough Thinking: Why We Must Change the Way We Solve Problems and the Seven Principles to Achieve This.* Rocklin, CA: Prima Publishing and Communications.

Nagy, E. (1983) Methodological problems of the implementation of QC circles. Proceedings, Twenty-Seventh EOQC Conference, Madrid. Appendix.

Naisbitt, John. (1982) *Megatrends: Ten New Directions Transforming Our Lives.* New York: Warner Books. (*4)

Naisbitt, John and Patricia Aburdene. (1986) *Reinventing the Corporation.* New York: Warner Books. (*3)

Naj, KuMarch (1986) The human factor. *New York Times.* (November 10) 11. (*2)

Nakajima, Sciichi. (1988) *Total Productive Maintenance.* Cambridge, MA: Productivity Press.

Nakajima, Sciichi. (1989) *Introduction to TPM.* Cambridge, MA: Productivity Press.

Nakajo, Takeshi and Hitoshi Kume. (1985) The principles of foolproofing and their application in manufacturing. *Reports of Statistical Application Research.* 32, (June) 10-29.

Nakane, Chie. (1970) *Japanese Society.* Berkeley, CA: University of California Press. (*3)

Nakayama, Ichiro. (1975) *Industrialization and Labor-Management Relations in Japan.* Tokyo: The Japan Institute of Labor.

Nakayama, M., and C. Wessman. (1979) Application of sensory evaluation to the routine maintenance of product quality. *Food Technology.* 33, 38.

Nanus, Burt. (1989) *The Leader's Edge: The Seven Keys to Leadership in a Turbulent World.* Chicago, IL and New York: Contemporary Books.

Nanus, Burt. (1992) *Visionary Leadership.* San Francisco, CA: Jossey-Bass.

Narver, John C., and Stanley F. Slater. (1990) The effect of a market orientation on business profitability. *Journal of Marketing.* 50, (October) 20-35.

Nashua History Committee. (1978) *The Nashua Experience: History in the Making, 1673/1978.* Canaan, New Hampshire: Phoenix Publishing.

Nassr, M. A. (1977) Productivity growth through work measurement. *Defense Management Journal.* 13, (April) 16-20.

National Association of Purchasing Agents. (1967) *Evaluation of Supplier Performance.* New York: National Association of Purchasing Agents.

National Business Council for Consumer Affairs. (1973) *Safety in the Market Place.* Washington, DC: NBCCA.

National Center for Community Risk Management and Insurance. (1991) *State Liability Laws for Charitable Organizations and Volunteers*. Washington, DC: NCCRMI.

National Center for Manufacturing Sciences. (1990) *Competing in World Class Manufacturing.* Homewood, IL: Irwin.

National Center for Productivity and Quality of Working Life. (1972) *Productivity, Report of the Commission.* Washington, DC: NCPQWL.

National Center for Productivity and Quality of Working Life. (1975) *Improving Productivity: A Description of Selected Company Programs*. (Series 1, December). Washington, DC: NCPQWL.

National Center for Productivity and Quality Working Life. (1975) *A National Policy for Productivity Improvement*. Washington, DC: NCPQWL.

National Center for Productivity and Quality of Working Life. (1975) *Plant-Wide Productivity Plan in Action: Three Years of Experience with the Scanlon Plan.* Washington, DC: NCPQWL.

National Center for Productivity and Quality of Working Life. (1976) *Annual Report to the President and Congress*. Washington, DC: NCPQWL.

National Center for Productivity and Quality of Working Life. (1976) *Improving Productivity Through Industry and Company Measurement*. (October). Washington, DC: NCPQWL.

National Center for Productivity and Quality of Working Life. (1977) *The Future of Productivity*. Washington, DC: NCPQWL.

National Institute of Standards and Technology. (1994) Malcolm Baldrige national quality award 1992 fact sheet. In Harry Ivan Costin (Ed.) *Readings in Total Quality Management.* (1994) Fort Worth, TX: Dryden Press, 567-597.

National Institute of Standards and Technology. (1994) Malcolm Baldrige Quality Award 1993 award criteria. In Harry Ivan

Costin (Ed.) *Readings in Total Quality Management.* (1994) Fort Worth, TX: Dryden Press, 499-556.

National league for nursing. (1982) *The Quality Circle Process.* (November) 492-93.

Natrella, Mary G. (1963) *Experimental Statistics.* National Bureau of Standards Handbook 91, Washington, DC: U.S. Government Printing Office. (*2)

Naumann, A. (1988) The importance of productivity. *Quality Progress.* 13, (June) 18-26.

NAVSHIP. (1972) *Maintainability Design Criteria Handbook for Designers of Shipboard Electronic Equipment.* NAVSHIP Document 0967-312-8010. Philadelphia, PA: U.S. Department of Defense, Naval Publications and Forms Center.

Nayak, P., and J. Ketteringham. (1986) *Breakthroughs.* Cambridge, MA: Arthur Little.

Nayak, Ranganath. (1992) Creating a high-performance business: It won't result from traditional TQM. *Industry Week.* (September 21) 46. (*2)

Nayatani, Yoshinobu. (1983) Policy deployment: Japanese management's new strategic tool. *An Introduction for Doing Business in and with Japan.* 4, (February) 24-26.

Naylor, T., and H. Schauland. (1976) A survey of users of corporate planning models. *Management Science.* 22, (May) 927-937.

Near, R., and D. Weckler. (1990) Organizational and job characteristics related to self-managing teams. Paper presented at International Conference on Self-managed Work Teams, Denton, TX, September.

Neave, Henry R. (1990) *The Deming Dimension.* Knoxville, TN: SPC Press. (*4)

Neimark, Jill. (1989) Shake it up! *Success.* (July/August) 48-49.

Nelson, Kelly. (1991) Building in the quality. *The Canadian Business Review*. 18, (Winter) 22-25.

Nelson, L. S. (1974) Factors for the analysis of means. *Journal of Quality Technology*. 6, (October) 175-181.

Nelson, L. S. (1975) Use of the range to estimate variability. *Journal of Quality Technology*. 7, (January) 46-48.

Nelson, L. S. (1978) Best target value for a production process. *Journal of Quality Technology*. 10, (April) 88-89.

Nelson, L. S. (1982) Control chart for individuals. *Journal of Quality Technology*. 14, (March) 172-173.

Nelson, L. S. (1983) Exact critical values for use with the analysis of means. *Journal of Quality Technology*. 15, (January) 40-44.

Nelson, L. S. (1983) Problem identification and solution. *Conference on Managing Systems of People and Machines for Improved Quality and Productivity*. Cambridge, MA: MIT Press.

Nelson, L. S. (1984) The Shewhart control chart—tests for special causes. *Journal of Quality Technology*. 16, (April) 237-239. (*4)

Nelson, L. S. (1984) Technical aids. *Journal of Quality Technology*. 16, (October) 11-14.

Nelson, L. S. (1985) Interpreting Shewhart mean control charts. *Journal of Quality Technology*. 17, (April) 114-116. (*2)

Nelson, R. (1981) Research on productivity growth and productivity differences: Dead ends and new departures. *Journal of Economic Literature*. 29, (September) 1029-1064.

Nelson, R., and S. G. Winter. (1982) *An Evolutionary Theory of Economic Change*. Cambridge, MA: Harvard University Press.

Nelson, W. (1979) How to analyze data with simple plots: Volume 1. *The ASQC Basic References in Quality Control: Statistical Techniques*. Milwaukee, WI: ASQC Quality Press. (*2)

Nelson, W. (1982) *Applied Life Data Analysis*. New York: John Wiley. (*2)

Nelson, W. (1983) *How to Analyze Reliability Data*. Milwaukee, WI: ASQC Quality Press.

Nelton, Sharon. (1993) The benefits that flow from quality. *Nation's Business*. 81, (March) 71. (*3)

Nemoto, Masao. (1987) *Total Quality Control for Management: Strategies and Techniques from Toyota and Toyoda Gosei.* Englewood Cliffs, NJ: Prentice-Hall.

Nester, Donald and Rolf Staal (1986) The universal sequence of events on the production floor of AHC. *The Juran Report*. (Winter) 99-105.

Neter, J., W. Wasserman, and M. H. Ku. (1985) *Applied Linear Statistical Models*. Homewood, IL: Irwin.

Neter, J., W. Wasserman, and M. H. Ku. (1987) *Targets for Excellence*. Detroit, MI: General Motors Publishing.

Neuhardt, J. B., and C. A. Mount-Campbell. (1978) Selection of cost-optimal 2k-P fractional factorials. *Communications in Statistics: Simulation and Computation*. San Francisco, CA, 369-383.

Neuman, D. (1939) The distribution of the range in samples from a normal population expressed in terms of an independent estimate of the standard deviation. *Biometrika*. 31, (2) 20.

Neustadt, Richard E. (1960) *Presidential Power: The Politics of Leadership*. New York: John Wiley. (*2)

Never acquire a business: The ten best-managed companies. (1970) *Dun's Review*. (December) 30.

Nevilles, J. E. (1986) Processing quality information. Unpublished technical report, IBM-Tucson.

Nevilles, J. E. (1987) Guide for choosing control charts. *Quality*. (March) 87.

Nevins, Allan. (1957) *Ford: Expansion and Challenge.* New York: Scribners.

Nevins, Allan. (1981) *Ford: Decline and Rebirth.* New York: Scribners.

Nevins, Allan and Frank Ernest Hill. (1954) *Ford: The Times, the Man and the Company.* New York: Scribners.

The new cutting edge in factories. (1987) *The Washington Post*. (April 14) 1.

The new economy. (1983) *Time*. (May) 16.

A new era for auto quality. (1990) *BusinesswWeek*. (October 22) 84-96.

A new era for quality. (1990) *BusinessWeek*. (October) 23.

New equal right: The close shave. (1993) *BusinessWeek*. (March 29) 58-59, A1.

New era is at hand in global competition: U.S. vs. United Europe. *Wall Street Journal*. (July 15) A1.

The new realism in office systems. (1992) *BusinessWeek*. (June 15) 128-133.

New way to wake up a giant. (1990) *Fortune*. (October 22) 91. (*2)

New York Stock Exchange. (1982) *People and Productivity*. New York: New York Stock Exchange. (*2)

Newbold, P. (1990) Quality improvement: Lessons from experience. *Decisions in Imaging Economics*. 14.

Newcomb, John E. (1989) Management by policy deployment. *Quality*. (January) 28-30.

Newman, William H. (1975) *Constructive Control.* Englewood Cliffs, NJ: Prentice-Hall.

Newton, Fred J. (1990) A 1990s agenda for auditors. *Internal Auditor.* (December) 33-39.

Nichols, Don. (1988) Unions play catch-up to today's work environment. *Management Review.* 77, (February) 16-20.

Nickell, Warren L. (1985) Quality improvement in marketing. *The Juran Report.* (Winter) 29-35.

Nickell, Warren L., and Sylvia J. McNeil. (1987) Process management in a marketing environment. Proceedings of the Fourth Annual Conference on Quality Improvement.

Nissen, Mark E. (1995) Knowledge-based organizational process redesign: Using process flow measures to transform procurement. Unpublished Ph.D. dissertation, School of Business Administration, University of Southern California, Los Angeles, CA.

Nissen, Mark E. (1996) A focused review of the reengineering literature: Expert frequently asked questions. *Quality Management Journal.* 3, (No. 3) 52-66.

Nissen, Mark E. (1996) Knowledge-based reengineering of military procurement: From mysterious art to learnable craft. Fisher Center for Information Technology and Management. Working paper number CITM-96-WP-1012 (February), Los Angeles, CA.

Nitobe, Inazo. (1969) *The Soul of Japan.* Tokyo: Charles E. Tuttle. (*2)

Nitta, Y., K. Nukada, K. Mori, and M. Ohkawa. (1980) Information retrieval for review support. *Proceedings, Annual Reliability and Maintainability Symposium.* New York: IEEE, 152-157.

Niven, D. (1993) When times get tough, what happens to TQM? *Harvard Business Review.* 71, (May-June) 20-34.

No-dicker sticker car deals ignite: Buyers tired of getting beaten up. (1992) *USA Today*. (August 4) A1.

Noakes, Merle E. (1985) The three-level quality council. *The Juran Report*. (Winter) 92-94.

Noble, A. C. (1975) Instrumental analysis of the food properties of food. *Food Technology*. 29, (December) 56.

Noble, David F. (1984) *Forces of Production*. New York: Alfred A. Knopf.

Noble, I. A. (1984) Flexible manufacturing systems in the foundry industry. *British Foundryman*. 77, 137-141.

Noether, Gottfried E. (1967) *Elements of Non-Parametric Statistics*. New York: John Wiley.

Nolan, T. W. (1990) Estimation and prediction in statistical studies. Paper presented at the Michigan Conference on Teaching and Use of Statistical Theory and Methods, Michigan State University, East Lansing, Michigan, October.

Nolan, T. W. (1990) Quality as an Organizational Strategy. Paper presented at Philadelphia Annual Quality Conference, Philadelphia Area Council for Excellence, May.

Nolan, T. W., and Lloyd P. Provost. (1990) Understanding variation. *Quality Progress*. 23, (May) 73-76.

Noonan, Martin. (1984) Operator quality control. *EOQC Quality*. (November) 7-11

Noori, H. (1989) The Taguchi methods: Achieving design and output quality. *The Executive*. 3, 322-326.

Nora, John, Raymond C. Rogers, and Robert Stanny. (1986) *Transforming the Workplace*. Princeton, New Jersey: Princeton Research Press.

Norman, E. H. (1975) *Origins of the Modern Japanese State: Selected Writings of E. H. Norman*. New York: Random House. (*2)

Normann, R. (1976) *Management and Statesmanship*. Stockholm: Scandinavian Institutes for Administrative Research. (*2)

Normann, R. (1984) *Service Management: Strategy and Leadership in Service Businesses*. New York: John Wiley.

Normile, Dennis. (1990) Japan Inc. bows to the customer. *CIO*. (August) 91-93.

Norquist, Warren E. (1983) Improving quality/purchasing teamwork. *ASQC Annual Technical Quality Congress Transactions*. Milwaukee, WI: ASQC Quality Press, 136-141.

Norris, William C. (1980) Ideas and trends. *BusinessWeek*. (January 23) 20.

Norsworthy, J. R. (1979) The slowdown in productivity growth: An analysis of some contributing factors. *Brookings Papers on Economic Activity*. Washington, DC: Brookings Institute, 2387-2421.

Northcraft, Gregory B., and Richard B. Chase. (1985) Managing service demand at the point of delivery. *Academy of Management Review*. (October), 66-75.

Now for quality comparisons. (1992) *Management Today*. (August) 80. (*2)

Now quality means service too. (1991) *Fortune*. (April 22) 100.

Now unions are helping run business. (1986) *BusinessWeek*. (December 24) 69. (*2)

Nowlan, F. S. (1980) Reliability centered maintenance. Symposium on Design to Cost and Life Cycle Cost. Amsterdam, Netherlands: North Atlantic Treaty Organization.

Nowlan, F. S., and H. F. Heap. (1978) *Reliability Centered Maintenance*. Alexandria, VA: Defense Documentation Center.

Noyes, Richard J. (1979) Quality measurement system. *ASQC Annual Technical Quality Congress Transactions*. Milwaukee, WI: ASQC Quality Press, 434-437.

Nuclear construction-doing it right. (1983) *Engineering News Record.* (April) 26-9. (*2)

Nulty, Peter. (1984) How personal computers change managers' lives. *Fortune*. (September 3) 38-48.

Number 1's awesome strategy. (1981) *BusinessWeek.* (June 8) 86.

Nurick, A. J. (1985) *Participation in Organization Change.* New York: Praeger. (*2)

Nystrom, Paul C. (1978) Managers and the high-high leader myth. *Academy of Management Journal*. 21, (April) 325-331.

Nystrom, Paul C., and William H. Starbuck. (1981) *Handbook of Organizational Design.* Oxford, UK: Oxford University Press. (*2)

Oakland, John S. (1986) *Statistical Process Control: A Practical Guide*. London, UK: Heinemann. (*3)

Oakland, John S. (1990) Total quality management. *Journal of the Operational Research Society*. 41, (August) 784-785.

Oakland, John S. (1993) *Total Quality Management*. Oxford, UK: Butterworth Heinemann.

Oakland, John S. (1994) *Cases in Total Quality Management*. Oxford, UK: Butterworth Heinemann.

Oberle, Joseph. (1990) Quality gurus: The men and their message. *Training*. 27, (January) 47-53. (*7)

O'Boyle, Thomas F. (1985) Loyalty ebbs at many companies as employees grow disillusioned. *Wall Street Journal.* 11, (July) 29. (*2)

O'Boyle, Thomas F. (1990) Last in, right out: Firms' newfound skill in managing inventory may soften downturn. *Wall Street Journal.* (November 19) A1, A6

O'Brien, D. O., and J. Wainwright. (1993) Winning as a team of teams: Transforming the mindset of the organization at National and Provincial Building Society. *Business Change and Reengineering.* 1, (No. 3) 19-25.

Obrams, Jim. (1983) What you train is what you get. *The Japan Times Weekly.* (March) 17-18.

Odaka, Kunio. (1975) *Toward Industrial Democracy: Management and Workers in Modern Japan.* Cambridge, MA: Harvard University Press.

O'Dell, C. (1981) *Gainsharing: Involvement Incentives and Productivity.* New York: AMACOM.

O'Dell, C. (1984) *Sharing the Productivity Payoff.* Texas: American Productivity Center.

O'Dell, C. (1989) Team play, team pay—New ways of keeping score. *Across the Board.* (November) 38-45. (*2)

Odiorne, George S. (1965) *Management by Objective: A System of Managerial Leadership.* Boston, MA: Pitman.

Odiorne, George S. (1974) *Management and the Activity Trap.* New York: Harper and Row.

Odiorne, George S. (1978) MBO: A backward glance. *Business Horizons.* 21, (October) 14-24.

Odiorne, George S. (1979) *MBO II.* Belmont: Fearon Publishers.

Office automation: Making it pay off. (1987) *BusinessWeek.* (October 12) 134-146.

Office of the Assistant Secretary of Defense. (1960) *Statistical Procedures for Determining Validity of Supplier's Attributes*

Inspection. Handbook 109. Washington, DC: U.S. Department of Defense, Naval Publications and Forms Center.

Ogawa, Eiji. (1984) *Modern Production Management: A Japanese Experience.* Tokyo: Asian Production Organization.

Ogilvy, David. (1965) The creative chef. In Gary A. Steiner (Ed.) *The Creative Organization.* Chicago, IL: University of Chicago Press. (*2)

Ogilvy, David. (1968) *Principles of Management.* New York: Ogilvy and Mather.

Ogilvy, David. (1980) *Confessions of an Advertising Man.* New York: Atheneum. (*2)

O'Grady, P. J. (1988) *Putting the Just-In-Time Philosophy Into Practice.* New York: Nichols Publishing.

Ogryzkov, V. M. (1979) Quality training of industrial workers by means of technical aids. Proceedings, EOQC Twenty Third Conference, Heidelberg. 78. (*2)

O'Guin, Michael C. (1990) Focus the factory with activity-based costing. *Management Accounting.* (February) 36-41.

O'Guin, Michael C. (1991) *The Complete Guide to Activity-Based Costing.* Englewood Cliffs, NJ: Prentice-Hall.

O'Hanlon, Thomas. (1979) A rejuvenated Litton is once again off to the races. *Fortune.* (October 15) 160. (*2)

Ohmae, Kenichi. (1981) Myths and realities of Japanese corporations. *Chief Executive.* (Summer) 11. (*3)

Ohmae, Kenichi. (1982) *The Mind of the Strategist.* New York: McGraw-Hill. (*4)

Ohmae, Kenichi. (1988) Getting back to strategy. *Harvard Business Review.* 66, (November-December) 149-156.

Ohmae, Kenichi. (1990) *The Borderless World: Power and Strategy in the Interlinked Economy.* New York: Harper Business.

Ohno, Taiichi. (1982) *Workplace Management.* Cambridge, MA: Productivity Press.

Ohno, Taiichi. (1988) *Toyota Production System: Beyond Large-Scale Production.* Cambridge, MA: Productivity Press. (*2)

Ohno, Taiichi and S. Mito. (1988) *Just-In-Time for Today and Tomorrow.* Cambridge: Productivity Press. (*3)

Oishi, O. (1981) The concept for perfect production. *CTM: The Human Element.* (February) 14-16.

O'Keefe, Daniel F., and Isley C. Willard. (1976) Dotterweich revisited: Criminal liability under the federal food, drug and cosmetic act. *Food-Drug-Cosmetic Law Journal.* 31, (February) 21-28.

O'Keefe, Daniel F., and M. H. Shapiro. (1975) Personal criminal liability under the federal food, drug and cosmetic act: the dotterweich doctrine. *Food-Drug-Cosmetic Law Journal.* 30, (January) 13-16.

Okita, Saburo. (1981) *Japan's Challenging Years.* Canberra: Australia Japan Research Center.

Okun, A. M. (1975) *Equality and Efficiency.* Washington, DC: Brookings Institution. (*2)

O'Leary, D. S. (1987) *The Joint Commission Agenda for Change.* Chicago, IL: Joint Commission on Accreditation of Healthcare Organizations, 1-10.

Olian, Judy D., and Sara L. Rynes. (1991) Making total quality work: Aligning organizational processes, performance measures, and stakeholders. *Human Resources Management.* 30, (Issue 3, Fall) 303-333.

Oliva, T., D. Day, and W. DeSarbo. (1987) Selecting competitive tactics: Try a strategy map. *Sloan Management Review*. 28, (March) 5-15.

Oliver, Larry R., and Melvin D. Springer. (1972) A general set of Bayesian attribute acceptance sampling plans. *American Institute of Industrial Engineers*. 443-455. (*2)

Olling, Gustav. (1978) Experts look ahead to day of the full-blown computer integrated. *IEEE Spectrum*. 15, 60-66.

Ollson, John Ryding. (1986) The market-leader method; user-oriented development. Proceedings, Thirtieth EOQC Conference, Berlin. 1, 59-68. (*2)

Olmstead, Denison. (1972) *Memoir of Eli Whitney, Esq.* New York: Arno Press.

Olmstead, Paul S. (1982) How to detect the type of an assignable cause: Clues for particular types of trouble. *Journal of Quality Technology*. 9, (January) 32. (*2)

Olmstead, Paul S., and John W. Tukey. (1947) A corner test for association. *Annual of Mathematical Statistics*. 18, (December) 495-513.

Olmsted, Barney and Suzanne Smith. (1985) *The Job Sharing Handbook*. New York: Ten Speed Press.

Olmsted, M. (1959) *The Small Group*. New York: Random House.

Olson, Lynn. (1992) Schools getting swept up in current of business's 'Quality' movement. *Education Week*. 11, (March) 25.

Olson, M. (1982) *The Rise and Decline of Nations*. New Haven, CT: Yale University Press.

Olson, M. (1987) An investigation of the impacts of remote work environments and supporting technology. Working paper, Graduate School of Business Administration, New York University.

Olson, S. (1971) *The Depletion Myth.* Cambridge, MA: Harvard University Press.

Omachonu, Vincent K. (1991) *Total Quality and Productivity Management in Healthcare Organizations.* Norcross, GA: Industrial Engineering and Management Press. (*5)

Omachonu, Vincent K., and Joel E. Ross. (1994) *Principles of Total Quality.* Delray Beach, FL: St. Lucie Press. (*2)

O'Mahoney, M. (1979) Psychophysical aspects of sensory analysis of dairy products. *Dairy Science.* 62, 1954.

On probability as a basic for action. (1975) *The American Statistician.* 146-52.

On the use of judgment-samples. (1976) *Reports of Statistical Applications.* (March) 25-31.

O'Neal, R. (1987) The buyer-seller linkage in a just-in-time environment. *Journal of Purchasing and Materials Management.* 23, 7-13.

Onoe, M. (1981) *Real-Time/Parallel Computing: Image Analysis.* New York: Plenum.

An open letter: TQM on campus. (1991) *Harvard Business Review.* 69, (November-December) 94-95.

Opsahl, R. L., and M. D. Dunnette. (1966) The role of financial compensation in industrial motivation. *Psychological Bulletin.* 66, 9-118.

Orbaugh, Pamela K., and Tim Orbaugh. (1983) Is your lab ready for quality circles. *Medical Laboratory Observer.* (February) 41-45.

Ordover, J. A., and Robert D. Willig. (1981) An economic definition of predatory product innovation. In Steven Salop (Ed.) Strategic Views of Prediction. Washington, DC: Federal Trade Commission, 301-396.

O'Rear, Clarence Michael. (1995) An analysis of the level of implementation of total quality management in the technical institutes in the State of Georgia. Unpublished Ph.D. dissertation, Georgia State University, Atlanta, GA.

O'Reilly, B. (1984) Lessons from the home phone wars. *Fortune.* (December 15) 83-86.

O'Reilly, Charles A., III. (1977) Personality job fit: Implications for individual attitudes and performance. *Organizational Behavior and Human Performance.* 18, (January) 36-46.

O'Reilly, Charles A., III. (1982) Variations in decision makers' use of information sources: The impact of quality and accessibility of information. *Academy of Management Journal.* 25, (September) 756-771.

Orfan, Constantine. (1981) In-process and end-product goals of quality circles. *Quality Circles Journal.* 4, (February) 26-27.

Orlicky, J. (1969) *The Successful Computer System.* New York: McGraw-Hill. (*3)

Orlicky, J. (1975) *Material Requirements Planning.* New York: McGraw-Hill.

Orme, Clifton N., Robert J. Parsons and Glen Z. McBride. (1992) Customer information and the quality improvement process: Developing a customer information system. *Hospital and Health Services Administration.* 37, (Summer) 197. (*2)

Orr, Daniel. (1971) *Management and the Demand for Money.* New York: Praeger.

Orsburn, Jack D., Linda Moran, Ed Musselwhite, John H. Zenger, with Craig Perrin. (1990) *Self-Directed Work Teams: The New American Challenge.* Homewood, IL: Business One Irwin.

Orsini, Joyce Nilsson. (1987) Bonuses: What is the impact? *National Productivity Review.* 6, (Spring) 187-193. (*3)

Orwell, George. (1954) *Animal Farm.* New York: Harcourt Brace Jovanovich.

Osborn, A. F. (1979) *Applied Imagination: Principles and Procedures of Creative Problem Solving.* New York: Scribners. (*2)

Osborne, David and Ted Gaebloer. (1992) *Reinventing Government: How the Entrepreneurial Spirit is Transforming the Public Sector.* Reading, MA: Addison-Wesley.

OSHA Safety Regulation. (1977) *American Enterprise Institute for Public Policy Research.* Washington, DC: American Enterprise Institute for Public Policy Research.

Osterhoff, R., W. Locander, and G. M. Bounds. (1991) Competitive benchmarking at Xerox. In Michael J. and G. M. Bounds. *Competing Globally Through Customer Value.* Westport, CT: Quorum Books, 792.

Ostle, Bernard (1967) Industry use of statistical test design. *Industrial Quality Control.* 24, (January) 24-33.

O'Toole, James. (1977) *Work, Learning, and the American Future.* San Francisco, CA: Jossey-Bass.

O'Toole, James. (1981) *Making America Work.* New York: Continuum.

O'Toole, James. (1985) *Vanguard Management.* Garden City, NY: Doubleday. (*3)

O'Toole, P. (1984) *Corporate Messiah.* New York: William Morrow.

Ott, Ellis R. (1953) A production experiment with mechanical assemblies. *Industrial Quality Control.* 9, (July) 21-26.

Ott, Ellis R. (1957) A scatter diagram used to compare before and after measurements. *Industrial Quality Control.* 13, (June) 12-19.

Ott, Ellis R. (1967) Analysis of means—A graphical procedure. *Industrial Quality Control*. 24, (August) 101-109.

Ott, Ellis R. (1969) Achieving quality control. *Quality Progress*. 5, (May) 5-14.

Ott, Ellis R. (1975) *Process Quality Control—Troubleshooting and Interpretation of Data*. New York: McGraw-Hill. (*8)

Ott, Ellis R., and August B. Mundel. (1954) Narrow-limit gaging. *Industrial Quality Control*. 10, (March) 21-28.

Ott, Ellis R., and Ronald D. Snee. (1973) Identifying useful differences in a multiple-head machine. *Journal of Quality Technology*. 5, (April) 47-57.

Ottensmeyer, E. J., and Charles C. Snow. (1988) Managing strategies and technologies. In L. R. Gomez-Mejia and M. W. Lawless (Eds.) *Proceedings, Managing the High Technology Firm*. Boulder, CO: University of Colorado Press, 50-57. (*2)

Ouchi, William G. (1979) A conceptual framework for the design of organization control mechanisms. *Management Science*. 25, (September) 833-848.

Ouchi, William G. (1980) Markets, bureaucracies and clans. *Administrative Science Quarterly*. 25, (November) 129-141.

Ouchi, William G. (1981) *Theory Z: How American Business Can Meet the Japanese Challenge*. Reading, MA: Addison-Wesley. (*6)

Ouchi, William G. (1984) *The M-Form Society: How American Teamwork Can Recapture The Competitive Edge*. Reading, MA: Addison-Wesley. (*5)

Ough, C. S., and G. A. Baker. (1961) Small panel sensory evaluations of whines by scoring. *Hildegardia*. 30, 587.

Owen, D. B. (1962) *Handbook of Statistical Tables*. Reading, MA: Addison-Wesley.

Owen, D. B., and W. H. Frawley. (1971) Factors for tolerance limits which control both tails of the normal distribution. *Journal of Quality Technology.* 3, (February) 69-79.

Owen, M. (1989) *PC and Continuous Improvement.* London, UK: IFS Publications.

Ozawa, Terutomo. (1982) *People and Productivity in Japan.* New York: Pergamon Press.

P and G's new new-product onslaught. (1979) *BusinessWeek.* (October 1) 80. (*2)

Pabst, William R., Jr. (1963) MIL-STD-105D. *Industrial Quality Control.* 19, (November) 4-9.

Pabst, William R., Jr. (1972) Motivating people in Japan. *Quality Progress.* 5, (October) 14-18.

Packard, David. (1974) Lessons of leadership. *Nation's Business.* 62, (January) 42.

Packard, George. (1966) *Protest in Tokyo: The Security Treaty Crisis of 1960.* Princeton, NJ: Princeton University Press.

Packer, Michael B. (1983) Measuring the intangible in productivity. *Technology Review.* (February/March) 48-57.

Page, E. S. (1954) Continuous inspection schemes. *Biometrika.* 14, (3) 100-115.

Pairo, J. S. (1943) Using ratio-delay studies to set allowance. *Factory.* 1106, (October) 94

Pall, Gabriel A. (1987) *Quality Process Management.* Englewood Cliffs, NJ: Prentice-Hall. (*2)

Paller, Alan. (1989) A guide to EIS for MIS directors. *CA-Insight: The Computer Associates Software Magazine.* 2, 5-9.

Paluev, K. (1941) How collective genius contributes to industrial progress. *General Electric Review.* (May) 254-261.

Pangborn, R. M. (1964) Sensory evaluation of foods: A look backward and forward. *Food Technology.* 18, (September) 63.

Pangborn, R. M. (1987) Sensory science in flavor research: Achievements, needs and perspectives. In M. Martenas, G. A. Dalen, and H. Russwurm (Eds.) *Flavor Science and Technology.* London, UK: John Wiley.

Pangborn, R. M., and W. L. Durkley. (1964) Laboratory procedures for evaluating the sensory properties of milk. *Dairy Science.* 26, (February) 55.

Panov, A. A. (1983) Production improvements through the introduction of FMS and industrial robots. *Soviet Engineering Research.* 3, 50-52.

Paola, Sztajn. (1992) A matter of metaphors: Education as a handmade process. *Educational Leadership.* (November) 35-37.

Papa, Frank A. (1993) Linkage of old and new. *Management Review.* 82, (January) 63. (*3)

Paperwork is avoidable (if you call the shots). (1977) *Wall Street Journal.* (June 17) 24.

Parasuraman, A. (1987) Customer-oriented corporate cultures are crucial to services marketing success. *The Journal of Services Marketing.* (Summer) 39-46.

Parasuraman, A., Valarie A. Zeithami, and Leonard L. Berry. (1984) A conceptual model of service quality and its implications for future research. Report published by Marketing Science Institute (August).

Parasuraman, A., Valarie A. Zeithami, and Leonard L. Berry. (1986) Servqual: A multiple-item scale for measuring customer perceptions of service quality. Marketing Science Institute research program working paper. (August).

Parker, Glenn M. (1990) *Team Players and Teamwork*. San Francisco, CA: Jossey-Bass.

Parker, H. V. (1981) A paper mill solves a quality control problem with process control data. *Quality Progress*. 14, (March) 18-22.

Parker, J. E. S. (1978) *The Economics of Innovation*. Second edition. New York: Longman, Green.

Parker, Kenneth T. (1984) Departmental activity analysis: Management and employees working together. Proceedings of the Annual Conference of the International Association of Quality Circles.

Parker, Mike and Jane Slaughter. (1988) Behind the scenes at Nummi Motors. *New York Times*. Business section. (December 4) 2.

Parker, Mike and Jane Slaughter. (1988) *Choosing Sides: Unions and the Team Concept*. Boston, MA: South End Press. (*2)

Parsons, H. M., and G. P. Kearsley. (1981) *Human Factors and Robotics: Current Status and Future Prospects*. Englewood Cliffs, NJ: Prentice-Hall.

Pascale, Richard Tanner. (1984) Fitting new employees into the company culture. *Fortune*. (May 28) 28-40.

Pascale, Richard Tanner. (1990) *Managing on the Edge: How the Smartest Companies Use Conflict to Stay Ahead*. New York: Simon and Schuster.

Pascale, Richard Tanner and Anthony G. Athos. (1979) *The Art of Japanese Management*. New York: Warner Books. (*10)

Pascarella, Perry. (1981) Fad of philosophy? QCs may become too popular. *Industry Week*. (March 6) 23-24.

Pascarella, Perry. (1982) Quality circles. *Industry Week*. (July 2) 50-55. (*2)

Pascarella, Perry. (1993) 15 ways to win people's trust. *Industry Week*. (February 1) 47-53.

Passell, P., and L. Ross. (1975) *The Best.* New York: Pocket Books.

Pasteelnick, L. A., and W. B. Leder. (1957) Statistical analysis in a polymerization process. *Chemical Engineering Progress*. 53, (August) 392-395.

Patchin, Robert I. (1981) Consultants: Good and bad. *Quality Circles Journal*. 4, (February) 11-12.

Patchin, Robert I. (1981) Facilitators, facilitation and ownership. *Quality Circles Journal*. 4, (February) 13-14.

Patchin, Robert I. (1981) Stairway to the stars. *Quality Circles Journal*. 5, (February) 10-15.

Patchin, Robert I., and Robert Cunningham. (1983) *The Management and Maintenance of Quality Circles*. Homewood, IL: Irwin.

Patel, M. S. (1962) Group screening with more than two stages. *Technometrics*. 4, (February) 209-217.

Patel, M. S. (1963) Partially duplicated fractional factorial designs. *Technometrics*. 5, (July) 83.

Pathways: New thoughts on the Road to Quality Improvements. (1989) Milwaukee, WI: ASQC Quality Press. (*2)

Patinkin, M. (1987) *Gamble on Assembly Teams Pays Off.* Pittsburgh, PA: Pittsburgh Press, B6-B7.

Patten, Thomas H., Jr. (1991) Beyond systems—The politics of managing in a TQM environment. *National Productivity Review*. 11, (Winter) 9-19.

Pattison, Diane d. (1993) Continuous process improvement at Brooktree. *Management Accounting*. (February) 69.

Paul, Bill. (1987) Coky Johnson's job is trimming inventory to help Sun Co. shine. *Wall Street Journal.* (April 20) 1,7.

Paul, William J., Jr., Keith B. Robertson, and Frederick Herzberg. (1969) Job enrichment pays off. *Harvard Business Review.* 47, (March-April) 61-78.

Pava, C. (1983) *Managing New Office Technology—An Organizational Strategy.* New York: Free Press. (*2)

Pavitt, K. (1984) Sectoral patterns of technical change: Toward a taxonomy and a theory. *Research Policy.* 13, 343-373.

Pavsidis, C. (1984) Total quality control: An overview of current efforts. *Quality Progress.* 17, (September) 28-29.

Payne, B. J. (1984) Statistical techniques in the management of quality improvement. *International Journal of Quality and Reliability Management.* 1, (March) 24-35.

Payne, Tom. (1992) Total quality: It's a good fix. *Telephone Engineer and Management.* 96, (July 1) 58. (*2)

Payoff from the new management. (1993) *Fortune.* (December 13) 103-110.

Peach Roben W. (1980) Defining hard to define customer quality expectations. *Quality Progress.* 13, (December) 14-16.

Peacore, E. J. (1975) Reliability developments AWACS. *Proceedings, Annual Reliability and Maintainability Symposium.* New York: IEEE 383-389.

Pearce, C. G. (1989) Doing something about your listening ability. *Supervisory Management.* (March) 29-34.

Pearce, C. G., R. Figgins, and S. Golen. (1984) *Principles of Business Communication.* New York: John Wiley.

Peck, M. Scott. (1978) *The Road Less Traveled: A New Psychology of Love, Traditional Values, and Spiritual Growth.* New York: Simon and Schuster.

Peck, M. Scott. (1987) *A Different Drum: Community Making and Peace.* New York: Simon and Schuster.

Pedraja, R. R. (1988) Role of quality assurance in the food industry: new concepts. *Food Technology.* 42, (December) 92.

Peeples, D. E. (1978) Measures for productivity. *Datamation.* 24, (May) 222-28.

Pefeffer, J., and Gerald R. Salancik. (1974) Organizational decision making as a political process: The case of a university budget. *Administrative Science Quarterly.* 19, (December) 135-151.

Pegels, C. Carl. (1976) *Systems Analysis for Production Operations.* New York: Gordon and Breach Science Publishers.

Pegg, J. (1985) The just-in-case mentality has to go. *Industrial Management (Canada).* 9, (June) 22-26.

Pelletier, B. P., and M. A. Rahim. (1993) Total quality management and drawbacks of incentive systems: Fact or fallacy? *Industrial Management.* 35, (January-February) 4. (*3)

Peloquin, J. J. (1980) Training: The key to productivity. *Training and Development Journal.* 34, (February) 49-52.

Pelz, C. (1952) Influence: A key to effective leadership in the first-line supervisor. *Personnel.* 29, (March) 31-38.

Pelz, C. (1957) *Motivation of the Engineering and Research Specialists.* New York: American Management Association.

Pelz, D., and D. Munson. (1980) The innovating process: A conceptual framework. Working Paper, Center for Research on Utilization of Scientific Knowledge. Ann Arbor, MI: University of Michigan.

Pelz, D., and F. Munson. (1982) Originality level and the innovating process in organizations. *Human Systems Management 3.* 173-187.

Pendeleton, W. E. (1984) Process planning optimization—The key to ZI/JIT success. Zero Inventory Philosophy and Practice Seminar Proceedings, APICS. (October).

Pennings, J. M., and F. Harianto. (1988) Innovation in an interorganizational context. In L. R. Gomez-Mejia and M. W. Lawless (Eds.) *Proceedings, Managing the High Technology Firm.* Boulder, CO: University of Colorado Press, 228-234.

Pennix, Gail B. (1987) Try a little TQC. *ARMA Records Management Quarterly.* 21, (October) 24-30.

Penrose, Edith. (1959) *The Theory of Growth of the Firm.* New York: John Wiley.

Penzias, A. (1989) *Ideas and Information: Managing in a High Tech World.* New York: W. W. Norton.

Pepper, T., E. Janow, and J. W. Wheeler. (1985) *The Competition: Dealing with Japan.* New York: Praeger.

Pereira, Armando (1987) Quality audits and international standards. *Quality Progress.* 20, (January) 27-29.

Performance appraisal and quality. (1985) *Quality Progress.* 18, (April) 12-13.

Perigord, Michel. (1992) Reussir la qualite totale. *Organizational Dynamics.* 20, (Spring) 71-72.

The perils of cutting quality. (1982) *New York Times.* (August) 22.

Perkins, D., V. Nieva, and E. Law. (1983) *Managing Creation: The Challenge of Building a New Organization.* New York: John Wiley. (*2)

Perlman, J. (1989) Devalued dollar prompts catalogers to develop new sourcing methods. *Catalog Age.* (Winter) 36-38. (*2)

Perrow, Charles. (1984) *Normal Accidents: Living with High-Risk Technologies*. New York: Basic Books.

Perrow, Charles. (1986) *Complex Organizations*. Third edition. New York: Random House.

Perry, B. (1984) *Enfield: A High Performance System*. Bedford, MA: Educational Services Development and Publishing. (*2)

Perry, John Curtis. (1980) *Beneath the Eagle's Wings: America is Occupied*. New York: Dodd, Mead.

Perry, R. L. (1973) Skip-lot sampling plans. *Journal of Quality Technology*. 5, (March) 123-130. (*2)

Perry, R. L. (1973) Two-level skip-lot sampling plans-operating characteristic properties. *Journal of Quality Technology*. 5, (October) 160-166.

Peryam, D. R. (1950) Quality control in the production of blended whesday. *Industrial Quality Control*. 7, (November) 17-21.

Peryam, D. R., and R. Shapiro. (1955) Perception, preference, judgement-clues to food quality. *Industry Quality Control*. 11, 1.

Peters, Bruce J. (1992) The quality revolution. *The Internal Auditor*. 49, (April) 20-24. (*4)

Peters, D. (1992) A new look for quality in home care. *Journal of Nursing Administration*, 22, 21-26.

Peters, J. (1970) *Tolerancing the Components of An Assembly for Minimum Cost*. New York: American Society of Mechanical Engineers.

Peters, M., and T. Oliva. (1981) *Operations and Production Management*. Boston, MA: Prindle, Weber and Schmidt.

Peters, Peter E. (1983) Axle plant Jura system and example of solving a non-quality problem. *The Juran Report*. (Winter) 77-81.

Peters, Thomas J. (1980) Management systems: The language of organizational character and competence. *Organizational Dynamics.* 3, (Summer) 15.

Peters, Thomas J. (1980) Putting excellence into management. *BusinessWeek.* (July 21) 196-205.

Peters, Thomas J. (1987) There are no excellent companies. *Fortune.* (April 27) 341. (*3)

Peters, Thomas J. (1987) *Thriving on Chaos: Handbook for a Management Revolution,* New York: Alfred A. Knopf. (*11)

Peters, Thomas J. (1991) The retooling of a nightmarish manufacturing process. *The Business Journal.* 4, (February) 16.

Peters, Thomas J. (1991) Total quality leadership: Let's get it right. *Journal for Quality and Participation.* (March) 10-15. (*2)

Peters, Thomas J. (1994) *The Pursuit of WOW!: Every Person's Guide to Topsy-Turvy Times.* New York: Vintage Books.

Peters, Thomas J., and Nancy Austin. (1985) *A Passion for Excellence: The Leadership Difference.* New York: Random House. (*5)

Peters, Thomas J., and Robert H. Waterman Jr. (1982) *In Search of Excellence: Lessons from America's Best Run Companies.* New York: Harper and Row. (*14)

Peterson, Esther. (1974) Consumerism as a retailer's asset. *Harvard Business Review.* 52, (May-June) 91-101.

Petrozzo, D. P., and J. C. Stepper. (1994) *Successful Reengineering.* New York: Van Nostrand Reinhold.

Pettigrew, Andrew M. (1973) *The Politics of Organizational Decision Making.* London, UK: Tavistock. (*2)

Pettijohn C. L. (1986) Achieving quality in the development process. *AT and T Technical Journal.* 65, (March-April) 85-93.

Petzinger, Thomas, Jr. (1981) Indiana standard continues its strategy for growth, bucking the takeover trend. *Wall Street Journal.* (December) 12.

Pfeffer, J. (1972) Merger as a response to organizational interdependence. *Administrative Science Quarterly.* 17, (January) 382-394.

Pfeffer, J., and Gerald R. Salancik. (1978) *The External Control of Organizations.* New York: Harper and Row. (*3)

Phadke, Madhav S. (1982) Quality engineering using design experiments. Proceedings of the American Statistical Association, Cincinnati. (August) 11-20.

Phadke, Madhav S. (1986) Design optimization case studies. *AT and T Technical Journal.* 65, (March-April) 51-68.

Phadke, Madhav S. (1989) *Quality Engineering Using Robust Design.* Englewood Cliffs, NJ: Prentice Hall.

Phadke, Madjav S., and Genichi Taguchi. (1984) Quality engineering through design optimization. *Proceedings of the Communications Society,* GLOBECOM 84. New York: IEEE.

Phadke, Madjav S., R. N. Kackar, D. V. Speeney, and J. M. Grieco. (1983) Off-line quality control in integrated circuit fabrication using experimental design. *Bell System Technical Journal.* 62, (May-June) 1273-1309. (*2)

Phillipp, Thomas J. (1982) Quality system concepts in the CAD/CAM era. *ASQC Annual Technical Quality Congress Transactions.* Milwaukee, WI: ASQC Quality Press, 569-573.

Phillips, G. J., and Fritz Hirschfeld. (1980) Rotating machinery bearing analysis. *Mechanical Engineering.* (July) 28-33.

Phillips, G. P. (1980) Design quality index. Internal document of the Cadillac Motor Car Division. Detroit, MI: General Motors.

Physical requirement guidelines for sensory evaluation laboratories. (1986) Philadelphia, PA: American Society for Testing and Materials.

Pickard, Jane. (1992) Job evaluation and total quality management come under fire. *Personnel Management.* 24, (May) 17.

Pickard, Jane. (1992) W. Edwards Deming. *Personnel Management.* 24, (June) 23.

Picking up the pace: The commercial challenge to American innovation. (1989) Booklet published by the Council on Competitiveness.

Piepel, G. F., and J. A. Cornell. (1985) Models for mixture experiments when the response depends on the total amount. *Technometrics.* 27, (May) 219-227.

Pierce, Richard J. (1986) *Involvement Engineering: Engaging Employees in Quality and Productivity.* Milwaukee, WI: ASQC Quality Press. (*2)

Pilgrim, A. (1983) Bar codes in industry. *Quality.* (March) 14-15.

Pilgrim, A. (1985) Talking to computers. *Quality.* (November) 28-29.

Pinchot, Gifford. (1985) *Entrepreneuring.* New York: Harper and Row.

Pinder, C. (1984) *Work Motivation.* Glenview, Il: Scott, Foresman. (*2)

Pines, Ellis. (1990) The gurus of TQM: After years of neglect, TQM thinkers now have an audience. *Aviation Week and Space Technology.* (May 21) 29-33. (*3)

Pinskey, Paul D. (1983) *Statpro, The Statistics and Graphics Database Workstation.* Boston, MA: Wadsworth Electronic Publishing Company.

Piori, J. (1982) Why unions don't work anymore. *Inc.* (March) 16-17.

Pipkin, F. M., and R. C. Ritter. (1983) Precision measurements and fundamental constants. *Science.* 29, (February 25) 913-921.

Pipp, F. J. (1981) The new lean, mean Xerox. *BusinessWeek.* 12, (October) 126-32.

Pipp, F. J. (1983) Management commitment to quality: Xerox. *Corporation Quality Progress.* 16, (August) 12-17.

Pirsig, Robert M. (1974) *Zen and the Art of Motorcycle Maintenance: An Inquiry into Values.* New York: William Morrow. (*4)

Pirsig, Robert M. (1976) *SPC and Continuous Improvement.* New York: William Morrow.

Pisano, Daniel J., Jr. (1987) Replanning the product development process. Proceedings of the Fourth Annual Conference on Quality Improvement.

Pitt, Hy. (1994) *SPC for the Rest of Us.* Reading, MA: Addison-Wesley.

Piturro, Marlene C. (1989) Employee performance monitoring . . . Or meddling? *Management Review.* (May 19) 31-33.

Placek, Chester. (1990) CMMs in automation. *Quality.* (March) 28-38.

Plackett, R. L., and J. P. Burman. (1946) The design of optimum multifactorial experiments. *Biometrika.* 33, (1) 305-325.

Plaistowe, Ian. (1992) Reputations at stake in the pursuit of quality. *Accountancy.* 110, (August) 11. (*2)

Plan for productivity/quality improvement, commercial division. (1980) *Sperry-Vickers Corporation.* (July) 9-24.

Plank, R. P. (1948) A rational method for grading food quality. *Food Technology*. 2, 241.

Platt, W. (1931) Scoring food products. *Food Industry*. 3, 108.

Plisher, Emily S. (1992) Seeking recognition: U.S. auditors build their base. *Chemical Week*. (November 11) 30-33.

PLMS. (1978) Pricing high-quality products. *The PLMSletter*. Cambridge, MA: The Strategic Planning Institute.

Plossl, G. W. (1971) How much inventory is enough? Production and inventory management. *APICS Journal*. (Second Quarter) 21-26. (*2)

Plossl, G. W. (1972) *MRP and Inventory Record Accuracy*. Decatur, GA: G. W. Plossl and Company. (*2)

Plossl, G. W. (1973) Getting the most from forecasts. Production and inventory management. *APICS Journal*. (First Quarter) 31-38. (*2)

Plossl, G. W., and O. W. Wight. (1967) *Production and Inventory Control: Principles and Techniques*. Englewood Cliffs, NJ: Prentice-Hall. (*2)

Plsek, P. E. (1987) Defining quality at the marketing/development interface. *Quality Progress*. 20, (June) 28-36.

Plsek. P. E. (1992) Introduction to control charts. *Quality Management in Health Care*. 1, (January) 65-74.

Plum. Kathryn S. (1987) A success story. *Quality Progress*. 20, (January) 32-34.

Plunkett, Lorne C., and Guy A. Hale. (1982) *The Proactive Manager: The Complete Book of Problem-Solving and Decision-Making*. New York: John Wiley.

Pocock, S. J. (1977) Group Sequential methods in the design and analysis of clinical trials. *Biometrika*. 64, (2) 191-199.

Polakoff, Joel C. (1987) Inventory accuracy: getting back to basics. *Management Review.* 76, (November) 44-46.

Poore, B. P. (1886) *Perly's Reminiscences.* Philadelphia, PA: Hubbard Brothers.

Pope, N. W. (1979) Mickey Mouse marketing. *American Banker.* (July) 167-168. (*2)

Port, Otis. (1987) The push for quality. *BusinessWeek.* (June 8) 130-135.

Port, Otis. (1988) Developments to watch. *BusinessWeek.* (December 12) 82. (*2)

Port, Otis. (1989) Psst? Want a secret for making superproducts? *BusinessWeek.* (October 2) 106-110.

Port, Otis. (1989) The best-engineered part is no part at all. *BusinessWeek.* (May 8) 150.

Port, Otis. (1992) Quality: Small and midsize companies seize the challenge—Not a moment too soon. *BusinessWeek.* (November 30) 66. (*3)

Port, Otis and Geoffrey Smith. (1992) Beg, borrow—And benchmark. *BusinessWeek.* (November 30) 74. (*2)

Portable gage lab provides flexibility and minimizes downtime. (1971) *Quality Management and Engineering.* (November) 23.

Porter, David B., Megan E. Bird, and Arthur Wunder. (1990-91) Competition, cooperation, satisfaction and the performance of complex tasks among Air Force Cadets. *Current Psychology: Research and Reviews.* 9, (Winter) 347-354. (*2)

Porter, Michael E. (1976) Please note location of nearest exit: Exit barriers and planning. *California Management Review.* 19, (Winter) 21-33.

Porter, Michael E. (1980) *Competitive Strategy: Techniques for Analyzing Industries and Competitors.* New York: Free Press. (*7)

Porter, Michael E. (1985) *Competitive Advantage: Creating and Sustaining Superior Performance.* New York: Free Press. (*7)

Porter, Michael E. (1986) *Competition in Global Industries.* Cambridge, MA: Harvard Business School Press.

Porter, Michael E. (1987) From competitive advantage to corporate strategy. *Harvard Business Review.* 65, (May-June) 43-59.

Porter, Michael E. (1990) *The Competitive Advantage of Nations.* New York: Free Press. (*2)

Porter, Michael E. (1992) Capital disadvantage: America's failing capital investment system. *Harvard Business Review.* 70, (September-October) 65-83.

Porter, Michael E., and V. Millar. (1985) How information gives you competitive advantage. *Harvard Business Review.* 63, (July-August) 149-159.

Posesorski, Sherrie. (1985) Here's how to put statistical process control to work for you. *Canadian Business.* (December) 163.

Posner, Bruce G. (1986) How to stop worrying and love the next recession. *Inc.* (April) 89-95.

Pounds, R. L., and R. Bryner. (1967) *The School in American Society.* New York: Macmillan. (*2)

Pounds, W. E. (1969) The process of problem finding. *Industrial Management Review.* 11, (Fall) 1-19.

Pournille, Jerry. (1986) The information revolution. Byte, problem/solution cross reference. *Quality.* (April) 15-25.

Powell, Gary N. (1990) One more time: Do female and male managers differ? *Academy of Management Executives.* 4, (January) 68-75. (*2)

Powell, Richard F. (1970) Analyzing and interpreting field failure data. *Proceedings, Annual Symposium on Reliability and Maintainability*. New York: IEEE, 94-100.

Power, Elizabeth. (1992) Basic TQM tools and the management of multiple personality disorder. In Harry Ivan Costin (Ed.) *Readings in Total Quality Management*. (1994) Fort Worth, TX: Dryden Press, 369-375.

Power, Elizabeth. (1992) *Managing Our Selves: Building A Community of Caring*. Nashville: Power and Associates.

Powers, J. J., and V. N. M. Rao. (1985) Computerization of the quality assurance program. *Food Technology*. 39, (November) 136.

Powers, J. J., D. R. Godwin, and R. E. Bargmann. (1977) Relations between sensory and objective measurements for quality evaluation of green beans. In R. A. Scanlon (Ed.) *Flavor Quality-Objective Measurement*. Washington, DC: American Chemical Society.

Powers, Thomas L. (1988) Identify and fulfill customer service expectations. *Industrial Marketing Management*. 17, (November) 273-276.

Powers, William. (1973) *Behavior: The Control of Perception*. Chicago, IL: Aldine Book Company.

Poza, Ernesto J. (1983) A do it yourself guide to group problem solving. *Personnel*. 60, (March-April) 69-77.

Poza, Ernesto J., and M. L. Markus. (1980) Success story: The team approach to work restructuring. *Organizational Dynamics*. 3, (March) 3-25.

Prahalad, C. K., and Gary Hamel. (1990) The core competence of the corporation. *Harvard Business Review*. 68, (May-June) 79. (*2)

Prairie, R. R., and W. J. Zimmer. (1973) Graphs, tables and discussion to aid in the design and evaluation of an acceptance sampling procedure based on cumulative sums. *Journal of Quality Technology*. 5, (April) 58-66.

Pranzag, L. (1963) Sampling procedures based on prior distributions and costs. *Technometrics.* 6, (June) 547-561.

Pranzag, L. (1970) The efficiency of sequential sampling plans based on prior distributions and costs. *Technometrics.* 12, (July) 299-310.

Pratt, W. K. (1978) *Digital Image Processing.* New York: John Wiley.

President's Commission Report on the Challenger. (1986) Report to the President by the Presidential Commission on the Space Shuttle *Challenger* Accident. Washington, D.C.

Prestowitz, C. V. (1988) *Trading Places: How We Allowed Japan to Take the Lead.* New York: Basic Books.

Price, F. (1984) *Right First Time.* Aldershot, UK: Gower Press. (*2)

Pricing of products is still an art. (1981) *Wall Street Journal.* (November) 25, 33.

Priestman, S. (1985) SQC and JIT: Partnership in quality. *Quality Progress.* 18, (May) 31-34.

Prince, G. (1970) *The Practice of Creativity.* New York: Harper and Row.

Pringle's vs the real thing (1975) *New York Times.* (November 30) 9.

The problem of being premium. (1978) *Forbes.* 56-57.

Procter and Gamble rewrites the marketing rules. (1989) *Fortune.* (November 6) 91.

Proctor, B. H. (1986) A sociotechnical work-design system at Digital Enfield: Utilizing untapped resources. *National Productivity Review.* 5, (Summer) 262-270.

Productivity and employment: Challenges for the 1990s. (1989) International Productivity Symposium III. (April 10-13)

Washington, DC: U.S. Department of Labor, Bureau of Labor-Management Relations and Cooperative Programs.

The productivity paradox. (1988) *BusinessWeek.* (June 6) 33-34. (*3)

Prokesch, Steven. (1986) Employees go to the rescue: Labor policy aids Miller Furniture. *New York Times.* (August 14) D1, D6.

Proske, Robert J. (1992) The quality quandary. *Financial Executive.* 8, (May-June) 35. (*2)

Provost, Lloyd P., and R. S. Elder. (1983) Cost-effective laboratory quality control. *ASQC Annual Technical Quality Congress Transactions.* Milwaukee, WI: ASQC Quality Press, 496-502.

Prowse, M. (1992) Is America in decline? *Harvard Business Review.* 60, (July-August) 162.

Pucik, Vladimir and Nina Hatvany. (1988) Management practices in Japan and their impact on business strategy. In Henry Mintzberg and James Brian Quinn (Eds.). *The Strategy Process: Concepts, Contexts and Cases.* Second edition. Englewood Cliffs, NJ: Prentice-Hall.

Pucik, Vladimir, Noel M. Tichy, and Carole K. Barnett (Eds.). (1992) *Globalizing Management: Creating and Leading the Competitive Organization.* New York: John Wiley.

Pugh, A. (1983) *Robot Vision.* New York: Springer-Verlag.

Pul-eeze! Will somebody help me? (1987) *Time.* (February 2) 98-116.

Purcell, Warren R. (1968) Sampling techniques in quality systems audits. *Quality Progress.* 1, (October) 13-16.

Puri, S. C., and J. R. McWhinnie. (1981) *Quality Management Through Quality Indicators: A New Approach. Quality Assurance: Methods, Management and Motivation.* Dearborn, MI: Society of Manufacturing Engineers, 34-40. (*2)

The push for quality. (1987) *BusinessWeek.* (June 8) 131.

Putnam, A. O. (1985) A redesign for engineering. *Harvard Business Review*. 63, (May-June) 139-144.

Putnam, A. O., E. R. Barlow, and G. N. Stilian. (1963) *Unified Operations Management*. New York: McGraw-Hill. (*2)

Pyhrr, Peter A. (1973) *Zero-Based Budgeting: A Practical Management Tool for Evaluating Expense*. New York: John Wiley.

Pyzdek, Thomas. (1976) The impact of quality cost reductions on profits. *Quality Progress*. 9, (November) 14-15.

Pyzdek, Thomas. (1984) *An SPQ Primer*. Milwaukee, WI: ASQC Quality Press. (*2)

Pyzdek, Thomas. (1984) *An SPQ Primer: Programmed Learning Guide to Statistical Process Control*. Tucson, AZ: Quality America. (*2)

Pyzdek, Thomas. (1986) *Certified Quality Engineer Examination Study Guide*. Tucson, AZ: Quality America.

Pyzdek, Thomas. (1989) *Pydzek's Guide to SPC*. Tucson, AZ: Quality America.

QC circle activities and the suggestion system. (1982) *Japan Labor Bulletin*. (January) 5-8.

Quality illustrated. (1985) *Brochure*. Milwaukee, WI: ASQC Quality Press.

The quality imperative. (1991) *BusinessWeek*. (October 25) 4, 7, 10, 38, 73 and 95.

Quality and productivity: America's revitalization. (1982) *BusinessWeek*. (November) 19-30.

Quality circle boom part of growing American trend. (1981) *Supervision*. (September) 8-11.

Quality management programs set; federation seminars focus on TQM, gauge measurement topics. (1992) *American Paint Coatings Journal*. (May 25) 14. (*2)

Quality management spotlighted at AGC convention. (1992) *Building Design and Construction*. (May) 17. (*2)

Quality plan, pay changes linked in study. (1992) *Pensions and Investments*. (November 9) 37. (*2)

Quality representative-certified vendor representative. (1981) *Quality*. (August) Q3-Q4.

Quality review standards interpretations. (1992) *Journal of Accountancy*. (July) 138. (*2)

Quality: A road to profits. (1993) *Agency Sales Magazine*. (January) 58. (*2)

Quality: The U.S. drives to catch up. (1982) *BusinessWeek*. (November) 66-80.

Quenouille, M. H. (1959) *Rapid Statistical Calculations*. Chicago, IL: Hafner Publishing Company.

Quest for quality. (1989) *Electronics Business Magazine Special Issue*. 15, (October 16).

Quible, Zane K. (1981) Quality circles: A well rounded approach to employee involvement. *Management World*. 10, (September) 10-11.

Quigley, Carroll. (1961) *The Evolution of Civilizations*. New York: Macmillan. (*2)

Quinby, E. (1970) Advanced requirements planning system cuts inventory costs, improves work flow. Production and inventory management. *APICS Journal*. (Third Quarter) 50-63. (*2)

Quinn, James Brian. (1977) Strategic goals: Process and politics. *Sloan Management Review*. 18, (Fall) 26. (*2)

Quinn, James Brian. (1979) Technological innovation, entrepreneurship and strategy. *Sloan Management Review.* 20, (Spring) 25. (*2)

Quinn, James Brian. (1980) *Strategies for Change.* Homewood, IL: Irwin. (*4)

Quinn, James Brian. (1981) Formulating strategy one step at a time. *Journal of Business Strategy.* (Winter) 57-59. (*2)

Quinn, James Brian. (1987) How to gain the JIT advantage. *Traffic Management.* (March) 39-52.

Quinn, James Brian. (1987) How to make just-in-time work for you. *Traffic Management.* (February) 40-52.

Rabushka, A. (1985) *From Adam Smith to the Wealth of America.* New Brunswick, NJ: Transaction Books.

Race for computerized booking systems is heating up among European airlines. (1988) *Wall Street Journal.* (December 1) B3.

Radcliffe College. (1987) *Project on Interdependence.* Cambridge, MA: Radcliffe College .

Radford, G. S. (1917) The control of quality. *Engineering Magazine.* (October) 9-12.

Radford, G. S. (1922) *The Control of Quality in Manufacturing.* New York: Ronald Press. (*4)

Radigan, R. A., and J. J. Zeccardi. (1976) Auditing systems which affect product quality. *ASQC Annual Technical Quality Congress Transactions.* Milwaukee, WI: ASQC Quality Press, 323-329.

Raelin, J., C. K. Sholl, and D. Leonard. (1985) Why professionals turn sour and what to do. *Personnel.* 62, (October) 28-41.

Raelin, J. (1985) The basis for the professional's resistance to managerial control. *Human Resource Management.* 24, (Spring/Summer) 147-176.

Raelin, J. (1987) Two track plans for one track careers. *Personnel Journal.* 1, (January) 96-101.

Raff, D. M. G. (1984) Making cars and making money in the interwar automobile industry: The manufacturing that stood behind the marketing. Unpublished paper.

Raheja, Dev. (1981) Failure mode and effects analysis: Uses and misuses. *ASQC Annual Technical Quality Congress Transactions.* Milwaukee, WI: ASQC Quality Press, 374-379.

Raheja, Dev. (1982) Fault tree analysis: How are we doing? *ASQC Annual Technical Quality Congress Transactions.* Milwaukee, WI: ASQC Quality Press, 355-359.

Raia, E. (1986) Just-in-time USA. *Purchasing.* 100, (March) 48-62.

Raktoe, B. L., A. Hedayat, and W. T. Federer. (1981) *Factorial Designs Jobs.* New York: John Wiley.

Ramaswamy, C. V. (1981) How good are you as a fabrication inspector? *PHEL.* (January) 8-10.

Ramberg, John S., Edward J. Dudewicz, Pandu R. Tadikamalla, and Edward F. Mykytka. (1979) A probability distribution and its uses in fitting data. *Technometrics.* 21, (February) 201-214.

Raming, P. F. (1983) Applications of the analysis of means. *Journal of Quality Technology.* 15, (January) 19-25.

Rampey, J., and Harry V. Roberts. (1992) Core body of knowledge working council: Perspectives on total quality. In *Report of the Total Quality Leadership Steering Committee and Working Councils.* Cincinnati, OH: Procter and Gamble (November) 2-2.

Ramquist, J. (1982) Labor-management cooperation: The Scanlon Plan at work. *Sloan Management Review.* 23, (Spring) 49-55.

Rand, Christopher. (1975) *Making Democracy Safe for Oil.* Boston, MA: Atlantic Monthly Press.

Randall, R. (1973) Job enrichment savings at Travelers. *Management Accounting*. 51, (January) 68-69, 72.

Randall, R. (1991) Results of quality function deployment as applied to focal plane arrays. Presented at 1991 Conference on the Producibility of Infrared Focal Plane Array Assemblies.

Ranganathan, J., and B. K. Kale. (1983) Outlier resistant tolerance intervals for exponential distributions. *American Journal of Mathematical and Management Sciences*. 3, (January) 5-25.

Rankin, Stewart C. (1992) Total quality management: Implications of educational assessment. *NASSP Bulletin*. 76, (September) 66. (*3)

Ranky, Paul. (1983) *The Design and Operation of Flexible Manufacturing Systems*. New York: Elsevier Science Publishing.

Rategan, Cathie. (1992) Total quality management. *Journal of Property Management*. 57, (September-October) 32. (*2)

Rau, Sri Y. R. (1981) Development of vendor quality control. *BHEL Quality Journal*. New Delhi: Bharat Heavy Electricals, Limited. 3-6.

Raudsepp, E. (1981) *How Creative Are You?* New York: Putnam.

Rawcliffe, R. H., and R. L. Randall. (1989) Concurrent engineering applied to an SDIO technology program. AIAA/ADPA/NSIA First National TQM Symposium, 89-3191, November.

Ray, M., and R. Myers. (1989) *Creativity in Business*. Garden City, NY: Doubleday.

Rayner, Bruce C. P. (1989) The Pentagon revives its interest in quality. *Electronic Business*. 15, (October 16) 149-150.

Rayner, Bruce C. P. (1990) Market-driven quality: IBM's six sigma crusade. Special report, Commitment to Quality. *Electronic Business*. 16, (October 15) 22-27.

Raynor, Michael E. (1992) Quality as a strategic weapon. *Journal of Business Strategy*. 13, (September-October) 3. (*2)

Raynor, Michael E. (1993) ISO certification. *Quality*. (May) 44-45.

Rea, John. (1981) *Nissan-Datsun: A History of the Nissan Motor Corporation in the U.S.A., 1960-80.* New York: McGraw-Hill.

Read, W. H. (1962) Upward communication in industrial hierarchies. *Human Relations*. 15, (February) 3-15.

Reark, Robert. (1989) Electronic mail speeds business communication. *Small Business Reports*. 14, (February) 73-77.

Rebuilding America: Start at the factory. (1988) *Wall Street Journal*. (May) 1.

Rechtschaffner, R. (1967) Saturated fractions of the second and third factorial designs. *Technometrics*. 9, (August) 569-575.

Recommended Practice for Sampling Industrial Chemicals. (1981) Philadelphia, PA: American Society for Testing and Materials.

Reddy, J. (1980) Incorporating quality in competitive strategies. *Sloan Management Review*. 21, (Spring) 53-60. (*2)

Reddy, J. (1983) Three essentials of product quality. *Harvard Business Review*. 61, (July-August) 153-159.

Reddy, W. Brendan, and Kaleel Jamison (Eds.). (1988) *Team Building, Blueprints for Productivity and Satisfaction.* San Diego, CA: NTL Institute for Applied Behavioral Science and University Associates.

Reece, R. N. (1979) A quality assurance perspective of sensory evaluation. *Food Technology*. 33, (September) 37.

Reed, Thomas W., and Mark R. Olson. (1982) Circle quality-Members remembered. IAQC Fourth Annual Conference Transactions. Cincinnati, OH: International Association of Quality Circles.

Rees, A. (1979) Improving the concepts and techniques of productivity measurements. *Monthly Labor Review.* 102, (September) 23-27.

Refashioning IBM: Don't just stand there, listen to something. (1990) *The Economist.* (November 17) 21-24.

Regis, Lesley. (1993) Driving quality up and cycle time down with design of experiment. *Industrial Engineering.* 25, (February) 54. (*3)

Rehder, Robert R. (1981) Japans' synergistic society: How it works and its implications for the United States. *Management Review.* 70, (October) 64-66.

Rehder, Robert R. (1981) What American and Japanese managers are learning from each other. *Business Horizons.* 24, (March-April) 63-70.

Rehder, Robert R., and Faith Ralston. (1984) Total quality management: A revolutionary management philosophy. *SAM Advanced Management Journal.* 49, (Summer) 24-33.

Rehder, Robert R., and Marta Smith. (1986) *Kaisen* and the art of labor relations. *Personnel Journal.* 65, (December) 83-93. (*2)

Reich, Cary. (1985) The innovator. *New York Times Magazine.* (April 21) 29. (*2)

Reich, Robert B. (1983) *The Next American Frontier.* New York: Times Books. (*5)

Reich, Robert B. (1985) The executive's new clothes. *New Republic.* (May) 23-28.

Reich, Robert B. (1987) *Tales of a New America.* New York: Times Books. (*3)

Reich, Robert B. (1991) *The Work of Nations.* New York: Random House. (*2)

Reich, Robert B., and John Donahue. (1985) *New Deals: The Chrysler Revival and the American System.* New York: Time Books.

Reichauer, Edwin. (1977) *The Japanese.* Cambridge: Harvard University Press.

Reichheld, F. F., and W. Earl Sasser Jr. (1990) Zero defections: Quality comes to services. *Harvard Business Review.* 78, (September-October) 105-111.

Reid, Laura. (1982) Nashua: Using statistics to solve hidden problems. *The Financial Times of Canada.* (November 22) 11-13.

Reid, Leigh. (1992) Continuous improvement through process management. *Management Accounting (USA).* 74, (September) 37. (*2)

Reid, P. C. (1989) How Harley beat back the Japanese. *Fortune.* (September 25) 24-31.

Reid, P. C. (1990) *Well Made in America: Lessons From Harley-Davidson on Being the Best.* New York: McGraw-Hill.

Reid, T. R. (1984) *The Chip.* New York: Simon and Schuster.

Reiff, Henry E. (1978) Practical application of the Duane reliability growth model. *Automotive Division Newsletter, American Society for Quality Control.* (January) 5-7.

Reiker, Wayne S., and Shaun J. Sullivan. (1981) Can the effectiveness of QC circles be measured. *Quality Circles Journal.* 4, (May) 29-31.

Reilly, Robert F. (1981) Developing a sales forecasting system. *Managerial Planning.* (July-August) 24-30.

Reimann, Curt W. (1990) America unites behind the Baldrige quality crusade. *Electronic Business.* 16, (October 15) 63.

Reimann, Curt W. (1991) Winning strategies for quality improvement. *Business America.* (March 25) 8-11. (*2)

Reischauer, Edwin. O. (1970) *The United States and Japan.* Cambridge, MA: Harvard University Press.

Reischauer, Edwin O. (1977) *The Japanese.* Cambridge, MA: Harvard and University Press.

Reischauer, Edwin O. (1988) *The Japanese Today: Change and Continuity.* Cambridge, MA: Harvard University Press.

Remboldt, Ulrich, Mahesh K. Seth, and Jeremy Weinstein. (1977) *Computers in Manufacturing.* New York: Marcel Dekker.

Rendall, Elaine. (1981) Quality circles: A third wave intervention. *Training and Development Journal.* 35, (March) 28-31.

Rendall, Elaine and Marjorie Maser. (1980) Using quality circles in the health service. *Human Resource Development.* 4, (June) 12-14.

Render, Barry and R. Stair. (1985) *Quantitative Analysis for Management.* Boston, MA: Allyn and Bacon.

Renna, Vincent F and Harry P. Howard. (1979) New product development-quality assurance system approach. *ASQC Annual Technical Quality Congress Transactions.* Milwaukee, WI: ASQC Quality Press, 848-856.

Rennie, D., W. Morris, and K. Blackburn. (1978) Quality assurance: The modern concept of the third party inspection. *Proceedings, International Conference on Quality Control.* Tokyo: JUSE. C1-27 through C1-32.

Renolds, Larry. (1988) Labor's leaders changing to meet the times. *Management Review.* 77, (February) 11-16.

Report on the survey of labor-management consultation systems at work as of 1980. (1981) *Japan Productivity Center.* (April) 21-28.

Resnick-West, Susan M. (1985) Pride in Xerox: A study of employee attitudes and morale. Technical Report. El Segundo: Xerox Corporation.

Resnick-West, Susan M., and Mary Ann Von Glinow. (1989) *Beyond the Clash: Managing High Tech Professionals*. Cambridge, MA: Ballinger.

Responsiveness to customers drives curriculum changes. (1992) *Newsline*. American Assembly of Collegiate Schools of Business (Summer) 15.

Rethinking IBM. (1993) *BusinessWeek*. (October 4) 88-89.

Retraining/adjustment data. (1986) *New York Times*. (August) 10.

Reuther, Victor. (1976) *The Brothers Reuther and the Story of the UAW*. Boston, MA: Houghton Mifflin.

ReVelle, J. B. (1988) *The New Quality Technology*. Los Angeles: Hughes Aircraft Company.

The revenge of Big Yellow. (1990) *The Economist*. (November 10) 77-78.

The revival of productivity. (1984) *BusinessWeek*. (February 13) 27.

Revolutionize your company. (1993) *Fortune*. (December 13) 114-118.

Reynolds, Larry. (1992) The feds join the quality movement. *Management Review*. 81, (April) 39-40.

Rhodes, Lewis A. (1992) On the road to quality. *Educational Leadership*. 49, (Issue 6, March) 76-80.

Rhodes, Lucien and Cathryn Jacobson. (1981) Small companies: America's hope for the 80's. *Inc*. (April) 44. (*2)

Riccio, Lucius J. (1984) Management science in New York's Department of Sanitation. *Interfaces*. 14, (March-April) 1-13.

Riccio, Lucius J. (1987) Sweeping changes at NYC sanitation. *Management Review*. 76, (May) 46-50.

Rice, A. K. (1958) *Productivity and Social Organizations: The Ahmedabad Experiment.* London, UK: Tavistock Publications, Ltd.

Rice, J. W., and T. Yoshikawa. (1982) A comparison on *Kanban* and MRP concepts of repetitive manufacturing systems. *Production and Inventory Management.* 23, (First Quarter) 1-13.

Rice, Judy. (1992-1993) Cascaded training at Hughes Aircraft helps ensure continuous measurable improvement. *National Productivity Review.* 11, (Winter) 111-116.

Rich, Barrett G., O. A. Smith, and Lee Korte. (1967) *Experience with a Formal Reliability Program.* Warrendale, PA: Society of Automotive Engineers.

Rich, H. (1975) The impact of material shortages on purchasing organization. *Journal of Purchasing.* 11, 13-17.

Richard, William C. (1948) *The Last Billionaire: Henry Ford.* New York: Scribners.

Richardson, Hugh W. (1981) Designing for customer setup. *Quality.* (October) 62-65.

Richardson, John H. (1983) Manpower and material overlooked elements of productivity. *Production Engineering.* 30, (August) 30-31.

Richman, Tom. (1986) Talking cost. *Inc.* (February) 105-108.

Richman, Tom. (1990) The language of business. *Inc.* (February) 41-50.

Richman, Tom and C. Koontz. (1993) How benchmarking can improve business process reengineering. *Planning Review.* 21, (No. 6) 26-27.

Rider, G. (1973) Performance review: A mixed bag. *Harvard Business Review.* 51, (July-August) 61-67.

Riding, Alan. (1978) Mexico's oil man proved his point. *New York Times*. (July) F5.

Riehl, Julian W. (1988) Planning for total quality: The information technology component. *SAM Advanced Management Journal*. 53 (Autumn) 13-19.

Rieker, Wayne S. (1976) What is the Lockheed quality control circle program. *ASQC Annual Technical Quality Congress Transactions*. Milwaukee, WI: ASQC Quality Press, 101-106.

Rieker, Wayne S. (1979) The QC circle phenomenon: An update. *ASQC Annual Technical Quality Congress Transactions*. Milwaukee, WI: ASQC Quality Press, 201-206.

Rieker, Wayne S. (1980) Management's role in QC circles. IAQC Second Annual Conference Transactions. (February). Cincinnati, OH: International Association of Quality Circles.

Riesman, David and Evelyn Riesman Thompson. (1967) *Conversations With the Japanese*. New York: Basic Books.

Riesz, P. C. (1979) Price-quality correlations for packaged food products. *Journal of Consumer Affairs*. (Winter) 244. (*2)

Rifkin, G. (1991) Pursuing zero defects under the six sigma. *New York Times*. (January 1) 1-5.

Riggan (1985) Employment security revisited in the 80's. *Personnel Administrator*. (December) 67-74.

Riggs, H. E. (1983) *Managing High-Technology Companies*. Belmont, CA: Lifetime Learning Publications. (*2)

Riggs, J. L. (1981) *Production Systems: Planning, Analysis, and Control*. New York: John Wiley. (*2)

Riley, F. D. (1979) Visual inspection. Time and distance method. *ASQC Annual Technical Quality Congress Transactions*. Milwaukee, WI: ASQC Quality Press, 483-490.

Rimondi, G., G. Tavazza, and U. Turello. (1976) Numerical simulation techniques in the tolerance settlement of product qualitative characteristics. *EOQC Quality*. (May) 19-26.

Ringle, M. (1981) The America who remade—Made in Japan. *Nations Business.* 69, 67-70. (*2)

Ris, Cindy. (1980) Big jam is watching at RMI Company and its workers like it just fine. *Wall Street Journal.* (August) 15.

Risen, James. (1986) GM taking back seat to rival Ford. *Los Angeles Times*. (December 6) . (*2)

Risen, James. (1989) GM's revolution in auto design. *Los Angeles Times*. (April 2) 1. (*2)

Ritter, Diane. (1991) *Education and Total Quality Management . . . A Resource Guide.* Methuen, MA: Goal/QPC.

Ritti, R. R., and R. Funkhouser. (1982) *The Ropes to Skip and the Ropes to Know.* Columbus, OH: Grid. (*2)

Robbins, K. (1973) *The Eclipse of a Great Power.* New York: Longman.

Robenstein, S. (1989) Don't fear the team, join it. *New York Times.* (June 11) 3, 2.

Roberts, Edward B (1978) Managing new technical ventures. *Technology, Innovation and Corporate Strategy: A Special Executive Seminar*. Cambridge, MA: Industrial Liaison Program, MIT, 121-122.

Roberts, G. W. (1983) *Quality Assurance in Research and Development*. New York: Marcel Dekker.

Roberts, Harry V., and Bernard F. Sergesketter. (1993) *Quality Is Personal: A Foundation for Total Quality Management*. New York: Free Press.

Roberts, K. H., and D. M. Rousseau. (1989) Research in nearly failure free, high reliability organizations: Having the bubble. *IEEE Transactions on Engineering Management*. 36, 132-139.

Roberts, K. H., J. Halpern, and S. Stout. (1988) Decision making in high reliability organizations: Four tensions. Working Paper, Univ. of California, Berkeley.

Roberts, Mary Lou. (1994) Becoming customer oriented. In Harry Ivan Costin (Ed.) *Readings in Total Quality Management*. (1994) Fort Worth, TX: Dryden Press, 305-319.

Roberts, Nancy. (1978) Teaching dynamic feedback systems thinking: An elementary view. *Management Science*. 24, (April) 27-36.

Robertson, James A. (1969) Analyzing field failure. *Quality Progress*. 2, (January) 12-13.

Robie, Richard S. (1996) Is your organization spooked by ghostly team performances? *Quality Progress*. 30, (May) 98-101.

Robinson, A. L. (1983) Using time to measure length. *Science*. 29, (June 24) 1367.

Robotics. (1983) *International Management*. (March) 31-36.

Robson, M. (1982) *Quality Circles: A Practical Guide*. Aldershot, UK: Gower Press.

Rockart, John F. (1973) An approach to productivity in two knowledge-based industries. *Sloan Management Review*. 15, (Fall) 23-33.

Rockart, John F. (1979) Chief executives define their own data needs. *Harvard Business Review*. 57, (March-April) 81-93. (*2)

Rodgers, T. J. (1990) No excuses management. *Harvard Business Review*. 78, (July-August) 91.

Roe, J. (1982) In-cycle gauging: A new concept in component size control. *Sixth International Conference on Automated Inspection and Product Control*. Bedford, UK: IFS Publications, 17-28.

Roemer, M. R., and J. W. Friedman. (1971) *Doctors in Hospitals: Medical Staff Organization and Hospital Performance,* Baltimore, MD: Johns Hopkins Press.

Roethlisberger, Fritz J. (1945) The foreman: Master and victim of double talk. *Harvard Business Review.* 23, (Spring) 283-98. (*2)

Roethlisberger, Fritz J., and William J. Dixon, with Harold A. Wright. (1939) *Management and the Worker: An Account of a Research Program Conducted by the Western Electric Company, Hawthorne Works, Chicago, IL.* Cambridge, MA: Harvard University Press. (*5)

Rogan, Helen. (1984) Top women executives find path to power strewn with hurdles. *Wall Street Journal.* (October 25) 35.

Rogers, Carl. (1951) *Client Centered Therapy.* Boston, MA: Houghton Mifflin.

Rogers, Carl. (1983) *Freedom to Learn for the '80's.* New York: Macmillan.

Rogers, Everett M. (1982) *Diffusion of Innovations.* New York: Free Press. (*2)

Rogers, Everett M. (1986) *Communication Technology: The New Media Society.* New York: Free Press.

Rogers, Everett M., and J. K. Larsen. (1984) *Silicon Valley Fever: Growth of High Technology Culture.* New York: Basic Books. (*2)

Rogers, Everett M., and T. Valente. (1988) Technology transfer in high technology industries. Paper Presented at the Second Annual International Business Education and Research Program (IBEAR) Research Conference, University of Southern California. (April 7-9). (*2)

Rogers, Harry G. (1991) Practicing what we preach. *The Canadian Business Review.* 18, (Winter) 16-18.

Rogers, W. T. (1962) Total quality control in an integrated steel plant. *ASQC Annual Technical Quality Congress Transactions.* Milwaukee, WI: ASQC Quality Press, 481-491.

Rohan, M. (1987) Bosses—Who needs 'Em? *Industry Week.* (February 2) 15. (*2)

Rohan, T. M. (1983) Quality or junk? Facing up to the problem. *Industry Week.* (December 12) 72-79.

Rohan, T. M. (1989) Sermons fall on deaf ears. *Industry Week.* (November 20) 35.

Rohlen, T. P. (1979) *For Harmony and Strength.* Berkeley, CA: University of California Press.

Rohlen, T. P. (1983) *Japan's High Schools.* Berkeley, CA: University of California Press. (*2)

Rokeach, M. (1960) *The Open and Closed Mind.* New York: Basic Books.

Rolland, I., and R. Janson. (1981) Total involvement as a productivity strategy. *California Management Review.* 24, (Winter) 40-48. (*2)

Rome Air Development Center. (1982) *RADC Testability Notebook.* Document number AD-A118881L. Springfield, VA: National Technical Information Service (NTIS).

Rome Air Development Center. (1983) *The Evolution and Practical Applications of Failure Modes and Effects Analyses.* Document number AD-A118881H. Springfield, VA: NTIS.

Romo, Cheryl. (1990) Quality thinking in an age of upheaval. *Public Utilities Fortnightly.* 125, (April) 17-21.

Rorty, A. (1987) Interdependence and the concept persons. Working paper series number 1, Radcliffe College.

Rosander, Aelyn Custer. (1976) A general approach to quality control in the service industries. *ASQC Annual Technical Quality Transactions Congress*. Milwaukee, WI: ASQC Quality Press.

Rosander, Aelyn Custer. (1985) *Applications of Quality Control in the Service Industries.* Milwaukee, WI: ASQC Quality Press. (*3)

Rosander, Aelyn Custer. (1989) *The Quest for Quality in Services.* Milwaukee, WI: ASQC Quality Press.

Rose, Frank. (1990) A new age for business. *Fortune.* (October 8) 156-164.

Rose, Frank. (1991) Now the quality means service too. *Fortune.* (April 15) 97.

Rose, John and E. L. Phelps. (1979) Cost of ownership application to airplane design. *Proceedings, Annual Reliability and Maintainability Symposium*. New York: IEEE, 47-50.

Rosecrance, R. (1986) *The Rise of the Trading State.* New York: Basic Books. (*2)

Rosenberg, Doris and Fred Ennerson. (1952) Production research in the manufacture of hearing aid tubes. *Industrial Quality Control*. 8, (May) 94-97.

Rosenberg, H., and J. H. Witt. (1976) Effects on LCC of test equipment standardization. *Proceedings, Annual Reliability and Maintainability Symposium*. New York: IEEE, 287-292.

Rosenberg, N., and E. Birdzell. (1986) *How the West Grew Rich.* New York: Basic Books.

Rosenburg, Jim. (1990) Philosophy and practice of quality: International Newspaper Group hears a new management gospel. *Editor and Publisher.* 123, (December 1) 32.

Rosenthal, Robert. (1983) Spare part quality assurance. *Quality Progress.* 16, (May) 27.

Rosenthal, Robert and Lenore Jacobson. (1968) *Pygmalion in the Classroom.* New York: Holt, Rinehart and Winston.

Rosenthal, Sanford T. (1975) Failure free warranty/reliability improvement warranty-seller viewpoints. *ASQC Annual Technical Quality Congress Transactions.* Milwaukee, WI: ASQC Quality Press, 80-86.

Rosenweig, R. M. (1982) *The Research Universities and Their Patrons.* Berkeley, CA: University of California Press.

Rosenzweig, G. (1968) Less steel in the scrap bucket, yield improvement program in a rolling mill. *ASQC Annual Technical Quality Congress Transactions.* Milwaukee, WI: ASQC Quality Press, 217-221.

Roslund, J. L. (1989) Evaluating management objectives with the quality loss function. *Quality Progress.* 22, (August) 45-49.

Rosner, J. (1990) Ways women lead. *Harvard Business Review.* 78, (November-December) 119-120.

Rosow, Jerome M. (1981) *Productivity Prospects for Growth.* New York: Van Nostrand Reinhold. (*2)

Rosow, Jerome M. (1984) *Employment Security in a Free Economy.* New York: Pergamon Press. (*2)

Rosow, Jerome M., and Robert Zager. (1985) *Employment Security in a Free Economy.* New York: Pergamon Press.

Ross, Alexander. (1993) Running scared on the fast track. *Canadian Business.* 66, (January) 64. (*3)

Ross, Colin. (1989) *Multiple Personality Disorder: Diagnosis, Clinical Features and Treatment.* New York: John Wiley.

Ross, Joel E. (1981) *Productivity, People and Profits*. Reston, VA: Reston Publishing Company.

Ross, Joel E., and David Georgoff. (1991) A survey of quality issues in manufacturing: The state of the industry. *Industrial Management*. 33, (January/February) 15-23.

Ross, Joel E., and J. Burkhead. (1974) *Productivity in the Local Government Sector*. Lexington, MA: Lexington Books.

Ross, Joel E., and Lawrence A. Klatt. (1986) Quality: The competitive edge. *Management Decision (UK)*. 24, (No. 5) 12-16.

Ross, Joel E., and William C. Ross. (1982) *Japanese Quality Circles and Productivity*. Reston, VA: Reston Publishing Company. (*4)

Ross, Lee. (1977) The intuitive psychologist and his shortcomings. In L. Berkowitz (Ed.) *Advances in Experimental Social Psychology*. New York: Academic Press, 173-220. (*2)

Ross, Phillip J. (1988) *Taguchi Techniques for Quality Engineering*. New York: McGraw-Hill.

Ross, R. L., and G. M. Jones. (1972) Approach to increased productivity: The Scanlon Plan. *Financial Executive*. 40, (February) 23-29.

Rosseau, D., and R. Cooke. (1984) Technology and structure. *Journal of Management*, 345-361.

Rossi, P. N., and H. E. Freeman. (1989) *Evaluation*. Fourth edition. Newbury Park, CA: Sage.

Rotfeld Herbert J., and Kim B. Rotzoll. (1976) Advertising and product quality: Are heavily advertised products better? *Journal of Consumer Affairs*. (Summer) 33-47.

Roth, Williams, Jr. (1987) What's going on down in Louisiana. *Pulp and Paper International*. 61, (September) 12-15.

Roth, Williams, Jr. (1988) Designing a new academic management training program. *SAM Advanced Management Journal*. 53, (Winter) 31-36.

Roth, Williams, Jr. (1988) Do safety programs really work. *Pulp and Paper International*. 62, (January) 24-26.

Roth, Williams, Jr. (1988) *Problem Solving for Managers*. New York: Praeger.

Roth, Williams, Jr. (1988) The great quality shell game. *Personnel*. 65, (December) 13-16.

Roth, Williams, Jr. (1989) Dos and don'ts of quality improvement. *Quality Progress*. 22, (August) 11-12.

Roth, Williams, Jr. (1989) Five phases to success. *Quality and Participation*. (June) 25-29.

Roth, Williams, Jr. (1989) Get training out of the classroom. *Quality Progress*. 22, (May) 15-16.

Roth, Williams, Jr. (1989) Quality through people: A hit for HR. *Personnel*. 66, (November) 24-31.

Roth, Williams, Jr. (1989) Try some quality improvement process glue. *Quality and Participation*. (December) 33-36.

Roth, Williams, Jr. (1989) *Work and Rewards: Redefining Our Work Life Reality*. New York: Praeger.

Roth, Williams, Jr. (1990) A new role for unions. *Quality and Participation*. (September) 25-28.

Roth, Williams, Jr. (1990) Keeping the jungle out of the MBA classrooms. *Personnel*. 67, (September) 13-16.

Roth, Williams, Jr. (1991) Quality: Rebirth of the systems approach. *Quality Digest*. (January) 27-29.

Roth, Williams, Jr. (1991) The missing hammer. *Quality and Participation.* (March) 11-12.

Roth, Williams, Jr. (1991) The second subtle link between quality and globalization. *Pulp and Paper International.* 65, (March) 7.

Rothfeder, Jeffrey and Michele Galen. (1990) Is your boss spying on you? *BusinessWeek.* (January 15) 74-75.

Rothfeder, Jeffrey. (1988) It's late, costly, incompetent—but try firing a computer system. *BusinessWeek.* (November 7) 164-165.

Rothman, Howard. (1992) You need not be big to benchmark. *Nation's Business.* 80, (December) 64. (*3)

Rothman, Steven. More than money. *D and B Reports.* (March) 12.

Rothschild, Emma. (1972) *Paradise Lost.* New York: Basic Books.

Rothschild, W. E. (1984) *How to Gain (And Maintain) The Competitive Advantage in Business.* New York: McGraw-Hill.

Rowen, Hobert. (1991) Restoring American superiority; the commitment needed goes far beyond begging the Japanese to buy something. *Washington Post.* 115, (December 26) A23.

Roy, Conner C., Jr. (1992) A success formula. *The Internal Auditor.* 49, (April) 33-36.

Rubenstein, Sydney P. (1970) New management concepts from Japan: A tale of two conferences. *Paperboard Packaging.* (January) 44-45.

Rubenstein, Sydney P. (1971) Participative quality control. *Quality Progress.* 4, (January) 24-27.

Rubenstein, Sydney P. (1976) QWL and technical societies. *Training and Development Journal.* 34, (August) 76-81.

Ruch, W. A., and J. C. Hershauer. (1974) *Factors Affecting Worker Productivity*. Bureau of Business and Economic Research, College of Business Administration. Tempe, AZ: Arizona State University.

Rudelius, William and Rogene A. Buchholz. (1979) Ethical problems of purchasing managers. *Harvard Business Review*. 57, (March-April) 8-14.

Rudnitsky, Howard. (1980) Will it play in Toledo. *Forbes*. (November) 198. (*2)

Rudintsky, Howard and Jay Grisen. (1981) Winning big by thinking small. *Forbes*. (September 28) 106. (*2)

Ruehrmund, M. E. (1985) Coconut as an ingredient in baking foods. *Food Technology in New Zealand*. (November) 21-25.

Ruiz, U., A. Karmele, R. Buenoventura, J. Coll, S. Coronado, A. Rivero, and S. Rocillo. (1992) Implementing Total Quality Management in the Spanish health care system. *Quality Assurance in Health Care*. 3, (April/May) 47-59.

Rukeyser, Louis. (1989) Frustrated unions take on corporate image—and smear it. *Los Angeles Times*. (August) B1.

Rumelt, Richard P. (1974) Strategy, structure and economic performance. *Graduate School of Business Administration, Harvard University*.

Rummler, Geary A., and Alan P. Brache. (1990) *Improving Performance: How to Manage the White Space on the Organization Chart*. San Francisco, CA: Jossey-Bass. (*2)

Runkle, S. F. (1976) *An Introduction to Japanese History*. Tokyo: International Society for Educational Information Press.

Russell, B. (1963) *Authority and the Individual*. Boston, MA: Beacon Press.

Russell, E. R., and Kenneth S. Stephens. (1970) An EVOP teaching game using a simulated process. *Journals of Quality Technology,* 2, (February) 61-66.

Russo, J. E., and P. J. H. Shoemaker. (1992) Managing overconfidence. *Sloan Management Review.* 33, (Winter) 7-17.

Rutenbeck, S. K. (1985) Initiating an in-plant quality control/sensory evaluation program. *Food Technology.* 39, (November) 124.

Rutherford, John R. (1971) A logic structure for experimental development programs. *Chemical Technology.* (March) 159-164.

Ryan, John M. (1983) The productivity/quality connection: Plugging in at Westinghouse Electric. *Quality Progress.* 16, (December) 26-29.

Ryan, John M. (1987) 1987 ASOC/Gallup survey. *Quality Progress.* 20, (December) 12-13.

Ryan, John M. (1988) Consumers see little change in product quality. *Quality Progress.* 21, (December) 15-16.

Ryan, John M. (1990) *The Human Side of Quality.* Milwaukee, WI: ASQC Quality Press.

Ryan, John M. (1992) *The Quality Team Concept in Total Quality Control.* Milwaukee, WI: ASQC Quality Press.

Ryan, John M., and H. Wong. (1984) Tiered data systems for statistical quality control. *Quality Progress.* 17, (September) 22-24.

Ryan, Kathleen D., and Daniel K. Oestreich. (1991) *Driving Fear out of the Workplace.* San Francisco, CA: Jossey-Bass. (*2)

Ryan, Nancy E. (1987) Tapping into Taguchi. *Manufacturing Engineering.* (May) 21-22.

Ryan, W. J. (1968) Procurement views of life cycle costing. *Proceedings, Annual Symposium on Reliability.* New York: IEEE, 164-168.

Saaty, T. L. (1982) *Decision Making for Leaders*. Belmont, CA: Lifetime Learning Publications. (*2)

Safford, H. F. (1946) The U.S. Army Ordnance Department use of quality control. *Industrial Quality Control*. (January) 4. (*2)

Sage, L. A. (1984) Just-in-time: A philosophy in manufacturing excellence. Zero Inventory Philosophy and Practices Seminar Proceedings, APICS.

Saharia, A. N, T. M. Barron, T. J. Davenport, J. K. Ho, and H. Mendelson. (1994) Is there a theory of reengineering? In Proceedings of the fifteenth international conference on information systems.

Sahrmann, Herman. (1979) Set-up assurance through time series analysis. *Journal of Quality Technology*. 11, (July) 105-115. (*2)

Salancik, Gerald R. (1977) Commitment and the control of organizational behavior and belief. In Barry M. Staw and Gerald R. Salancik (Eds.) *New Directions in Organizational Behavior*. Chicago, IL: St. Clair Press, 20ff.

Salinger, M. A., and H. Summers. (1983) *Behavioral Simulation Methods in Tax Policy Analysis*. Chicago, IL: University of Chicago Press.

Salkin, Stephanie and William Edwards Deming. (1992) Total quality management: Fast track for the '90s. *Institutional Distribution*. 28, (April) 56. (*2)

Salmans, Sandra. (1980) Demerging Britain's G.E. *Wall Street Journal*. (July) F7.

Salomon, Daniel and John E. Biegel. (1984) Assessing economic attractiveness of FMS applications in small businesses. *IE*. 88-96.

Salzman, H. (1985) The new Merlins or Taylor's automations? The impact of computer technology on skills and workplace organization. Department of Sociology, Brandeis University and Center for Applied Social Science. Boston University, Boston.

Sampling procedures and tables for life and reliability testing based on the weibull distribution (mean life criterion). (1961) Quality Control and Reliability Technical Report TR 3. (September).

Sampling Procedures and Tables for Life and Reliability Testing Based on Exponential Distribution. (1960) MIL-HDBK-108 Washington, DC: U.S. Government Printing Office.

Sampling Procedures and Tables for Inspection by Attributes. (1981) Milwaukee, WI: ASQC Quality Press.

Sampling Procedures and Tables for Inspection by Variables for Percent Defective. (1968) MIL-STD-414 Washington, DC: U.S. Government Printing Office. (*2)

Sampson, Anthony. (1975) *The Seven Sisters.* New York: Viking Press.

Sampson, R. C. (1955) *The Staff Role in Management.* New York: Harper and Row.

Sanders, George. (1974) Total process control. *Quality Progress.* 7, (January) 22-25.

Sanders, R. S., M. Leitnaker, and G. Ranney. (1991) Managing in the presence of variation. In Michael J. Stahl and G. M. Bounds. *Competing Globally Through Customer Value.* Westport, CT: Quorum Books, 253-274.

Sanders, Sol. (1975) *Honda: The Man and His Machine.* Tokyo: Charles E. Tuttle.

Sandholm, Lennhart. (1981) Education and training in developing countries. *ASQC Annual Technical Quality Congress Transactions.* Milwaukee, WI: ASQC Quality Press, 862-868.

Sandholm, Lennhart. (1983) Japanese quality circles—a remedy for the west's quality problems? *Quality Progress.* 16, (February) 20-23.

Sandras, William A., Jr. (1988) *Just-in-Time: Unleashing the Powers of Continuous Improvement*. Essex Junction, VT: Oliver Wight Limited.

Sansom, G. (1963) *A History of Japan, 1615-1867*. Tokyo: Charles E. Tuttle.

Sanson, Sir George. (1950) *The Western World and Japan*. New York: Alfred A. Knopf.

Saporito, Bill. (1984) Allegheny Ludlum has steel figured out. *Fortune*. (June 25) 40-44.

Saporito, Bill. (1984) Hewlett-Packard discovers marketing. *Fortune*. (October 1) 50-56.

Saporito, Bill. (1987) Cutting cost with cutting people. *Fortune*. (May 25) 11. (*2)

Sarason, Seymour B. (1991) *The Predictable Failure of Educational Reform*. San Francisco, CA: Jossey-Bass.

Sarazen, J. Stephen. (1990) Cause-and-effect diagrams. In Harry Ivan Costin (Ed.) *Readings in Total Quality Management*. (1994) Fort Worth, TX: Dryden Press, 177-185.

Sashkin, Marshall and Kenneth J. Kiser. (1993) *Putting Total Quality Management to Work*. San Francisco, CA: Berrett-Koehler.

Sashkin, Marshall and William C. Morris. (1985) *Phases of Integrated Problem Solving*. King of Prussia, PA: Organization Design and Development.

Sashkin, Marshall. (1972) *Making Participative Management Work*. King of Prussia, PA: Organization Design and Development.

Sasser, W. Earl, Jr. (1979) *Service Management*. Boston, MA: Harvard Business Review Reprints.

Sathe, V. (1983) Implications of corporate culture: A manager's guide to action. *Organizational Dynamics*. 6, (Autumn) 5-23.

Satisfaction-action. (1991) *Marketing News*. (February 4) 4.

Sato, Kinko. (1982) More and more Japanese women are hoping to get lifetime jobs. *The Japan Economic Journal*. (March 30) 11.

Satoshi, Kamata. (1982) *Japan in the Passing Lane*. New York: Pantheon Books.

Satterthwaite, F. E. (1946) An approximate distribution of estimates of variance components. *Biometrics*. 2, (September) 110-114.

Saunders, David, Mark Cary, Bonnie Kay, Paul Orleman, Wayne Robertshaw, Gabriel Ross, Wallace Wallace, and John Wittenbraker. (1987) The customer window. *Quality Progress*. 20, (June) 13-14.

Sawyer, W. W. (1956) *Mathematician's Delight*. Baltimore, MD: Penguin Books.

Sayle, Allen J. (1988) *Management Audits*. London, UK: McGraw-Hill.

Scanlon, Frank and John T. Hogan. (1983) Service industry quality management. *Quality Progress*. 16, (June) 30-35.

Schaaf, Dick. (1992) Selling quality. *Training*. 29, (June) 53-59. (*4)

Schaffer, G. (1984) Machine vision: A sense for CIM. *American Machinist*. Special Report 767, (June) 101-120.

Schaffer, R. H. (1981) Productivity improvement strategy: Make success the building block. *Management Review*. 70, (August) 46-52. (*2)

Schaffer, R. H., and H. A. Thomson. (1992) Successful change programs begin with results. *Harvard Business Review*. 70, (January-February) 80-89.

Schaffir, Kurt H. (1985) Information technology for the manufacturer. *Management Review*. 74, (November) 61-62.

Schaffitzel, W., and U. Kersten. (1985) Introducing CAD systems: Problems and the role of user-developer communication in their solution. *Behavior and Information Technology*. 4, (January) 41-61.

Schainblatt, A. H. (1982) How companies measure the productivity of engineers and scientists. *Research Management*. 25, (May) 10-18.

Scheer, A. L. (1993) A new approach to business processes. *IBM Systems Journal*. 32, (No. 1) 80-98.

Scheffe, H. (1952) An analysis of variance for paired comparisons. *Journal of the American Statistical Association*. 47, (201) 381-400.

Scheffe, H. (1953) A method for judging all contrasts in an analysis of variance. *Biometrika*. 40, (3) 87.

Scheffe, H. (1958) Experiments with mixtures. *Journal of the Royal Statistical Society*. (Series B) 20, (June) 344-360.

Scheffe, H. (1963) The simplex centroid design for experiments with mixtures. *Journal of the Royal Statistical Society*. (Series B) 25, (May) 235-251.

Scheid, Phil N. (1965) Charter of accountability for executives. *Harvard Business Review*. 43, (July-August) 88.

Schein, Edgar Henry. (1967) *Process Consultation: Its Role in Organizational Development*. Reading, MA: Addison-Wesley.

Schein, Edgar Henry. (1981) SMR forum: Does Japanese management style have a message for American managers?. *Sloan Management Review*. 23, (Fall) 55-68.

Schein, Edgar Henry. (1984) Coming to an awareness of organizational culture. *Sloan Management Review*. 25, (Winter) 3-16.

Schein, Edgar Henry. (1985) *Organizational Culture and Leadership*. San Francisco, CA: Jossey-Bass. (*4)

Schein, Edgar Henry. (1985) Organizational socialization and the profession of management. In L. Boone and D. Bowen. *The Great Writings in Management and Organizational Behavior*. Tulsa, OK: Penn Well Books.

Scherer, F. M. (1982) Industry technology flows in the U.S. *Research Policy*. 11, 227-245.

Scherkenbach, William W. (1985) Quality in the driver's seat. *Quality Progress*. 18, (April) 40-46.

Scherkenbach, William W. (1986) *The Deming Route to Quality and Productivity: Road Maps and Roadblocks*. Rockville, MD: CEE Press. (*7)

Scherkenbach, William W. (1986) *The Deming Route to Quality and Productivity: Roadmaps and Roadblocks*. Milwaukee, WI: ASQC Quality Press. (*3)

Scherkenbach, William W. (1986) *The Deming Route to Quality and Productivity: Roadmaps and Roadblocks*. Rockville, MD: Mercury Press. (*3)

Scherkenbach, William W. (1991) *Deming's Road to Continual Improvement*. Knoxville, TN: SPC Press. (*3)

Schermerhorn, J. R., Jr. (1984) *Management for Productivity*. New York: John Wiley.

Schifrin, Matthew. (1989) Who checks the checkers? *Forbes*. (August 7) 64.

Schiller, Zachary. (1988) The refrigerator that has GE feeling the heat. *BusinessWeek*. (April 25) 65-66.

Schilling, Edward G. (1973) A systematic approach to the analysis of means: Analysis of treatment effects. *Journal of Quality Technology*. 5, (July) 93-108.

Schilling, Edward G. (1974) Variables sampling and MIL-STD 414. *Quality Progress*. 7, (May) 16-20.

Schilling, Edward G. (1981) ANSI/ASQC Z1.9—A modernization. *Quality Progress*. 14, (March) 26-29.

Schilling, Edward G. (1981) Revised variables acceptance sampling standards—ANSI Z1.9 and ISO 3951. *Journal of Quality Technology*. 13, (February) 131-138.

Schilling, Edward G. (1982) *Acceptance Sampling in Quality Control*. New York: Marcel Dekker. (*2)

Schilling, Edward G. (1982) Revised attributes acceptance sampling standard—ANSI/ASQC Z1. *Journal of Quality Technology*. 14, (December) 215-218.

Schilling, Edward G. (1983) Two new ASCQ acceptance sampling standards. *Quality Progress*. 16, (March) 14-17.

Schilling, Edward G. (1984) An overview of acceptance control. *Quality Progress*. 23, (April) 24-25.

Schilling, Edward G. (1984) The role of statistics in the management of quality. *Quality Progress*. 16, (March) 32-35.

Schilling, Edward G. (1985) The role of acceptance sampling in modern quality control. *Common Statistics—Theory and Methods*. 14, (November) 2769-2783.

Schisgall, Oscar. (1981) *Eyes on Tomorrow: The Evolution of Procter and Gamble*. Chicago, IL: J. G. Ferguson. (*2)

Schlaifer, R. (1959) *Probability and Statistics for Business Decisions*. New York: McGraw-Hill.

Schlesinger, Jack M. (1988) GM's new compensation plan reflects general trend tying pay to performance. *Wall Street Journal*. (January 26) 39. (*2)

Schlesinger, L. (1984) Quality of worklife and the manager: Muddle in the middle. *Organizational Dynamics*. (Summer) 21-32. (*4)

Schlosstein, S. (1984) *Trade War: Greed, Power, and Industrial Policy On Opposite Sides of the Pacific.* New York: Congdon and Weed. (*2)

Schmenner, R. W. (1984) *Production/Operations Management: Concepts and Situations.* Chicago, IL: Science and Research Associates.

Schmenner, R. W., and R. L. Cook. (1985) Explaining productivity differences in North Carolina factories. *Journal of Operations Management.* 5, (May) 273-89.

Schmidt, E. (1990) Hard work can't stop hard times. *New York Times.* (November 25) 1.

Schmidt, F., and J. Stuart Hunter. (1981) Employment testing. *American Psychologist.* 36, (October) 1128-1137.

Schmidt, J. W., and E. Taylor. (1970) *Simulation and Analysis of Industrial Systems.* Homewood, IL: Irwin.

Schmidt, Jerry L. (1980) Participative management—Challenge to competition. *ASQC Annual Technical Quality Congress Transactions.* Milwaukee, WI: ASQC Quality Press, 662-668.

Schmidt, W., and J. Finnigan. (1992) *The Race Without a Finish Line: America's Quest for Total Quality.* San Francisco, CA: Jossey-Bass, 268-279.

Schmitt, G. A., N. P. Preston, and B. S. Mitchell. (1980) Successful application of a quality circle program in a utility environment. AIIE Proceedings, Fall Annual Conference. (Fall) 365-371.

Schmoker, Michael J., and Richard B. Wilson. (1993) *Total Quality Education.* Bloomington, IN: Phi Delta Kappa Educational Foundation.

Schmoker, Michael J., and Richard B. Wilson. (1993) Transforming schools through total quality education. *Phi Delta Kappan.* 74, (January) 389.

Schmuckler, Eric. (1990) Eyes on the prize. *Forbes*. (February 5) 14. (*3)

Schoeffler, Sidney, Robert D. Buzzell, and Donald F. Heany. (1974) Impact of strategic planning on profit performance. *Harvard Business Review*. 52, (March-April) 137-145.

Scholtes, Peter R. (1987) *An Elaboration on Deming's Teachings on Performance Appraisal*. Madison, WI: Joiner Associates.

Scholtes, Peter R. (1993) *Total Quality or Performance Appraisal: Choose One*. Madison, WI: Joiner Associates.

Scholtes, Peter R., and other Joiner Associates. (1988) *The Team Handbook-How to Use Teams to Improve Quality*. Madison, WI: Joiner Associates. (*5)

Schon, D. A. (1967) *Technology and Change*. New York: Delacorte Press.

Schonberger, Richard J. (1982) *Japanese Manufacturing Techniques: Nine Hidden Lessons in Simplicity*. New York: Free Press. (*13)

Schonberger, Richard J. (1982) Production workers bear major quality responsibility in Japanese industry. *Industrial Engineering*. 14, (December) 34-40.

Schonberger, Richard J. (1983) Plant layout becomes product-oriented with cellular, just-in-time production concepts. *Industrial Engineering*. 15, (November) 66-77.

Schonberger, Richard J. (1984) *Operations and Management*. Plano, TX: BPI.

Schonberger, Richard J. (1986) *World Class Manufacturing: The Lessons of Simplicity Applied*. New York: Free Press.

Schonberger, Richard J. (1987) *World Class Manufacturing Casebook: Implementing JIT and TQC*. New York: Free Press. (*2)

Schonberger, Richard J. (1990) *Building a Chain of Customers: Linking Business Functions to Create the World Class Company.* New York: Free Press. (*2)

Schonberger, Richard J. (1992) Is strategy strategic? Impact of total quality management on strategy. *Academy of Management Executive.* 6, (August) 80-87. (*2)

Schonberger, Richard J. (1992) Total quality management cuts a broad swath through manufacturing and beyond. *Organizational Dynamics.* 20, (Spring) 16-28.

Schonberger, Richard J., and J. P. Gilbert. (1983) Just-in-time purchasing: A challenge for U.S. industry. *California Management Review.* 26, (Fall) 54-68.

Schoonhoven, C. B. (1980) The management of innovation revisited: Volatile environments, structure and effectiveness in high technology corporations. Paper presented at Pacific Sociological Association. San Francisco, CA. (April 20).

Schoonhoven, C. B. (1985) High technology firms: Where strategy really pays off. *Columbia Journal of World Business.* (Winter) 49.

Schoonhoven, C. B. (1986) Organizational adaptation caused by technological change: Issues and analysis. A paper presented at the Western Academy of Management. Los Angeles, CA.

Schoonhoven, C. B., and K. M. Eisenhardt. (1985) Influence of organizational, entrepreneurial and environmental factors on the growth and development of technology-based start up firms 12-14. A research proposal funded by U.S. Department of Commerce, Economic Development Administration.

Schoonhoven. C. B., and K. M. Eisenhardt. (1987) Surviving the liability of newness: A model for successful entrepreneurship in technology-based ventures. Paper presented at the Academy of Management. New Orleans.

Schorr, Burt. (1983) Schools use new ways to be more efficient and enforce discipline. *Wall Street Journal.* (December 15) 1, 16.

Schostack, G. L. (1984) *Designing Services that Deliver*. New York: Random House.

Schrader, L. J. (1986) An engineering organization's cost of quality program. *Quality Progress*. 19, (January) 29-34. (*2)

Schrock, Edward M., and H. L. Lefevre. (1988) *The Good and the Bad News About Quality*. Milwaukee, WI: ASQC Quality Press. (*2)

Schroeder, Michael. (1990) Heart trouble at Pfizer. *BusinessWeek*. (February 26) 47-48.

Schroeder, Roger G. (1981) *Operations Management*. New York: McGraw-Hill.

Schroeder, Roger G. (1989) *Operations Management*. Third edition. New York: McGraw-Hill.

Schultz, Jack. (1992) Quality management. *Stores*. 74, (November) 19. (*2)

Schultz, V. (1967) The real low-down on materials. *Management Factory*. (December) 49.

Schumacher, R. B. F. (1973) *Small is Beautiful: Economics as if People Mattered*. New York: Harper and Row. (*2)

Schumacher, R. B. F. (1976) Quality control in a calibration laboratory: Part I. *Quality Progress*. 9, (January) 25-28.

Schumacher, R. B. F. (1976) Quality control in a calibration laboratory: Part II. *Quality Progress*. 9, (February) 16-20.

Schumacher, R. B. F. (1981) Systematic measurement error. *Journal of Quality Technology*. 13, (January) 10-24.

Schumpeter, J. A. (1947) *Capitalism, Socialism and Democracy*. New York: Harper and Row. (*2)

Schuster, John. (1984) *Management Compensation in High Technology Companies*. Lexington, MA: D. C. Heath.

Schuster, John. (1985) Compensation plan design. *Compensation Plans*. (May) 5-8.

Schuster, Lynda. (1982) Wal-Mart chief's enthusiastic approach infects employees, keeps retailer growing. *Wall Street Journal.* (April) 21. (*2)

Schuster, M. H. (1984) *Union Management Cooperation: Structure, Process, Impact.* Kalamazoo, MI: W. E. Upjohn. Institute for Research.

Schutz, Howard G., and Marianne Casey. (1981) Consumer perceptions of advertising as misleading. *Journal of Consumer Affairs.* (Winter) 340-357.

Schvaneveldt, Shane J., Takao Enkawa, and Masami Miyakawa. (1991) Consumer evaluation perspectives of service quality: Evaluation factors and two-way model of quality. *Total Quality Management*. 2, (February) 149-161.

Schwartz, H. (1987) On the psychodymanics of organizational disaster: The case of the space shuttle *Challenger*. *The Columbia Journal of World Business*. 22, (Spring) 1.

Schwarz, Robert A. (1990) *Midland City, Recovering Prosperity Through Quality.* New York: John Wiley.

Schwartz, Stephen B. (1990) Quality: The key to success in the '90s—Beyond. *ASQC Annual Technical Quality Congress Transactions*. Milwaukee, WI: ASQC Quality Press.

Schweber, W. (1982) Programming for control-computerizing measurement and control. *Quality*. (March) 38-42.

Schweiger. D. M., W. R. Sandberg, and J. W. Ragan. (1986) Group approaches for improving strategic decision making: A comparative analysis of dialectical inquiry, devil's advocacy and consensus. *Academy of Management Journal.* 29, (March) 51-71.

Scott, A. J. (1982) Why should I use automated inspection? *Sixth International Conference on Automated Inspection and Product Control.* Kempston, UK: IFS Publications, Kempston, (April) 1-5.

Scott, B. (1993) USAF using TQM to exploit scaled-back forces. *Aviation Week and Space Technology.* 38, (July) 59.

Scott, B., and C. Lodge. (1985) *U.S. Competitiveness in the World Economy.* Cambridge, MA: Harvard Business School Press.

Scott, Harold A., et al. (1983) Hierarchal control model for automated manufacturing systems. *Computer and Industrial Engineering.* 7, 241-255.

Scott, Rachel. (1974) *Muscle and Blood.* New York: E. P. Dutton.

Scott, William B. (1989) TQM expected to boost productivity, ensure survival of U.S industry. *Aviation Week and Space Technology.* 131, (December) 64-65.

Scott, William B. (1990) Aerospace/defense firms see preliminary results from application of TQM concepts. *Aviation Week and Space Technology.* 132, (January) 61-62.

Scott, William B. (1993) USAF using TQM to exploit scaled-back forces. *Aviation Week and Space Technology.* 138, (February 15) 59. (*2)

Sculley, John. (1987) *Odyssey: Pepsi to Apple.* New York: Harper and Row.

Sculley, John. (1990) The human use of information. *Journal for Quality and Participation.* (January/February) 10-13.

The search for the organization of tomorrow. (1992) *Fortune.* (May 18) 95.

Sears, J. A. (1982) Changing role of the quality inspection function. *ASQC Annual Technical Quality Congress Transactions.* Milwaukee, WI: ASQC Quality Press, 506-512.

Sears, James A. (1983) Changing role of the quality inspection function. *Quality Progress.* 16, (July) 12-17.

Seashore, Stanley E. (1981) Quality of working life perspective. In A. Van de Ven and W. F. Joyce (Eds) *Perspectives on Organization Design and Behavior.* New York: John Wiley. (*2)

Seashore, Stanley E., and D. G. Bowers. (1970) The durability of organizational change. *American Psychologist.* 25, (March) 227-233. (*2)

Seashore, Stanley E., Phillip H. Mirvis, and Cortland Cammann. (1983) *Observing and Measuring Organizational Change: A Guide to Field Practice.* New York: John Wiley.

Secrest, D. (1968) Time sharing experimental control on a small computer. *Industrial and Engineering Chemistry.* 60, (September) 9.

Sedam, Scott, M. (1982) QC circle training process should cover relating, supporting, problem solving skills. *Industrial Engineering.* 14, (January) 70-74.

Seder, Leonard A. (1950) Diagnosis with diagrams. *Industrial Quality Control.* 6, (January) 23. (*2)

Sederberg, George W. (1982) The role of the steering committee. IAQC Fourth Annual Technical Conference Transactions. Cincinnati, OH: International Association of Quality Circles.

Seelye, H. Ned, Edward C. P. Stewart, and Joyce A. Sween. (1982) *Evaluating Quality Circles in U.S. Industry: A Feasibility Study.* Washington, DC: U.S. Department of Defense, Office of Naval Research.

Seghezzi, H. D. (1981) What is quality? Conformance with requirements or fitness for the intended use? *EOQC Quality.* (April) 3-4.

Seidler, Edouard. (1976) *Let's Call It Fiesta.* Newfoundland: Haessner.

Seifert, Laurence C. (1988) AT&T's full-stream quality architecture. *Total Quality Performance.* (Research Report Number 909) New York: The Conference Board, 56-58.

Seliger, G., et al. (1986) Decision support for planning flexible manufacturing systems. Simulation in Manufacturing Conference. San Francisco, CA, 201-222.

Seller, J. (1967) *Systems Analysis in Organization Behavior.* Homewood, IL: Irwin Dorsey.

Selwitchka, R. (1980) The priority list on measures for reducing quality related costs. *Quality.* (May) 3-7.

Selznick, Philip. (1949) *TVA and the Grass Roots.* Berkeley, CA: University of California Press.

Selznick, Philip. (1957) *Leadership in Administration: A Sociological Interpretation.* New York: Harper and Row. (*2)

Semler, R. (1989) Managing without managers. *Harvard Business Review.* 67, (September-October) 75-84. (*2)

Semmer, Robert H. (1990) Keeping in step with the environment: Applying TQC to energy supply. *National Productivity Review.* 9, (Autumn) 439-455.

Semple, Jack. (1992) Why we need TQM-PDQ. *Management Today.* (May) 84. (*3)

Senge, Peter M. (1984) *Transforming Leadership.* Alexandria: Miles River Press.

Senge, Peter M. (1990) *The Fifth Discipline: The Art and Practice of the Learning Organization.* New York: Doubleday/Currency. (*7)

Senge, Peter M. (1992) Building learning organizations. In Harry Ivan Costin (Ed.) *Readings in Total Quality Management.* (1994) Fort Worth, TX: Dryden Press, 59-72.

Senge, Peter, M., Art Kleiner, Charlotte Roberts, Richard B. Ross, and Bryan J. Smith. (1994) *The Fifth Discipline Fieldbook: Strategies and Tools for Building a Learning Organization.* New York: Doubleday/Currency.

Senker, P., and E. Arnold. (1984) Implications of CAD/CAM for training in the engineering industry. In P. Arthur (Ed.) *CAD/CAM in Education and Training*. London, UK: Kogan Page.

Sentry Insurance. (1976) *Consumerism at the Crossroads*. Stevens Points, WI: Sentry Insurance Co.

Sepehri, M. (1985) How *Kanban* is used in an American Toyota motor facility. *Industrial Engineering*. 17, (February) 33-37.

Sepehri, M. (1985) JIT and FMS—A working team for factory of the future. *P and I M Review and APICS News*. (April) 20-22.

Sepehri, M. (1985) Quality circles—A vehicle for just-in-time implementation. *Quality Progress*. 18, (July) 13-14.

Serrin, William. (1973) *The Company and the Union.* New York: Alfred A. Knopf.

Servan-Schreiber, J. J. (1969) *The American Challenge.* New York: Atheneum. (*2)

Service quality: Measuring customer expectations. (1988) Booklet published by Metropolitan Life and affiliated companies.

Setzer, Susan R. (1986) Quality assurance for scrubber operation R and D. *ASQC Annual Technical Quality Congress Transactions*. Milwaukee, WI: ASQC Quality Press, 484-491.

Sewell, Carl J., and Paul B. Brown. (1990) *Customers for Life: How to Turn That One-Time Buyer into a Lifetime Customer*. New York: Doubleday/Currency.

Seymour, Daniel T. (1992) *On Q: Causing Quality in Higher Education.* New York: Macmillan.

Seymour, Daniel T., and Casey Collett. (1991) *Total Quality Management in Higher Education: A Critical Assessment.* Methuen, MA: Goal/QPC.

Shaffer, James C. (1982) Project your production. *Quality.* (April) 33-35.

Shaffer, James C. (1992) Quality where it doesn't count. *Across the Board.* (October) 11. (*2)

Shaffer, Robert H. (1988) *The Breakthrough Strategy.* Cambridge, MA: Ballinger.

Shah, M. J., and R. E. Stillman. (1970) Computer control and optimization of a large methanol plant. *Industrial and Engineering Chemistry.* 62, (December) 12.

Shaiken, H. (1984) *Work Transformed: Automation and Labor in the Computer Edge.* New York: Holt, Rinehart and Winston.

Shaiken, H. (1985) The automated factory: The view from the shop floor. *Technology Review.* (January) 17-24.

Shainin, Dorian. (1972) Unusual practices for defect control. *Quality Management and Engineering.* (February) 30.

Shainin, Dorian. (1976) *Tool and Manufacturing Engineers Handbook.* New York: McGraw-Hill.

Shainin, Dorian. (1978) Test: Tolerances and measuring—both vitally weak in Q.C. *ASQC Annual Technical Quality Congress Transactions.* Milwaukee, WI: ASQC Quality Press, 39-43.

Shainin, Dorian. (1984) Better than good old X and R charts asked by vendees. *ASQC Annual Technical Quality Congress Transactions.* Milwaukee, WI: ASCQ Quality Press, 302-307.

Shainin, Peter D. (1990) Control charts. In Harry Ivan Costin (Ed.) *Readings in Total Quality Management.* (1994) Fort Worth, TX: Dryden Press, 187-194.

Shank, J., and N. Churchill. (1977) Variance analysis: A management-oriented approach. *Accounting Review.* (October) 950-957.

Shannon, Robert E., and Richard Mayer. (1985) Expert systems and simulation. *Simulation Magazine.* 42, (June) 275-284.

Shapiro, Benson P. (1968) The psychology of pricing. *Harvard Business Review.* 46, (July-August) 17-18.

Shapiro, Benson P. (1988) What the hell is 'Market Oriented'? *Harvard Business Review.* 66, (November-December) 119-125.

Shapiro, Isaac. (1981) Second thoughts about Japan. *Wall Street Journal.* (June 5) .

Shapiro, Samuel S. (1990) *How to Test Normality and Other Distributional Assumptions.* Revised edition. Milwaukee, WI: ASQC Quality Press.

Sharda, Ramesh, Steve H. Barr, and James C. McDonald. (1988) Decision support system effectiveness: A review and an empirical test. *Management Science.* 34, (April) 139-159.

Sharp, D. B. (1976) Inching toward the metric system. *ASQC Annual Technical Quality Congress Transactions.* Milwaukee, WI: ASCQ Quality Press, 381-388.

Sharpe, W. F., and G. J. Alexander. (1990) *Investments.* Fourth edition. Englewood Cliffs, NJ: Prentice-Hall.

Shaw, George Bernard. (1950) *Man and Superman.* New York: Penguin Books.

Shaw, J. C. (1978) *The Quality-Productivity Connection in Service Sector Management.* New York: Van Nostrand Reinhold.

Shaw, J. C., and R. Capoor. (1979) Quality and productivity: Mutually exclusive or interdependent in service organizations? *Management Review.* 68 (March) 25-28, 37-39.

Shaw, M. (1981) *Group Dynamics*. Third edition. New York: McGraw-Hill.

Shaw, Robert J. (1982) Middle management's role in quality circles. *Management Focus*. 29, (May-June) 34-36.

Shea, Gregory P. (1986) Quality circles: The danger of bottled change. *Sloan Management Review*. 27, (Spring) 33-46.

Shearman, Robert W. (1979) How can America increase productivity in the next decade? *Quality Progress*. 12, (January) 22-26.

Shedd, Tom. (1992) UP's quest for quality. *Railway Age*. 193, (February) 22-24.

Sheesley, J. H. (1977) Tests for outlying observations. *Journal of Quality Technology*. 9, (January) 38-41.

Sheesley, J. H. (1980) Attributes comparison of k samples involving variables or data using the analysis of means. *Journal of Quality Technology*. 12, (May) 47-52.

Sheets, R. G. (1985) The political economy of interorganizational relations in central cities: CETA and economic development. Unpublished Ph.D. dissertation, Department of Sociology, University of Illinois, Chicago, IL.

Shein, E. H. (1967) *Process Consultation: Its Role in Organizational Development*. Reading, MA: Addison-Wesley.

Shelp, R. K., C. Stephenson, and N. S. Truitt. (1984) *Service Industries and Economic Development*. New York: Praeger.

Shelton, Sandra and George Allger. (1993) Who's afraid of level 4 evaluation?: A practical approach. *Training and Development Journal*. 47, (June) 43-46.

Shepard, A. (1956) Supervisors and subordinates in research. *Journal of Business*. 29, (April) 16.

Shepard, Clovis. (1964) *Small Groups: Some Sociological Perspectives*. San Francisco, CA: Chandler.

Shepard, H. R., and Robert R. Blake. (1962) Changing behavior through cognitive maps. *Human Organization*. 21, 88-96.

Shepard, Mark, Jr., and J. Fred Bucy. (1979) Innovation at Texas Instruments. *Computer*. (September) 84. (*4)

Shepherd, G. (1972) The elements of market structure. *Review of Economics and Statistics*. 54, (February) 25-36.

Sheppard, John W. (1977) Case is now 12 years old. *Quality Progress*. 10, (November) 38-39.

Sheppard, T. I. (1986) Silent signals. *Supervisory Management*. (March) 31-33.

Sheppeck, Michael and Stephen Cohen. (1985) Put a dollar value on your training program. *Training and Development Journal*. 39, (November) 23-28.

Sherer, F. M. (1980) *Industrial Market Structure and Economic Performance*. Second edition. Chicago, IL: Rand McNally.

Sheridan, David. (1990) Getting the picture. *Training*. 27, (September) 12-15.

Sheridan, John H. (1990) America's best plants. *Industry Week*. (October 3) 27-64.

Sheridan, John H. (1990) World-class manufacturing: Lessons from the gurus. *Industry Week*. (August 6) 35-41. (*2)

Sheridan, John H. (1991) Racing against time. *Industry Week*. (June 20) 22-24.

Sheridan, John H. (1993) Where bench-markers go wrong. *Industry Week*. (March 15) 28. (*3)

Sherif, Muzafer. (1951) Experimental study of intergroup relations. In J. Rohrer and Muzafer Sherif (Eds.) *Social Psychology at the Crossroads.* New York: Harper and Row.

Sherman, G. (1976) The Scanlon concept: Its capabilities for productivity improvement. *The Personnel Administrator.* 21, (July) 17-20.

Sherman, H. (1966) *It All Depends.* Tuscaloosa, AL: University of Alabama Press. (*2)

Sherman, Stratford P. (1989) The mind of Jack Welch. *Fortune.* (March 27) 11.

Sheth, J., and G. Eshghi. (1989) *Global Marketing Perspectives.* Cincinnati, OH: South-Western.

Shetty, V. K. (1987) Product quality and competitive strategy. *Business Horizons.* 30, (May-June) 46-52. (*2)

Shetty, Y. K. (1982) Key elements of productivity improvement programs. *Business Horizons.* 25, (March-April) 15-22.

Shetty, Y. K. (1982) Management's role in declining productivity. *California Management Review.* 25, (Fall) 33-37.

Shetty, Y. K., and J. Barrett. (1981) *Productivity: A Resource Guide.* Roy, UT: Barrett Management Services.

Shetty, Y. K., and Joel E. Ross. (1985) Quality and its management in service businesses. *Industrial Management.* 27, (November/ December) 7-12.

Shetty, Y. K., and Vernon M. Buehler. (1983) *Quality and Productivity Improvements: U.S and Foreign Companies.* Cincinnati, OH: Manufacturing Productivity Center.

Shetty, Y. K., and Vernon M. Buehler. (1985) *Productivity and Quality through People.* Westport, CT: Greenwood Press. (*2)

Shetty, Y. K., and Vernon M. Buehler. (1988) *Competing Through Productivity and Quality*. Cambridge, MA: Productivity Press.

Shewhart, William A. (1931) *The Economic Control of Quality of Manufactured Products.* New York: Van Nostrand. (*14)
Reprinted (1980) by ASQC Quality Press.

Shewhart, William A. (1939) *Statistical Method from the Viewpoint of Quality Control.* Washington, DC: Graduate School, Department of Agriculture, George Washington University. [also reprinted by Dover, 1986] (*5)

Shiba, B. (1989) Quality knows no bounds. *Look Japan*. (May) 30-31.

Shiffer, Marion. (1992) Total quality management in contract clinical research. *Drug and Cosmetic Industry*. 151, (October) 42. (*2)

Shilliff, Karl A and Milan Bodis. (1975) How to pick the right vendor. *Quality Progress*. 8, (January) 12-14.

Shimoda, Y., and H. Miyazaki. (1981) The selection of inspectors for sensory tests. *ASQC Annual Technical Quality Congress Transactions*. Milwaukee, MI: ASQC Quality Press, 884-891.

Shimoyamada, Kaoru. (1987) The president's audit: QC audits at Komatsu. *Quality Progress*. 20, (January) 44-49. (*2)

Shingo, Shigeo. (1981) *A Study of Toyota Production System from Industrial Engineering*. Tokyo: Japan Management Association. (*2)

Shingo, Shigeo. (1986) *A Revolution in Manufacturing: The SMED System*. Cambridge, MA: Productivity Press. (*2)

Shingo, Shigeo. (1986) *Zero Quality Control: Source Inspection and the Poka-Yoke System*. Cambridge, MA: Productivity Press. (*3)

Shingo, Shigeo. (1988) *Non-Stock Production: The Shingo System for Continuous Improvement.* Cambridge, MA: Productivity Press. (*2)

Shinklin, W. L., and J. K. Ryans Jr. (1984) *Marketing High Technology*. Lexington, MA: D. C. Heath.

Shinohara, I. (1988) *New Production System-JIT Crosses Industry Boundaries*. Cambridge: Productivity Press. (*2)

Shirley, R. C., M. H. Peters, and A. I. El-Ansary. (1981) *Strategy and Policy Formation*. New York: John Wiley, 238-250.

Shisgall, Oscar. (1981) *Eyes on Tomorrow: The Evolution of Procter and Gamble*. Chicago, IL: J. G. Ferguson.

Shook, Robert L. (1980) *Ten Greatest Salespersons: What They Say About Selling*. New York: Harper and Row. (*2)

Shook, Robert L. (1990) *Turnaround: The New Ford Motor Company*. Englewood Cliffs, NY: Prentice-Hall.

Shores, A. R. (1988) *Survival of the Fittest*. Milwaukee, WI: ASQC Quality Press. (*2)

Short, J. E., and N. Venkatraman. (1992) Beyond business process redesign: Redefining Baxter's business network. *Sloan Management Review*. 33, (Fall) 7-21.

Shortell, S. M., and J. P. LoGerfo. (1981) Hospital medical staff organization and quality of care: Results for myocardial infarction and appendectomy. *Medical Care*. 19, (January) 104-154.

Should an ad identify brand X? (1979) *Media and Advertising*. (September) 24, 156-161.

Showalter, Michael J. (1992) Integrating total quality management into the business school curriculum. *Decision Sciences*. 23, (May) 14. (*2)

Shrinking supplier bases. (1991) *Wall Street Journal*. (August 16) B1.

Shrivastava, P. (1987) *Bhopal: Anatomy of a Crisis*. Cambridge, MA: Ballinger.

Shumaker, M. J., and J. C. DuBuisson. (1976) Tradeoff of thermal cycling vs. life cycle costs. *Proceedings, Annual Reliability and Maintainability Symposium*. New York: IEEE, 300-305.

Shuster, J. (1984) *Management Compensation in High Technology Companies*. Lexington, MA: Lexington Books. (*2)

Sibson, R. E. (1976) *Increasing Employee Productivity*. New York: American Management Association.

Sick, Gary. (1985) *All Fall Down*. New York: Random House.

Sidel, J. L., and J. Bloomquist. (1983) Industrial approaches to defining quality. In A. A. Williams and R. K. Atkin (Eds.) *Sensory Quality in Food and Beverages: Definitions, Measurement and Control*. London, UK: Ellis Horwood Limited.

Sidel, J. L., H. Stone, and J. Bloomquist. (1981) Use and misuse of sensory evaluation in research and quality control. *Dairy Science*. 64, 2296-2302.

Siefel, Irving. (1966) A practical approach to vendor ratings. *Industrial Quality Control*. 22, (July) 17-19.

Siegal, Irving. (1982) *Productivity Measurement: An Evolving Art*. New York: Pergamon Press.

Siege, J. C. (1982) Statistical management methods to improve quality, productivity and competitive position. Industrial Liason Program Symposium, Massachusetts Institute of Technology. (August 17). (*2)

Siegel, I. H. (1980) *Company Productivity: Measurement for Improvement*. Kalamazoo, MI: W. E. Upjohn Institute for Employment Research.

Siegel, J. C. (1982) *Managing with Statistical Methods*. SAE Technical Paper Series #820520. Warrendale, PA: Society of Automotive Engineers. (*2)

Siegel, S. (1956) *Non-Parametric Statistics for the Behavioral Sciences*. New York: McGraw-Hill.

Siehl, C., Gerald E. Ledford, Jr., R. Silverman, and P. Foy. (1988) Managing cultural differences in mergers and acquisitions: The role of the human resource function. *Mergers and Acquisitions*. (March-April) 22. (*5)

Sierra, E. (1983) Quality control systems in developing countries: Some experiences of the international trade center UNCTAD/GATT (ITC). Proceedings, Twenty-Seventh EOQC Conference. Madrid.

Siff, Walter C. (1984) The strategic plan of control: A tool for participative management. *ASQC Annual Technical Quality Congress Transactions*. Milwaukee, WI: ASQC Quality Press, 384-390.

Silver, D. A. (1985) *Venture Capital*. New York: John Wiley.

Simmons, J. (1989) Partnering pulls everything together. *Journal for Quality and Participation*. (June) 12-16.

Simmons, J., and W. J. Mares. (1983) *Working Together: Participation from Shopfloor to Boardroom*. New York: Alfred A. Knopf.

Simon, Herbert A. (1957) *Research in Industrial Human Relations*. New York: Harper and Brothers.

Simon, Herbert A. (1977) What computers mean for man and society. *Science*. 23, (March 18) 1186-1192.

Simon, Herbert A. (1979) Information processing models of cognition. *Annual Review of Psychology*. 30, 363.

Simon, Herbert A. (1987) Making management decisions: The role of intuition and emotion. *The Academy of Management Executive*. 4, (February) 57-63.

Sims, Henry. P., and J. W. Dean. (1985) Beyond quality circles: Self-managing teams. *Personnel*. 62, (January) 25-32.

Sinbaldi, Frank J. (1985) Pre-control-does it really work with non-normality? *ASQC Annual Technical Quality Congress Transactions.* Milwaukee, WI: ASQC Quality Press, 428-433.

Singhvi, Suren S. (1987) A quantitative approach to site selection. *Management Review.* 76, (November) 61-62.

Singleton, Jack. (1982) Quality circles in a state psychiatric hospital. IAQC Fourth Annual Conference Transactions. Cincinnati, OH: International Association of Quality Circles.

Sinha, M. N., and W. Willborn. (1985) *The Management of Quality Assurance.* New York: John Wiley.

Sinibaldi, Frank J. (1983) Nested designs in process variation studies. *ASQC Annual Technical Quality Congress Transactions.* Milwaukee, WI: ASQC Quality Press, 484-491.

Sink, D. S. (1985) *Productivity Management: Planning, Measurement and Evaluation, Control.* New York: John Wiley.

Sink, Scott. (1991) The role of measurement in world class quality. *Industrial Engineering.* 13, (June) 31-35.

Siotani, Minoru, T. Hayakawa, and Y. Fujikoshi. (1985) *Modern Multivariate Statistical Analysis: A Graduate Course and Handbook.* Columbus OH: American Sciences Press.

Sirkin, H., and George Stalk Jr. (1990) Fix the process, not the problem. *Harvard Business Review.* 78, (July-August) 30.

Sjostrom, L. B. (1968) Correlation of objective-subjective methods as applied in the food field. *Correlation of Objective-Subjective Methods in the Study of Odors and Taste.* Philadelphia, PA: American Society for Testing and Materials.

Skagen, Anne E. (1989) Nurturing relationships, enhancing quality with electronic data interchange. *Management Review.* 78, (February) 28-32.

Skinner, B. F. (1953) *Science and Human Behavior.* New York: Macmillan.

Skinner, B. F. (1971) *Beyond Freedom and Dignity.* New York: Alfred A. Knopf. (*2)

Skinner, B. F. (1974) *About Behaviorism.* New York: Vintage Books.

Skinner, Wickham. (1969) Manufacturing: The missing link in corporate strategy. *Harvard Business Review.* 47, (May-June) 136-145.

Skinner, Wickham. (1974) The focused factory. *Harvard Business Review.* 52, (May-June) 113-121. (*2)

Skinner, Wickham. (1978) *Manufacturing in the Corporate Strategy.* New York: John Wiley. (*2)

Skinner, Wickham. (1986) The productivity paradox. *Harvard Business Review.* 64, (July-August) 55-59.

Skolnik, Michael, Steve Lawrence, and Karen Smyth. (1990) Total quality management is the substance, not slogan. *Marketing News.* 24, (May) 24-25.

Slater, Stanley F., and John C. Narver. (1992) Market Orientation, Performance, and the Moderating Influence of Competitive Environment. Report, No. 92-118, July. Cambridge, MA: Marketing Science Institute.

Slatin, Peter D. (1992) Now, organized management. *Architectural Record.* 180, (April) 32. (*2)

Sloan, Alfred P. (1964) *My Years with General Motors.* Garden City, NY: Doubleday.

Sloan, Alfred P. (1972) *My Years with General Motors.* New York: Anchor Books. (*2)

Sloan, Alfred P. (1990) *My Years with General Motors*. Edited by John McDonald with Catharine Stevens. With a new introduction by Peter F. Drucker. New York: Doubleday/Currency.

Sloan, Allen. (1983) *Three Plus One Equals Billions: The Bendix-Martin-Marietta War*. New York: Arbor House.

Small, Bonnie B. (1956) *Statistical Quality Control Handbook.* Indianapolis, IN: Western Electric Company.

Small business administration (1993) Quality: A road to profits. *Agency Sales Magazine.* 23, (January) 58.

Smart factories: America's Turn? (1989) *BusinessWeek.* (May 8) 142

Smircich, Linda, et al., eds. (1992) New intellectual currents in organization and management theory. Theory development forum. Special Issue. *Academy of Management Review.* (July) 41-48.

Smith, Adam. (1965) *An Inquiry into the Nature and Causes of the Wealth of Nations.* New York: The Modern Library.

Smith, Adam. (1965) *The Wealth of Nations.* New York: Modern Library. (*2)

Smith, Bruce A. (1989) Total quality management will require procurement changes, perseverance. *Aviation Week and Space Technology.* 131, (December) 59-60.

Smith, Douglas K., and Robert C. Alexander. (1988) *Fumbling the Future: How Xerox Invented, then Ignored, the Personal Computer.* New York: William Morrow. (*3)

Smith, Emily T. (1985) Turning an expert's skills into computer software. *BusinessWeek.* (October 7) 104-108.

Smith, Frederick W. (1990) Creating an empowering environment for all employees. *Journal for Quality and Participation.* (June) 6-10.

Smith, Frederick W. (1990) Our human side of quality. *Quality Progress.* 23, (May) 19-21.

Smith, G. L. (1988) Statistical analysis of sensory data. In J. R. Piggott (Ed.) *Sensory Analysis of Foods*. New York: Elsevier Science Publishing.

Smith, H. (1957) *Social and Rational Behavior in a Social Setting.* New York: John Wiley.

Smith, H. A., and J. D. McKeen. (1993) Reengineering the corporation: Where does I.S. fit in? *Proceedings of the Twenty-sixth Annual Hawaii International Conference on System Sciences*. Los Alamitos, CA: IEEE Computer Society Press.

Smith, H. T. (1983) *The Office Revolution.* Willow Grove, PA: Administrative Management Society Foundation.

Smith, I. G. (1969) *The Measurement of Productivity*. New York: McGraw-Hill.

Smith, Jack E., and Ronald B. Morgan. (1996) *Staffing the New Workplace: Selecting and Promoting for Quality Improvement.* Milwaukee, WI: ASQC Quality Press.

Smith, J. R., and H. Duvier, III. (1984) Effect of inspector error on inspection strategies. *ASQC Annual Technical Quality Congress Transactions*. Milwaukee, WI: ASQC Quality Press, 146-151.

Smith, Jim and Mark Oliver. (1992) Quality programs aren't enough. *Machine Design*. 64, (December 10) 113. (*2)

Smith, Lee. (1980) The lures and limits of innovation. *Fortune.* (October 15) 84. (*4)

Smith, Lee. (1980) A superpower enters the soft-drink wars. *Fortune.* (June 30) 77.

Smith, Lee. (1981) J and J comes long way from baby. *Fortune.* (June 1) 66. (*2)

Smith, Martin R. (1992) Quality scams. *Across the Board.* (April) 14. (*2)

Smith, R. Jeffrey. (1979) Shuttle problems compromise space program. *Science*. 25, (November) 910-911.

Smith, Wilma and Richard Andrews. (1989) *Instructional Leadership: How Principals Make a Difference.* Alexandria, VA: Association for Supervision and Curriculum Development.

Snedecor, George W., and William G. Cochran. (1980) *Statistical Methods*. Ames, IA: Iowa State University Press.

Snee, Ronald D. (1973) Design and analysis of mixture experiments. *Journal of Quality Technology*. 3, (June) 159-169.

Snee, Ronald D. (1979) Experimental design for mixture systems with multicomponent constraints. *Communications in Statistics.* A8, 303-326.

Snee, Ronald D. (1985) Computer-aided design of experiments: Some practical experiences. *Journal of Quality Technology.* 17, (October) 222-236.

Sobel, Robert. (1981) *Colossus in Transition.* New York: Times Books. (*2)

Soffer, S. B. (1981) Transformed p charts for variable sample size. *Journal of Quality Technology*. 13, (March) 189-191.

Sokol, Marc and V. Hurwitz. (1982) Evaluation equals growth and survival. *Quality Circles Journal*. 5, (August) 15-20.

Solomon, L. C., and M. A. LaPorte. (1987) The educational implications of the high technology revolution. In A. Kleingartner and C. S. Anderson (Eds.) *Human Resource Management in High Technology Firms.* Lexington, MA: D. C. Heath, 47-66.

Solovy, Alden T. (1993) Champions of change: Today's CEOs learn to say 'yes'. *Hospitals.* 67, (March 5) 14. (*3)

Solovy, Alden T. (1993) Retooling the hospital: Moving into second phase. *Hospitals*. 67, (March 5) 18. (*2)

Sonnenberg, Frank K. (1989) Service quality: Forethought, not afterthought. *Journal of Business Strategy*. (September/October) 56-57.

Sorensen, Charles. (1956) *My Forty Years With Ford.* New York: W. W. Norton.

Sorge, Marjorie. (1981) Work smarter, not harder, advises quality consultant. *Automotive News*. (July 27) 6.

Souder, William E. (1981) Encouraging entrepreneurship in the large corporations. *Research Management*. (May) 19. (*2)

Southard, Rod. (1996) Developing a business process approach to ISO 9000. *Quality Digest*. (August) 31-33.

Soyka, David. (1981) Honeywell pioneers in quality circle movement. *World of Work Report*. 6, (September) 65-67.

Spechler, Jay W. (1988) *When America Does it Right: Case Studies in Service Quality*. Norcross, GA: Industrial Engineering Press.

Spekman, R. E., and L. W. Stern. (1979) Environmental uncertainty and buy group structure: An empirical investigation.

Spence, L. (1978) *The Politics of Social Knowledge.* University Park, PA: Pennsylvania State University Press.

Spencer, James L. (1986) The highs and lows of reliability predictions. *Proceedings, Annual Reliability and Maintainability Symposium*. New York: IEEE, 156-162.

Spendley, W., G. R. Hext, and F. R. Himsworth. (1962) Sequential application of simplex designs in optimization and evolutionary operation. *Technometrics*. 4, (August) 441-461.

Spendolini, Michael. (1991) *The Benchmarking Book*. New York: AMACOM.

Spizizen, Gary. (1992) The ISO 9000 standards: Creating a level playing field for international quality. *National Productivity Review.* 11, (Summer). (*4)

Sports car drivers start your engines. (1986) *Newsweek.* (June 6) 51. (*2)

Spow, E. E. (1984) Automatic assembly. *Tooling and Production.* (October) 46-47.

Sproul, R. C. (1980) *Stronger than Steel: The Wayne Alderson Story.* New York: Harper and Row.

Sprow, Eugene. (1982) Made in USA. *Tooling and Production.* (February) 73-80.

Sprow, Eugene. (1982) The quality commitment. *Tooling and Production.* (March) 73-80.

Sprow, Eugene. (1992) Insights into ISO 9000. *Manufacturing Engineering.* (September) 73.

Staffiery, Richard A. (1975) A semiconductor traceability plan that avoids confusion. *Quality Management and Engineering.* (April) 20, 21.

Stagner, R. (1956) *The Psychology of Industrial Conflict.* New York: John Wiley.

Stahl, Michael J. (1986) *Managerial and Technical Motivation: Assessing Needs for Achievement, Power, and Affiliation.* New York: Praeger.

Stahl, Michael J. (1989) *Strategic Executive Decisions: An Analysis of the Difference Between Theory and Practice.* Westport, CT: Quorum Books.

Stahl, Michael J. (1992) Protectionism or total quality management? *Quality Progress.* 25, (November) 21-16.

Stahl, Michael J. (1995) *Management: Total Quality in a Global Environment.* Cambridge, MA: Basil Blackwell.

Stahl, Michael J., and G. M. Bounds. (1991) *Competing Globally Through Customer Value: The Management of Strategic Suprasystems.* Westport, CT: Quorum Books.

Stahl, Michael J., and D. W. Grigsby. (1992) *Strategic Management for Decision Making.* Boston, MA: PWS-Kent.

Stahl, Michael J., and A. Harrell. (1981) Modeling effort decisions with behavioral decision theory: Toward an individual differences version of expectancy theory. *Organizational Behavior and Human Performance.* 27, (May) 303-325.

Stalk, George, Jr., and Thomas M. Hout. (1990) *Competing Against Time: How Time Based Competition Is Reshaping Global Markets.* New York: Free Press. (*2)

Stalk, George, Jr., P. Evans, and L. E. Shulman. (1992)Competing on capabilities: The new rules of corporate strategy. *Harvard Business Review.* 70, (March-April) 57-69.

Stalker, A. H. (1980) The inspection record. *Quality.* (August) 33.

Staneas, Al P. (1987) The metamorphosis of the quality function. *Quality Progress.* 20, (November) 30-33.

Stansbury, James F. (1981) Financial incentives for circles?. *Quality Circles Journal.* 4, (February) 7.

Stanton, Burr. (1974) Consumer appliance reliability: Closing the feedback loop. *Proceedings, Annual Reliability and Maintainability Symposium.* New York: IEEE, 30-34.

The star of the oil fields tackles semiconductors. (1981) *BusinessWeek.* (February) 60.

Starr, C. G. (1983) *A History of the Ancient World.* New York: Oxford University Press.

Starr, M. K. (1978) *Operations Management*. Englewood Cliffs, NJ: Prentice-Hall.

Statement of Purpose. (1993) Cincinnati, OH: Procter and Gamble.

Statistical Quality Control. (1984) Special Report #762, *American Machinist*. (January) 97-108. (*2)

Stayer, R. (1990) CEO opinion: The flight of the buffalo. *Target*. (Spring) 21.

Stayer, R. (1990) How I learned to let my workers lead. *Harvard Business Review*. 78, (November-December) 66-83.

Staying power: Motorola illustrates how an aged giant can remain vibrant. (1992) *Wall Street Journal*. (December 11) A1.

Stebbing, Lionel. (1989) *Quality Assurance: The Root to Efficiency and Competiveness*. Ellis Horwood Limited.

Steber, H. (1985) Qualitatskontrolle bei fruchtzubereitungen. *Deutsche Molkerei-Zeitung*. 46, 1547-1550.

Steel, Robert G. D., and James H. Torrie. (1962) *Principles and Procedures of Statistics*. New York: McGraw-Hill. (*2)

Steeples, M. M. (1993) *The Corporate Guide to the Malcolm Baldrige National Quality Award: Proven Strategies for Building Quality in Your Organization*. Second edition. Milwaukee, WI: ASQC Quality Press.

Steers, R., and L. Porter. (1991) *Motivation and Work Behavior*. Fifth edition. New York: McGraw-Hill.

Stein, Barry A., and Rosabeth Moss Kanter. (1980) Building the parallel organization: creating mechanisms for permanent quality of work life. *The Journal of Applied Behavioral Science*. 16, (April) 371-386.

Stein, R. E. (1993) *The Next Phase of Total Quality Management: TQM II and the Focus on Profitability*. New York: Dekker.

Steinbeck, John. (1941) *The Log from the Sea of Cortez.* New York: Viking Press. (*2)

Steinberg, D. M., and William G. Hunter. (1984) Experimental design: Review and comment. *Technometrics.* 26, (February) 71-97. (*2)

Steinbruner, John D. (1974) *The Cybernetic Theory of Decision: New Dimensions of Political Analysis.* Princeton, NJ: Princeton University Press. (*2)

Steiner, George A. (1979) *Strategic Planning: What Every Manager Must Know.* New York: Free Press. (*2)

Steiner, George A. (1983) *The New CEO.* New York: Macmillan.

Steiner, George A., and J. F. Steiner. (1988) *Business, Government, and Society*, New York: Random House.

Stephens, Kenneth S. (1979) *Preparing for Standardization, Certification and Quality Control.* Tokyo: Asian Productivity Organization.

Stephens, Kenneth S. (1982) *How to Perform Skip-Lot Sampling and Chain Sampling, Volume 4, The ASCQ Basic References in Quality Control.* Milwaukee, WI: ASQC Quality Press.

Stephens, L. S. (1978) A closed form solution for single sample acceptance sampling plans. *Journal of Quality Technology.* 10, (April) 159-163.

Sterett, W. Kent (1987) Commitment and involvement: Vital components in a successful quality improvement program. *The Juran Report.* (Winter) 35-37. (*2)

Sterman, John. (1987) *Misperceptions of Feedback in Dynamic Decision Making.* Cambridge: Harvard University Press.

Sterman, John. (1989) Modeling managerial behavior: Misperceptions of feedback in a dynamic decision making experiment. *Management Science.* 35, (March) 335-347. (*2)

Stertz, Bradley A. (1988) GM will discontinue the Fiero, citing slump in 2-seater market. *Wall Street Journal.* (March 2) 3. (*2)

Stevens, Mark. (1979) *Like No Other Store in the World: The Inside Story of Bloomingdale's.* New York: Crowell. (*2)

Stevens, Roger T. (1978) *Operational Test and Evaluation: A Systems Engineering Process.* New York: Springer-Verlag.

Stevens, W. L. (1948) Control by gauging. *Royal Statistical Society Journal.* 10, (September) 54-108.

Stevenson, Harold W., and James W. Stigler. (1992) *The Learning Gap: Why our Schools Are Failing and What We Can Learn from Japanese and Chinese Education.* New York: Summit Books.

Stevenson, S. G., M. Vaisey-Genser, and N. A. M. Eskin. (1984) Quality control in the use of deep frying oils. *JAOCS.* 61, (June) 1102-1108.

Stevenson, W. J. (1982) *Production/Operations Management.* Homewood, IL: Irwin.

Stewart, R. (1971) *How Computers Affect Management.* New York: Macmillan.

Stewart, Thomas A. (1989) Westinghouse gets respect at last. *Fortune.* (July 3) 92-98.

Stewart, Thomas A. (1993) Reengineering: The hot new management tool. *Fortune.* (August 14) 33-37.

Stewart, W. T. (1978) A yardstick for measuring productivity. *Industrial Engineering.* 10, (February) 34-37.

Stickler, Michael J. (1989) Going for the globe, Part II: Eliminating waste. *Production and Inventory Management Review and APICS News.* (November) 104.

Stockman, David. (1986) *The Triumph of Politics.* New York: Harper and Row.

Stockton, J. R., and T. Clark. (1985) *Introduction to Business and Economic Statistics.* Cincinnati, OH: South-Western.

Stoddard, D. B., and S. L. Jarvenpaa. (1995) Business process redesign: Tactics for managing radical change. *Journal of Management Information Systems.* 12, (No. 1) 81-107.

Stoddard, D. B., and C. J. Meadows. (1992) Capital Holding Corporation—Reengineering the direct response group. Harvard Business School Case No. 9-192-001. Cambridge, MA: Harvard Business School.

Stogdill, Ralph Melvin. (1948) Personal factors associated with leadership: A survey of the literature. *Journal of Psychology.* (January) 35-64.

Stogdill, Ralph Melvin. (1974) *Handbook of Leadership.* New York: Free Press.

Stogdill, Ralph Melvin and A. E. Coons. (1957) *Leader Behavior.* Research Monograph Number 88. Columbus, OH: Ohio State University, Bureau of Business Research.

Stokes, R. G., and F. N. Stehle. (1968) Some life-cycle cost estimates for electronic equipment: Methods and results. *Proceedings, Annual Reliability and Maintainability Symposium.* New York: IEEE, 169-183.

Stolte-Heiskanen, Veronica. (1980) A managerial review view of research. *Science.* 26, (January 4) 48.

Stone, Byron and Carol North. (1988) *Risk Management and Insurance for Nonprofit Managers.* First Non Profit Risk Pooling Trust.

Stone, H., and J. Sidel. (1985) *Sensory Evaluation Practices.* New York: Academic Press.

Stone, Herbert. D., and T. A. Guith. (1984) Buick city: Strategy for quality and productivity. *Quality Progress.* 17, (April) 34-38.

Stone, Thomas H., and Jack Fiorito. (1986) A perceived uncertainty model of human resource forecasting technique use. *Academy of Management Review*. (November) 635-642.

Stoner, James A. F., and R. Edward Freeman. (1989) *Management*. Englewood Cliffs, NJ: Prentice-Hall.

Storey, Christopher. (1989) Excellence: It's in the cards. *Training and Development Journal*. 43, (September) 46-49. (*3)

Stouffer, J. C. (1985) Coordinating sensory evaluation in a multi-plant operation. *Food Technology*. 39, (November) 134.

Stowell, Daniel M. (1989) Quality in the marketing process. *Quality Progress*. 22, (October) 57-62.

Stratton, Brad. (1990) A beacon for the world. *Quality Progress*. 23, (May) 19-21.

Stratton, Brad. (1990) Making the Malcolm Baldridge Award better. *Quality Progress*. 23, (March) 12-13.

Stratton, Brad. (1991) The value of implementing quality. *Quality Progress*. 24, (July) 70-71.

Stratton, Donald A. (1987) Force field analysis: A powerful tool for facilitator. *The Juran Report*. (Winter) 105-111.

Stressing the system approach. (1969) *Manufacturing Engineering*. (August) 75.

Strickland, Jack. (1988) Total quality management. *Army Research Development and Acquisition Bulletin*. (March-April) 1-4.

Striner, Herbert E. (1984) *Regaining the Lead: Policies for Economic Growth*. New York: Praeger.

Strolle, Alfred. (1991) Creating a total quality management culture is everyone's business. *Research Technology Management*. 34, (August) 8-9.

Strong, E. P. (1962) *Increasing Office Productivity: A Seven-Step Program*. New York: McGraw-Hill.

Strongrich, A. L., G. E. Herbert, and T. J. Jacoby. (1983) *Simple Statistical Methods*. SAE Paper 830299. Warrendale, PA: Society of Automotive Engineers, 31-38. (*2)

Strother, Deborah Burnett. (1991) *A Measure of Excellence.* Bloomington, IN: Phi Delta Kappa.

Struthers, J. E. (1981) Canada-Japan essay: Long road back. *Canada-Japan Council*. (February) 6-10.

Struthers, J. E. (1981) Why can't we do what Japan does? *Canadian Business Review*. 8, (Summer) 24-26.

Stubin, Robert J. (1978) Temperature monitoring and control system for MLRB's. *ASQC Annual Technical Quality Congress Transactions*. Milwaukee, WI: ASQC Quality Press, 273-278.

Studer, Kimberly J., and Mark D. Dibner. (1988) Robots invade small businesses. *Management Review*. 77, (November) 26-31.

Stuelpnagel, Thomas R. (1989) Total quality management in business and academia. *Business Forum*. 14, (Issue 1, Fall 1988-Winter) 4-9.

Stuckey, John. (1983) *Vertical Integration and Joint Ventures in the Aluminum Industry*. Cambridge, MA: Harvard Univrsity Press.

Stuller, Jay. (1993) Practical matters. *Across the Board*. (January-February) 36-40.

Substituting rules for judgement: The iconoclast who made Visa number 1. (1980) *BusinessWeek*. (December) 44.

Sugarman, Aaron. (1988) Success through people: A new era in the way America does business. *Incentive*. (May) 40-43.

Sugimori, Y., K. Kusinoki, F. Cho, and S. Uchikawa. (1977) Toyota production system and *Kanban* system—Materialization of just-in-time and respect for human system. *International Journal of Production Research.* (October) 553-564.

Sugimoto, T. (1968) QC audit by the top management. *Hinshitsu Kanri.* 19, (April) 1136-1140.

Sugimoto, Yasuo. (1972) The advancing QC circle movement. *Japan Quality Control Circles.* Tokyo: Asian Productivity Organization, 31-45.

Sullivan, Barry F. (1981) What I am really talking about. *International Service Products: The Opportunity of the 80's.* (March) 13.

Sullivan, L. P. (1984) Reducing variability: A new approach to quality. *Quality Management.* (July) 15-21. (*2)

Sullivan, L. P. (1985) Letters. *Quality Progress.* 18, (April) 7-8.

Sullivan, L. P. (1986) Quality function deployment. *Quality Progress.* 19, (June) 39-50. (*3)

Sullivan, L. P. (1986) The power of Taguchi methods. *Target.* (Summer) 21-26.

Sullivan, L. P. (1986) The seven stages in company-wide quality control. *Quality Progress.* 19, (May) 50-52. (*2)

Sullivan, N., and K. U. Frentzel. (1992) A patient transport pilot quality improvement team. *Quality Review Bulletin,* 18, (July) 215-221.

Sullivan, T. (1983) Quality sharpens Corning's edge. *Quality.* (May) 27-30.

Sundstrom, E., K. Demeuse, and D. Futrell. (1990) Work teams: Applications and effectiveness. *American Psychologist.* 55, (February) 120-133.

Suntag, Charles. (1993) *Inspection and Inspection Management.* Milwaukee, WI: ASQC Quality Press.

Support group formed for companies seeking ISO 9000. (1993) *Industrial Engineering*. 25, (March) 8.

Surprise! CEOs blame workers for poor quality. (1990) *The Quality Executive*. (August) 3.

Suszko, M., and J. Breaugh. (1986) The effects of realistic job previews on applicant self-selection and employee turnover, satisfaction and coping ability. *Journal of Management*. (Fall) 513-523.

Sutermeister, Robert A. (1973) *People and Productivity*. New York: McGraw-Hill.

Suto, K. (1978) Standardization in the CMEA and its realization in Hungary. *Proceedings, Conference on International Quality Control*. Tokyo: JUSE Press, A6, 7. (*2)

Sutton, Judy. (1992) Quality focus is heightened at steel centers. *American Metal Market*. 100, (September 9) 14A.

Sutton, R. I., K. M. Eisenhardt, and J. V. Jucker. (1986) Managing organizational decline: Lessons from Atari. *Organizational Dynamics*. 9, (Spring) 17-29.

Suver, James D., Bruce R. Nuemann, and Keith E. Boles. (1992) Accounting for the costs of quality. *Healthcare Financial Management*. 46, (September) 29. (*2)

Suzaki, Kiyoshi. (1987) *The New Manufacturing Challenge: Techniques for Continuous Improvement*. New York: Free Press.

Sward, Keith. (1948) *The Legend of Henry Ford*. New York: Rinehart.

Swartz, G., and V. Constock. (1979) One firm's experience with quality circles. *Quality Progress*. 12, (September) 14-16. (*2)

Swartz, Steve. (1987) Wall Street's growth is seriously outpacing management systems. *Wall Street Journal*. (July 27) 1.

Swatman, P. M. C., P. Swatman, and D. C. Fowler. (1994) A model of EDI integration and strategic business reengineering. *Journal of Strategic Information Systems*. 3, (No. 1) 41-60.

Swaton, Lawrence E., and C. P. Green. (1973) Automated process audit and certification program. *Quality Management and Engineering*. (March) 24.

Swiss, James E. (1992) Adapting total quality management (TQM) to government. *Public Administration Review*. 52, (July-August) 356-362. (*3)

Switzer, R. (1984) The determinants of industrial R and D: A funds flow simultaneous equations approach. *Review of Economics and Statistics*. (February) 163-68.

Swoyer, J. (1983) OPT: Zero inventory for all. *Wall Street Journal*. 18, (February) 1.

Sylvester, D. L. (1984) Statistical techniques to improve quality and production in non-manufacturing operations. *Survey of Business*. 19, (Spring) 11-17.

Szczesniak, A. S. (1973) *Texture Measurements of Foods*. Dordrecht, Holland: D. Reidel Publishing Company.

Szczesniak, A. S. (1987) Correlating sensory with instrumental texture measurements. *Texture Studies*. 18, 1-15.

Szilagyi, Andrew D., Jr., and Marc J. Wallace Jr. (1990) *Organizational Behavior and Performance,* Fifth edition. Glenview, IL: Scott, Foresman.

Tabak, Lawrence. (1993) Can quality save business? *Ingram's*. 19, (January) 42. (*2)

Tagliaferri, L. E. (1982) As quality circles fade, a bank tries top down teamwork. *ABA Banking Journal*. 74, (July) 98-100.

Taguchi, Genichi. (1970) *Quality Assurance and Design of Inspection During Production-Reports of Statistical Applications and Research.* Tokyo: JUSE Press.

Taguchi, Genichi. (1978) Off-line and on-line quality control systems. *Proceedings, International Conference on Quality Control.* Tokyo: JUSE Press, B4-1 through B4-5. (*3)

Taguchi, Genichi. (1978) *Systems of Experimental Design.* New York: Kraus International Publications.

Taguchi, Genichi. (1981) *On Line Quality Control During Production.* Tokyo: Japanese Standards Association.

Taguchi, Genichi. (1985) Quality engineering in Japan. *Common Statistics—Theory and Methods.* 14, (November) 2785-2801.

Taguchi, Genichi. (1986) *Introduction to Quality Engineering: Designing Quality into Products and Process.* Tokyo: Asian Productivity Organization. (*4)

Taguchi, Genichi. (1987) *System of Experimental Design.* White Plains, NY: UNIPUB.

Taguchi, Genichi, and Don Clausing. (1990) Robust quality. *Harvard Business Review.* 78, (January-February) 65.

Taguchi, Genichi, and S. M. Wu. (1979) *Introduction to Off Line Quality Control.* Magaya, Japan: Meieki Nakamura Ku. (*2)

Tague, Nancy R. (1995) *The Quality Toolbox.* Milwaukee, WI: ASQC Quality Press.

Taha, H. (1988) *Operations Research: An Introduction.* New York: Macmillan, 1-2.

Takamiya, Susumu. (1981) The characteristics of Japanese management. *Management Japan.* 14, (Summer) 6-9.

Takanashi, M. (1978) Quality assurance system for the integrated circuit. *Proceedings, International Conference on Quality Control.* Tokyo: JUSE Press, C1-51 through C1-56.

Takayanagi, A. (1974) Quality control activities at a shipyard. *Hinshitsu Kanri.* 24, (April) 515-519.

Takeda, Yutaka. (1980) Autonomous self-management activity: A key to high productivity at Nippon Steel Corporation. A paper presented at the Japan Society (May).

Takei, Fumio. (1986) Engineering quality improvement through TQC activity. *IEEE Transactions on Engineering Management.* 33, (May) 92-94.

Takeuchi, H. (1981) Productivity: Learning from the Japanese. *California Management Review.* 23, (Summer) 5-19. (*3)

Takeuchi, H., and I. Nonaka. (1986) The new, new product development game. *Harvard Business Review.* 64, (January-February) 137-146. (*2)

Takeuchi, H., and J. A. Quelch. (1983) Quality is more than making a product. *Harvard Business Review.* 61, (July-August) 139-145. (*2)

Talley, D. J. (1986) The quest for sustaining quality improvement. *The Juran Report.* (Summer) 188-192.

Talwar, R. (1993) Business reengineering—A strategy-driven approach. *Long Range Planning.* 26, (No. 6) 22-40.

Tamarkin, Bob. (1980) The country slicker. *Forbes.* (January) 40.

Tanaka, T. (1989) Two giants, Mitsubishi and Toyota: A Historical study of management accounting in Japan. Unpublished paper.

Tannenbaum, Arnold S. (Ed.). (1968) *Control in Organizations.* New York: McGraw-Hill.

Tannenbaum, Jeffrey A. (1992) Small companies are finding it pays to think global: Firms win new business by adopting international quality standards. *Wall Street Journal.* (November 19, Section B) 2.

Tannenbaum, Robert and Warren H. Schmidt. (1957) How to choose a leadership pattern. *Harvard Business Review.* 35, (March-April) 95-101. (*3)

Tape controlled machines at Sunstrand Aviation (1980) *Quality Assurance.* 6, (June) 30-40.

Tarrant, J. J. (1972) *Data Communications and Business Strategy: A Working Source Book for Modern Managers.* Princeton, NJ: Auerbach Publishers.

Tarver, Mae-Goodwin. (1984) Multi-station process capability: Filling equipment. *ASQC Annual Technical Quality Congress Transactions.* Milwaukee, WI: ASQC Quality Press, 281-288.

Tatsuno, Sheridan M. (1986) *Technopolis Strategy.* Englewood Cliffs, NJ: Prentice-Hall. (*2)

Tatsuno, Sheridan M. (1990) *Created in Japan: From Imitators to World-Class Innovators.* New York: Harper and Row.

Tavenier, Gerard. (1981) Awakening a sleeping giant: Ford's employee involvement program. *Management Review.* 70, (June) 15-20.

Tawara, N. (1980) A case study on measuring inspection job design. *International Journal of Production Research.* 18, 353.

Taylor, Alex, III. (1990) Here come the new luxury cars. *Fortune.* (July 1) 58-65.

Taylor, Alex, III. (1990) The new drive to revive GM. *Fortune.* (April 9) 52-61.

Taylor, Alex, III. (1990) New lessons from Japan's carmakers. *Fortune.* (October 22) 165, 168.

Taylor, Alex, III. (1990) Why Toyota keeps getting better and better and better. *Fortune.* (November 19) 69. (*3)

Taylor, B. W., and K. R. Davis. (1977) Corporate productivity: Getting it all together. *Industrial Engineering.* 9, (March) 30-36.

Taylor, C. W. (1964) *Creativity: Progress and Potential.* New York: McGraw-Hill.

Taylor, Ervin F. (1981) Product quality and the media. *ASQC Annual Technical Quality Congress Transactions.* Milwaukee, WI: ASQC Quality Press, 825-830.

Taylor, Frederick Winslow. (1911) *Principles of Scientific Management.* New York: Harper and Row. (*3)

Taylor, Frederick Winslow. (1919) *Shop Management.* New York: Harper and Row. (*2)

Taylor, Frederick Winslow. (1923) *Fredrick W. Taylor: Father of Scientific Management.* New York: Harper and Row.

Taylor, Frederick Winslow. (1947) *Principles of Scientific Management.* New York: Harper and Row. (*3)

Taylor, Frederick Winslow. (1947) *Scientific Management.* New York: Harper and Row. (*2)

Taylor, Frederick Winslow. (1967) *The Principles of Scientific Management.* New York: W. W. Norton.

Taylor, Frederick Winslow. (1985) *The Principles of Scientific Management.* Easton, PA: Hive Publishing.

Taylor, J. (1983) *Shadows of the Rising Sun.* New York: William Morrow. (*2)

Taylor, J. A., and H. Williams. (1994) The 'transformation game': Information systems and process innovation in organizations. *New Technology, Work and Employment.* 9, (No. 1) 54-65.

Taylor, J. C., and D. G. Bowers. (1972) *Survey of Organizations: A Machine Scored Standardized Questionnaire Instrument.* Ann Arbor, MI: Institute for Social Research. (*2)

Taylor, Mark. (1982) BankCal quality circles. IAQC Fourth Annual Conference Transactions. (March). Cincinnati, OH: International Association of Quality Circles.

Taylor, S. (1993) Eastman Chemical strives for better than world class. *Industrial Engineering.* 25, (November) 28-34.

Taylor, T. C. (1993) Plugging into the future. *Sales and Marketing Management.* (June) 20-24.

Taylor, William R. (1981) Quality assured in new products via comprehensive system approach. *Industrial Engineering.* 13, (March) 28-32.

Tazewell, W. L. (1986) *Newport News Shipbuilding: The First Century.* Newport, VA: Newport News, The Mariners Museum.

Team spirit: A decisive response to crisis brought Ford enhanced productivity. (1992) *Wall Street Journal.* (December 15) A1.

Technical Information Center. (1961) *Engineering Management.* (MIL-STD-449A). Washington, DC: Defense Document Distribution Center.

Technical Information Center. (1969) *Requirements for System Safety Programs for Systems and Associated Subsystems and Equipment.* (MIL-STD-882). Philadelphia, PA: U.S. Department of Defense, Naval Publications and Forms Center.

Technical Information Center. (1973) *Maintainability Verification/ Demonstration/Evaluation.* (MIL-STD-471A). Philadelphia, PA: U.S. Department of Defense, Naval Publications and Forms Center.

Technical Information Center. (1977) *System Safety Program Requirements.* (MIL-STD-882A). Philadelphia, PA: U.S. Department of Defense, Naval Publications and Forms Center.

Technical Information Center. (1980) *Procedures for Performing a Failure Mode, Effects and Criticality Analysis.* (MIL-STD-1629A). Philadelphia, PA: U.S. Department of Defense, Naval Publications and Forms Center.

Technical Information Center. (1980) *Reliability Program for Systems and Equipment Development and production.* (MIL-STD-785B). Philadelphia, PA: U.S. Department of Defense, Naval Publications and Forms Center.

Technical Information Center. (1981) *Definitions of Terms for Reliability and Maintainability.* (MIL-STD-721C). Philadelphia, PA: U.S. Department of Defense, Naval Publications and Forms Center.

Technical Information Center. (1981) *Reliability Design Qualification and Production Acceptance Tests Exponential Distribution.* (MIL-STD-781C). Philadelphia, PA: U.S. Department of Defense, Technical Information Center.

Technical Information Center. (1982) *Reliability Prediction of Electronic Equipment.* (MIL-DBK-217D). Washington, DC: U.S. Department of Defense.

Technical Information Center. (1983) *Maintainability Program Requirements for System and Equipment.* (MIL-STD-470A). Philadelphia, PA: U.S. Department of Defense, Naval Publications and Forms Center.

Technical Information Center. (1986) *Reliability Program for Systems and Equipment Development and Production.* (MIL-STD-785B). Philadelphia, PA: U.S. Department of Defense, Technical Information Center.

Technology: No Compromises. (1992) *Wall Street Journal.* (November 16) R8.

Tedaldi, Michael, Fred Scaglione, and Vincent Russotti. (1992) *A Beginner's Guide to Quality in Manufacturing.* Milwaukee, WI: ASQC Quality Press.

Teece, D. J. (1987) *The Competitive Challenge: Strategies for Industrial Innovation and Renewal.* New York: Harper and Row.

Teitelbaum, R. S. (1991) LBO's really didn't pay, say the chiefs. *Fortune.* (August 14) 73-76.

Tellier, R. D. (1978) *Operations Management: Fundamental Concepts and Methods.* New York: Harper and Row.

Telschow, Roger. (1993) Quality begins at home. *Nation's Business.* 81, (January) 6. (*2)

Temin, T. R. (1983) Ford to suppliers: Get serious about quality. *Purchasing Magazine.* (February 27) 21-24. (*2)

The ten best managed companies. (1970) *Dun's Review.* (December) 30.

Teradyne, Inc. (1974) *High-Volume Testing for Electronic Device Users.* Boston, MA: Teradyne.

Tersine, R. J., and H. Campbell. (1977) *Modern Materials Management.* New York: North Holland.

Teshner, H. G. (1968) Controlling data flow in a steel mill. *Control Engineering.* 15, (April) 76-80.

Tetzeli, Rick. (1992) Making quality more than a fad. *Fortune.* (May 18) 12. (*3)

Tetzeli, Rick. (1993) A day in the life of Ed Deming. *Fortune.* (January 11) 74.

Thackray, J. (1993) Fads, fixes and fictions. *Management Today.* (June) 40-42.

Thamhain, H. J. (1990) Managing technologically innovative team efforts toward new product success. *Journal of Product Innovation Management.* 7, (March) 5-18.

Thayer, Ann M. (1992) Chemical industry group introduces new system for quality management. *Chemical and Engineering News*. 70, (December 7) 17. (*2)

Theisen, E. C. (1972) *How to Obsolete Inventory Obsolescence*. Decatur, GA: G. W. Plossl. (*2)

Thelen, H. (1954) *Dynamics of Groups At Work*. Chicago, IL: University of Chicago Press.

Thietart, R. A., and R. Vivas. (1984) An empirical investigation of success strategies for businesses along the product life cycle. *Management Science*. 30, (December) 1405-1423.

This company has never left: P and G's new new-product on-slaught. (1979) *BusinessWeek*. (October) 79.

Thoday, Wilfred R. (1981) Additional reflections on quality terminology. *EOQC Quality*. (January) 11.

Thoday, Wilfred R. (1983) A solution to multiple assessment. *ASQC Annual Technical Quality Congress Transactions*. Milwaukee, WI: ASQC Quality Press, 653-655.

Thoman, D. R., L. J. Bain, and C. E. Antle. (1970) Maximum likelihood estimation, exact confidence intervals for reliability and tolerance limits in the Weibull distribution. *Technometrics*. 12, (September) 363-371.

Thomas, Berry H. (1990) *Managing the Total Quality Authoritarian*. New York: McGraw-Hill. (*2)

Thomas, D. W., et al. (1956) *Statistical Quality Control Handbook*. Indianapolis, IN: AT and T.

Thomas, E. F (1981) Shortcomings of current motivational techniques. In H. J. Bajaria (Ed.) *Quality Assurance: Methods, Management and Motivation*. Dearborn, MI: Society of Manufacturing Engineers, 87-96. (*2)

Thomas, H., and D. Gardner. (1985) *Strategic Marketing and Management*. New York: John Wiley.

Thomas, J. H. (1977) Productivity in the quality control department. *ASQC Inspection Division Newsletter*. 8, (March) 2-3.

Thomas, J. W., and D. L. Longo. (1990) Applications of severity measurement systems for hospital quality management. *Hospital and Health Services Administration*. 35, (February) 221-243.

Thomas, Kenneth W., and Betty A. Velthouse. (1990) Cognitive elements of empowerment. *Academy of Management Review*. (October) 668-681.

Thomas, Michael M. (1980) Businessmen's shortcomings. *New York Times*. (August 21) A 1. (*2)

Thomas, R. (1994) *What Machines Can't Do*. Berkeley, CA: University of California Press.

Thomas, Veronica. (1966) The wizard of Plockropool. *Atlantic Monthly*. (July) 124-126.

Thompson, D. B. (1987) Everybody's a boss. *Industry Week*. (February 23) 16-17. (*2)

Thompson, H. A., and E. A. Reynolds. (1964) Inspection and testing as a problem in man-machine systems control engineering. *Industrial Quality Control*. 22, (July) 21-23.

Thompson, J. (1967) *Organizations in Action*. New York: McGraw-Hill. (*2)

Thompson, P. C. (1981) Management circles—Number. *Quality Circles Journal*. 4, (November) 7.

Thompson, P. C. (1981) Voluntary circles. *Quality Circles Journal*. 4, (May) 9.

Thompson, P. C. (1982) *Quality Circles: How to Make Them Work in America*. New York: AMACOM. (*2)

Thompson William O., and Raymond H. Myers. (1968) Response surface designs for mixture problems. *Technometrics.* 10, (April) 739-756.

Thomson, J. E. (1950) *Inspection Organization and Methods.* New York: McGraw-Hill.

Thon, Heinz-Jurgen, and Reinhard Willinger. (1983) FMS—Modular automation for the factory of the future. *Siemens Power Engineering.* 5, 330-331.

Thor, Carl G. (1991) How to measure organizational productivity. *CMA—The Management Accounting Magazine.* (March) 17-19.

Thorelli, H. B., and S. C. Burnett. (1981) The nature of product life cycles for industrial goods businesses. *Journal of Marketing.* 45, (Fall) 31-40.

Thornburg, Linda. (1992) Pay for performance: What you should know. *H R Magazine.* 37, (June) 58-61. (*4)

Thorndike, E. (1911) *Animal Intelligence.* New York: Macmillan.

Thurow, Lester C. (1980) *The Zero-Sum Society: Distribution and the Possibilities for Economic Change.* New York: Basic Books. (*8)

Thurow, Lester C. (1983) *Dangerous Currents.* New York: Random House.

Thurow, Lester C. (1985) *Management Challenge.* Cambridge, MA: MIT. (*2)

Thurow, Lester C. (1985) A time to dismantle the world economy. *The Economist.* (November 9) 21-61.

Thurow, Lester C. (1987) A weakness in process technology. *Science* (December) 1659-1663.

Thurow, Lester C. (1990) The state of American competitiveness and how it can be improved. Report of proceedings from The Xerox Quality Forum II, July 31-August 2. Leesburg, VI: Xerox, 13-16.

Thurow, Lester C. (1992) *Head to Head, The Coming Economic Battles Between Japan, Europe, and America*. New York: William Morrow. (*2)

Tichy, Noel M. (1983) *Managing Strategic Change: Technical, Political and Cultural Dynamics*. New York: John Wiley. (*2)

Tichy, Noel M. (1993) The handbook for revolutionaries. In Noel M. Tichy and Stratford Sherman. *Control Your Destiny or Someone Else Will: Lessons in Mastering Change—From the Principles Jack Welch Is Using to Revolutionize GE*. Garden City, NY: Doubleday, 367-447.

Tichy, Noel M., and Mary Anne Devanna. (1986) *The Transformational Leader*. New York: John Wiley.

Tichy, Noel M., Charles J. Fombrun, and Mary Anne Devanna. (1982) Strategic human resource management. *Sloan Management Review*. 23, (Winter) 47-61.

Tichy, Noel M., and Stratford Sherman. (1993) *Control Your Destiny or Someone Else Will: Lessons in Mastering Change—From the Principles Jack Welch Is Using to Revolutionize GE*. Garden City, NY: Doubleday.

Tichy, Noel M., and Stratford Sherman. (1993) Walking the talk at GE. *Training and Development Journal*. 47, (June) 26-35.

Tichy, Noel M., and D. O. Ulrich. (1984) The leadership challenge—A call for the transformational leader. *Sloan Management Review*. 26, (Fall) 59-68.

Timms, H. L. (1966) *The Production Function in Business*. Homewood, IL: Irwin.

Tindill, B. S., A. F. Al-Assaf, and S. Gentling. (1993) Total quality improvement: A study of Veterans Affairs directors and Quality

Assurance coordinators. *American Journal of Medical Quality*. 8, (February) 45-52.

Tinnin, David B. (1981) The heady success of Holland's Heineken. *Fortune*. (December 15) 169. (*2)

Tipnis, V. A. (1980) Computer aided process planning. *ASQC Annual Technical Quality Congress Transactions*. Milwaukee, WI: ASQC Quality Press, 129-134.

Tippett, L. H. C. (1925) On the extreme individuals and the range of samples taken from a normal population. *Biometrika*. 17, (2) 13-16.

Tippett, L. H. C. (1935) Ratio-delay study. *Journal of Textile Institute Transactions*. 36, (February) 21-32.

Tippett, L. H. C. (1944) *Statistics*. Oxford, UK: Oxford University Press.

Tippett, L. H. C. (1950) *Technological Applications of Statistics*. New York: John Wiley. (*2)

Tippett, L. H. C. (1952) *The Methods of Statistics*. New York: John Wiley.

Tkachenko, V. V. (1973) *Principles of Standardization and Quality Control*. Moscow: Gosstandart. (*2)

Tobey, D. (1979) Metrology = calibration. *ASQC Annual Technical Quality Congress Transactions*. Milwaukee, WI: ASQC Quality Press, 513-520.

Tobin, Lawrence M. (1990) The new quality landscape: Total quality management. *Journal of Systems Management*. 41, (November) 10-14.

Tocqueville, A. (1898) *Democracy in America*. New York: The Century Company.

Toffler, Alvin. (1970) *Future Shock*. New York: Random House. (*2)

Toffler, Alvin. (1980) *The Third Wave.* New York: William Morrow. (*2)

Toffler, Alvin. (1990) *Powershift: Knowledge, Wealth, and Violence at the Edge of the Twenty-First Century.* New York: Bantam Books. (*2)

The Tokyo stock market: And how its swings affect you. (1990) *BusinessWeek.* (February 12) 74-84.

Toland, John. (1970) *The Rising Sun.* New York: Random House.

Tomlinson, L. H. (1983) Silicon crystal termination, an application of the analysis of means for percent defective. *Journal of Quality Technology.* 15, (January) 26-32.

Tompkins, M. D., and G. B. Pratt. (1959) Comparison of flavor evaluation methods for frozen citrus concentrates. *Food Technology.* 13, 149-152.

Toohey, Edward F., and Alberto B. Calvo. (1980) Cost analyses for avionics acquisition. *Proceedings, Annual Reliability and Maintainability Symposium.* New York: IEEE, 85-90.

Torbeck, D. (1985) A bibliography of quality in the service industries. *Quality Progress.* 18, (June) 74-83.

Tornatzky, L. G., J. D. Eveland, M. G. Boylan, W. A. Hetzner, E. C. Johnson, D. Roitman, and J. Schneider. (1983) *The Process of Technological Innovation: Reviewing the Literature.* Washington, DC: National Science Foundation. (*2)

Tortorich, R., R. Thompson, C. Orfan, D. Layfield, C. Dreyfus, and M. Kelly. (1981) Measuring organizational impact of quality circles. *Quality Circles Journal.* 4, (November) 26-33.

Towey, John F. (1988) Information please: What are quality costs? *Management Accounting.* (March) 40.

Townsend, Patrick L., and Joan E. Gebhardt. (1990) *Commit to Quality.* New York: John Wiley. (*2)

Townsend, Patrick L., and Joan E. Gebhardt. (1990/91) The quality process: Little things mean a lot. *Review of Business.* (Winter) 15-20.

Townsend, Patrick L., and Joan E. Gebhardt. (1992) *Quality in Action.* New York: John Wiley.

Townsend, Robert. (1970) *Up The Organization.* New York: Alfred A. Knopf. (*2)

Townsend, Robert. (1980) Why the Japanese are so successful. *Management Review.* 69, (October) 29-47.

Townsend, Robert. (1984) *Further up the Organization.* New York: Random House.

Toynbee, Arnold. (1979) *A Study of History.* New York: Weathervane Books. (*2)

Toyoda, Eiji. (1985) *Toyota: Fifty Years in Motion.* Tokyo, Japan and New York: Kodansha International.

TQM: More than a dying fad? (1993) *Fortune.* (October 18) 66-72.

TQM: You need it to survive. (1992) *Florida Trend.* (October) 25.

Training America: Learning to work for the 21st Century. (1989) Booklet published by the American Society for Training and Development.

Training Magazine's 1986 industry report on training. (1986) *Training.* 23, (October) 22-60.

Trant, A. S., R. M. Pangborn, and A. C. Little. (1981) Potential fallacy of correlating hedonic responses with physical and chemical measurements. *Food Science.* 46, (February) 583-588.

Travel broadens shop-floor minds. (1980) *International Management.* (November) 16-17.

Travelers Insurance Co. (1972) *The Act and Its Principal Features.* The Travelers Insurance Companies.

Travelers Insurance Co. (1973) *A Management Guide to Protect Quality and Safety.* The Travelers Insurance Companies.

Traver, R. W. (1983) Locating the key variables. *ASQC Annual Technical Quality Congress Transactions.* Milwaukee, WI: ASQC Quality Press, 231-237.

Traver, R. W. (1984) Locating the key variable. *Quality Progress.* 17, (February) 21-27.

Traversa, L. L. (1984) High-touch requirements for high-tech CAD/CAM. *Autofact 6.*

Traylor, W. S. (1948) Use of statistical methods for time study of batch processes. *Industrial Quality Control.* 4, (January) 25-28.

Treece, James B., Mark Maremont, and Larry Armstrong. (1988) Will the auto glut choke Detroit?. *BusinessWeek.* (March 7) 54-62.

Tregoe, B. B. (1983) Productivity in America: Where it went and how to get it back. *Management Review.* 72, (February) 23-45.

Tregoe, B. B., and W. Zimmerman. (1980) *Top Management Strategy.* New York: Simon and Schuster.

Tremper, Charles and James Goldberg. (1991) *Hiring and Firing Within the Law: A Guide for Nonprofit Organizations.* Pittsburgh, PA: National Union Fire Insurance Company of Pittsburgh.

Tribus, Myron. (1987) *Quality First: Selected Papers on Quality and Productivity Improvement.* Washington, DC: National Society of Professional Engineers.

Tribus, Myron. (1990) *The Systems of Total Quality.* Privately published.

Tribus, Myron. (1992) Lean on quality. *National Productivity Review.* 11, (Spring) 277.

Tribus, Myron. (1992) Ten management practices. In Frank Voehl (Ed.). *Total Quality: Principles and Practices within Organizations.* Coral Springs, FL: Strategy Associates. (*2)

Tribus, Myron and Geza Szonyi. (1989) An alternative view of the Taguchi approach. *Quality Progress.* 22, (May) 46-52.

Trippi, R. R. (1975) The warehouse location formulation as a special type of inspection problem. *Management Science.* 21, (May) 986-988.

Trist, E. (1981) *The Evolution of Socio-Technical Systems.* (Occasional Paper, Number 2). Toronto: Quality of Working Life Centre. (*2)

Trist, E., and K. W. Bamforth. (1951) Some social psychological consequences of the longwall method of coal-getting. *Human Relations.* 4, (June) 3-38. (*2)

Trist, E., G. W. Higgins, H. Murray, and A. B. Pollock. (1963) *Organizational Choice.* London, UK: Tavistock Institute.

The trouble with auto warranties. (1979) *Consumer Reports.* (October) 598-601.

Troy, Kathryn. (1992) Will TQM run out of steam? *Across the Board.* (March) 57.

Trumpold, H. (1976) Experience with education and training of mechanical engineers in QC. Proceedings, Twentieth EOQC Conference, Berlin. 1, 31-48. (*2)

Tsurumi, Yoshi. (1981) American management has missed the point—The point is management itself. *The Dial.* (September) 7.

Tsurumi, Yoshi. (1981) Productivity: The Japanese approach. *Pacific Basin Quarterly.* 6, (Summer) 7-9.

Tsurumi, Yoshi and Rebecca Tsurumi. (1982) A closer look at Japan's lifetime employment system. *Pacific Basin Quarterly.* 8, (Fall) 5-6.

Tuchman, Barbara W. (1965) Developmental sequence in small groups. *Psychological Bulletin.* 63, (June) 384-399. (*2)

Tuchman, Barbara W. (1980) The decline of quality. *New York Times.* (November 2) 38-41, 104.

Tuchman, Barbara W. (1984) *The March of Folly: From Troy to Vietnam.* New York: Alfred A. Knopf.

Tucker, Allan. (1984) *Chairing the Academic Department.* Second edition. New York: Macmillan.

Tucker, W. W., and R. L. Clark. (1984) *From Drafter to CAD Operator: A Case Study in Adaptation to the Automated Workplace.* SME Paper 84-629. Dearborn, MI: Society of Manufacturing Engineers.

Tuckman, Bruce. (1955) Development sequence in small groups. *Psychological Bulletin.* 55, (June) 111-146.

Tufte, E. (1990) *Envisioning Information.* Cheshire, CT: Graphics Press.

Tukey, John W. (1949) Comparing individual means in the analysis of variance. *Biometrics.* 5, (April) 99.

Tukey, John W. (1959) A quick, compact, two-sample test to Duckworth's specifications. *Technometrics.* 1, (February) 31-48.

Tukey, John W. (1977) *Exploratory Data Analysis.* Reading, MA: Addison-Wesley. (*3)

Turner, R. E. (1974) Today and tomorrow for NDT. *Quality Management and Engineering.* (December) 36-41.

Tushman, M. L., and P. Anderson. (1986) Technological discontinuities and organizational environments. *Administrative Science Quarterly.* 31, (January) 165.

Tushman, M. L., and W. L. Moore. (1982) *Readings in the Management of Innovation.* Boston, MA: Pitman.

Tustin, W. (1980) Selecting a testing laboratory. *Quality*. (June) 24-26.

Tuttle, C. (1985) Assessing performance and productivity in white-collar organizations. *National Productivity Review*. 4, (Summer) 211-224.

Tuttle, Howard C. (1971) The shortest distance to employee ideas is a circle. *Production*. (June) 73-75.

Tversky, Armos and Daniel Kahneman. (1971) The belief in the law of numbers. *Psychological Bulletin*, 105-110.

Tversky, Armos and Daniel Kahneman. (1974) Judgment under uncertainty: Heuristics and biases. *Science*. 20, (September) 1124-1131.

TWA may go to creditors, employees: Rescue plan needs union, investor approval. (1992) *USA Today*. (August 4) B1.

Twiss, B. C. (1986) *Managing Technological Innovation*. New York: Longman.

Tyler, R. D. (1991) From QA to TQM. *Physician Executive*. (May/June) 19-23.

Tyson, Thomas N. (1987) Quality and profitability: Have controllers made the connection? *Management Accounting*. (November) 38-42.

Tyworth, John E., Pat Lemons, and Bruce Ferrin. (1989) Improving LTL delivery service quality with statistical process control. *Transportation Journal*. (Spring) 4-12.

Tzu, Sun. (1963) *The Art of War*. Oxford, UK: Oxford University Press. (*2)

U.S. punctures tire grading. (1983) *Consumer Reports*. (April) 166.

U.S. cars come back. (1992) *Fortune*. (November 16) 58.

U.S. Department of Commerce. (1974) *Report of the Task Force on Appliance Warranties and Service*. Washington, DC: U.S. Government Printing Office.

U.S. Department of Commerce. (1993) *Malcolm Baldrige National Quality Award: 1993 Award Criteria*. Washington, DC: U.S.D.C.

U.S. Department of Defense. (1963) *Military Standard 105D: Sampling Procedures and Tables for Inspection by Attributes*. MIL-STD-105D. Washington, DC: U.S. Government Printing Office.

U.S. Department of Defense. (1977) *General Specifications for Microcircuits*. MIL-M-38510D. Washington, DC: U.S. Department of Defense.

U.S. Department of Labor, Bureau of Labor Statistics. (1971) *The Meaning and Measurement of Productivity*. Washington, DC: U.S. Government Printing Office.

U.S. Department of Labor, Bureau of Labor Statistics. (1973) *Productivity: A Selected Annotated Bibliography, Bulletin 1776*. Washington, DC: U.S. Government Printing Office.

U.S. firms lag in meeting global quality standards. (1993) *Marketing News*. (February 15) 12-13.

U.S. General Accounting Office. (1991) *Management Practices: U.S. Companies Improve Performance through Quality Efforts*. GAO/NSIAD-91-190. Washington DC: USGAO.

UAW president defends policy of cooperation. (1989) *Los Angeles Times*. (June) 1.

Udovichenko, E. J. (1977) *Integrated System of Quality Control*. Kiev: Publishing House of Technology. (*2)

Ulla, F. M. (1982) Productivity measurements of inspectors. *ASQC Annual Technical Quality Congress Transactions*. Milwaukee, WI: ASQC Quality Press, 108-117.

Ulvila, J. W., and R. V. Brown. (1982) Decision analysis comes of age. *Harvard Business Review*. 60, (September-October) 130-141.

Unfortunately, most cars are ruined when they run into barriers like these. *BusinessWeek*. (October 26) 1.

Ungson, G. R. (1988) International competition between Japanese, U.S. and European high technology firms: An institutional approach. In L. R. Gomez-Mejia and M. W. Lawless (Eds.) *Proceedings, Managing the High Technology Firm*. Boulder, CO: University of Colorado Press, 1-40. (*2)

Ungson, G. R. (1988) A research agenda on the management of high technology firms. In L. R. Gomez-Mejia and M. W. Lawless (Eds.) *Proceedings, Managing the High Technology Firm*. Boulder, CO: University of Colorado Press, 41-58.

Ungson, G. R., and N. Van Dijk. (1987) Concurren in de postindustriele semeleving: de verenigde statedn lapan en Europa. *M and O*. 41, (September-October) 378-389.

Ungson. G. R, A. W. Bird, and R. M. Steers. (1988) The institutional foundations of competitive strategies: Comparing Japanese and U.S. high technology firms. Working Paper, Graduate School of Management, University of Oregon.

United Nations Industrial Development Organization (UNIDO). (1984) *Guide to Training Opportunities for Industrial Development*. Vienna: UNIDO.

United States Department of Defense. (1957) *Sampling Procedures and Tables for Inspection by Variables for Percent Defective*. MILI-STD 414. Washington, DC: U.S. Government Printing Office.

United States Department of Defense. (1981) *Single- and Multi-Level Continuous Sampling Procedures and Tables for Inspection by Attributes*. MIL-STD 1235B. Washington, DC: U.S. Government Printing Office.

United States Department of Defense. (1989) *An Education and Training Strategy for Total Quality Management in the Department of Defense.* Washington, DC: U.S. Government Printing Office. (*2)

United States Department of Defense. (1990) *Failure Rate Sampling Plans and Procedures: Military Standard.* MIL-STD-690B. Washington, DC: U.S. Government Printing Office.

United States Department of Defense. (1990) *Total Quality Management Guide.* Volumes 1 and 2. Department of Defense 5000. 51-G. Washington, DC: U.S. Government Printing Office.

UPIU's Wayne Glenn discusses his union's current goals. (1985) *Pulp and Paper International.* 59, (May) 5-6.

Urban, G. L., and E. A. von Hippel. (1988) Lead user analysis of new industrial product concepts. *Management Science.* 34, (May) 41-44.

Urwick, L. (1944) *The Elements of Administration.* New York: Harper and Row.

Uttal, Brothers. (1979) The gentlemen and the upstarts meet in a great mini battle. *Fortune.* (April 15) 98-108.

Uttal, Brothers. (1981) Storage technology goes for the gold. *Fortune.* (April 15) 58.

Uttal, Brothers. (1981) The animals of Silicon Valley. *Fortune.* (January 1) 94. (*2)

Uttal, Brothers. (1984) Japan's latest assault on chipmaking. *Fortune.* (September 15) 81.

Uttal, Brothers. (1987) Companies that serve you best. *Fortune.* (December 7) 98.

Uttal, Brothers. (1987) Speeding new ideas to market. *Fortune.* (March 2) 7. (*2)

Vail, Peter B. (1978) Toward a behavioral description of high-performing systems. In Morgan W. McCall Jr., and Michael M. Lombardo (Eds.) *Leadership: Where Else Can We Go*. Durham, NC: Duke University Press, 109-111. (*2)

Van De Ven, A. H. (1983) Review of *In Search of Excellence. Administrative Science Quarterly*. 28, 621-24.

Van De Ven, A. H. (1986) Central problems in the management of innovation. *Management Science*. 32, (June) 590-607. (*2)

Van De Ven, A. H. (1988) Processes of innovation and organizational change. Technical report of the Strategic Management Research Center. University of Minnesota. (February).

Van Dine, H. A. (1980) Quality auditing-familiar land explored. *Quality Progress*. 13, (November) 13-14.

Vance, F. P. (1966) An economic basis for setting confidence limits. *Industrial and Engineering Chemistry*. 58, (February) 2.

Vance, L. C. (1983) A bibliography of statistical quality control chart techniques. *Journal of Quality Technology*. 15, (April) 59-62. (*2)

Vance, L. C. (1986) Average run lengths of cumulative sum control charts for controlling normal means. *Journal of Quality Technology*. 18, (March) 189-193.

Vancil, R. F. (1973) What kind of management control do you need? *Harvard Business Review*. 51, (March-April) 75-85.

Vancil, R. F. (1980) Decentralization: Managerial ambiguity by design. New York: Financial Executives Research Foundation.

VanGrundy, A. B. (1985) *Techniques of Structured Problem Solving*. New York: Van Nostrand Reinhold.

Vani, Jagdish. (1995) *Certified Quality Engineer Examination Guide*. New York: McGraw-Hill.

Vansina, Leopold S. (1989) Total quality control: An overall organizational improvement strategy. *National Productivity Review.* 9, (Winter) 59-73.

VanWolferen, K. (1989) *The Enigma of Japanese Power.* New York: Alfred A. Knopf.

Varadarajan, P. Rajan. (1978) *An Empirical Investigation of the Relationship Between Market Share and the Competitive Market Position of a Firm.* Amherst, MA: University of Massachusetts.

Varadarajan, P. Rajan and W. R. Dillion. (1981) Competitive position effects and market share: An exploratory investigation. *Journal of Business Research.* 9, 49-64.

Varadarajan, P. Rajan, Terry Clark, and William M. Pride. (1992) Controlling the uncontrollable: Managing your market environment. *Sloan Management Review.* (Winter) 39-47.

Vardeman, S. B. (1986) The legitimate role of inspection in modern SQC. *The American Statistician.* 24, (April) 325-328.

Vasilash, Gary S. (1989) Hearing the voice of the customer. *Production.* (February) 66-68.

Vasilash, Gary S. (1992) Driving beyond satisfaction at Rockwell Automotive. *Production.* 104, (April) 40. (*2)

Vasiliev, V. N. (1985) Simulation and FMS planning. *CIM.* 10, 8-9.

Vaswani, Sundari and Ellis R. Ott. (1954) Statistical aids in locating machine differences. *Industrial Quality Control.* 2, (July) 40-42.

Vaughn, R. C. (1974) *Quality Control.* Ames, IA: Iowa State University Press.

Veen, B. (1981) Integration of TQC and motivation programs. In H. J. Bajaria (Ed.) *Quality Assurance: Methods, Management, and Motivation.* Dearborn, MI: Society of Manufacturing Engineers. (*2)

Vellman, P., and D. C. Hoaglin. (1981) *Applications, Basics and Computing for Data Analysis*. Belmont, MA: Wadsworth.

Velocci, Anthony L., Jr. (1991) TQM makes Rockwell tougher competitor. *Aviation Week and Space Technology*. 135, (December) 68-69.

Vendor Delivery Problems? Are You Victim or Culprit? (1970) Decatur, GA: G. W. Plossl and Company.

Venn, B. (1971) Standardization of flow charts for process quality control systems. *EOQC Quality*. (February) 35-39.

Venkatraman, N. (1991) IT-induced business reconfiguration. In Scott M. Morton (Ed.) *The Corporation of the 1990s: Information Technology and Organizational Transformation*. Oxford, UK: Oxford University Press.

Venkatraman, N. (1994) IT-enabled business transformation: From automation to business scope redefinition. *Sloan Management Review*. 35, (Winter) 73-87. (*2)

Veraldi, L. C. (1985) The team Taurus story. Paper presented at MIT conference, Chicago, IL. (August) 22.

Verba, S., and R. Orren. (1985) *Equality in America*. Cambridge, MA: Harvard University Press.

Verespej, Michael A. (1990) Yea, teams? Not always. *Industry Week*. (June 18) 103-105.

Verschoor, J. T. (1982) PPM management—A tool for IC quality improvement. *Electronic Components and Applications*. 4, (April) 215-222.

Victor, B. (1990) Coordinating work in complex organizations. *Journal of Organizational Behavior*, 187-199.

Vinacke, E. (1957) An experimental study of coalitions in the triad. *American Sociological Review*. 22, 406-414.

Vinson, William D., and Donald F. Heany. (1977) Is quality out of control? *Harvard Business Review.* 55, (November-December) 114-122. (*2)

Voehl, Frank W. (1992) *Strategy Management.* Coral Springs, FL: Strategy Associates. (*2)

Voehl, Frank W. (1992) *Total Quality: Principles and Practices within Organizations.* Coral Springs, Fla.: Strategy Associates. (*2)

Voehl, Frank W. (1992) *TQM Implementation Models and Critical Success Factors.* Coral Springs, FL: Strategy Associates.

Voehl, Frank W. (1993) *Quality Council Handbook.* Coral Springs, FL: Strategy Associates.

Voehl, Frank. (1993) ISO 9000 Adapted to Various Business Industries and Institutions of Higher Learning. Unpublished manuscript, Coral Springs, FL: Strategy Associates.

Vogel, E. F. (1975) *Modern Japanese Organization and Decision-Making.* Berkeley and Los Angeles, CA: University of California Press.

Vogel, E. F. (1963) *Japan's Middle Class: The Salary Man and His Family in a Tokyo Suburb.* Berkeley, CA: University of California Press.

Vogel, E. F. (1979) *Comeback.* New York: Simon and Schuster.

Vogel, E. F. (1979) *Japan as Number One: Lessons for America.* Cambridge, MA: Harvard University Press. (*4)

Vogel, Todd. (1989) Big changes are galvanizing General Electric. *BusinessWeek.* (December 18) 100-102.

Voice entry system gives quality inspectors a hand (1973) *Quality Progress.* 6, (July) 12-14.

Volk, William (1956) Industrial statistics. *Chemical Engineering.* (March) 165-190.

Vollman, T. E., W. L. Berry, and D. C. Whybark. (1984) *Manufacturing Planning and Control Systems*. Homewood, IL: Irwin.

Von Bertalanffy, L. (1968) *General Systems Theory.* New York: G. Braziller.

Von Glinow, Mary Ann. (1988) *The New Professionals: Managing Today's High Tech Employees.* Cambridge, MA: Ballinger. (*2)

Von Glinow, Mary Ann and M. B. Teagarden. (1988) The impact of contextually embedded influences on cooperative strategic alliances: The case of Sino-U.S. joint ventures. Working paper, University of Southern California.

Von Glinow, Mary Ann and Susan Albers Mohrman. (1990) *Managing Complexity in High Technology Organizations*. New York: Oxford University Press.

Von Hippel, E. A. (1978) Users as innovators. *Technology Review.* (January) 31-39. (*2)

Von Oech, Roger A. (1983) *A Whack on the Side of the Head: How to Unlock Your Mind for Innovation.* New York: Warner Books.

Vough, C. F., and B. Asbell. (1975) *Tapping the Human Resource: A Strategy for Productivity*. New York: AMACOM.

Vrakking, W. J. (1991) Customer orientation within the organization. In W. Mastenbroek (Ed.) *Managing for Quality in the Service Sector*. Oxford, UK: Basil Blackwell.

Vroom, Victor Harold. (1974) *Work and Motivation*, New York: John Wiley. (*2)

Vroom, Victor Harold and Arthur G. Jago. (1988) *The New Leadership*. Englewood Cliffs, NJ: Prentice-Hall.

Vroom, Victor Harold and Philip W. Yetton. (1973) *Leadership and Decision-Making*. Pittsburgh, PA: University of Pittsburgh Press. (*3)

Vuori, H. (1989) Research needs in quality assurance. *Quality Assurance in Health Care.* 1, (February/March) 147-159.

Wachniak, R. (1983) Development and implementation of a project support review program. *The Juran Report.* (Autumn) 87-90.

Wadsworth, G. P., and J. G. Bryan (1974) *Applications of Probability and Random Variables.* New York: McGraw-Hill.

Wadsworth, Harrison M., Kenneth S. Stephens, and Blanton A. Godfrey. (1986) *Modern Methods for Quality Control.* New York: John Wiley. (*3)

Wagel, William H. (1987) Corning zeroes in on total quality. *Personnel.* 64, (July) 4-9.

Waggoner, D. M. (1992) Applications of continuous quality improvement techniques to the treatment of patients with hypertension. *Health Care Management Review.* 17, (March) 33-42.

Wagner, H. (1984) Profit wonders, investment blunders. *Harvard Business Review.* 62, (September-October) 121-35. (*2)

Wait, D. J. (1979) Productivity measurement: A management accounting challenge. *Management Accounting.* 61, (May) 24-30.

Wakefield, Ted. (1993) No pain, no gain. *Canadian Business.* 66, (January) 50. (*3)

Walberg, J. (1983) Scientific literacy and economic productivity. *International Perspective.* (Spring) 11-12.

Walbert, Herbert J. (1983) Scientific literacy and economic productivity in international perspective. *Daedalus.* (Spring)

Wald, A. (1947) *Sequential Analysis.* New York: John Wiley.

Walden, C. H., and P. L. Widener. (1967) Quality control of an aluminum sheet mill. *ASQC Annual Technical Quality Congress Transactions.* Milwaukee, WI: ASQC Quality Press, 23-24.

Walden, James C. (1987) Integrating customer satisfaction into daily work. *The Juran Report.* (Spring) 30-34. (*2)

Walker, C. R. (1957) *Towards the Automatic Factory.* New Haven, CT: Yale University Press.

Walker, C. R., and R. H. Guest. (1952) *The Man on the Assembly Line.* Cambridge, MA: Harvard University. (*2)

Walker, C. R., R. H. Guest, and A. N. Turner. (1956) *The Foreman on the Assembly Line.* Cambridge, MA: Harvard University Press.

Walker, H. M. (1951) *Mathematics Essential for Elementary Statistics.* New York: Holt, Rinehart and Winston.

Walker, Terry. (1992) Creating total quality improvement that lasts. *National Productivity Review.* 11, (Autumn) 473.

Wall, J. F. (1970) *Andrew Carnegie.* New York: Oxford University Press. (*4)

Wallace, Thomas F. (1985) *MRP II: Making it Happen.* New York: Van Nostrand Reinhold.

Walleck, Steven A. (1991) Manager's journal: A backstage view of world-class performers. *Wall Street Journal.* (August 26) A10.

Walleigh, R. C. (1985) SQC and JIT: Partnership in quality. *Quality Process.* (May) 31-34.

Walleigh, R. C. (1986) What's your excuse for not using JIT? *Harvard Business Review.* 64, (March-April) 38-54.

Wallis, Claudia. (1989) Onward women! *Time.* (December 4) 80-89. (*2)

Wallis, W. Allen. (1980) Statistical research group, 1942-1945. *Journal of the American Statistical Association.* 85, (June) 320-321.

Wallis, W. Allen and Harry V. Roberts. (1956) *Statistics: A New Approach.* New York: Free Press.

Walsh, D. S. (1980) Analyzing and solving productivity problems. *Training and Development Journal*. 34, (July) 70-74.

Walsh, L. (1974) Back to 100% inspection? Editorial comment. *Quality Management and Engineering.* (March) 9.

Walsh, L. (1976) 100% inspection at production line rates. *Quality.* (November) 30-31.

Walsh, L. (1978) Steel wheel maker tests hardness 100%. *Quality.* (November) 37.

Walsh, L. (1979) 100% inspection plus. *Quality.* (September) 102-104.

Walsh, L. (1979) Can 100% testing be eliminated? *Quality.* (May) 42-43.

Walsh, L., et al. (1986) *Quality Management Handbook.* New York: Marcel Dekker.

Walsmann, M. R. (1981) The check list—A powerful inspection tool. *ASQC Annual Technical Quality Congress Transactions.* Milwaukee, WI: ASQC Quality Press, 348-351.

Walter, C. (1983) Management commitment to quality: Hewlett-Packard Company. *Vital Speeches.* 16, (August) 22-24.

Walters, R. W., and Associates, Inc. (1975) *Job Enrichment for Results: Strategies for Successful Implementation.* Reading, MA: Addison-Wesley.

Walther, G. R. (1990) Reach out to accounts. *Success.* (May) 24.

Waltking, A. E. (1982) Progress report of the AOCS flavor nomenclature and standards committee. *JAOCS.* 59, (February) 116A-120A.

Walton, E. (1985) The diffusion of new work structures: Explaining why success didn't take. *Organizational Dynamics.* 8, (Winter) 25-32.

Walton, E. (1977) Successful strategies for diffusing work innovations. *Journal of Contemporary Business.* (Spring) 32-36.

Walton, E. (1979) Do supervisors thrive in participative work systems? *Organizational Dynamics.* 2, (Winter) 34-37.

Walton, Mary. (1986) *The Deming Management Method.* New York: Dodd Mead. (*8)

Walton, Mary. (1990) *Deming Management at Work.* New York: Putnam. (*6)

Walton, Mary. (1991) Deming management at work. *Small Business Reports.* 16, (June) 59.

Walton, Richard E. (1976) Quality of working life: What is it? *Sloan Management Review.* 17, (April) 13-22.

Walton, Richard E. (1977) Successful strategies for diffusing work innovations. *Journal of Contemporary Business.* 6, (Winter) 1-22.

Walton, Richard E. (1979) Work innovations at Topeka: After six years. *The Journal of Applied Behavioral Science*, 13 (March) 422-433. (*2)

Walton, Richard E. (1985) From control to commitment in the workplace. *Harvard Business Review.* 63, (March-April) 76-84. (*4)

Walton, Richard E. (1987) *Innovating to Compete: Lessons for Diffusing and Managing Change in the Workplace.* San Francisco, CA: Jossey-Bass.

Walton, Richard E. (1988) How to counter alienation in the plant. *Harvard Business Review.* 50, (November-December) 70-81.

Walton, Richard E., and R. Lawrence. (1985) *Human Resources Management: Trends and Challenges.* Cambridge, MA: Harvard Business School Press.

Walton, Richard E., and R. B. McKersie. (1965) *A Behavioral Theory of Labor Negotiations.* New York: McGraw-Hill. (*2)

Walton, Richard E., and L. A. Schlesinger. (1979) Do supervisors thrive in participative work systems? *Organizational Dynamics.* 8, (March) 24-39. (*3)

Wambach, G. W., and A. S. Raymond (1977) The optimum sampling plan. *ASQC Annual Technical Quality Congress Transactions.* Milwaukee, WI: ASQC Quality Press. 574-578.

Wampler, R. H. (1970) On the accuracy of least squares computer programs. *Journal of the American Statistical Association.* 65, (330) 549-565.

Wang Labs challenges the goliaths. (1979) *BusinessWeek.* (June 4) 100.

Wang, S. C. (1975) Human reliability in visual inspection. *Quality.* (September) 24-25.

Wang, S. C. (1981) A system simulation for inspection planning. *ASQC Annual Technical Quality Congress Transactions.* Milwaukee, WI: ASQC Quality Press, 769-776.

Ward, A. (1993) TQM vs. business process innovation. Paper presented at USC COMER roundtable XVIII seminar on business process reengineering.

Ward, S. S. (1992) Quality monitoring for maintenance of skin integrity. *Journal of ET Nursing.* 19, (March) 91-94.

Wastell, D. G., P. White, and P. Kawalek. (1994) A methodology for business process redesign: Experiences and issues. *Journal of Strategic Information Systems.* 3, (No. 1) 23-40.

Waterman, Robert H., Jr. (1987) *The Renewal Factor: How the Best Get and Keep the Competitive Edge.* New York: Bantam Books. (*2)

Waterman, Robert H., Jr., Thomas J. Peters, and J. R. Phillips. (1980) Structure is not organization. *Business Horizons.* 23, (June) 1-13.

Waters, Craig R. (1985) Profit and loss. *Inc.* (April) 103-112.

Waters, R. (1984) Why everybody's talking about just-in-time. *Inc.* 6, (March) 77-90.

Watkins, Edward. (1992) How Ritz-Carlton won the Baldrige Award. *Lodging Hospitality.* (November) 16-18. (*2)

Watkins, J. (1994) Business process redesign in the UK retail financial services sector. *Business Change and Reengineering.* 1 (No. 4) 38-48.

Watkins, J., C. Skinner, and J. Pearson. (1993) Business process reengineering: Hype, hazard or heaven. *Business Change and Reengineering.* 1, (No. 2) 41-46.

Watson, G. S. (1961) A study of the group screening method. *Technometrics.* 3, (March) 371-388.

Watson, H., and P. Marrett. (1979) A survey of management science implementation problems. *Interfaces.* 9, (August) 124-128.

Watson, Thomas J., Jr. (1963) *A Business and Its Beliefs: The Ideas That Helped Build IBM.* New York: McGraw-Hill. (*2)

Waxler, Robert P., and Thomas Higginson. (1994) TQM: Labor-management cooperation. In Harry Ivan Costin (Ed.) *Readings in Total Quality Management.* (1994) Fort Worth, TX: Dryden Press, 421-429.

We have created a monster: Don't blame the system, blame the managers. (1980) *Dun's Review.* (September) 88.

Weatherly, Jonathen D., and Bill Leonard. (1992) Dare to compare for better quality. *H R Magazine.* 37, (September) 42. (*2)

Weaver, Henry. (1978) Quality deterioration (economic marketplace). *Quality Progress.* 11, (February) 28-30.

Weaver, L. A. (1975) Inspection accuracy sampling plans. *ASQC Annual Technical Quality Congress Transactions.* Milwaukee, WI: ASQC Quality Press, 34-39.

Webb. S. R. (1968) Non-orthogonal designs of even resolution. *Technometrics.* 10, (October) 291-299.

Webb, S. R. (1968) Saturated sequential factorial design. *Technometrics.* 10, (November) 535-550.

Webber, Ross A. (1979) Staying organized. *Wharton Magazine.* (Spring) 22.

Webbink, D. W. (1977) The semiconductor industry: A survey of structure, conduct and performance. An Economic Report to the Federal Trade Commission by the Bureau of Economics. (January).

Weber, Max. (1947) *The Theory of Social and Economic Organization.* New York: Oxford University Press.

Webster, James J. (1988) Pulling—not pushing—for higher productivity. *Mechanical Engineering* . (April) 42-44.

Weick, K. E. (1976) Educational organizations as loosely coupled systems. *Administrative Science Quarterly.* 21, (March) 1-19. (*4)

Weick, K. E. (1977) Organizational design: Organizations as self-designing systems. *Organizational Dynamics.* 1, (Autumn) 31-36. (*2)

Weick, K. E. (1979) *The Social Psychology of Organizing.* Reading, MA: Addison-Wesley. (*2)

Weil, Frank A. (1979) Management's drag on productivity. *BusinessWeek.* (December 3) 14.

Weinberg, E. (1976) Labor-management cooperation: A report on recent initiatives: Effect on employee productivity. *Monthly Labor Review.* 99, (April) 13-22.

Weinberg, G. M. (1971) *The Psychology of Computer Programming.* New York: Van Nostrand Reinhold.

Weinberger, C. W. (1984) *Memorandum to Secretaries of the Military Departments*. Alexandria, VA: Development to Production of Defense, Technical Information Center.

Weindling, J. L., S. B. Littauer, and J. T. Oliveira. (1970) Mean action time of the mean control chart with warning limits. *Journal of Quality Technology*. 2, (February) 79-85.

Weinstein, Martin E. (1989) Our debt to Henry Ford. *Business Tokyo*. (April) 42-45.

Weir, M., and S. Mills. (1973) The supervisor as a change catalyst. *Industrial Relations Journal*. 4, (Winter) 11-13.

Weisberger, Bernard. (1979) *The Dream-Maker: William C. Durant*. Boston, MA: Little, Brown.

Weisbord, Marvin R. (1990) *Productive Workplaces*. San Francisco, CA: Jossey-Bass.

Weitzman, M. L. (1984) *The Share Economy: Conquering Stagflation*. Cambridge, MA: Harvard University Press.

Welbourne, T. M., and L. R. Gomez-Mejia. (1988) Gainsharing revisited. *Compensation and Benefits Review*. 20, (July-August) 19-29.

Welch, Cas and Pete Geissler. (1992) Measuring the total quality of the sales function. *National Productivity Review*. 11, (Autumn) 517.

Welch, J. L., and D. Gordon. (1980) Assessing the impact of flextime on productivity. *Business Horizons*. 23, (December) 61-62.

Welch, John F., Jr. (1980) Quality—The marketing mission. Speech presented to the 1980 General Electric Marketing Management Conference. The Homestead, Hot Springs, Virginia. (April 10).

Welch, John F., Jr. (1983) Quality recovery for world competitiveness. *Financier*. (April) 7.

Welch, John F., Jr. (1989) Speed, simplicity, self-confidence: Keys to leading the '90s. Speech presented at The General Electric Annual Meeting of share owners, Greenville, South Carolina.

Welch, W. E. (1956) *Tested Scientific Inventory Control.* Greenwich, CT: Management Publishing Company. (*3)

Wellborn, John M., and G. W. Lawson. (1978) Maintainability by design. *Proceedings Annual Reliability and Maintainability Symposium*. New York: IEEE, 478-485.

Wellins, Richard S., et. al. (1990) *Self-Directed Teams: A Study of Current Practice.* Survey report. Pittsburgh, PA: Development Dimensions International, Association for Quality and Participation.

Wellins, Richard S., William C. Byham, and Jeanne M. Wilson. (1991) *Empowered Teams.* San Francisco, CA: Jossey-Bass. (*2)

Wells, H. G. (1956) *The Outline of History.* New York: Garden City Books.

Wellstood, Sybil A., and Linda Wright. (1983) Using quality circles to spot and solve lab problems. *Medical Laboratory Observer.* (February) 32-37.

Wels, Alena. (1980) How Citicorp restructured for the eighties. *Euromoney*. (April) 13.

Welsh, John J. (1983) Pre-acquisition audit: Verifying the bottom line. *Management Accounting*. (January) 32-37.

Welty, Gus. (1992) How TTX tracks quality. *Railway Age*. 193, (April) 29.

Wensley, R. (1982) PIMS and BCG: New horizons or false dawn? *Strategic Management Journal*. 3, (January-February) 147-158.

Werley, H. H., E. C. Devine, C. R. Zorn, R. Ryan, and B. L. Westra. (1991) The nursing minimum data set: Abstraction tool for standardized, comparable, essential data. *American Journal of Public Health.* 81, (April) 421-426.

Werner, G. W., and E. Zetzsche. (1982) Working methods and means of quality and reliability assurance in large industrial plants. *EOQC Quality.* (May) 8-13.

Wernimont, G. (1950) Precision and accuracy of test methods. *ASTM Symposium on Applications of Statistics.* Special Technical Publication 103. Philadelphia, PA: American Society for Testing and Materials, 13-26.

Wernimont, G. (1951) Design and interpretation of interlaboratory studies of test methods. *Analytical Chemistry.* 23, (June) 1572.

Wernimont, G. (1967) Evaluation of laboratory performance of spectrophotometers. *Analytical Chemistry.* 39, (May) 554.

Wertner, William, B., Jr. (1982) Quality circles: Key executive issues. *Journal of Contemporary Business.* 11, (Second Quarter) 17-26.

Wescott, Mason E. (1990) *Mimeo Notes.* Rochester NY: Rochester Institute of Technology.

Wesner, Mason E., and C. Egan. (1990) Self-managed teams in operator services. Paper presented at International Conference on Self-Managed Work Teams, Denton, TX, September.

Westbrook, D. (1993) Organizational culture and its relationship to TQM. *Industrial Management.* 35, (January) 1. (*2)

Westbrook, Robert A. (1980) A rating scale for measuring product/service satisfaction. *Journal of Marketing.* 40, (Fall) 68-72.

Western Electric. (1956) *Statistical Quality Control Handbook.* Indianapolis, IN: Western Electric.

Wetherill, G. B. (1977) *Sampling Inspection and Q.C.* London, UK: Chapman and Hall. (*2)

Wettach, R. (1985) Function or focus? The old or new view of quality. *Quality Progress.* 18, (November) 65-68.

Wetzstein, Carl (1982) Take the hassle out of managing experimental data. *ASQC Annual Technical Quality Congress Transactions.* Milwaukee, WI: ASQC Quality Press, 254-261.

What if Japan triumphs? (1992) *Fortune.* (May 18) 61.

What makes Harry Gray run. (1979) *BusinessWeek.* (December) 77.

What U.S. scientists discover, the Japanese convert into profit. (1990) *Wall Street Journal.* (June 25) 1.

What us worry? Big unions' leaders overlook bad news, opt for status quo. (1993) *Wall Street Journal.* (October 5) B1.

What workers want: The gap in management's perception. (1988) *Behavioral Sciences Newsletter.* (June 27) 1.

Whatsell, George W. (1991) Total quality management. *Topics in Health Care Financing.* 18, (Winter) 12-20.

Wheeler, Donald J. (1993) *Understanding Variation: The Key to Managing Chaos.* Knoxville, TN: SPC Press. (*2)

Wheeler, Donald J., and David S. Chambers. (1986) *Understanding Statistical Process Control.* Knoxville, TN: SPC Press. (*3)

Wheeler, Donald J., and R. W. Lyday. (1989) *Evaluating the Measurement Process.* Knoxville, TN: SPC Press.

Wheelwright, S. C. (1984) Quality and productivity in the new industrial competition. Presented at the AT and T Managerial Workshop on Quality and Productivity. Somerset, NJ.

Wheelwright, S. C., and S. Makridakis. (1973) *Forecasting Methods for Management.* New York: John Wiley.

When a new product strategy wasn't enough. (1980) *BusinessWeek.* (February 18) 143.

When companies tell business schools what to teach. (1986) *BusinessWeek.* (February) 11.

When the employees are the entrepreneur. (1980) *Venture.* (June) 21-22.

Where managers will go. (1992) *Fortune.* (January 27) 51.

Where quality control is a part time job. (1979) *BusinessWeek.* (November 26) 44.

Whethan, C. D. (1980) *A History of Science.* Fourth edition. New York: Macmillan.

Whewhart, W. A. (1931) *Economic Control of Quality of Manufactured Product.* New York: Van Nostrand Reinhold.

Whisler, L. (1958) Performance appraisal and the organization man. *Journal of Business.* 3, (January) 11-14.

White, M. (1984) Japanese education: How do they do it? *The Public Interest.* (Summer) 96. (*3)

White, R. (1981) *Structural Context, Strategy and Performance.* Cambridge, MA: Harvard University Press.

White, S. (1966) The analysis of a simple class of multi-stage inspection plans. *Management Science.* 12, (July) 685-93.

White, Theodore H. (1985) The danger from Japan. *New York Times Magazine.* (July 28) 1.

Whitehill, M. (1978) Workplace harmony: Another Japanese miracle? *Columbia Journal of World Business.* 13, (Fall) 25-39.

Whiteley, Richard C. (1990) Creating a customer focus. *Executive Excellence.* (September) 9-10.

Whiteley, Richard C. (1991) *The Customer Driven Company: Moving from Talk to Action.* Reading, MA: Addison-Wesley. (*2)

Whiteside, David E. (1986) Artificial intelligence finally hits the desktop. *BusinessWeek.* (June 9) 68-70.

Whiteside, David, Richard Brandt, Zachery Schiller, and Andrea Gabor. (1985) How GM's Saturn could run things around old-style carmakers. *BusinessWeek.* (January 28) 126-128.

Whiteside, Thomas. (1972) *The Investigation of Ralph Nader.* New York: Arbor House.

Whiting, Rick. (1990) Digital strives for a consistent vision of quality. *Electronic Business.* 16, (November 26) 55-56.

Whiting, Rick. (1990) Hewlett-Packard educates from within. *Electronic Business.* 16, (October 15) 113-114.

Whiting, Rick. (1991) Benchmarking: Lessons from the best-in-class. *Electronic Business.* 17, (October 7) 128-134.

Whiting, Robert. (1977) *The Chrysanthemum and the Bat.* New York: Dodd, Mead.

Whitmore, Elaine. (1997) *Product Development Planning for Health Care Products Regulated by the FDA.* Milwaukee, WI: ASQC Quality Press.

Whitney, John O. (1993) *The Trust Factor: Liberating Profits and Restoring Corporate Vitality.* New York: McGraw-Hill. (*2)

Whittaker, Barrie. (1991) The path to excellence. *The Canadian Business Review.* 18, (Winter) 19-21.

Whittingham, P. R. (1982) Practical operator control. *Quality Assurance.* 8, (December) 99-102.

Who gains from the new Europe? (1989) *Fortune.* (December 18) 84.

Why Hewlett-Packard overhauled its management. (1984) *BusinessWeek.* (July 30) 111-112.

Why industrial productivity is as important as military arms. (1981) *Government Executive.* (October) 38-40.

Why Japan will emerge stronger. (1992) *Fortune.* (May 18) 46-56.

Whyte, G. (1989) Groupthink reconsidered. *Academy of Management Review*, (March) 40-56.

Whyte, W. F. (1955) *Money and Motivation.* New York: Harper and Row.

Whyte, William H., Jr. (1956) *The Organization Man.* New York: Simon and Schuster. (*2)

Widtfeldt, James R. (1982) How IES can contribute to, gain from a quality circle. *Industrial Engineering.* 14, (January) 64-68.

Wiegner, Kathleen K. (1980) Corporate samurai. *Forbes.* (October) 172. (*2)

Wiegner, Kathleen K. (1981) The one to watch. *Forbes.* (March 2) 60. (*2)

Wiersema, Fred. (1983) *Price-Cost Dynamics: An Empirical Study.* Cambridge, MA: Harvard University Press.

Wiggenhorn, William. (1990) Motorola U: When training becomes an education. *Harvard Business Review.* 78, (July-August) 71-83.

Wiggins, S. N., and W. J. Lane. (1983) Quality uncertainty, search and advertising. *American Economic Review.* (December) 881-894.

Wight, Oliver W. (1970) Input/output control—A real handle on lead time, production and inventory management. *APICS Journal.* (Third Quarter) 21-28. (*2)

Wight, Oliver W. (1972) *The Executives New Computer*. Reston, VA: Reston Publishing Company. (*2)

Wight, Oliver W. (1981) *Manufacturing Resource Planning: MRP II.* New York: Van Nostrand Reinhold.

Wight, Oliver W. (1981) *MRP II: Unlocking America's Productivity Potential.* Boston, MA: CBI Publishing Company. (*2)

Wiig, Karl W. (1986) AI: Management's newest tool. *Management Review.* 75, (August) 24-28.

Wild, R. (1977) *Concepts for Operations Management.* New York: John Wiley.

Wilder, C. (1995) The internet pioneers—The emergence of the World Wide Web and Mosaic has convinced early corporate adopters of the viability of doing business online. *Information Week.* 9, (January) 38.

Wilder, C., K. Bull, and C. Gillooly. (1995) Intranet tools—Corporations seek internal Web applications and major vendors are happy to help. *Information Week.* 6, (November) 14.

Wilensky, H. L. (1957) *Human Relations in the Workplace.* New York: Harper and Row.

Wilensky, R. (1983) *Planning and Understanding: A Computational Approach to Human Reasoning.* Reading, MA: Addison-Wesley. (*2)

Wiley, Ann L. (1992) The meaning of continuous improvement. *Technical Communication.* 39, (November) 709. (*2)

Wilhelm, Wilbert and Subhash C. Sarin. (1983) Models for the design of flexible manufacturing systems. *AIIE Conference Presentation.*

Wilkinson, A., and B. Witcher. (1991) Fitness for use? Barriers to full TQM in the UK. *Management Decision (UK).* 29, (No. 3) 34-36.

Wilkes, M. V. (1972) *Timesharing Computer System.* Second edition. London, UK: MacDonald and Company, New York: Elsevier Science Publishing.

Wilkie, William L., and Paul W. Farris. (1975) Comparison advertising: Problems and potential. *Journal of Marketing*. 39, (October) 7-15.

Wilks, S. S. (1948) *Elementary Statistical Analysis*. Princeton, NJ: Princeton University Press.

Will the slide kill quality circles. (1982) *BusinessWeek*. (January) 108-109.

Will the U.S stay number one? (1987) *U.S. News and World Report*. (February 2) 17.

Willard, Irving E. (1979) Reliability growth curves. *ASQC Annual Technical Quality Congress Transactions*. Milwaukee, WI: 321-328.

Williams, A. A. (1978) Interpretation of the sensory significance of chemical data in flavor research. *IFFA*. (March) 80-85.

Williams, E. E. (1896) *Made in Germany*. London, UK: William Heinemann. (*2)

Williams, F. (1986) *Reasoning with Statistics*. New York: Holt, Reinhart and Winston.

Williams, K. (1981) Enhancing productivity through automation. *Management Accounting*. 63, (July) 54-55.

Williams, K. (1991) TQM improves companies' performance. *Management Accounting*. 73, (August) 14.

Williams, Robert. (1991) Putting Deming's principles to work. *Wall Street Journal*. (November 4) A18.

Williams, T. J. (1976) Trends in the development of process control computer system. *Journal of Quality Technology*. 8, (April) 63-73.

Williamson, D. T. N. (1968) A better way of doing things. *Science Journal*. (June) 53-5.

Williamson, E., and M. H. Bretherton. (1963) *Tables of the Negative Binomial Probability Distribution.* New York: John Wiley.

Williamson, H. (1951) *Growth of the American Economy.* Englewood Cliffs, NJ: Prentice-Hall.

Williamson, J. W., E. Reerink, A. Donabedian, C. W. Turner, and A. Christensen. (1991) Health science information management. *Quality Assurance in Health Care.* 3, (February) 95-114.

Williamson, O. E. (1975) *Markets and Hierarchies: Analysis and Antitrust Implications.* New York: Free Press. (*2)

Willis, Roger G., and Kevin H. Sullivan. (1984) CIMS in perspective: Costs, benefits, timing, payback periods are outlined. *Industrial Engineering.* 16, (February) 23-36.

Willmot, H. C. (1994) Business process reengineering and human resource management. *Personnel Review.* 23, (No. 3) 46-51.

Wilmot, Robert W. (1988) Computer integrated management—The next competitive breakthrough. *Long Range Planning.* (December) 65-70.

Wilrich, P. T. (1971) *Frontiers in Statistical Quality Control 2.* Wurzburg, W. Germany: Physica-Verlag.

Wilson, A. H. (1977) Engineering and productivity. *Engineering Journal.* 60, (March) 22-26.

Wilson, C., and M. Kennedy. (1991) Improving the product development process. In Michael J. Stahl and G. M. Bounds. *Competing Globally Through Customer Value: The Management of Suprasystems.* Westport, CT: Quorum Books, 428-477.

Wilson, J. T. (1985) Strategic planning at R. J. Reynolds Industries. *Journal of Business Strategy.* 6, 22 28.

Wilson, Lawrence A. (1983) Generative quality assurance planning. *ASQC Annual Technical Quality Congress Transactions.* Milwaukee, WI: ASQC Quality Press, 95-100.

Wilson, Myron F. (1967) The quality your customer sees. *ASQC Journal of the Electronics Division.* (July) 3-16. (*2)

Wilson, Myron F. (1968) *The Quality Your Customer Needs.* Washington, DC: Collins Radio Company.

Wilson, Rob. (1992) Changing customer needs means changes for instrument supplier. *Diesel Progress Engines and Drives.* 58, (July) 10.

Wind, Y. J. (1982) *Product Policy: Concepts, Methods, and Strategies.* Reading, MA: Addison-Wesley.

Wing, R. (1988) *The Art of Strategy.* New York: Dolphin Books.

Wingert, B., M. Rader, and U. Riehm. (1981) Changes in working skill in the fields of design caused by use of computers. In J. Mermet (Ed.). *CAD in Medium Sized and Small Industries.* Amsterdam: North Holland.

Winner, R. I., J. P. Pennell, E. H. Bertrand, and M. M. C. Slusarczuk. (1988) The Role of concurrent engineering in weapons system acquisition. Institute for Defense Analysis (IDA) Report R-338, December.

Winter, Robert S. (1993) Applying TQM principles in the classroom. *Explorations in Teaching and Learning.* 3, (January) 1, 7.

Wirkus, Stephen R. (1982) Quality awareness-control where it counts. *ASQC Annual Technical Quality Congress Transactions.* Milwaukee, WI: ASQC Quality Press, 225-229.

Wise, J. (1980) Setting up a company productivity program. *Management Review.* 69, (June) 15-18.

Wiseman, Charles. (1985) *Strategy and Computers: Information Systems as Competitive Weapons.* Homewood, IL: Irwin.

Wiseman, Charles. (1988) *Strategic Information Systems.* Homewood, IL: Irwin.

Witoshynssky, Mary. (1991) Total quality for success. *Business Mexico*. 1, (October) 48-49.

Witzenberg, Gary. (1986) *Fiero*. Tucson, AZ: HP Books.

Wojahn, Ellen. (1986) Will the company please come to order. *Inc.* (March) 78-86.

Wolak, Jerry. (1988) Manage the process. *Quality*. (September) 14-15.

Wolf, John D. (1983) Quality is management at McDonnell Douglas. *The Juran Report*. (Spring) 116-123.

Wolf, John D. (1985) Quality improvement: The continuing operational phase. Proceedings of the Second Annual Conference on Quality Improvement.

Wolf, M. J. (1983) *The Japanese Conspiracy: The Plot to Dominate Industry World-Wide*. New York: Empire Books.

Wolfe, K. A. (1979) Use of reference standards for sensory evaluation of product quality. *Food Technology*. 33, 43-44.

Wolkenhauer, Steve. (1992) Total quality management: Beyond the hype. *Institutional Distribution*. 28, (July) 20.

Woltz, J. R. (1963) Product quality audit system. *ASQC Annual Technical Quality Congress Transactions*. Milwaukee, WI: 291-295.

Womack, James P., Daniel T. Jones, and Daniel Roos. (1990) *The Machine That Changed The World*. New York: Rawson Associates. (*3)

Woo, C. Y. (1983) Evaluation of the strategies and performance of low ROI market share leaders. *Strategic Management Journal*. 4, (May-June) 123-135.

Woo, C. Y. (1984) Market share leadership—not always so good. *Harvard Business Review*. 62, (January-February) 50-54.

Woo, C. Y., and A. C. Cooper. (1985) Corporate settings of effective low share business. *Harvard Business Review*. 63, (March-April) 465-481.

Wood, Buddy B. (1982) Development of the reliability program for the advanced medium range air to air missile (AMRAAM). *Proceedings, Annual Reliability and Maintainability Symposium*. New York: IEEE, 510-514.

Wood, C. (1988) The prophets of quality. *Quality Review*. (Winter) 18-25.

Wood, N. (1979) Contract inspection service. *Quality*. (May) 13-14.

Wood, R. A. (1991) Hero without a company. *Forbes*. (March 18) 112-114.

Wood, R., F. Hull, and K. Azumi. (1983) Evaluating quality circles: The American application. *California Management Review*. 26, (Fall) 37-53. (*2)

Wood, Robert Chapman. (1988) The prophets of quality. *The Quality Review*. (Fall) 20-27.

Wood, Robert Chapman. (1989) A lesson learned and a lesson forgotten. *Forbes*. (February 6) 70-78. (*2)

Woodruff, R. B. (1990) A new era for auto quality. *BusinessWeek*. 22, (October) 84-96.

Woodruff, R. B., and E. Cadotte. (1987) Analyzing market opportunities for new ventures. *Survey of Business*. (Summer) 10-15.

Woods, D. G., and C. Zeiss. (1981) Coordinate measuring and finite metrology. *ASQC Annual Technical Quality Congress Transactions*. Milwaukee, WI: ASQC Quality Press, 232-237.

Woods, K. C. (1978) Calibration system for measuring and testing equipment. *Quality Progress*. 11, (March) 20-21.

Woods, Michael D. (1989) How we changed our accounting. *Management Accounting*. 70, (February) 42-5. (*2)

Woodward, James D. (1985) Not just another training program. *The Juran Report*. (Winter) 24-27.

Woodward, Joan. (1965) *Industrial Organizations: Theory and Practice*. London, UK: Oxford University Press.

Woodward, W. A., A. C. Elliott, and H. L. Gray. (1985) *Directory of statistical computer software*. New York: Marcel Dekker.

Woollen, A. (1988) How Coca-Cola assures quality with QUACS. *Soft Drinks Management International*. (March) 21-24.

Wooten, L. M., and J. L. Tarter. (1976) The productivity audit: A Key tool for executives. *MSU Business Topics*. 24, (Spring) 31-41.

Work in America. (1973) Cambridge, MA: MIT Press. (*2)

Work revolution in U.S. industry. (1984) *BusinessWeek*. (May 16) 22.

Worker motivation in Japan (II). (1982) *Japan Labor Bulletin*. (March) 5-8.

Workman, J. P., Jr. (1988) Linking technology with market opportunities: An ethnography of new product development in the Micro-Electronics sector. Unpublished working paper. Cambridge, MA: MIT.

Workplace basics: The skills employers want. (1988) Booklet published by the American Society for Training and Development and the U.S. Department of Labor, Employment and Training Administration.

World business. (1992) *Wall Street Journal*. (September 24) R26-R27.

Wortham, W. (1971) A backward recursive technique for optimal sequential sampling plans. *Naval Research Logistics Quarterly*. 18, 203-213.

Wortham, W., and G. F. Heinrich (1972) Control charts using exponential smoothing techniques. *ASQC Annual Technical Quality Congress Transactions*. Milwaukee, WI: ASQC Quality Press, 451-458.

Worthy, Ford S. (1987) Accounting bores you? Wake up. *Fortune*. (October 12) 43-52.

Wray, D. E. (1949) Marginal men of industry: The foremen. *American Journal of Sociology 54*. 298-301.

Wrege, Charles D., and Ronald G. Greenwood. (1991) *Frederick W. Taylor: The Father of Scientific Management; Myth and Reality*. Homewood, IL: Irwin.

Wren, D. (1994) *The Evolution of Management Thought*. Fourth edition. New York: John Wiley.

Wright, J. Patrick. (1979) *On a Clear Day You Can See General Motors: John Z. De Lorean's Look Inside the Automotive Giant*. Grosse Point, NY: Wright Enterprises. (*3)

Wyden, Peter. (1987) *The Unknown Iacocca*. New York: William Morrow.

Wynholds, Hans W., and John P. Skratt. (1977) Weapon system parametric life cycle cost analysis. *Proceedings, Annual Reliability and Maintainability Symposium*. New York: IEEE, 303-309.

Wysocki, L. (1990) Implementation of self-managed teams within a non-union manufacturing facility. Paper presented at International Conference on Self-Managed Work Teams. Denton, TX. (September).

Xerox unlocks the future with training, teamwork. (1990) *Purchasing World*. (April) 34.

Yager, Edwin G. (1979) Examining the quality control circle. *Personnel Journal.* 58, (October) 682-84.

Yager, Edwin G. (1980) Quality circle: A tool for the 80's. *Training and Development Journal.* 34, (August) 60-63.

Yager, Edwin G. (1981) The quality control circle explosion. *Training and Development Journal.* 35, (April) 98-105.

Yakabe, Katsumi. (1974) *Labor Relations in Japan: Fundamental Characteristics.* Tokyo: International Society for Educational Information.

Yamada, Katsuyoshi. (1977) Reliability activities at Toyota Motor Company. *Reports of Statistical Applications and Research.* Tokyo: JUSE, 24, (September) 22-39.

Yamada, Mutsuhiko. (1981) Japanese-style management in America: Merits and difficulties. *Japanese Economic Studies.* 10, (Fall) 1-31.

Yamagiwa, Takashi. (1988) Computer use in the Japanese educational system. *Business Japan.* (March) 38-39.

Yamamoto, Tadashi. (1976) *The Silent Power.* Tokyo: Simul Press.

Yamamura, M. (1986) Joint research and antitrust: Japanese vs. American strategies. In H. Patrick and L. Meissner (Eds.) *Japan's High Technology Industries.* Seattle, WA: University of Washington Press.

Yamashita, Toshihiko. (1989) *The Panasonic Way: From a Chief Executive's Desk.* Translated by Frank Baldwin. Tokyo: Kodansha International.

Yang, Charles Y. (1977) Management styles: American vis-a-vis Japanese. *Columbia Journal of World Business.* 12, (Fall) 23-31. (*2)

Yankelovich, Daniel. (1981) *New Rules: Searching for Self-Fulfillment in a World Turned Upside Down.* New York: Random House. (*4)

Yankelovich, Daniel. (1983) *Putting the Work Ethic to Work.* New York: Public Agenda Foundation. (*2)

Yardley, Jonathan. (1990) Should universities remain shelters for the slothful. *Los Angeles Times*. (January) 1, 7.

Yasuda, Yuzo. (1991) *40 Years, 20 Million Ideas: The Toyota Suggestion System*. Cambridge, MA: Productivity Press.

Yates, Brock. (1983) *The Decline and the Fall of the American Automobile Industry.* New York: Empire Books.

Yates, Frank. (1937) *The Design and Analysis of Factorial Experiments.* Rothamsted, Harpenden, UK: Imperial Bureau of Soil Science. (*2)

Yee, Kenneth W. (1982) *An On-line Method of Determining Tool by Timex-developed Analysis*. SME Technical Paper MR82-901. Dearborn, MI: Society of Manufacturing Engineers.

Yin, R. K. (1984) *Case Study Research: Design and Methods.* Beverly Hills, CA: Sage.

Yip, G. S. (1982) *Barriers to Entry: A Corporate Strategy Perspective.* Lexington, MA: Lexington Books.

Yip, G. S. (1982) Gateways to entry. *Harvard Business Review*. 60, (September-October) Reprint # 82512.

Yoder, K. (1990) All that's lacking is Bert Parks singing, Cadillac, Cadillac. *Wall Street Journal.* (December) 1, 15.

Yoffie, D. B. (1983) *Power and Protectionism.* New York: Columbia University Press.

Yoji, A. (1987) *Datamyte Handbook.* Tokyo: Datamyte.

Yoji, A. (1990) *Quality Function Deployment: Integrating Customer Requirements into Product Design.* Cambridge, MA: Productivity Press.

Yoneyama, T. (1969) *Hinshitsu Kanri no Hanashi.* Tokyo: JUSE Press.

Yoshida, Kosaku. (1989) Deming management philosophy: Does it work in the U.S. as well as in Japan?. *Columbia Journal of World Business*. (Fall) 10-18.

Yoshida, Kosaku. (1992) New economic principles in America—competition and cooperation. *Columbia Journal of Business*. 26, (Winter) 21-26.

Yoshida, Mitsukuni. (1980) The concept of labor in Japan: The wheel extended. *Toyota Quarterly Review*. 9, (Spring) 2-8.

Yoshida, Shigeru. (1962) *The Yoshida Memoirs*. Boston, MA: Houghton Mifflin.

Yoshino, M. Y. (1968) *Japan's Managerial System: Tradition and Innovation*. Cambridge, MA: MIT Press.

Yost, John C. (1979) Quality circles: Is everybody ready and willing. IAQC 1st Annual Conference Transactions. (February) Cincinnati, OH: International Association of Quality Circles.

Youden, William John. (1951) *Statistical Methods for Chemists*. New York: John Wiley.

Youden, William John. (1951) Statistics for chemists. *Technometrics*. 1, (May) 234-267.

Youden, William John. (1959) Evaluation of chemical analyses on two rocks. *Technometrics*. 1, (April) 409-417.

Youden, William John. (1959) Graphical diagnosis of interlaboratory tests. *Industrial Quality Control*. 15, (November) 1-5.

Youden, William John. (1962) *Experimentation and Measurement*. Washington, DC: National Science Teachers Association.

Youden, William John. (1963) Ranking laboratories by round robin tests. *Materials Research Standards*. 3, (January) 9-13.

Youden, William John. (1967) *Statistical Technique for Collaborative Tests*. Washington, DC: Association of Official Analytical Chemists.

Youden, William John., and J. Stuart Hunter. (1955) Partially replicated latin squares. *Biometrics*. 5, (April) 99-104.

Young, John A. (1988) Speech, Matsushita Quality Conference, Tokyo, July.

Young, Robert E., and S. F. Simon Chen. (1984) A supervisory control system for a flexible manufacturing system. AIIE Conference Presentation.

Young, S. Mark. (1992) A framework for successful adoption and performance of Japanese manufacturing practices in the United States. *Academy of Management Review*. (October) 647-676.

Young, Stanley. (1966) *Management: A Systems Analysis*. Glenview, IL: Scott, Foresman and Company.

Your digital future. (1992) *BusinessWeek*. (September 7) 56.

Yovovich, B. G. (1991) Becoming a world-class customer. *Business Marketing*. (September) 11. (*2)

Yu, Shawn S., and Kenneth E. Case. (1984) An updated look at NLG for process control. *ASQC Annual Technical Quality Congress Transactions*. Milwaukee, WI: ASQC Quality Press, 308-314.

Yucht, Madelyn. (1992) The voices of implementation: Real life perspectives on implementing TQM. In Harry Ivan Costin (Ed.) *Readings in Total Quality Management*. (1994) Fort Worth, TX: Dryden Press, 377-389.

Yuhasz, L. S. (1991) The functional requirements for TQ. *The Quality Leader*. 2, (January) 1-3.

Yukosawa, Toshiharu. (1983) The QC circle movement applied to shop requirement. *Japan Quality Control Circles*. Tokyo: Asian Productivity Organization, 51-65.

Zabel, Diane and Christine Avery. (1992) Total quality management: A primer. *RQ*. 32, (Winter) 206. (*2)

Zablocki, Elaine. (1993) Quality management targets health care. *Nation's Business*. 81, (February) 40. (*3)

Zacks, Shelemyahu. (1983) *Workshop on Statistical Methods of Reliability Analysis for Engineers.* Binghampton, NY: State University of New York.

Zagarow, H. W. (1990) The training challenge. *Quality*. (August) 6.

Zager, Robert and Michael P. Rosow. (1982) *The Innovative Organization: Productivity Programs in Action.* New York: Pergamon Press.

Zahniser, J. Stuart and D. Lehmen. (1951) Quality control at Talon Incorporated. *Industrial Quality Control*. 7, (March) 32-36.

Zairi, M. (1994) *Measuring Performance for Business Results.* London, UK: Chapman and Hall.

Zairi, M., and P. Leonard. (1994) *Practical Benchmarking: The Complete Guide*. London, UK: Chapman and Hall.

Zalenznick, Abraham. (1977) Managers and leaders: Are they different? *Harvard Business Review*. 55, (May-June) 67-78. (*2)

Zalenznick, Abraham. (1989) *The Managerial Mystique.* New York: Harper and Row.

Zaludova, A. H. (1981) Some reflections on quality terminology. *EOQC Quality*. (January) 3-10.

Zander, Alvin and T. Curtis. (1962) Effects of social power on aspiration setting and striving. *Journal of Abnormal and Social Psychology*. 64, 63-74.

Zani, William M. (1970) Blueprint for MIS. *Harvard Business Review*. 48, (November-December) 95-100.

Zayac, S. A. (1985) Training for productivity—An engineers perspective. Proceedings of the Fourteenth American Statisticians Association Meetings.

Zbaracki, Mark Joseph. (1994) The rhetoric and reality of total quality management. Unpublished Ph.D. dissertation, Stanford University, Stanford, CA.

Zeithami, C. P. (1984) Stage of the product life cycle, business strategy and business performance. *Academy of Management Journal.* 27, (March) 134-145.

Zeithami, C. P., and W. F. Louis. (1984) Contextual and strategic differences among mature business in four dynamic performance situations. *Academy of Management Journal.* 27, (November) 841-860.

Zeithami, Valarie A., A. Parasuraman, and Leonard L. Berry. (1990) *Delivering Quality Service: Balancing Customer Perceptions and Expectations.* New York: Free Press. (*2)

Zemke, Ronald E. (1980) Quality circles: Can they work in the U.S.? *Journal of Applied Management.* 5, (September-October) 16-21.

Zemke, Ronald E. (1985) The case of the missing managerial malaise. *Training.* 22, (November) 9-10.

Zemke, Ronald E. (1991) Bashing the Baldrige. *Training.* 28, (March) 36.

Zemke, Ronald E. (1992) Faith, hope and TQM. *Training.* 29, (January) 8.

Zemke, Ronald E. (1992) TQM: Fatally flawed or simply unfocused? *Training.* 29, (October) 8. (*2)

Zemke, Ronald E. (1993) Bluffer's guide to TQM. *Training.* 30, (April) 49-55.

Zemke, Ronald E., and Dick Schaaf. (1989) *The Service Edge: 101 Companies that Profit from Customer Care.* New York: New American Library. (*2)

Zemke, Ronald E., and T. J. Kramlinger. (1982) *Figuring Things Out: A Trainers Guide to Task and Needs Analysis.* Reading, MA: Addison-Wesley.

Zemsky, Robert, William Massy, and Penney Oedel. (1993) On reversing the ratchet. *Change.* 25, (March) 56.

Zero-based budgeting. (1988) *Small Business Report.* (April) 52-57.

Zero-based budgeting: Justifying all business activity from the ground up. (1983) *Small Business Report.* (November) 20-25.

Ziegler, August H. (1981) Vendor quality's new challenge: Public Law 95-507. *ASQC Annual Technical Quality Congress Transactions.* Milwaukee, WI: ASQC Quality Press, 281-286.

Ziegler, August H., and James Diggs. (1982) An integrated approach to subcontract support. *ASQC Annual Technical Quality Congress Transactions.* Milwaukee, WI: ASQC Quality Press, 947-954.

Zif, J., R. F. Young, and I. Fenwick. (1984) A transnational study of advertising-to-sales ratio. *Journal of Advertising Research.* 24, (June-July) 58-63.

Zimmer, Ken and Subir Chowdhury. (1996) QS-9000 *Pioneers: Registered Companies Share Their Strategies for Success.* Milwaukee, WI: ASQC Quality Press.

Zimmerman, M. (1985) *How to do Business with the Japanese.* New York: Random House.

Zingheim, Patricia K., and Jay R. Schuster. (1992) Linking quality and pay. *H R Magazine.* 37, (December) 55. (*2)

Zipfel, H. J. (1983) Quality control circles—An efficient instrument for product quality. *Standardization and Quality.* 29, (February) 52. (*2)

Zorpette, G. (1988) Government oversight: Fighting waste and fraud. *IEEE Spectrum.* (Fall) 44-47. (*2)

Zuboff, Shoshana. (1988) *In the Age of the Smart Machine: The Future of Work and Power.* New York: Basic Books. (*2)

Zuckerman, Amy. (1996) *International Standards Desk Reference.* Milwaukee, WI: ASQC Quality Press.

Zuckerman, Marilyn R., and Lewis J. Hatala. (1992) *Incredibly American: Releasing the Heart of Quality.* Milwaukee, WI: ASQC Quality Press.

Zumwalt, Elmo R. (1976) *On Watch: A Memoir.* New York: Time Books.

Zweig, Philip L. (1981) Quality circles—a kind of employee brainstorming—helping banks solve problems, improve performance. *American Banker.* 146, (January 19) 1-4.

SUBJECT INDEX

I

COCONTRIBUTOR INDEX

A

B

C

D

H

I

J

K

L

M

P

S

ABOUT THE AUTHOR

Robert E. Kemper is a professor of management at Northern Arizona University, Flagstaff. He obtained his Ph.D. in business administration from the University of Washington (Seattle). Dr. Kemper teaches, researches, consults, and writes on a variety of management and organizational behavior topics—values and ethics, strategy, personnel, communications, operations, negotiations, and conflict management. He is the author of *Experiencing Strategic Management* (Dryden Press, 1989), the co-author of *Experiencing Operations Management* (PWS-Kent Publishing Company, 1991), the co-author of *The Conflict: The People Who Nobody Knows* (McGraw-Hill, College Custom Series, 1994), and the co-author of *The Resolution: Handbook for Win-Win-WIN Organizations* (McGraw-Hill, College Custom Series, 1994). Professor Kemper was a visiting professor of management at Inter-American University of Puerto Rico, San German Campus, in the fall of 1992. He was a consultant and taught teachers of management how to teach global-quality management in Slavjansk, Ukraine in the summer of 1995 for the International Executive Service Corps (IESC). Also for the IESC, he was a consultant and professor for the Slovak Management Training Center (SMTC) is Bratislava, Slovakia during January through March, 1997. In Slovakia, he designed, for executives, experiential courses in management, operations, and financial management.